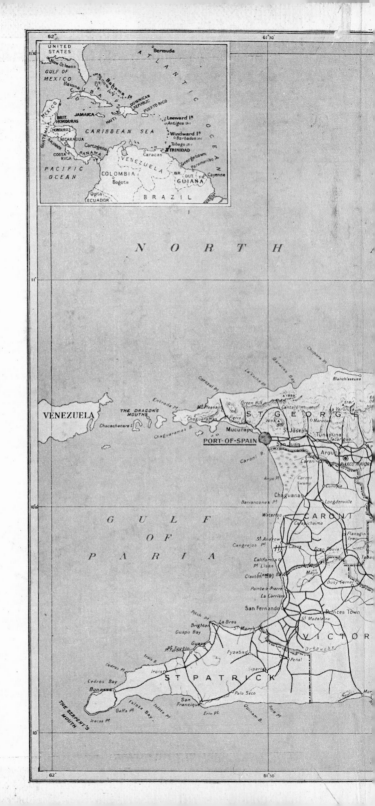

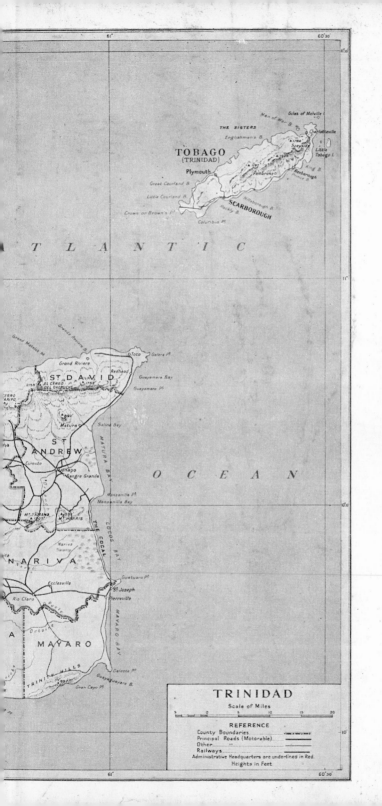

TOBAGO
(TRINIDAD)

THE SISTERS

Man of War B.

Giles or Melville I.

Englishman's B.

Charlotteville

Speyside

Little
Tobago I.

Plymouth

Pembrokeo

King B.

Roxborough

Prince B.

Hillsborough R.

Great Courland B.

Little Courland B.

SCARBOROUGH

Crown or Brown's Pt.

Columbus Pt.

Rocky B.

A T L A N T I C

Grand Matelot Pt.

Grande Riviere

Grand Riviere

Toco

Galera Pt.

ST. DAVID

Redhead

2150 EL CERRO
DEL ARIPO

Guayamare Bay

CERRO
ARIPO

Guayamare Pt.

Matura

Salina Bay

ST.
ANDREW

MATURA BAY

O C E A N

Cumuto

Guanapo

Sangre Grande

Manzanilla Pt.

Manzanilla Bay

MT. TAMANA
1027

MT. HARRIS

THE COCAL

COCOS BAY

Nariva
Swamp

N A R I V A

Ecclesville

Guatuaro Pt.

St. Joseph

Rio Claro

Pierreville

Ortoire

MAYARO BAY

M A Y A R O

TRINITY HILLS

Galeota Pt.

Guayaguayare B.

Gran Cayo Pt.

THE HISTORY OF THE WEST INDIAN ISLANDS OF TRINIDAD AND TOBAGO
1498–1900

THE HISTORY OF THE WEST INDIAN ISLANDS OF TRINIDAD AND TOBAGO

1498-1900

by

GERTRUDE CARMICHAEL

Lately Librarian to the Trinidad and Tobago Historical Society and Assistant Librarian, Imperial College of Tropical Agriculture, Trinidad, W.I.

ALVIN REDMAN

LONDON

First published by
ALVIN REDMAN LIMITED
107 Jermyn Street, St. James's,
London S.W.1
1961

PRINTED IN GREAT BRITAIN BY
BRISTOL TYPESETTING CO. LTD.
YORK STREET - ST. PHILIPS
BRISTOL 2

CONTENTS

ILLUSTRATIONS

FOREWORD

A PEOPLE without books lack a national identity. Many of Britain's one time possessions have for too long been in need of national literatures of their own, whether of the imagination or of scholarship. In particular their histories have been written and taught more as parts of the imperial pattern rather than as chronicles in their own right. But with the rapid emergence of new independent sovereign nations the situation is changing quickly. In a decade a flourishing school of West Indian literature has sprung up, and scholarship grows ever deeper roots through the activities of the University College of the West Indies. In particular independence produces the desire to know one's own history: and knowing that history is a vital feature of true independence.

It is for these reasons that, as President of the West India Committee, I would like to welcome and recommend Mrs. Gertrude Carmichael's *History of the West Indian Islands of Trinidad and Tobago*. It is an erudite work which keeps solidly in the foreground the key idea that the history of Trinidad has taken place in Trinidad and not elsewhere. Only someone who had immersed herself in the documentation could have pieced together so completely the story that began with Columbus, and I am sure that all Trinidadians will be grateful to Mrs. Carmichael for the labour she has devoted over so many years to this work.

It is a happy coincidence that such a history should appear just as Trinidad is about to achieve full nationhood in the wider community of the Federation of The West Indies. No more timely moment could have been chosen for its publication. May I express the hope that a similar substantial work will follow to deal with Trinidad's history since 1900, an era dominated by two features completely unknown in Mrs. Carmichael's much longer sweep of four hundred years—rapid communication by aeroplane and radio, and the revolution of rising expectations amongst the people of the Caribbean.

Meanwhile I feel certain that Mrs. Carmichael's hope that her book will meet a long felt need in the teaching of the history of Trinidad and Tobago will be fulfilled.

Jock Campbell.

The West India Committee,
40 Norfolk Street,
London W.C.2.

PREFACE

IN 1928, when I first arrived in Trinidad, my surprise at finding how many different nations were represented in the population was succeeded by a strong desire to find out all I could about the history of the island and neighbouring Tobago. At once I was confronted with the difficulty that no written history was readily available; those written in the early days were out of print, hard to come by and went no further than 1837.

By 1930, when I became Assistant Librarian at the Imperial College of Tropical Agriculture, I had found out a little, but real progress began when I took charge of the Trinidad and Tobago Historical Society's Library, which was housed at the College.

The Trinidad and Tobago Historical Society was founded by the late Dr. K. S. Wise, who at that time was Director of Medical Services, and when he left the Colony the work was carried on by the late Dr. C. Y. Shephard, Carnegie Professor of Economics at the Imperial College of Tropical Agriculture. It was due to these two enthusiasts, who opened up new avenues for research, arranged lectures and reproduced papers and old documents, more than 1,000 of which I indexed for the Society, that eventually I was able to piece together this history. I hope that the results of that work, which occupied many years, will prove of use to students and others interested in the history of the Caribbean islands and encourage further research.

The history of Tobago up to the time when she became a Ward of Trinidad was an entirely separate study.

I owe a debt of gratitude to Dr. Wise and Dr. Shephard. Also, I must thank the Rev. J. Hawkes, M.A.(Cantab.) who for a time was Chaplain to the Mariners' Club in Port of Spain for his assistance in arranging the subject matter. My thanks are also due to Booker Brothers, McConnell & Co. Limited, to Caroni Limited, to the West Indies Sugar Company Limited, and to Dr. Philip Sherlock, Vice-Principal of the University College of

The West Indies, and those who supported him, all these for their generous help in procuring the publication of this history. Without the help of Mr. A. E. V. Barton, Secretary of the West India Committee in London, this book could not have been published. To him I express my sincere appreciation. Finally I would like to thank Mr. G. Norman Knight, M.A., M.S. Ind. for the care he has bestowed on compiling the index and on correcting the proofs.

For a very long time the majority of the people in Trinidad and Tobago have remained ignorant and uninterested in past history, but with the coming of independence and the establishment of the Federation of The West Indies there is a widespread thirst for knowledge. As far as I know, there are no text books for the teaching of the history of Trinidad and Tobago. I hope therefore that this book will fill a long-felt want and be useful to all who are interested in the subject.

GERTRUDE CARMICHAEL.

Curepe,
  Trinidad.
January, 1961.

CHAPTER ONE

DISCOVERY, 1498

ON WEDNESDAY, May 30th, 1498, Christopher Columbus, "The Admiral of the Ocean Sea", weighed anchor at the bar of Sanlucar de Barremeda in the mouth of the Guadalquivir. The third great voyage of discovery had begun. With his little fleet, flagship the 100-ton *Santa Maria* and the caravels *El Correo* and *La Vaquenos,* he had two purposes to fulfil : to test the truth of the assertion of Don Joao II of Portugal, that athwart the Equator lay a great continent; and to discover lands lying to the south of the Antilles.

The journey did not have an auspicious start. A hostile French fleet off Cape St. Vincent meant that Columbus was unable to sail direct to Porto Santo and had to take a south-easterly sweep almost to the African coast. When he arrived his little fleet was mistaken for a detachment of the French and he was unable to complete supplies of wood and fresh water, the inhabitants having fled to the safety of the hills with their flocks and herds. Soft winds were encountered over the next forty miles, and two days passed before the ships were anchored in Funchal Roads,* where Columbus remained six days, being feted by the inhabitants. Stores were taken for the passage to the Canaries and the Cape Verde Islands.

On July 4th, with a slight breeze to assist them, the fleet finally set sail for the Indies. The breeze was so slight that at the end of a week it failed altogether and left Columbus becalmed and drifting in the doldrums. In his journal he wrote :

> "The heat was so excessive that there was none on board who dared go below to look after the casks of wine and water, which burst, snapping the hoops of the pipes; the wheat burned like fire, the bacon and salted meat roasted and putrefied. This heat lasted for eight days."

* Funchal had been his home in his early married life and this was his first visit since he had become famous.

Fortunately the sun shone only on the first day of the becalming; the remainder were overcast and accompanied by light rain. On the eighth day a steady wind sprang up and the fleet sailed on, making an average of 183 miles a day. This steady run to the west delighted the Admiral but not his crew, for, after a week of drifting, food was short and water rationed, and every mile westward meant a mile further from home. Columbus sensed the dissatisfaction of his men and decided to turn north and run for Dominica to replenish supplies before continuing his search for Don Joao's supposed continent.

At noon on Tuesday, July 31st,

"Alonzo Perez (Nirando), the Admiral's servant from Huelva, climbed to the crow's nest and saw land to the westward, distant fifteen leagues, and it appeared to be in the form of three rocks or mountains." (The Three Sisters.)

There was great rejoicing, the "Salve Regina" was repeated and prayers of thanksgiving were offered up. Columbus named the island "La Ysla de la Trinidad", as he had determined previously that the first land he reached should be dedicated to the Trinity.*

Course was altered at once and land approached at the point where the rocky formation resembled a ship's sail. This Columbus named La Cabo de la Galera (now Galeoto Point). In bright moonlight the fleet sought a safe anchorage, but were forced to sail close-reefed along the south coast of the island, unable to anchor owing to the steeply shelving sea bed. The search for a river mouth which would afford shelter and a supply of fresh water was started the next morning (August 1st). The need for water was urgent—even after rationing, the flagship was down to her last cask. At Cabo de la Playa, as Columbus called Erin Point, a sandy bay and fresh water in plenty were found. The crews of the three ships relaxed, bathing, and washing their clothes, seeing no sign of life, though they had observed a few thatched huts as they skirted the coast.

After two uncomfortable months at sea the island looked green and beautiful. Columbus thought it so fresh that he compared it with the beauty of the gardens of Valencia in the month of May.

From Erin Point, land was sighted to the south-west and the Admiral, taking it for another island, christened it "Ysla

---

* It is also held that the three mountains seen from the ship reminded Columbus of the Holy Trinity and that the island was named Trinidad as he had invoked the protection of the Trinity before sailing.

Sancta " (Holy Island), little realizing that this was Punta Bombeador at the Orinoco Delta, and was in fact part of the great continent he had come so far to find.

Erin Bay offered insufficient protection against an easterly wind, and on August 2nd, the fleet sailed once more. Rounding Punta del Arenal* (Icacos Point) they made the dangerous passage to the Boca de la Sierpe (Serpent's Mouth) at slack water and dropped anchor just inside the Gulf de la Ballena† (Gulf of Paria), in shelter from the wind and within easy reach of the shore.

Once again no inhabitants were seen, the only sign of life being unidentified animal footprints in the sand. It was not until August 3rd that contact was made with any living person. A large canoe containing some twenty-five young men approached the flagship. To the disappointment of the Admiral, who hoped to be met by orientals, the natives of Trinidad were light in colour and appeared of much the same stock as the Caribs and other Indians he had met in the West Indies. In his journal Columbus describes them as being graceful and handsome, with long dark hair cut according to the Spanish style, but wrapped round their heads in gaily coloured scarves, their only clothing a short tunic.

These visitors, armed with bows and arrows and carrying round wooden shields, did not approach the larger vessels too closely, lying off at a safe distance and calling out in a language which none aboard could understand. Columbus, in an effort to arouse their curiosity and draw them nearer, ordered a display of mirrors, brass pots and pans on the deck of the *Santa Maria*. To this the Indians appeared indifferent and the crew were ordered to dance to the pipe and tabor in the hopes that the natives might be amused. The effect was far from amusing. The natives interpreted the dancing and leaping of the seamen as some kind of war dance, seized their bows and arrows and began shooting at the flagship whilst themselves taking shelter under the lee of the *Vaquenos,* whose pilot treated them kindly and gave them as presents a coat and hat. The Indians, having nothing to offer in exchange, intimated that the pilot should accompany them ashore. On seeing him approach the *Santa Maria* for the Admiral's permission to land, they grew suspicious and withdrew and were not seen again.

Two days were spent in Icacos Bay, the sailors enjoying them-

* Punta del Arenal—Sandy Point.
† Ballena—Whale.

selves fishing, gathering oysters and catching parrots as large as chickens. The Admiral spent most of his time watching the currents in the Serpent's Mouth with great wonder. He noted that the tide continually set northwards through the Boca, slacking at the turn but roaring with great fury on the flood and on the ebb. The shelving sea bed made progress dangerous but there could be no going back. On August 4th preparations were made to sail up the gulf in the hopes that there might be another exit. As the fleet was about to leave a large wave was seen approaching from the west. Mast high, with a crest of foam, it came roaring down on the little vessel. Columbus was afraid he might lose his whole fleet in such a sea but, apart from snapping the *Vaquenos** cable and the loss of her anchor (she being a little slow in weighing), the ships rode the great wave in safety as it passed roaring through the Boca de la Sierpe.

Taking advantage of a steady breeze the fleet stood out and, leaving the barren rock of El Gallo (The Cock) behind, sailed northwards towards two lofty headlands at the head of the gulf. The point to the east was part of Trinidad. The other Columbus named Ysla Gracia (The Isle of Grace), not realizing that it was part of the mainland. Here he discovered even more narrow channels between the islands than those at the Serpents' Mouth, and named them Boca Del Dragón (Dragon's Mouth) and the islands El Caracol (The Snail), later called Chacachacare,† El Delfín (The Dolphin), now Huevos (Eggs), and Cabo Boto (Blunt Cape), believing Monos (Apes) to be part of the mainland.

After a short exploration of the Venezuelan coast as far as Rio Grande, the fleet returned to Trinidad and anchored for the night of August 12th in Puerto de Gatos (Monkey Harbour) on Chacachacare. Fresh water was taken from a neighbouring bay on Huevos, where fishermen's huts were discovered and the inlet named Puerto de las Cabañas (The Harbour of the Cabins). In the early hours of August 13th the fleet set sail through the Grand Boca, having claimed the Island of Trinidad for the Spanish Crown. Tobago, which was named Bellaforma, was seen on the distant horizon but not visited.

The latest recruits to the Spanish Empire, people with whom Columbus had had but the smallest contact, were Indians of

* In 1877 while workmen were digging a ditch on Constant Estate, Cedros, a bronze anchor was brought to light. This anchor is now in the Victoria Institute in Port of Spain and is believed to be the one lost.

† Chacachacare, supposedly an Indian onomatopoeic word resembling the chattering of the monkeys on the island or possibly a corruption of the Spanish "Chacarachaca", meaning continuous chatter.

14

the Arawak tribe. They were on the whole a short, muscular people, of mild disposition, and, for their time, peace-loving. They were a marked contrast to their fighting neighbours, the Caribs from the Essequibo, who attacked many of the West Indians islands and put thousands of Arawaks to death.

At the time of the discovery of Trinidad, the Arawaks had reached a state of civilization comparable to that of the South Sea Islanders when discovered by Captain Cook. They lived in villages in forest clearings, and where possible on high ground overlooking the sea near to either a stream or a river and exposed to the wind, to avoid the menace of both mosquito and sand fly. The villages were scattered over the island in clearings created by firing the bush, the trees being allowed to fall and burn themselves out, whereupon crops were planted between the fallen trunks. In the centre of the clearings huts, almost circular in shape, were built of closely placed wooden posts, between which canes were lashed with lianas. Wooden beams were laid across the tops of the posts and secured to form a conical roof, which was then thatched with palm leaves, making the whole secure from rain and draught. Their furniture consisted of a few wooden stools, which rested on the beaten earth floor, and hammocks made of cordage woven from the fibres of palms and other plants.

Each hut housed a single family, a large village having as many as fifteen huts, though most had fewer. The headman or cacique ruled the village, inheriting his position from his mother, the honour always passing to the eldest son of the previous cacique's sister.

These primitive peoples wore the minimum of clothing, men wearing short tunics and women aprons. They had one habit which has proved invaluable to archaeologist and historian alike —all the domestic rubbish was thrown into a communal dump or "midden" to the leeward of the village, or down the slope from their huts. It is from these "middens" that knowledge of their habits has been and still is being revealed; specimens of their pottery, tools and weapons and even the bones from their food have been excavated.

As a race, they were chiefly fish eaters, but did not cavil at reptiles or birds. Knowing little of agriculture, it is doubtful if they ate much vegetable food; cassava and peppers were indigenous, but the wild fruits, which were mostly sea grapes and hog plums,* were not very palatable. Their method of making fire for cooking was by twisting a hardwood stick between two

* Sea grape—Coccoloba uvifera. Hog plum—Spondias Mombin.

15

pieces of softwood tied together. The "middens" have provided many examples of Arawak pottery. Clay was moulded by hand to the desired shape and polished inside and out with a stone or bone polisher before being fired. Though they had no potter's wheel, they were not restricted in ingenuity, for vessels ranging from small saucers and plates to large bowls have been found. Handles, some of which were elaborate, were often attached in the shape of animal or human effigies, and it was common for spouts of vessels holding liquids to be modelled in the shape of animal heads. Nor was pottery plain, for, after firing, some was coloured with a true paint, the medium used being either animal fat or blood plasma, and the most usual colours red and blue or black and white.

Metals were unknown in the island. Weapons and tools were made from stone, shell, bone or wood, axe and hammer heads from conveniently sized and weighted stones, small knives from chips of flint. Awls and needles of bone have also been found in the "middens". Bows and arrows were of wood, the arrows with hardwood heads; shields and primitive spades were also wooden.

Joseph in his *History of Trinidad* writes of the amusements and religion of the Arawaks. They were, he says, fond of dances, which were chiefly of a warlike nature held in public. In these dances called Arcetoes, men and women danced together, keeping very strict time and singing as they danced. The music was provided by drums and conch shells. Dances of a private nature were also held, but these appear to have been somewhat licentious. Another of their amusements was a ball game known as Bato. The players, divided into opposing teams, played the ball with skill and gusto, striking it with the head, heel or elbow. Unfortunately the rules for playing and scoring have not come down to us.

The Arawaks' religion was for the greater part based on superstition and fear, the idea of an after life being vague and confused. They believed in several gods, the chief being Jocahuna. The priests, the Bohitos, controlled the people by oracles and through idols called Zemi. They also acted as judges in the villages and as physicians, curing the sick with herbs and charms.

CHAPTER TWO

EARLY GOVERNORS, 1500–1600

AFTER THE death of Christopher Columbus on May 20th, 1506, all his property and privileges passed to his son, Don Diego Columbus, Governor of Santo Domingo, who became "Admiral of the Ocean Sea" and "Viceroy and Governor of the Islands and Mainlands therein", and consequently Governor of Trinidad.

Neither Don Diego nor the Spanish King was interested in colonizing Trinidad; it was not until 1510 that there was any record of a Spanish vessel visiting the island. This ship arrived only under the pretence of trading. No sooner had the Indians become friendly than the Spaniards fell upon them, killed many and took some two hundred to Puerto Rico and Santo Domingo for sale as slaves. When news of this outrage reached Spain, the King, who was interested in Trinidad as a potential source of gold or other precious metals and jewels, sent word to Diego Columbus instructing him to treat the natives well as he believed them to be "as good and kind as any in the Indies". General permission was given for the capture of Carib war Indians. Instructions were also included for an exploration of the island and for a thorough search to be made for gold and other mineral wealth.

Diego's exploratory expedition was not successful. He failed to find gold and the natives, having no wish to be exploited by Spain, were hostile. In spite of this failure, the King, still hoping to find the colony a source of wealth, granted the right of conquest and pacification to the wealthy Captain Roderigo de Bastidas. Diego Columbus at once opposed the appointment on the grounds that it was a breach of the agreement between the King and his father, whereby all the Admiral's discoveries should be ruled by his descendants. Bastidas, realizing that discretion was the better part of valour, waived his claim rather than face what might become an interminable battle in the Spanish courts of law.

In accordance with the policy of Christopher Columbus, attempts were made to convert the Indians to Christianity* but with no great measure of success. Even with the help of Fray Francisco de Arevalo, the Bishop of the Indies, who attempted to build a church on the island, there was still little progress to report. By 1526, when Diego Columbus died, the impression made on the island by Spain and by Christianity was negligible.

The death of the discoverer's son was followed by a short inter-regnum before the first conquistador,† Antonio Sedeno, lately a Contador of Puerto Rico, was appointed Captain General of Trinidad for life. He was an ideal man for the task of putting Trinidad firmly on to the Spanish map. His previous career had been remarkable; although an official, he had been in gaol on various occasions. Once he had escaped by burning the prison over his own head. He had been banished as a disturber of the peace and the other officials had made it clear that San Juan would be a better place without his presence. Spain regarded him as a wealthy but turbulent man of unlimited courage, en-dowed with all the characteristics of the successful conquistador.

On July 12th, 1530, he was appointed Governor by the Queen of Spain, wife of the Holy Roman Emperor, Charles V.

"Inasmuch as you, Antonio Sedeno, our Contadour of the Island of San Juan, zealous for the service of the Kingdom of God and of our realms, have offered to construct a fort in the Island of Trinidad and to establish a priest there to baptize the Indians and that you will do all that is necessary to settle people in the said Island and to encourage the Indians there to accept the knowledge of our Holy Catholic Faith, in con-sequence of which we have approved an agreement with you, the terms and conditions of which you have signed, agreeing to comply with them all in our service and to carry out the pacification of this Island and the administration and execu-tion of our laws, therefore for the honour of your person we promise and do hereby appoint you to be our Governor of this said Island for all the days of your life provided that for the Governorship you receive no salary whatsoever until such time as we order that a residencia‡ be taken to assess your Governorship.

* It was his hope that the wealth of the New World could be used for the furtherance of Christianity and a crusade to recapture Jerusalem.
† Conquisitador—conqueror, discoverer, pacifier or settler. The bearer of the title Conquistador Adalantado was raised to the nobility.
‡ A periodic enquiry into a Governor's past dealings, at which all citizens had the right to lodge complaints. Until all complaints had been answered satisfactorily, the Governor's bonds and salary were withheld.

18

"Furthermore we do grant you the office of Alquazil*
Mayor of this same Island for all the days of your life and
that you may appoint to it any such person as you may wish
so long as he is diligent and attentive to the conditions of this
agreement . . ."

Sedeno, who was in Spain when he received his appointment,
at once set about preparations for his journey and the consequent settling of Trinidad. In September, 1530, he set sail with
three caravels and seventy men, most of whom were from the
Canary Islands, these islanders being regarded as more suitable
for life in the Indies than the metropolitan Spaniards. Early in
1531 he arrived at a point which he named Punta de las Palmas,
where he solemnly read his commission over to his men and was
accepted by them as Governor of Trinidad.

Sailing on, he entered the Gulf of Paria in search of an
Indian cacique, named Turpiari, who lived on the mainland
near the Bocas. This man was known to be a friend of Spain
and Sedeno needed an interpreter who was a man of influence
with him if he was to penetrate into Trinidad in a peaceful
manner.

Turpiari and Sedeno struck up a friendship which was to
last through some dangerous years, based on the mutual trust
of two strong men who knew what they wanted. Turpiari first
took Sedeno to the southern province of the island, Chaco-
mare, where he met the friendly cacique, Maruana. In the
northern province, Camocorabo, the population centre of which
was based at Cumucurape,† which is now Mucurapo, Sedeno
found the Indians so suspicious, unfriendly and untrustworthy,
that he decided it would be unwise to settle until he had
organized supplies from Paria. Here he built a small fort which
he left garrisoned whilst he went to San Juan and Margarita
for supplies and reinforcements.

Whilst Sedeno was away, Diego de Ordas, one of Cortez's‡
leading captains, who had recently been appointed Governor of
Guayana (including Paria) attacked and took the little fort, on
the grounds that it had been built without his permission on his
territory. Sedeno, meanwhile, was making preparations, and sent
out supplies without realizing that his fort had changed hands.
His advance guard, arriving at Paria, found it safer to move
over to Trinidad where they settled temporarily in the northern

* Alquazil (Alguacil) Mayor—equivalent of Chief Constable.
† Cumucurape—Cumaco and abo " the place of the silk cotton tree "
(Carib).
‡ Cortez (1485-1547) was conqueror of Mexico.

19

sector of the island. The Indians received them well, but in the course of a few days turned against them, massacred twenty-one and nearly captured the remainder of the party who only escaped by cutting the cables of their caravel.

In May, 1532, Sedeno, accompanied by eighty men from Margarita, set out for Trinidad to punish the treachery of the northern Indians. He launched a surprise attack and played havoc with the sleeping enemy, who put up a desperate struggle, preferring death by the sword to surrender. Only about ten of the attacking force were killed, most of these by the poisoned arrows of the Indians.

Having achieved his immediate object and still being unprepared to settle permanently in a hostile country, Sedeno withdrew to Margarita to re-equip and remuster. Here he was persuaded to include in his party Alonzo de Herrera, an old friend of Ordas, who was to take charge of the fort which Sedeno proposed to build in Trinidad, on the Caroni River.

In June, 1533, the full expedition landed at Cumucurape without resistance and a stockaded camp was quickly constructed. Food supplies were dangerously low, and Sedeno was forced to await attack from the Indians rather than carry out any offensive tactics. Before a ship reached them from Paria, the men were reduced to eating herbs and roots from the woods. The vessel which brought the food brought also bad news. Herrera, who had been left in Paria to look after the sending of supplies, was trying to undermine his captain's authority. Sedeno had therefore to return to Paria to fetch Herrera so that he could keep an eye on him. When he returned, it was to face an attack from the combined forces of all the Indians in the north of the island, an attack which was only broken by a cavalry charge and the fact that the Indians could not face mounted horsemen. Though Sedeno and his men could claim the victory, the situation after the engagement was not very encouraging. Some of the invaluable horses had been killed and all the rest were injured in one way or another. Of his men, only thirty were really fit and many were so dispirited that, when prompted by Herrera, they were quite ready to mutiny. In addition to the hostility of the local Indians, watch had to be kept for attacks from the Caribs from the mainland. They were particularly warlike and their attacks a constant menace to communications.

To raise the men's spirits and to secure himself against the Indians, Sedeno worked hard on increasing the fortifications of the little settlement before the next attack. Soon he had everybody in good humour, with regular supplies coming in from Paria and from the south of the island. To keep things going, he even sold his prisoners as slaves at Cabagua and invested the money in fishing nets so that his garrison might be as independent as possible.

Two incidents completely changed the plans on which Sedeno had proposed to work. Herrera was appointed to command in Paria until a Governor was nominated and Pizarro's reports of treasure in Peru turned the eyes of Spain away from her smaller possessions.

Herrera's appointment meant that the supplies from Paria would be closed down. The old enmity between Sedeno and Ordaz, and now between Sedeno and Herrera, would put an end to any co-operation between the mainland and the island. Pizarro's reports meant that it would be impossible to obtain reinforcements of any kind for minor expeditions. Even the soldiers of fortune would look naturally to Peru for their riches and not to a hard struggle in Trinidad, which at the moment showed no prospect of producing any dividends except hard work and danger.

Mutiny broke out amongst the men under his command. Many deserted to the mainland and eventually Sedeno was left holding his settlement with only twenty men and four horses. It became increasingly obvious that when the Indians attacked, as attack they must, the Spaniards would get short shrift.

On the instance of Herrera, the last remaining soldiers imprisoned Sedeno and made arrangements to move to the mainland in two small boats (pirogues) which had been sent for them. Sedeno was offered a passage, but had to leave his last four horses behind. On arrival at Paria he demanded immediate passage to San Juan but was taken ashore and imprisoned by Herrera for six months. He would have remained a prisoner longer had not a handful of loyal followers continually demanded his release. Herrera at first refused their demands, fearing the reprisals which might be taken against him, but after the Indians under Turpiari had attacked in an effort to release Sedeno, he came to an amicable agreement with his prisoner and released him. Sedeno had left the island with perhaps a few less Indians in it but with little to show for the influence of Spain. When he died in 1538 it was still uncolonized, unconverted and untamed.

A further attempt to convert the island was made by Fray Gregorio de Betata, Bishop of Cartagena, and Fray Francisco de

Montesinos, Provincial of the Order of St. Dominic. Again there was little success, though the principles of Fray Bartolome de las Casas,* " The Apostle of the Indies ", were followed.

A subsequent effort to conquer the island was made by Juan Troche Ponce de Leon in 1569 and a report by the Franciscan priest, Fray Miguel Diosdade, stated that by 1570 de Leon had finished the task assigned to him and that the conquest was now complete.

The report describes the islands as being very beautiful; green with many hills, valleys, forests, savannahs, springs and rivers of fresh water; all this with a temperate climate. It was abundant with food and there were many animals including very many monkeys and great numbers of birds with brilliant plumage. The Indian inhabitants were described as being of good disposition, noble in appearance, going about in a state of nature as they were born, both men and women. They were willing enough for the Spaniards to settle, but some were in league with the French† from whom there was great danger.

On receipt of this report the King of Spain made Juan Ponce de Leon Governor and Captain General. This title he retained until 1591. He was succeeded by Antonio de Berrio, who had strict orders to subdue the Indians completely. Berrio was also Governor of Margarita and proceeded there, after only a short stay in Trinidad, to arrange with Domingo de Vera for an expedition against the Trinidad Indians. De Vera had already been to Caracas negotiating with the Governor to raise men and money for the expedition. With the supplies he had obtained, he was sent, together with an extra thirty men, to settle Trinidad as a port and base from which " El Dorado ", the dream treasure chest of the Indies, might be sought.

Vera arrived in 1592 to take possession of the island in the name of Antonio de Berrio, announcing that Christianity would be brought to the Indian inhabitants, who would be protected from the attacks of the marauding Caribs from the mainland and other islands. The town of San Josef de Oruña (St. Joseph) was founded in May as the seat of Government.

"In the name of the King and Antonio de Berrio, he (Domingo de Vera) took possession of the Island of Trenydad so as to settle it as a port and principal base from which to enter and settle ' El Dorado ' . . .

---

* The protection of American Indians was the guiding principle of Las Casas's life. In his efforts on their behalf he advocated the introduction of African Negroes to labour on the plantations of the New World.
† Chiefly visiting French privateers.

"Domingo de Vera then made a wooden cross, forty feet high, and placed it with his own hands, assisted by Fray Domingo de Santa Agueda, Friar of the Order of St. Francis, Chaplain to this expedition . . .

"Domingo de Vera then swept his sword around, cutting down the plants and declared the Island to be taken for the King and that he would defend it against any challenger armed or unarmed.

"The soldiers and everyone shouted 'Biba el ray' . . .

"The authority for this settlement in Trinidad was given by Antonio de Berrio in Margarita on April 8th, 1592. Domingo de Vera named this place 'San Josephe de Oruña' and called upon all to testify that this place is called Caroni by the Indians, that it is upon the highlands of the River Caroni and has for boundaries, on the East, a high hill bare of trees, on the South a flat vega of the river, on the West rolling hilly land and on the North a high mountain with a pass."

A site was marked out for a church where Mass was immediately celebrated.

Berrio reported on his arrival that there were signs of gold in some of the ravines and that the island was very fertile. He suggested that unless the island was properly settled soon it would be impossible to conquer Guayana or to find "El Dorado". Though Trinidad was considered one of the largest of the Indies, there were, in 1592, only twenty-two resident Spaniards and some six thousand "war Indians".

Berrio was not left long in peaceful possession of his new colony. In 1593 Francisco de Vides, Governor and Captain General of the province of Cumana, was declaring that he had been granted Trinidad as one of his dependencies. Each side presented its case to Madrid, Berrio claiming the island as a base for his lengthy expeditions in search of "El Dorado"; Vides presenting legal claims based on Royal Cedulas. On January 18th, 1594, the Council of the Indies decided in favour of Vides and ordered Berrio to leave the colony. This did not finish the case, for Berrio refused to relinquish his claims, and appeals against the Council's decision were sent to the King by his supporters, who referred to him as "our General and Governor". He also continued to make use of Trinidad as the base for his expeditions up the Orinoco.

A report to the King from Cumana in 1595 pointed out that Berrio still regarded the island as his and refused to have anything to do with any representative of Vides, who was engaged

23

in raising an armed force to make good his claim. It was suggested that Berrio should be officially appointed to explore and conquer Guayana and Vides to conquer and settle Trinidad, or better still, that a new General be sent from Spain to do both.

In recent years the island had been used as a base for French corsairs and pirates of all nations in need of food, fuel and water. Amongst others, in 1592, the English ship *Wildman*, under command of Captain Benjamin Wood and John Chudley, was in the gulf.

The following year Captain Jacob Whidden arrived in the Gulf of Paria and established amicable relationship with Berrio. Whidden was advance guard for Sir Walter Raleigh, with whom he had served on many former occasions. He was trying to gain information as to the position of " El Dorado " so that his master might lay before the Queen of England the treasures of the Indies and regain his former favour in her eyes. Whilst in the gulf he met another great English navigator, Captain James Lancaster, who, after rounding the Cape of Good Hope, had run for Trinidad to replenish his water and food stocks before continuing his journey to England.

An unfortunate incident occurred during Whidden's stay. His men were invited ashore by a party of local Indians and were ambushed by Spaniards, though Berrio had given his word that the English should be unmolested. As he had not a strong force to take the matter up under arms, Whidden had to be content with reporting it to Raleigh when he returned to England.

The year 1595 saw the arrival of Robert Dudley, a young English privateer of note, who spent six weeks in the south of the island recuperating and exploring after a bad passage in his ship *The Bear*.

He in his turn was followed by Sir Walter Raleigh, called by the Spaniards "Count Milor Guaterral",* who arrived on April 4th with a fleet of three well equipped ships, seven barges and about three hundred men. He stayed in the south for several days, exploring bays and creeks and noting various aspects of the island's coast. He mentions in his notes the oysters growing on the mangrove roots. Whilst there he visited the Pitch Lake at La Brea, and used some of the pitch to caulk his ships, claiming that it was better than anything else he had ever used. A small party was put ashore to arrange a peaceful meeting between Governor Berrio and Raleigh; this party carried a letter to the island's chief citizen and a gold ring as a token of good faith,

* Guaterral—Bird of Passage.

but Berrio refused to meet one who might prove to be an unwelcome visitor.

Raleigh, as a gesture of defiance, landed his main force, marched on San Josef, sacked and fired the town and seized the person of Berrio, whom he later released unconditionally after a setback to his forces at Cumana. He then went on his way to lead another search which was fated not to find the wealth of " El Dorado ".

Berrio, undeterred by his capture, at once organized another expedition to the Orinoco, confident that with this final effort he would reach his goal. Vides hastily sent his envoy, Philipe de Santiago, after him to make some agreement about the situation in Trinidad. Nothing was settled and Berrio pressed on with his venture whilst Santiago returned to Trinidad, where he rebuilt San Josef, which he renamed San Philipe de Montes in 1596.

The following year Domingo de Vera heard that Berrio was a tired and broken old man. His expedition had cost him dearly and had met with no success. His interest in Trinidad was flagging. He hurried to the little township of San Thomé in Guayana only to find that Berrio was already dead and that his son Fernando had succeeded to the title of Governor of Trinidad and Guayana. So impressed was Vera with Fernando's grasp of the situation, his Christian zeal and his general ability at the youthful age of twenty-one, that though he himself had been offered the Governorship, he thought it better to leave it in this young man's hands.

CHAPTER THREE

THE SEVENTEENTH CENTURY, 1600–1700

SPAIN still had her eyes on "El Dorado" at the beginning of the seventeenth century, and, rather than raise the standard of living and prosperity of Trinidad, she put her insatiable desire for gold before that of creating a stable trading outpost. That there was room for trade is shown by the presence in 1600 of English, French and Dutch ships bartering manufactured goods for local hides, tobacco and salt.

Fernando de Berrio, the young Governor, brought up in the "El Dorado" tradition, with its legends of gold mines and people wearing fine clothes and living in great houses, determined to lead an expedition to the mainland in an effort to discover for his country and himself the source of this fabulous wealth. The expedition was not a success, for Berrio was overwhelmed by the Caribs, who drove him from the mainland. Disillusioned, he returned to Trinidad to find that in his absence the Illustrious Cabildo* had constituted itself in San Josef and had formed an offensive alliance with the Tibitibi Indians (Warraus) of the Orinoco delta. To their aid had been sent a party of twenty Spaniards under Captain Pedro de Beltranilla, whose purpose it was to punish the Caribs who continually harassed the colony.

Berrio might not have found the gold mines of "El Dorado", but nevertheless he had a prosperous colony to govern. Its source of wealth was tobacco, and a flourishing trade existed with the English and Dutch, who paid for their purchases in manufactured goods. So well did the trade flourish that the town of San Josef was rebuilt and the acreage under tobacco was continually increased; and 400 Negro slaves were purchased from the Dutch.† The Council of the

---

* In Spanish Dominions a local body appointed to conduct police and government of cities and towns. *See* Appendix X.

† It was not until the beginning of the eighteenth century that estate owners in Trinidad began to rely on slave labour for their plantations.

26

Indies* took note of this extensive foreign trade and ordered
Berrio to put an end to it and to cease the cultivation of tobacco
forthwith. This was in conformity with the current Spanish
policy of insisting that all her colonial trade must be with or
through the mother country. Berrio flouted the order and, by
1610, the cultivation of tobacco had so increased that there
were more than twenty vessels engaged in the forbidden trade.

As a result of this open disobedience by the Governor, Don
Sancho de Alquiza was instructed to hold a Residencia which
ended by depriving Berrio of his post for five years. Don Sancho
undertook the Governorship and found himself faced with a
difficult task, for the trade was well established, as was a growing trade with the Main. No Spanish vessels visited the colony
to create an alternate outlet for the island's produce, or to
crush the Caribs who were continually harrying the coasts.

In 1611, Sir Thomas Roe† (best known for his work in the
Middle East) visited the island and reported to his Government
that the Spanish in Trinidad were a proud and indolent people,
yet both needy and weak. The town of San Josef was rich, but
neither it nor the Caroni River was properly defended and the
island could easily be taken and held.

The year 1614 saw the arrival of the first Spanish vessel to
visit the island for nineteen years. Promises were made that there
would be a regular call each October to supply the needs of the
colony and to take the island's produce. This promise was never
fulfilled and trade with the mother country remained at a standstill.

In 1615 Diego Palameque de Acuña was appointed Governor.
He arrived in the colony towards the end of the year, and
carried out the instructions given to him to punish, as enemies
of Spain, all who had any dealings with foreigners. He reported
that the island was in extremely bad condition and that the
inhabitants all seemed to be very poor.

In February, 1618, a report was sent from the Cabildo to the
Governor of Cumana that 'the Corsair Guaterral' (Sir Walter
Raleigh) had passed by the island, had left five ships at Punta

* The supreme authority over all Spanish dominions in America and
the West Indies. It had jurisdiction in all ecclesiastical, civil, military
and commercial matters, appointed colonial officers and approved
colonial laws.
† Sir Thomas Roe was sent from England to report on the Spanish
settlements in the West. He submitted his report to the Lord High
Treasurer of England and Trinidad on February 28th, 1611. He
claimed to have seen in Trinidad "Fifteen sayle of ships, freighting
smoke (tobacco), English, French and Dutch."

27

Gallo and proceeded to San Thomé where he had killed Palameque de Acuña. It was later reported that Acuña had not died at the hands of the English but at those of a Spanish faction, presumably those he had stopped trading illegally in tobacco. They had taken advantage of the English attack, murdered the Governor and hung him like any common malefactor exposed to public view. Fernando de Berrio was reappointed Governor by the Council of the Indies, but soon after had the misfortune to be captured by Moors while returning to Spain, and died in Algiers before he could be released.

Appeals to the mother country for financial aid now met with no response. Conditions on the island went from bad to worse, and by 1633 they had deteriorated so far that there was a grave shortage of clothing and other supplies necessary to maintain life. Wine was in such short supply that it was impossible to celebrate Mass and the colonists were seriously considering vacating the island.

In 1632, when Don Diego Lopez de Escobar arrived to take over the Governorship, he had found the Indians rebellious, a Dutch settlement at Toco in league with the rebels, and preparations in hand for an attack on San Josef, where the defending force was reduced to forty men and boys. Whilst the Dutch were awaiting supplies from Holland, Escobar attacked and drove them from Toco. He followed this in 1636 with an attack on Tobago where he took many Dutch prisoners including Cornelis de Moor, the son of Jan de Moor, founder of the settlement.* Most of the prisoners were sent to Margarita to be hanged, for the Governor of that island had assisted in the attack. The Dutch on the Essequibo, hearing this news, planned a counter-attack in 1637 against the fort of San Thomé in Guayana, where they nearly captured Escobar and managed to release Cornelis de Moor. Encouraged by this success, they descended on San Josef, which they sacked, leaving the few remaining Spaniards to turn their thoughts once more to abandoning such an unprofitable island.

It was in this year that the colony was heavily attacked by the Caribs from the Main under their leader who styled himself "Carib Captain Baron".

Meanwhile Charles I of England had, in 1628, granted the islands of Trinidad, Tobago, Barbados and Fonseca† to Philip,

---

* The date of the attack is erroneously given as 1637 by Bryan Edwards in *The History Civil and Commercial of the British Colonies in the West Indies"* (1793). See also p. 302.
† Fonseca was one of the mythical West Indian islands believed to lie somewhere between 10° and 12° north of the Equator.

Earl of Montgomery (later Earl of Pembroke), though there is no record of the new owner ever visiting his possessions. In 1638, the Earl of Warwick took over Pembroke's patent for Trinidad and Tobago and a company was formed to exploit them. Warwick was Chairman and John Pym* was Treasurer. Other members of Parliament were on the board.

The first attempt by the company to form an English settlement was made from Tobago in 1640. Relying on the support of the Indians, an attack was launched on San Josef, but after four days' fighting the attackers had to withdraw with heavy losses. Another attempt was made in the Punta Galera area and, although twice expelled, a footing was eventually obtained and Major Jeremiah Hartley was formally elected Governor. A second settlement was formed at Moruga and, like its counterpart in the north, was supplemented by people driven from Bermuda by the Spaniards. This southern settlement was almost wiped out by fever, the few survivors leaving for Barbados. The northern settlement under Hartley continued for five years, but fear of disease and of attack by the Spaniards against their ever decreasing numbers eventually forced Hartley and his followers to withdraw.

An earlier settlement had been formed near Punta Galera when Sir Henry Colt, of Colt's Hall, Suffolk, had landed in 1631, and started a settlement at Toco, erecting buildings and starting cultivation. By ill-fortune, a Spanish frigate, blown off her course, put in for water and discovered the newly-founded settlement. After a short skirmish, the Spaniards withdrew, and on making Margarita reported this violation of Spanish territory to the Governor. The evidence was borne out by the crew of a Portuguese sloop which had also called at the settlement for supplies. The Governor of Margarita, Don Juan de Eulate, decided to wipe out the English settlement before it became too difficult to handle. He despatched under his son's command three companies of soldiers and fifty Guayquerie archers who, on arrival, attacked the settlement at dawn and killed all but eleven of the settlers. Colt was one of those who were taken to Margarita, where they were tried and executed late in 1632.

A new Governor was appointed in 1641, Martin Mendoza de la Hoz y Berrio, nephew of Antonio de Berrio. His first duty was to hold a Residencia on the conduct of Escobar, who was suspected of profiteering at the expense of the Spanish

* John Pym (King Pym), one of the most energetic opponents of Charles I, whose eloquence was largely responsible for the impeachment of the Earl of Strafford.

Metropolitan Government. Mendoza's chief claim to fame in the history of the colony was that he refused permission to Père Dionisio Misland, a French Jesuit, to introduce the Inquisition into his territory.*

Progress was as slow in the realm of religion as it was in the fields of economic stability, politics and colonization.

The efforts of Don Manuel Farfan de los Godes, who founded the "Hermandad del Santísimo Sacramento" (the Confraternity of the Blessed Sacrament) at San Josef in 1644, and of Padre Thomas Martinez de Leyba, who founded a similar organization for the Indians, had not produced any great results. Of a total of about four thousand Indians, only two hundred and fifty had been converted and they, with thirty residents in San Josef, were all that stood to the credit of the Roman Church. Nor had the abortive English settlements at Punta Galera and Moruga had any noticeable effect in converting the inhabitants to the Protestant faith.

Trinidad had a reputation for being unhealthy for Europeans and for this reason the French, except the Corsairs, kept clear of the island. Spanish ships still only visited the colony once in twenty years and the coasts were infested with pirates and privateers who used it as a base for repairs and watering. Again and again the crops failed through lack of skilled attention. Trinidad's chief bastions in keeping outsiders at a distance were the reputation of her unhealthy climate, her barren soil, and the lurking dangers of piratical attack. Nevertheless settlers did arrive occasionally, one of the earliest of whom was Fermin y Pradas, an ancestress of the Farfan family of San Josef, whose tombstone dated 1682 still marks the family grave.

In 1686, Father Thomas de Barcelona, Prefect of the Capuchins, acting under a Royal decree of the previous year, landed near Naparima, where San Fernando now stands. Thence he travelled with the Indians along trails through "monstrous thick wood", visiting Indian villages and selecting sites for Capuchin Missions. He chose Purísima Concepción de Naparima; Annunciation de Nazareth, on the Savannah east of Savannah Grande (now known as the Mission of Princetown); and Santa Anna at Savonetta (Couva). The San Fernando Mission is thought to have been founded just to the north of St. Vincent

* Two reasons are given for Mendoza's action. (1) That in the colonies where the Inquisition existed, the powers of the Governor were circumscribed. (2) By this time the Dutch and English influence on the Indians in Trinidad was negligible but in Guiana much stronger. Mendoza sent Père Misland to Guiana.

Street, as an old tumbled down church was situated there before the town was founded by the Spaniards.*

In 1684 the Alcaldes reported to the Governor of Margarita that the French had carried off the Governor, Ponce de Leon, whilst on a visit to Guayana, and that there remained very few Spaniards in the colony. The capture of the Governor was tragedy enough, even though he was held only for a matter of months, but worse was to follow.

In 1699 the Alcaldes Ordinarios reported that they had been obliged to take over the government of the island in conformity with the law of the Indies. The Governor, Don José de Leon y Eschales, and certain officials and missionaries, had been murdered at San Francisco de las Arenales (San Rafael). Here the Capuchins had a Mission and Fathers Estevan de San Felix and Marcos de Viqueand, with Raymondo de Figuerola, a lay brother, had worked successfully amongst the Indians. In that year they had begun work on a large church with the help of a number of the local Indians. Father Estevan, whilst directing operations, instructed some of these Indians to place a beam in a certain position. This the Indians refused to do and started blaspheming as they lost their tempers. Father Estevan, fearing that the situation might get out of hand, as his remonstrances were having no effect, warned the men that the Governor was due to visit the district and would use stern measures if they persisted in their foolishness. This incensed the Indians so much that one of them struck the good Father over the head, mortally wounding him. He managed to struggle into the church, where he knelt before the altar and prayed for the forgiveness of his assailants. Four of the Indians, armed with bows and arrows, then entered the church, shot at him and followed this up by chopping off his head. This victory over an unarmed and peaceful man increased their excitement, and they dragged his body to the site of the new building, where they flung it into the foundations. Next they turned on Father Marcos, who was reading the Hours in the Presbytery. He was similarly attacked, clubbed to death and flung into the foundations. Brother Raymondo was treated in a like fashion by the ever-increasing crowd.

To mark their victory over the Spaniards, a mock Mass was celebrated in the church. The chalice and paten were broken up so that pieces could be worn as charms or ornaments. The vest-

* Other Missions were founded about this time at Montserrat, Arima, Guayaguayare, Mayaro and Moruga. The two last were soon abandoned owing to the hostility of the Indians. One Mission was established at La Cocos (The Cocal) c. 1694.

31

ments also were torn up and used as gugyucos—little skirts—
and the images were dragged out of the building and smashed to
pieces.

Once the final flush of excitement was over, the fear of punishment descended on the Indians, and after discussing what
was best to be done they decided to meet trouble half-way. They
successfully ambushed the Governor in a gully, killing him and
several of his retinue before withdrawing. Some of the official
party managed to escape, though wounded, and took back the
news of the massacre to San Josef.

The Indians now realized the full extent of their crime and
fled with their families into the hills. The legend has it that they
met the Devil, who advised them to go to Punta Galera and to
make a stand. Before they could get away, an expedition from
San Josef caught up with them and killed some of their number.
The remainder pushed on towards a small island off the Cocal
in the hopes of finding safety from the avenging Spaniards.

So serious a matter as the murder of a Governor could not
go unpunished and the Cabildo sent a force of one hundred
Christian Indians under General Antonio de la Cruz to find and
capture the fugitives. A skirmish took place on the Cocal and
the remnant of the rebel force was driven on to Punta Galera.
Here, surrounded by the sea and their enemies, many threw
themselves and their children into the water. Those who were
captured were taken to San Josef, where they were tortured,
and a total of sixty-one were killed. The women and children
were condemned to slavery.

By the end of the century the condition of the island was
critical. Many of the Indian inhabitants had died during the
recurrent waves of smallpox, malaria and yellow fever, and
there only remained fifteen villages in the colony, whilst the
number of Spaniards was negligible.

CHAPTER FOUR

THE LAST DAYS OF THE SPANISH GOVERNMENT, 1700–1797

THE EARLY years of the eighteenth century were uneventful under the successive Governors, Francisco Ruiz de Aguirre (1701–1705); Felipe de Alcieda (1705–1711) and Cristoval de Guzman (1711–1716). The last named had the distinction of being the first Governor to climb the mountain of Maracas (Tucuche), though in the hot and humid climate his exertions to reach the look-out from which the approach of a seaborne enemy could be observed almost overcame him.

There was still a grave shortage of household commodities and, it appears, of priests, for one of the Capuchin missionaries at Naparima was unable to leave the island even after ten years' unbroken service. In 1721, when Martin Perez de Anda y Salazar, the new Governor of Trinidad and Guayana arrived, he at once requested Spain to send more priests to carry out the complete conversion of the Indians.

Nor was the colony safe from the invader. Edward Teach (Blackbeard) entered the Gulf of Paria in 1716, attacked shipping and burned, amongst others, a ship loaded with cacao for Cadiz. It was only the unexpected arrival of a Spanish frigate that put an end to his depredations.

Cacao, first grown in the colony in about 1615, was becoming more and more important to the island, so much so that the complete failure of the crop in 1725 was disastrous to the inhabitants. The planters blamed their ill-fortune on the presence of a comet; Father Gamella (or Gumilla) on the fact that they had not been regular in paying tithes!

By the turn of the century there was still no improvement in conditions. The surviving Indians were perpetually in need of food and medical attention. The repeated failure of the crops made it impossible to pay taxes. Appeals for assistance to the mother country fell on deaf ears, for Spain had tried to colonize on too vast a scale and considered the value of each colony on

B   33

its ability to produce precious metals and gems. Neither gold nor diamonds to adorn the Spanish crown could be found in Trinidad, whose wealth lay almost untouched in her soil. Untouched, for industrious cultivators were few and far between, owing to lack of encouragement from home. The revenue of the colony was so small that it was of little account to Spain. As long as it was sufficient to pay for the garrison of twenty soldiers stationed in the fort at the mouth of the Caroni, the colony was not to be abandoned. The few Spanish families lived in poverty near San Josef, the capital, and this neglected outpost of the Spanish Empire received a visit from its Bishop only once every five or six years. Disease was constantly spreading from the mainland and, though extra guards were placed in the Bocas, smallpox took a steady toll, particularly of the Indians.

By 1750, the morale of the colony was at its lowest ebb. The island had been attacked by a party of English who landed at Las Cuevas Bay and tried to reach San Josef by the hill path into Maracas Valley. They abandoned the attempt as the prospect of plundering the capital showed little promise of making the journey over the hills worth while.

The inhabitants were apathetic, indolent and poverty-stricken, making no effort to help themselves. Under the Governorship of Francisco Manclares (1752–1757) there was a slight revival of the cacao trade and a rise in the population. This seems only to have been a flash in the pan for, when Manclares was replaced by General Pedro de la Modena, a report was sent to Spain giving the new Governor's impression of his territory. The people, he declared, were too lazy to build houses or to mend the roads, claiming that they had not even the time to weed their gardens because they had to mount guard at the Caroni fort, as the garrison had been reduced to ten. They had no desire to repair the road, for they considered it would take twelve months to complete the work and they were not interested in working so long. With a food shortage, which the inhabitants blamed on the bad state of the fishing industry, they stated it was impossible to set about building houses. Beside this, they claimed that there was only one carpenter in the island and it was cheaper and easier to live in the woods.

The shortage of qualified people in the colony was shown by the Illustrious Cabildo's attempt to stop Gabriel Infanta, a medical man, leaving the island to visit his family. The Cabildo feared that it would be impossible to replace the man who had looked after the sick and provided medicine free of charge.

34

With inadequate medical facilities, the perpetual presence of malaria, yellow fever and intermittent outbreaks of smallpox on the mainland, it is little wonder that extra guards were posted at Point Gourde, Chaguaramas and Point la Brea to prevent foreigners landing. The arrival of a French doctor, Juan Bey, was greeted with the utmost joy in 1765.

Not only did the island suffer from disease, but in 1765 there was a strong earth tremor which damaged the church and many flimsily built houses in San Josef. Damage was confined to property, for most of the inhabitants merely maintained a house in town to satisfy the law, and lived in huts in the neighbouring woods.

The year 1772 saw the complete failure of the cacao crop through drought. In consequence there was a relapse into extreme poverty, so much so that two years later the Illustrious Cabildo declared that its members were unable to travel to Port of Spain, where the Governor, Juan de Dios Valdez, was in residence. It was the custom at this time for members of the Cabildo to wait upon the Governor on the occasion of the birth-day of the King of Spain to pay their respects. They now suggested that the Governor ought to make it his business to visit the Cabildo at San Josef, the capital of the colony.

At long last Spain began to take an interest in Trinidad. Foreign immigration to the island was permitted under restrictions in 1776. Until the following year both Trinidad and Margarita were in the Vice-Royalty of the New Kingdom of Grenada with its capital at Santa Fé. Being so far distant from their base, little was known about the two islands, but now they were transferred to the Government and military command of the Captain General of Venezuela. Engineers were sent out from Spain to advise on the steps to be taken to encourage and develop agriculture and commerce in Trinidad. While this economic mission was in the colony, the Governor was entertaining two Frenchmen, Mons. E. M. Nol, later to become a large landholder in the island, and Mons. P. R. Roume St. Laurent from Grenada, who later reported his findings on the island to his Governor.

That St. Laurent was impressed with what he saw, even if he did not like it all, is evident from his description of the island. Healthy, with many plants and animals, the woods full of howler monkeys and many species of flying quadrupeds and snakes—some venomous. There were, he claimed, many types of table birds, plenty of fish in the rivers and surrounding sea but a large number of frogs, whose croaking was most disagreeable. He mentions that the coconuts on the east coast (the Cocal) were by tradition the cargo of a ship from Africa which had been wrecked, the coconuts being washed ashore and taking root. Cacao and coffee flourished and several crops of corn were harvested every year without the use of manure and with only the most primitive cultivation. He reported on two pitch lakes and a mine of pitcoal (charbon du terre). On the strength of what he saw, he advocated French immigration to Trinidad. So enthusiastic was his advocacy of this policy that he visited the Spanish Court at Madrid and succeeded in persuading the King to pass the famous Royal Cedula on Colonization in 1783.* This offered generous grants of land to settlers on condition that they took the oath of allegiance to the King of Spain and that they were Roman Catholics. Additional grants were made to all immigrants who brought slaves with them. This encouragement to settlers with slaves by grants of extra land was very unpopular in Tobago and the Grenadines as it encouraged slave stealing. In Grenada most stringent laws were passed against visitors from Trinidad. These included a bond of $1,000 on landing and very severe penalties for attempts to steal or coerce slaves.

The new immigration policy saw the beginning of a new era in the life of Port of Spain. Governors had been living in this town since General Pedro de la Modena had refused to remain at San Josef in 1757. It was a small township of a few houses on the east side of St. Ann's River where boats made their landings across the mud. A church was built in 1781 on a site later known as Tamarind Square, and on August 21st of 1783 the Illustrious Cabildo, having abandoned the old capital, held their first meeting in Port-of-Spain.

The following year saw the arrival of the last and perhaps the greatest of the Spanish Governors, in the person of José Maria Chacon, an ex-naval officer. Under his guidance the colony prospered as never before, the population increased and it was rumoured that Trinidad might even replace Cartagena as the West Indian arsenal. A fort was built on the Laventille hills overlooking both town and sea and a new town was founded at San Fernando on the site of an old Indian settlement. The Rio Santa Anna (now the Dry River) was diverted into a new course along the foot of the hills in an effort to improve the health of Port of Spain. Chacon himself bore one-third of the

* See Appendix I.

cost of this work, which was carried on under the guidance of José del Poza at a cost of about three thousand dollars.

As the town grew (by 1787, it had seven streets running north and south and three running east and west), so its protection was increased. A small stone battery was erected offshore and connected to the mole with a wooden bridge. This was known as Fort San André or "the Mole Battery" and was protected by five cannon. The mole itself was constructed for the convenience of shipping. A new Government House was completed near the waterfront on the corner of the present Charlotte Street and Marine Square, and here Chacon took up residence.

Chacon did his utmost to develop the natural resources of the island and in so doing created the posts of Commissaries of Population, dividing the colony into three parts, over which each Commissary was to have charge.

1. Las Cuevas, Salibia, Guanapo, Tacarigua, Cimaronero, Ventilla (Laventille), Santa Anna, Tragarete, Maraval, Diego Martin and Carenero.
2. Naparima, Galeota, Cocal and Guatero.
3. Guapo, Los Gallos and Guayaguayare.

Their principal duties were to obtain "with the greatest exactitude, a knowledge of the lands" in their division

". . . to know those lands which have been granted and those which remain to be granted; to know the estate of each inhabitant and the cultivation which each carries on; to examine the navigable rivers therein and the roads which have already been opened and those which ought to be made to facilitate the transport of produce; also whatsoever can further conduce to the agriculture, the commerce and population of these Divisions, the peace and happiness of the inhabitants."

Chacon also endeavoured to raise a loan of a million dollars from the Royal Exchequer in Spain for the purchase of fresh slaves to overcome labour conditions. His application was refused owing to lack of funds but he was given permission to work with the Illustrious Cabildo in finding any European country which would grant the money on condition that the interest and capital were repaid entirely from the profits made in the colony. To assist in financing the day to day work of the Cabildo, he arranged for the islands of Patos, Huevos and Monos to be transferred to the Illustrious body so that they would receive the benefit of their rents.

Relations between Spain and England were friendly when Chacon became Governor and H.M. Sloop *Boneta*, under the command of Captain Ricketts, paid a courtesy visit. The captain reported to his superior officers that the defences of the island were very feeble, confined as they were to Fort San André and the Bocas. The forests, he noted, were full of fine timber but all mahogany was reserved for the Spanish Navy. The people he described as Spaniards, French, people of colour, Negroes, Indians (natives), some American adventurers and some English at Tacarigua and more in Port of Spain.

European events had their reflection in Trinidad, for, in 1790, Jean Villoux,* the editor of a weekly paper, was expelled from the colony for publishing extracts from the foreign Press which Chacon considered unsuitable reading for those under his care. Though his policy appeared reactionary, on occasions Chacon could be progressive; witness the support he gave to Don Cosmo de Churruca in 1792, in establishing an observatory at Fort San André. From here the correct latitude of Port of Spain was fixed, the first town in the new world to be placed accurately on the map. Chacon also encouraged the pitch industry and a factory was opened at La Brea, where pitch was prepared for export at a rate of about seven hundred barrels per year, the first shipment being sent to the Royal Arsenal in Spain.

With the outbreak of the French Revolution, the population of the island was increased by an influx of refugees who, in their turn, were followed by Republicans, for France cast envious eyes on an island in which England had started interesting herself, particularly when such an island was well placed for its owners to use it as a base for attacks on shipping.

Chacon's position was extremely delicate. He was Governor of a Spanish island whose population was largely French, even though they had taken an oath of allegiance to the Spanish Crown. Spain and England were not at war and English ships used the port regularly. The situation was intolerable, for there were constant fights between the French inhabitants and the English seamen.

In May, 1796, such a battle took place between the French in Port of Spain and the sailors from an English frigate. Starting as a simple brawl, it nearly led to the destruction of the town, with the French breaking into the arsenal to arm themselves, and the English under Captain Vaughan landing with drums playing and colours flying. Chacon had such a small force that

* See Appendix II.

38

it was almost impossible to stop the frequent breaches of the peace and it was not until England and Spain were finally at war that his position was eased.

England did not so much need Trinidad as desire to have the island under her control. Ever since the publication of the Cedula on Colonization there had been raids on other West Indian islands to steal slaves so that increased grants of land could be obtained in the colony. The French Republicans who had arrived in the island made no secret of the fact that they would seize the place for France as soon as a suitable opportunity occurred. Thus, in Abercromby's instructions, Trinidad was described as

"a source of great mischief to British Islands, being a shelter for privateers who annoyed their trade and as an asylum for bad people of every description who make depredations on the coasts carrying off slaves and property."

CHAPTER FIVE

CAPITULATION, 1797

AT THE outbreak of war, the British fleet started raiding Spanish shipping in the West Indies and effected a virtual blockade of Trinidad. In anticipation of attack, Chacon constructed additional forts on the island of Gasparee, on the property of Nicholas de Percin. The situation with which he was faced was not encouraging. The troops in his garrison were in poor health, many being laid low by fever of a type which Dr. Williams, a resident of the colony, declared to be curable only by the removal of the sufferers to high ground or out to sea. Sickness was also raging in the several vessels anchored in Chaguaramas Bay and the consequent lack of protection had brought trade with the mainland to a virtual standstill.

The units of the Spanish fleet in the island were inadequate to give the protection which Chacon considered necessary against the attack which was sure to come from the British force. Rear-Admiral Apodoca arrived in January, 1797, and brought the total force to four ships and one frigate, but within a month Chacon's worst fears materialized. On February 17th, Admiral Harvey appeared off Trinidad with seventeen armed ships and forty transports containing some eight thousand men under the command of Sir Ralph Abercromby.* With his greater force, Harvey considered that he could dictate the course of any engagement that might take place and anchored off Five Islands and prepared to attack on the following day.

Chacon, who was entertaining Admiral Apodoca when the British fleet was sighted, implored his guest to return to his ships at Chaguaramas to attack and destroy the invader at all costs. Apodoca, seeing that he was outgunned and outnumbered, preferred to destroy his fleet rather than suffer defeat.† At two o'clock in the morning of February 18th, he ordered the burning

* See Appendix III.
† See Appendix IV.

40

of his ships, all of which, with the exception of *San Damaso* were a total loss. At dawn Harvey engaged the new forts on Gasparee, which were evacuated after a brief exchange and at noon made his first landing at Mucurapo* whence the troops advanced towards Port of Spain against only slight opposition. It was not until the site of the present St. James's Barracks was reached that shots were exchanged in earnest.

When the size of the British force was seen, many of the Republican French overpowered the guard at the arsenal, armed themselves and took to the woods, where they were followed by the Spanish reinforcements sent out from the town. This diversion did not affect Abercromby, who continued his advance through the Maraval valley and entered Port-of-Spain without further opposition. On arrival he discovered that Chacon had sent the archives to San Josef for safety and had retired with his staff to the fort on the Laventille hills. Having taken the town without loss (his only battle casualty in the whole operation being Lt. Villeneau, who died from wounds a few days after the capitulation), he sent a messenger to Chacon with instructions to :—

"State to the Governor that I see with sorrow his troops are without hope of being able to carry out his wishes; that the undeniable superiority of the troops under my command has rendered me master of the town, and that he is surrounded on all sides, both by sea and land, without the slightest chance of assistance. With such unequal forces resistance is for him impossible, and before causing a considerable amount of bloodshed without any hope of ultimate success, I beg of him to name a place for conference. I offer him an honourable capitulation on such terms as are due to good and faithful soldiers who would otherwise be sacrificed in vain."

This message was accepted and the Articles of Capitulation were signed at Valsayn,† the site of the present Government Stock Farm, on February 18th, 1797.

The fall of Trinidad was a bitter blow to the King of Spain, who at once set up a Council of War under the Governor of Cadiz, to enquire into the behaviour of Chacon and Apodoca. The Council sifted the evidence and recommended to the King that the innocence of his officers, including Chacon and Apodoca, should be proclaimed in all the Royal Domain in Europe and

* Invaders' Bay, near Wrightson Road, Port of Spain.
† See Appendix V.

41

America, especially in the Province of Caracas and the islands. All concerned with the capitulation and the burning of the fleet should be exonerated from blame and compensation was suggested for the rigorous imprisonment they had suffered after their return to Spain. The King refused to accept the recommendations of his Council, holding that Chacon had failed to defend the colony and that Apodoca had prematurely burned his ships. He deprived both officers of their posts and Chacon was banished from the Royal Domain for life, without the right of appeal against the Royal Decree. Perpetual silence was enjoined on all concerned, including the captains who had carried out Apodoca's orders, who were also punished by being suspended for a period of four years. Chacon was unable to gain his restitution and died in exile, but Apodoca's case was reconsidered in 1809, and he was reinstated.

In the simplest engagement of the war and with the minimum number of casualties, Trinidad passed into British possession.

CHAPTER SIX

TRINIDAD UNDER PICTON, 1797–1803

(1) *Settling In*

THE CAPITULATION did not at first make a great difference
to the life of the island, as the laws of Spain were to remain in
force until such time as the British Government saw fit to make
alterations or to return the island to its Spanish owners. The inhabitants were ordered to swear allegiance to the King of
England before February 22nd, and all persons of French origin
were compelled to report to the British Commandant by March
1st. Apart from this change of allegiance, there was little that
could be done, for the future of the colony was uncertain. War
was still being waged and there was always the chance that the
island would be attacked and retaken. Trinidad was also expected
to have a good bargaining value when the time came for a final
settlement. There was, too, the problem of language, which
would have to be faced. Spanish was the language of the law
courts and the government offices. Any attempt at a rapid change
from Spanish ways to English would be difficult owing to the
scarcity of English officials who could speak Spanish; and there
was the added difficulty that under any future peace treaty
Trinidad might be returned to Spain.

Admiral Harvey and Sir Ralph Abercromby did not delay
long after receiving Chacon's capitulation, but moved on to
Martinique, leaving Lt. Colonel Thomas Picton, of the 50th
Regiment, as Governor of the island.* They also appointed John
Nihell, an Irish immigrant under the Cedula of 1783, and expert
in Spanish law and procedure, to be Chief Justice.

Picton, a man of action, with a heavy responsibility on his
shoulders, determined that at all costs the island must be properly
held. The immediate threat of counter-attack from the mainland
was removed when the Governor of Caracas, faced with insurrection in his own province, was forced to withdraw the

* See Appendix VI.

43

force he had assembled against Angostura. Nevertheless, Picton created a police force in the capital and slowly extended it through the colony. With this force he was able to impose an eight o'clock curfew on all shops and to restrict the sale of liquor to soldiers. This action was necessary as many of the men under his command were Germans of the Hompsesch Fusiliers, in which regiment there was such a lively spirit of insubordination that the Governor was forced to confine them to barracks in Port of Spain under his own watchful eye. Even after taking this precaution he was obliged by the number of desertions to offer rewards for the apprehension of missing men either alive or dead, and to keep firm control he was forced to make a stern example of four men who had assaulted and robbed a free Negro woman. To make sure that the civil life of the colony was conducted properly he removed from office many corrupt officials and lawyers, including the Assessor for Spanish Law.*

Relations with the Spanish mainland were naturally difficult. The Governors of Caracas and Cumana collected information from the French and Spanish malcontents and openly offered rewards to all who deserted from the British forces and reached their provinces. They realized that a British-held Trinidad would always be a menace to the Spanish American Empire and, in their eagerness to recapture the island, without a fight, placed a price on Picton's head. When Picton received news of this, he wrote to the Governor of Caracas :—

" Sir :
Your Excellency has highly flattered my vanity by the handsome value which you have been pleased to fix on my head. $20,000 is an offer which would not discredit your Master's munificence. As the trifle has had the good fortune to recommend itself to Your Excellency's attention, come and take it; and it will be very much at your service; in expectation of which I have the honour, etc., etc.,

Thomas Picton.

The price put on Picton's head was occasioned by information which the Audiencia of Caracas had received secretly from a French priest resident in Trinidad. He stated that the English Government was very unpopular in the island and that the discontented French, Spanish and Germans far outnumbered the British garrison. It was recommended that action be taken if the reports were true, and the French were as numerous and as

* Equivalent of Attorney General.

influential as was claimed. The information was supported by a report from Chacon that before he left Trinidad he had heard Picton was ready and willing to carry the war to the Main. Before embarking on such a campaign, Picton was carrying on a propaganda war by distributing leaflets and notices to the inhabitants of the coastal areas.

The Secretary of State for the Colonies* in London instructed Picton to do all possible to promote trade with the Spanish Main, even by contraband means, in spite of the continued war between the two countries. To encourage this, the port of St. Josef (Port of Spain), the most convenient and obvious place, was on June 6th, 1797, declared a " free port ". Picton issued a Proclamation stating :—

" By virtue of an official paper which I, the Governor of this Island of Trinidad, have received from the Rt. Hon. Henry Dundas, Minister of His Britannic Majesty's foreign affairs, which is literally as follows :

The object which at present I desire most particularly to recommend to your attention, is the means which might best be adopted to liberate the people of the continent near to the Island of Trinidad from the oppressive and tyrannic system which supports with so much vigour the monopoly of commerce, under the title of exclusive registers which their government licences demand; also to draw the greatest advantages possible, and which the local situation of the Island presents, by opening a direct and free communication with the other parts of the world without prejudice to the commerce of the British Nation. In order to fulfil this intention with the greater facility, it will be prudent for your Excellency to animate the inhabitants of Trinidad in keeping up the communication which they had with those of Tierra Firma previous to the reduction of that Island, under the assurance that they will find there an entrepot or general magazines of every sort of goods whatsoever. To this end His Britannic Majesty has determined in Council to grant freedom to the ports of Trinidad, with a direct trade to Great Britain. With regard to the hopes you entertain of raising the spirits of those persons with whom you are in correspondence towards encouraging the inhabitants to resist the oppressive authority of their government, I have little more to say, than that they may be certain that whenever they are in that disposition they may receive at your hands all the succours to be expected from His Britannic Majesty, be it with forces, or with arms and ammunition to

* Prior to 1854 the post of Secretary of State for the Colonies was held in conjunction with the War Department.

45

any extent; with the assurance that the views of His Britannic Majesty go no further than to secure to them their independence, without pretending to any sovereignty over their country, nor even to interfere in the privileges of the people, nor in their political, civil, or religious rights."

Unfortunately lack of naval support enabled enemy privateers to cut communications with the mainland and ships were constantly attacked and captured in the Gulf of Paria. Frequently, Picton drew Abercromby's attention to this fact and informed him that the coast from Toco to Mayaro was infested with French pirates and privateers and was, consequently, cut off from the island's capital. Eventually Abercromby agreed to the arming of launches and there was an immediate increase in contraband trade with the Spanish colonies.

Picton was eager to carry the war to the Spanish Main, and even went so far as to advocate the issue of arms to would-be Spanish American insurgents. With the care of Trinidad on his hands he was unable to say too much about prospects of initiating an attack, particularly as his troops were in sickly condition and there was a constant danger of a revolt by the French people of colour. To counteract this threat, he arrested the ringleaders of a potential rising and formed the Militia, his aim being a force of three thousand infantry, cavalry and artillery in five divisions—The Port of Spain Division, The Diego Martin Corps, the St. Joseph Rifle Corps, the Couva and Pointe-a-Pièrre Battalion, and the North and South Naparima Corps.

The Militia and all the defences of the island were paid for out of a 3½ per cent tax imposed by Abercromby on all imports and exports since the capitulation, one quarter of the income being reserved to pay the expenses of the Illustrious Cabildo. Picton, by careful and economic administration, managed to keep the actual tax down to 1¾ per cent, much to the satisfaction of the local merchants and indeed of the Home Government in the United Kingdom who, in January, 1798, advised him that:—

" In consideration of the extraordinary expense attending civil and military command of the Island an allowance of £1,200 per annum should be made to the Governor."

This was to be charged against the island's revenue.

The first year of Picton's administration was taken up more largely with the civil life of the colony than the military. Now in 1798, Lt. General Cuyler, temporary successor to Abercromby, as Commander West Indies Station, visited Trinidad and made recommendations for its defence, favouring St. Joseph* as a suitable location for the garrison and stores. Admiral Harvey, Commander-in-Chief Naval Forces, despatched the sloop *Bee* and the tender *Regulator* from his base at Martinique with a detachment of troops who, with men from the Trinidad Rangers, under Captain Soter, made an expedition against the French privateers. These privateers, by banding together, had become so great a menace to shipping in the gulf that active steps had to be taken against them. The expedition was successful though the *Regulator* was lost with all hands in the Boca Grande on the return journey.

Picton was still interested in attacking the Spanish Main and despatches to Abercromby, Cuyler,† Harvey and the Secretary of State, show how low he considered the morale of the population. He asked for three thousand men, one ship of the line and a frigate, together with some pieces of artillery to throw into the Caracas and Cumana provinces, where he firmly believed the Spaniards would soon be forced to capitulate if the attacking force was properly handled. Permission to undertake this venture was not granted and Picton had to concentrate his energies on defence.

At the end of 1798, the peace of the island was threatened by the presence of a force of refugees from Trinidad who had found shelter on the Main and now wished to return. They assembled fully armed on the coast of Paria, intent on joining their discontented friends in the colony. When Picton received news of this move he sent detachments of Trinidad Rangers and Soter's Corps to deal with the menace. At their approach the refugees fled, leaving their stocks and supplies behind them.

Picton now pressed for a sloop to be based permanently on the island for trade protection and built Fort Abercromby at Las Cuevas Bay as a suitable base for this protective work. The nearest he got to fulfilling his plan to attack the Main was when a naval force under command of Captain Dickson arrived in the colony. To H.M. ships *Victorieuse* and *Invincible* and the sloop *Zephyr* was added a picked body of Royal Rangers under Major Laureal, for an expedition against the batteries on the Rio Caribe and at Carruseano (Caruspano). The attack was successful and in addition to putting the batteries out of action, two French privateers were captured. The expedition, though seemingly trivial in material results, was important in that it

* The modern name for San Josef de Oruña.
† See Appendix VII.

47

removed all doubts from the minds of the inhabitants of the Orinoco area as to the nature of British policy in South America. No longer did they regard invitations to trade as a ruse to betray them and seize their property. Trinidad itself was delighted that trade had been so happily opened up and the merchants presented Captain Dickson with a sword as a token of their appreciation of his good work.

Picton's chief difficulty with defence was the impossibility of doing anything adequate with only six hundred and fifty effective men scattered throughout an island whose inhabitants were for the most part of colour, and many of whom had been obliged to leave other West Indian islands for a variety of reasons. He summed them up as " irredeemably republicans ", whom nothing but the arm of authority, exercised without relexation, could keep in order. He required a force of at least two thousand effectives to replace the 57th Regiment, which, after long years in the tropics, was fit for light duty only, and to relieve his coloured battalion of the 12th West India Regiment. A surprise attack on the island would mean its loss and communication with other islands was so slow that reinforcements could not arrive in time to be of assistance. Strong fortifications were another necessity if the island was to remain in British hands, as the inhabitants were on the whole of a disposition which made it difficult, if not impossible, to turn them into loyal citizens. They were ready, Picton knew, to join the enemies of Britain, whether French or Spanish. He took up with the Commander-in-Chief West Indies the question of support in case of attack, pointing out that Tobago and Grenada were his only sources of aid, but that they were of little worth unless communications could be guaranteed by a British naval force.

His reports on Trinidad to the Secretary of State gave his reasons for considering the colony one of the most important held by England. Port of Spain harbour he described as large, safe, the healthiest in the West Indies and the only one in which a fleet could safely shelter during the hurricane season. The Pitch Lake contained an inexhaustible supply of the finest quality pitch, there was ample timber on the island for repairs to ships, a good place for careenage and sufficient water for the largest ship afloat. The commercial value of the port he considered to be enormous. The land generally was fertile; sugar, coffee, cotton and cacao could be cultivated successfully, and whereas in some of the other islands the soil was being worked out, in Trinidad it was in good condition. Capital, he thought, should be invested

48

in the colony. Already settlers from the Bahamas and from the Danish and Swedish islands were purchasing land in Trinidad. He considered that the "poor whites" from Barbados and the other colonies should be encouraged to settle, as well as a certain number of free coloured peoples, but he did not think it advisable at the time to entrust such a mixed and illiterate population with any legislative powers. It would be better to wait until the country was more settled and had acquired the necessary degree of constitutional consistency.

Picton saw that the best way to increase trade for Trinidad would be to encourage and help Spanish colonials who were ready to rise in rebellion. In return for assistance it should not be impossible to obtain concessions on a free Venezuelan coast from Point Peña to Rio Guardapeche, thus ensuing safety for shipping in the Gulf of Paria and facilitating the introduction of cattle and mules into the colony. If arrangements could be made for the free navigation of the Orinoco, there appeared no reason why British manufactured goods should not be sold throughout South America.

When events in Europe made it appear that peace was imminent, Picton earnestly represented to the Secretary of State the inadvisability of returning the colony to Spain, as all who had co-operated with the British administration were marked men. The memories of what had happened in Havana when it had been returned to Spain in 1763* still lingered on and it would make an indelible impression on the minds of all South Americans if the same happened in Trinidad. It would turn the rebellious Spanish colonies against British policy and against her trade in the western world.

(2) *Peaceful Penetration*

The turn of the century saw an improvement in Picton's position. With peace not far off and negotiations already begun, the likelihood of invasion of the island declined. Napoleon, now First Consul, strongly opposed the cession of Trinidad to the British, but the British Government held out against his views and on June 29th, 1801, appointed Picton as Civil Governor of Trinidad, at a salary of £3,000 per annum.

The colony was reserved as an "island of experiment" without a Legislative Assembly, chiefly on account of the growing anti-slavery campaign. The abolitionists were gaining influence with the English Government who, whilst not yet being

---

* Those who had co-operated with the British were ill-treated.

49

prepared to promote legislation, were ready to see that the evils of the system were not extended. Canning* expressed the Government's view when he declared that laws passed by an assembly of owners and merchants could only bring misery to the helpless slaves. "Trust not the masters in what concerns the slaves." As a result of this and other influences, Governors of colonies which had slave populations were instructed to do all in their power to improve the conditions of the slaves. Picton, in response to this instruction, published one of the most humane codes of slavery ever drawn up,† but, as it did not receive the Royal Assent within the necessary two years, it was allowed to lapse.

There being no Legislative Council, Picton was instructed to appoint a Council of Advice having neither legislative powers nor control over the Governor to whom it would be responsible in an advisory capacity only. To this Council Picton appointed John Black, John Nihell, St. Hilaire de Bégorrat, Don Christoval de Robles, and John Nugent,‡ and he gradually extended its field of working until the Illustrious Cabildo was limited merely to the affairs of Port of Spain.§ He also revived the Court of Consulado, or Mercantile Court under the eye of John Nihell. To further the good of his colony, he appointed in England a Mr. William Knox, already Agent for New Brunswick and Dominica, to be Colonial Agent for Trinidad at a salary of £500 per year.

Though peace had not yet been signed between France and England, it had been clear since the appointment of Picton as Civil Governor that England intended to retain the colony. The Cabildo sent a petition to the King expressing :—

"the universal joy and satisfaction of the inhabitants on learning that Trinidad is to become part of Your Majesty's dominions . . ."

and asking that Spanish Law and religion might continue until a permanent form of Government was settled. They also suggested that an Assembly should be elected from the island's twenty-three parishes and the eight barrios of Port of Spain, should include two members of the Governor's Council of Advice and be presided over by the Governor. They desired that this

* George Canning was leader of the House of Commons. In 1827 he became Prime Minister.
† See Appendix VIII.
‡ See Appendix IX.
§ See Appendix X.

Assembly should at a later date determine " the system of government and administration of justice most appropriate to the situation."

Picton was not wholeheartedly in favour of this suggestion. He considered that with only one-sixth of the population English, and not all those reliable, the concession of a free legislature might prove ruinous. He countered the suggestion with a proposal that certain picked planters and merchants should be given temporary legislative powers.

In 1801 occurred a case which, though insignificant in itself, was to have a profound effect on Picton's subsequent career.

Pedro Ruis, a small government contractor and owner of a waterfront shop, found one evening that his savings of about $2,000 had been stolen from a trunk on his premises. There were three possible suspects—his partner, Pedro Perez, his mistress, Louisa Calderon, and her young friend, Carlos Gonzales. Ruis reported the facts to Picton, who was taking his evening walk in the vicinity, and a little later the three suspects were arrested.

Before the First Alcalde, St. Hilaire de Bégorrat, Louisa Calderon denied all knowledge of the theft, but she left the impression that she was not telling the whole truth. Under the current Spanish law, torture could be applied to a refractory witness. The question was laid before Picton who agreed with the normal procedure of the law and signed the certificate permitting the use of torture. As a result, Carlos Gonzales was ordered to pay a fine of $1,800, to be put to hard labour until the fine was paid, and finally to be banished from the colony.

Louisa Calderon seems to have suffered no ill effects for she required no medical attention and within a few minutes of being released walked over a mile to the store to explain how the money had been taken. As she walked, it is reported that she was smoking a cigar! In defence, at her trial, she pleaded only her youth as a reason that she should not undergo torture, claiming falsely that she was only fourteen years of age. She was finally released and no further notice of the trial was taken in Trinidad. Though not a very pleasant story of contemporary justice, it is more than likely that had the case been heard in England both Calderon and Gonzales would have been hanged.

With the cessation of hostilities, numbers of English adventurers arrived in Trinidad seeking to exploit the colony before any final settlement for its future might be made. In Picton they found themselves up against a stern Governor who was determined that they should not have their way. In an effort to force his hand, they formed the "English Party" and set about making things as difficult as possible for the administration.

On March 25th, 1802, the formal Treaty of Amiens was signed. Under Article IV of this document, "His Catholic Majesty ceded and guaranteed in full property and sovereignty the Island of Trinidad to His Britannic Majesty."

The "English Party" now came into the open with an address to the King asking for free representation in a House of Assembly and for trial by jury. To collect signatures for this petition, a dinner, ostensibly for celebrating the signing of the treaty, was organized in Mr. Wharton's tavern. Picton deemed the arrangement for the dinner to be seditious and warned Wharton that he would be held personally responsible for any consequences of the meeting. The dinner was postponed, but at a public meeting held on December 18th a previously prepared address to the King was put forward. A number of respectable inhabitants had already signed, not realizing its importance, but when it was suggested that the address be sent to the King through the Agent in England rather than through the Governor, many withdrew from the meeting, which gradually became more and more violent until at last the Chairman, William Harrison, retired. Thomas Higham, one of the merchants involved, was called before Picton, who demanded a copy of the address, and on his refusal to part with it, was arrested. The following day a copy was handed to the Governor, who released Higham but removed both his name and that of his friend, John Shaw, from the roll of officers of the Militia.

Picton acted strongly in suppressing the "English Party" owing to the tension between them and the free coloured population over the change from Spanish to English law.

The "English Party" rallied to the attack, and one night a seditious handbill was placed on the sentry box at the King's Wharf. A copy was placed before the Council of Advice by the Governor at their next meeting.

"Sanguinary Punishment corrupts Mankind. The Effect of Cruel Spectacles exhibited to the Populace is the destruction of all tender emotions; it more frequently excites Disgust than Terror; it creates Indifference rather than Dread; it operates on the lower orders as an incentive to the practices of Torture, etc., for the purpose of Revenge; when they have the power of exercising what they have been taught, they will.
Par Ordre d'Alcalde de Barrio. Humanity."

The result of the discussion which followed the appearance of this notice was the expulsion from the colony of its supposed author, William Minchin, a self-styled barrister and attorney-at-law, who had but recently come from Tobago. Commandants of Quarters and Alcaldes of Barrios were instructed to be more diligent in seeking out seditious characters who were attempting to disturb the peace.

Picton, answering a query from the Secretary of State concerning the affairs of the colony, wrote :

> " The white inhabitants in general have shown a disposition to tranquillity and good order . . . A few despicable characters amongst the English merchants are alone excepted from this general observation."

A large number of the landed proprietors were foreigners, largely Italians (Corsicans) and French, who had become rich and were considering returning to their own countries. There were a few French gentlemen, refugees from the Revolution, who under no circumstances could be reconciled to the new form of government in their homeland. These persons Picton described as being loyal and deserving of consideration. There were, he reported, only six or seven respectable Spaniards in the island, who from their behaviour deserved well of His Majesty's Government.

> " French free people of colour amounting to nearly 3,000, a dangerous class who must be gradually got rid of. It is hoped that a great majority of them will emigrate on the giving up of the French Islands. The adoption of proper measures will gradually reduce their numbers."

Trade with the Spanish Main was still forbidden by the Spanish authorities. Picton was, however, able to report that the traders were so full of daring and enterprise that they would follow the market and would take all that the English could provide. He referred also to the general laxity of the police forces of the West Indies and enclosed a copy of the new regulations he had issued in Trinidad and which had passed all expectations in results.

Once again he expressed the view that Trinidad society was not yet ready for the form of government which could be applied to some of the older of the colonies. He concluded by stating that :

> " All intelligent planters who had resided in Trinidad agree that the soil is more congenial to the sugar-cane than that of

53

any of the other islands and that with much less art and intelligence in the mode of manufacture the sugar is of much finer quality and the return much larger."

This despatch of Picton's crossed, in the mail, one from the Secretary of State in which he restated the very great objection in England to the importation of slave labour, suggesting that in future arrangements should be made to procure labour elsewhere. Indians from the Main were proposed, to be paid for by the planters through loans subsidized from revenue. Another idea was the establishment of a colony of white labourers to cultivate the hilly and therefore healthier parts of the island, this to be supplemented by the settlement of deserving and trustworthy soldiers from the West India Regiment in the plains and low lying areas.

Picton's reply named sugar, cotton, coffee and cacao as the most suitable crops to be grown in the colony. Sugar was by far the best but had to be supported by large capital and slave labour forces. Cotton was more restricted in area but required less capital and labour. Coffee production was lighter work but required many hands for picking and, as much work had to be done during the wet season, the death rate among the workers was high. Cacao, he thought, was the most suitable crop for the island, for Trinidad cacao had a fine reputation and could be cultivated by white people. He thought that the " poor whites "* from Barbados and other islands might be persuaded to come by an offer of land and assistance in its cultivation. As far as the West India Regiment was concerned, he considered that settlement of its members should be encouraged, provided that selection of the possible immigrants was made with caution. He concluded with a reference to slavery :

" It is much to be wished that those who declaim so violently against the inhumanity of the system would give themselves the trouble to examine it more nearly and not wholly depend for their information upon the representations of pretended philanthropists whose humanity too frequently resides upon the tongue without ever visiting the heart.

I came to this country nine years ago with a strong impression against the system. Few, I believe, can pretend to more experience or better opportunities of examining the state of slavery in these Islands than I can and I shall not hesitate

* The " poor whites " were descended from the Royalists who had emigrated to the islands and had lost their fortunes prior to and during the Civil War. Some were descendants of prisoners taken during Monmouth's Rebellion, who were deported from England.

to say that the slaves of this Island, generally taken, are in point of comfort and care at least equal to a great majority of European peasantry . . . A few masters, blind to their own interests, probably do treat their slaves with less humanity. The law should in such cases take cognisance of such conduct and punish it as they do here."

The Secretary of State agreed to the appearance in the London newspapers of advertisements offering grants of land in Trinidad to labouring men and craftsmen willing to emigrate. The major portion of these grants was, however, taken up by white settlers from islands which had been returned to the French by treaty. They were men who had tried to exploit the new colonies and now found themselves with nowhere to go. On arrival they joined their counterparts in Trinidad, the " English Party ", and became fellow conspirators against Picton. He, in a despatch to London, complained that he found himself after six years' hard work " attacked by all that is rascally in the land." He was, he stated,

" well aware that these people of bankrupt fortunes were capable of every species of infamy . . . It is a conspiracy to vilify me in the public opinion by every kind of misrepresentation and calumny."

Even after the appointment of Mr. Archibald Gloster as Attorney General, and Mr. George Woodyear as Public (or Colonial) Secretary, he still had to continue wasting time and energy combating the attacks of the " English Party ".

In 1802 Trinidad was attracting a good deal of attention in the British Parliament, particularly with reference to its cultivation and to its share in the slave trade. The two subjects formed one problem, for it was difficult to see how the island's agriculture could be properly developed without the use of slaves. Mr. Canning moved an address to the King, praying him

". . . not to alienate any of the uncleared lands of Trinidad, unless upon condition that they were not cultivated by Negroes newly imported from Africa."

He added that the 34,000 acres of land cultivated already employed 10,000 slaves and the remaining land still suitable for the cultivation of sugar would, if it were allocated, employ about one million additional persons. He further suggested that the island be turned into a Naval Station, Military Post and Sanatorium for the use of all British troops in the West Indies. In July of the same year, Picton received a reply to his despatch about the activities of the "English Party". The Secretary of State pointed out that this was the first official intimation that he had received concerning any dissatisfaction in the colony. He stated the British Government's agreement with all that Picton had done during the critical years of his Governorship, and that "His Majesty's Ministers were in perfect unison" with his suggestions for the future of the island's government.

The despatch ended with what must have been one of the most amazing decisions in Picton's experience. His Majesty's Government considered it

"'expedient' to place the Government of Trinidad in Commission, judging that, from the union of Civil, Military and Naval talents combined in the persons selected for this service, advantages must arise which could not be expected from any one individual."

CHAPTER SEVEN

COMMISSION GOVERNMENT, 1803

(1) *Three Heads*

THE COMMISSION appointed to govern Trinidad consisted of Colonel William Fullarton, Civil and First Commissioner; General Picton, who on account of his experience was appointed Military Commissioner; and Commodore Samuel Hood, R.N., Naval Commissioner.

A despatch from the Secretary of State addressed to the three Commissioners gave the reasons for their appointment and detailed instructions as to what was expected of them.* The Home Government expected great things, hoping that each, in his own sphere, would suggest the best way in which to administer the colony and obtain the co-operation of all parties, and thus create a sound and popular government policy.

The First Commissioner arrived in Trinidad on January 4th, 1803. He was a man of many years' experience in the service of the East India Company, from which he had retired to take a position as Under Secretary to Lord Buckingham, and had been a Member of Parliament for Ayr for many years. Picton, though his senior in rank, greeted him with the cordiality and respect due to his office, but from the start it was obvious that the new arrangement was not to be the success that London had hoped. Fullarton seemed to think that his mission was to criticize all that Picton had done during the course of his Governorship. Almost at once he reversed a decision made by Picton for the expulsion from the island of a certain Madame Duval, as being an undesirable character. At the first meeting of the Council, on February 15th, he tabled a motion for the production of a certified statement of all criminal proceedings, a complete list of all persons who had been expelled from the island, and all who had suffered any sort of punishment during Picton's administration.

* See Appendix XI.

This unwarranted action caused a breach between the two Commissioners, which was only healed on the withdrawal of the papers and the promise of their destruction. The reconcilation did not last long, for at the next meeting Fullarton proposed and secured, through his own casting vote, the suspension of the Public Secretary, Mr. Woodyear, whom he accused of causing the breach between himself and Picton.

The arrival of the third Commissioner, Commodore Hood, brought Picton a little peace of mind, for, with the support of this outspoken and straightforward naval officer, differences ought to be settled and the business of government conducted harmoniously. At the first meeting of the three Commissioners with the Council, Fullarton again demanded a certified copy of all criminal proceedings over the past six years. Picton, realizing that Fullarton was trying to undermine his authority, answered this challenge by suggesting that the originals should not only be placed before the Council but also forwarded to the Secretary of State in London. This was agreed and the Registrar was instructed to produce the documents. Picton, sensing that even with the presence of Hood, administration of the Government would be no easier, sent in his resignation to the King.

The inhabitants of the colony soon realized that there was dissension amongst the Commissioners, and took sides. The old colonists, the clergy and the respectable inhabitants supported Picton; the " English Party ", with their new adherents, supported Fullarton.

Relations were more strained at the next meeting of the Council on March 24th, when Fullarton stated that :

" It would be necessary to produce lists of all persons who have been confined without specific offence, and of those who had been executed, banished or otherwise punished without any trial whatsoever . . . In order to prevent all possibility of misapprehension, Colonel Fullarton added, Brigadier General Picton cannot remove the heavy imputation under which he labours, until he undergoes public trial, and acquittal for the following charges. (Here followed a list of alleged illegal acts including the case of Louisa Calderon).

Four days later, when the Council met again, St. Hilaire de Bégorrat announced that Colonel Fullarton, who was absent, had removed all records relating to the charges against Picton from the custody of De Castro, the Registrar of the Council. De Castro had been arrested for neglect of public duty and Fullarton had tried to obtain his release. Having failed in his immediate object, Fullarton decided to leave for Barbados. Two days later, aboard the *Start*, he wrote to the Secretary of State informing him that he had the records in a safe place and would hand them over in exchange for an official receipt.

When the Council received the news of Fullarton's departure, they passed a series of resolutions condemning his conduct. The two remaining Commissioners passed a further resolution stating that as he had left without informing them, Fullarton could no longer be considered a member of the Commission.

In due course, the news that Picton had resigned spread through the island, and the colonists began to show their appreciation of his administration. Many documents solemnly declaring his integrity and honesty were laid before the Council. At the end of May, the principal inhabitants and owners of property sent him an address, together with a gold mounted sword, whose damascened blade was inscribed : " The inhabitants of Trinidad to Governor Picton for a Colony preserved ". The Cabildo voted that a portrait of the Governor should be painted and hung in the Cabildo Hall.

It was in May of 1803 that war between Britain and France was renewed, and Hood left at once to join the fleet at Barbados. Thus Picton, as the only remaining member of the Commission, was to all intents and purposes Governor again. This state of affairs did not continue long. At the end of the month he was informed that his resignation had been accepted and that Brigadier-General Maitland would take over command of the armed forces in the island and that Colonel Thomas Hislop would become Lieutenant-Governor of the colony. It took Picton only a short time to arrange his affairs, and on June 14th he boarded the armed schooner *Nelly* for Barbados.

(2) *Fullarton v. Picton*

Picton's arrival in Barbados coincided with the departure of an expedition under General Grinfield and Commodore Hood to recapture St. Lucia and Tobago. In spite of having had no leave since he arrived in Trinidad, Picton volunteered to serve and was in command of the troops when St. Lucia was taken from the French on June 22nd. At the end of the month he commanded the advance column of the 3rd West India Regiment in Tobago. On the surrender of the island, he was appointed Military Governor, whilst Grinfield and Hood returned to Barbados to organize an expedition against the Spanish Main.

59

Picton did not retain his second Governorship for long. No sooner had he left Trinidad than Fullarton had returned and, in the teeth of the Council's passing a resolution stating that his presence in the island would endanger peace, he had insisted on calling a meeting. One member attended. Fullarton, nothing daunted, appointed new members, but thanks to the early arrival of Governor Hislop, he was unable to upset the life of the colony. Almost at once he left for England with all the evidence he could muster against Picton, who on hearing this resigned his commission in the army and hurried home before Fullarton could do too much damage to his reputation.

On August 11th, 1803, Grinfield wrote to the Secretary of State :—

> "Circumstances, unexpected by Colonel Picton, or by any other person have placed him, for a little time, in a disagreeable situation, but I am fully persuaded that his general conduct has been such as will convince the world of his merits and his fame will rise higher for the unmerited persecution under which he now labours."

Fullarton was determined that notice should be taken of his charges against Picton, and on his arrival in London brought them at once to the notice of the Secretary of State. Because of their seriousness, they were laid before the Privy Council for consideration as to whether criminal proceedings should be taken against Picton. In the meantime Fullarton published a pamphlet which was widely read and noted in the Press. One paper stated, before the Privy Council had reached any conclusions :

> "His Majesty's Government is to institute an enquiry into the conduct of a late Governor whose unheard-of cruelties will harrow up the feelings and call forth the indignation of every sensitive and virtuous mind."

Picton, on his arrival, called upon the Secretary of State and placed before him the details of his administration and presented him with a Memorandum refuting all charges.

Whilst this private battle was going on, the Privy Council decided to take proceedings against Colonel Thomas Picton, former Governor of Trinidad, under an Act of 1542, on the charge of applying torture to extort confession from Louisa Calderon, who was said to have been under fourteen years of age at the time.

Picton was arrested in December, 1803, and allowed bail in the sum of £40,000. At his trial he was found guilty. Fullarton was delighted—"now humanity is satisfied." This may or may not have been the case but Picton, his friends and advisers were not satisfied, and in 1806 Mr. (later Lord Chief Justice) Dallas obtained a retrial in the Court of the King's Bench. The Privy Council had by this time decided that there were no grounds for any proceedings on other charges made by Fullarton.

Two months before the second trial, Picton was gazetted Major-General. He then had the pleasure of hearing the Court bring in the special verdict :—

"That by the Law of Spain torture existed in Trinidad at the time of the cession of the Island to Great Britain and that no malice existed against Louisa Calderon independent of the illegality of the act."

In February, 1810, the Court ordered the defendant's recognisance "to be respited until they should order further." There was no further order, as the cause of the trouble, Colonel Fullarton, had died just before the second trial began.

It is worthy of note that Picton's friends and supporters in Trinidad, when they heard of the trial, realized the tremendous expense which would be involved. Between them they sent the sum of £4,000, asking that it be used in obtaining justice and in refuting the many libellous charges brought against him. Picton gratefully accepted this kind gift, but when he heard of the devastation caused by the great fire in Port of Spain in 1808 he returned the same amount to be used for the relief of those who suffered. The expenses of the defence were borne for Picton by his uncle, the wealthy General W. Picton, and amounted to over £7,000. The expenses of prosecution were borne by the British Government.

Picton himself was undismayed by the length and course of the trial and in 1809, seeking further active service for his King and country, was appointed Chief of Staff to the Earl of Chatham. He was killed at Quatre Bras in 1815. His last resting place was the family vault in the graveyard of St. George's Church in Hanover Square, London, where he was buried on July 3rd, 1815. A little later a monument to his memory was erected in St. Paul's Cathedral. It was suggested that a monument should be erected in Trinidad, but nothing was done, although an excellent painting by Reinagle adorned the walls of the Town Hall for many years. This portrait perished in a recent fire.

(3) *Defence and Immigration*

The short time that the Commissioners worked in Trinidad was not taken up exclusively with the fight between Picton and Fullarton. A move was made towards the goal of all Governors, the safey of the colony. It had already been suggested to the Secretary of State by a Mr. John Dawson that the Island of Shargrem (Chaguaramas) be used for a military post. Fullarton had discussed this point with General Grinfield, the British Commander-in-Chief in Barbados, when on his way to take up his duties as First Commissioner. The Surveyor General, Colonel Rutherford, and his Chief Engineer, Colonel Shipley, started a martitime survey of the island. Beginning at Chaguaramas and the surrounding lands, they followed in the steps of Captain Columbine who, in H.M.S. *Ulysses*, had already charted Gaspar Grande and the Carenage.

As defence and improvements to the colony were likely to prove expensive, the Commissioners had instructions to raise the import and export duty. They were to aim at collecting the full $3\frac{1}{2}$ per cent to which the Government of the island was entitled, rather than be satisfied with $1\frac{3}{4}$ per cent on which Picton had been able to manage.

Fullarton's departure from the island did not ease the difficulties of the two remaining Commissioners, for

> "by his intrigues he had weakened all public institutions and deprived the law of the energy necessary for prompt and effective application."

As a result there was general apprehension throughout the colony over the future. The Commissioners were forced to take all possible steps to restore order and confidence. Their first move was the re-forming and re-establishment of the Militia, in the course of which work they were forced to deport a Mr. P. McCullum* for attempting to stop militiamen carrying out their duties.

Certain merchants and planters, mostly affiliated to the "English Party", had already forwarded a petition to London asking for British law to run in the colony. To meet this demand, the two Commissioners set up a special court for the determination of all commercial and transitory suits and permitted the use of languages other than Spanish. They recommended to London that new Laws of Mortgage as proposed by the Attor-

---

* Author of *Travels in Trinidad*, 1803.

ney-General (Mr. Gloster) be adopted, but they felt that they could not, at this stage, suggest to the Secretary of State with any confidence that British law should be adopted throughout the colony. They suggested that there should be a gradual change, with its ultimate object a constitution similar to that already granted to Canada, which had a Governor and a Legislative Council.

The Commissioners had to tackle the problem of immigration. They were approached by many ex-officers from the British forces for grants of land, one of the most notable being Brigadier-General Maitland, who was prepared to cultivate a long stretch on the banks of the Caroni River. British subjects who wished to leave the Dutch colonies were also applying for land, and there were already in the colony over one hundred Germans from the 5th Battalion of the 60th Regiment, and about ninety Dutch from Surinam. Housing these settlers and arranging for the arrival of more was a difficult problem. The Commissioners had to order the building or hiring of houses in or near town until land could be cleared. In their report on this problem they mentioned the bad arrangements recently made in Cayenne to support their case for the gradual settlement of the island. The fear of fever and tropical diseases amongst the Europeans, through inadequate housing during their initial period in the colony, was a strong argument for a very gradual process of immigration. They also forwarded Picton's idea that British people who had been disappointed in the land settlement in America should be given first priority in grants on account of the growing necessity for a larger British population in the island. The figures they sent to the Secretary of State show how precarious was the position of a British government.

	White	Free Coloured	Total
French	1095	2925	4020
Spanish	505	1751	2256
British	663	599	1262
			7538

Racial feeling ran high in the colony, and on March 21st, 1803, the Cabildo addressed a long memorandum to the Commissioners.

"The Cabildo of this Island, whose duty it is to watch over

the public welfare and to remonstrate when necessary, cannot remain silent when the state of the Police lately so well ordered is completely relaxed."

The memorandum pointed out that peace had brought to Trinidad conflict between the nations. The reason given was the failure of the Commissioners to publish an edict promulgating whatever alterations in the law they believed necessary for the improvement of the colony and for its safety. This was customary with newly appointed Governors so that the inhabitants could understand what was in store for them. The silence of the Commissioners, together with the First Commissioner's " interference in the affairs of the Police, has produced arrogance in the people of colour and insubordination among the slaves." The difference in number between white and coloured people made the Cabildo uneasy lest the disturbances which had taken place in St. Vincent, Grenada and Hispaniola might spread to Trinidad through indecisive government. " If the inhabitants are not controlled untold trouble is inevitable." The Cabildo looked back to the days after the capitulation when Picton's strong military government had saved the island from disturbance. " To relax the Police when we still have 5,000 of these people and daily increasing, would be an act of moral madness. Most of them are the scum of the Revolution who find here a ' Refugium Peccatorum ' and against whom every precaution is necessary."

It is noted in the memorandum that many of the people of colour were those who had left Trinidad after the capitulation. They had later been exiled from French colonies for their crimes, and settled temporarily on the Main. They were now being driven out by the Spanish Government, and were returning to their old homes in the colony. To remedy this it was suggested that a panel of three older inhabitants be set up to advise the Government on the coloured people entering the colony. They also proposed that a proclamation be issued in English, French and Spanish specifying the laws and regulations in force. The memorandum ended :—

" The Cabildo relies on the purity of its intention, to secure a favourable reception of these views which would encourage its vigilance and efforts in promoting the good of the Colony and its inhabitants."

That the views taken by the Cabildo were serious is borne out by a letter from the Attorney-General to the Secretary of State.

" My Lord,

I beg to urge the importance of which I write here to every Proprietor in the Colony. The First Commissioner started with fair outward professions, but later showed that his object was to overset Brigadier-General Picton and afterwards get rid of Commodore Hood.

We dread more than the party differences. From the presence of the First Commissioner we may expect the massacres and conflagrations that have marked San Domingo, Grenada and St. Vincent; and they may not be far distant. Before his arrival, the Coloured people were tranquil, loyal and in fact happy, due to a firm rule. Now that an Apostle of Liberty, a Philanthropist and a voluble talker upon the Rights of Man shows his face, their hopes are excited and expectations buoyed up. He has weakened the authority of the Commandants of Quarters as he deems any authority as an Invasion of his own prerogatives; he opens the door to tumult, disorder and riot in distant Parishes. Overbearing insolence of this class is already increasing.

Both France and Spain look at Trinidad with a jealous eye and will not fail to take advantage of our foolishness. We are surrounded by the worst class of coloured persons joined to French and Spanish freebooters and brigands. If they attacked with such a host of enemies within, we are lost and with us the whole archipelago of the West Indies.

Pray remove from us this improper character; all rascals here profess his friendship. His prevailing passions are lust of power, however obtained; and his greediness for money, to support his miserably shattered fortunes. The truth is not in him; he has all the vices and none of the virtues of the Scotch, and is a living libel on the King's Ministers :

Not only I, but other members of Council, will not act with Colonel Fullarton, neither will the Cabildo, even though he be forced on us.

Yours most respectfully and faithfully,
Arch. Gloster.

The Right Honourable Lord Hobart.

P.S.—I have not any objections that you should show that I write to Mr. Addington (Prime Minister), he is a good wise man, too sincerely open in his Politics to countenance, much less patronize, Jesuits and weak intriguing Governors. If you wish to keep Trinidad, keep General Picton in it, so long as he will stay. If not send us out some man of Honour and experience as a Soldier; none of your East Indian Commissioners, My Dear Lord, in times like these, to govern West Indian conquered settlements.

A.G."

CHAPTER EIGHT

GOVERNOR HISLOP, 1804–11

(1) *Immigration and Defence*

BRIGADIER THOMAS HISLOP arrived in the colony to take over duties as Governor in July, 1804.

His first major problem was the immigration of people of colour. He found that many had not taken the oath of allegiance and fidelity to the King, nor had they enrolled in the Militia, and in many cases they had disobeyed other regulations for the preservation of the peace and safety of the colony. Within a few days he issued a Proclamation instructing the Commandants of the various districts to search out and present to Government House all illegal immigrants. Heavy penalties were imposed for " concealing, comforting and aiding persons remaining in the Colony without the sanction of the Government."

In Port of Spain all houses were to be numbered and a list of residents, lodgers, servants and slaves was to be posted on each door with the times of arrival and departure and the nature of the business of all those within. Refusal to comply was punishable by a fine of twenty dollars, or ten days' imprisonment.

A Board was set up to examine immigrants whom the Harbour Master was instructed to bring before it. On receipt of the Board's report, the Governor himself would decide who might stay in the island.

All ships, particularly Spanish launches from the Main, were to be searched on arrival by the Harbour Master, who was responsible for forwarding a full list of those on board each vessel, to the Governor. A similar check was to be made before the ship sailed, and any vessel trying to put out from the harbour without its full complement was to be detained.

In April, 1803, a Memorandum had been issued by the Colonial Department concerning Chinese immigration to the West Indies, as a means of solving the problem of labour shortage. It had been suggested that it might be a good plan to introduce " a race of free cultivators, kept distinct from the

Negroes and by their interest attached to the White Planters."

The Chinese were represented as "inured to industry and anxious to become proprietors themselves," and were the most obvious solution to the problem. Similar schemes had been tried with success in Java, Manila and Prince of Wales Island.* It was thought that Chinese from Prince of Wales Island might be induced to emigrate to Trinidad and thence to other West Indian islands.

Mr. Kenneth McQueen was selected by the British Government to go to the island, where he had previously served at the naval station, and had learned to understand Chinese manners and customs. He was to make arrangements for the Chinese to travel in comfort to Trinidad, in the hope that good results might be achieved if the first venture proved a success.

As there was a growing demand for Indian goods in America, it was also suggested that Trinidad be turned into the main depot for the trade if the East India Company were agreeable.

Early in 1806, McQueen wrote to the Secretary of State from Calcutta to say that he had arrived there with 147 Chinese from Prince of Wales Island and that all were well behaved and were temporarily housed ashore, awaiting transport to Trinidad. Another hundred men could easily be raised in Calcutta if necessary. He felt that it would have been much more satisfactory to have recruited labour in China itself, where a favourable report would have resulted in a steady flow of Chinese to the West Indies.

On October 26th, Hislop reported to London that McQueen had arrived in Port of Spain on board the East Indiaman *Fortitude* with 192 Chinamen, including one woman, eight men having died during the five month passage and another after arrival in port. He also reported that on board was a cargo of Indian goods about which he had received no instructions. The ship and her cargo had therefore been seized by the Chief Naval Officer on behalf of the Admiral of the Station for an alleged breach of the laws relating to Plantation and Trade. He and the Collector of Customs had held a conference on this " extraordinary and unprecedented predicament " but had seen no way out and had been forced to let the vessel be held by the Vice-Admiralty Court in Trinidad.

Most of the Chinese wished to be hired to work on the plantations on Government terms; for those who preferred to work independently a small estate was rented for £300, to be culti-

* Now known as Penang in Malaya.

vated as market gardens. The colony's finances were unable to meet the needs of McQueen and the settlers, and Hislop, with the Council's advice, drew £500 on His Majesty's Treasury.

Mr. Black, a member of the Council, was charged with the direction of the Chinese settlers. He reported in July, 1807, that $2,800 was needed to pay wages due to them and that between thirty and forty had applied to return home on the *Fortitude* at the end of their contract. He did not consider the experiment a success and the West Indies were not likely, in his view, to benefit from the presence of these settlers in the island. They would, he was sure, always be an expense on the Government and if support was withdrawn they would "perish in misery and want." He therefore suggested that at the conclusion of their contract in the following October they should all be shipped off to Bengal as, with a few exceptions, their industry would never equal their maintenance.

The Secretary of State approved the measure taken by the Governor for the settlement of the Chinese and recommended to the Lords of the Treasury that they accept bills up to the £500 which had been drawn. To this Hislop replied :—

". . . The approbation of the measures adopted for settling the Chinese is very gratifying. I feel confident that a very great advantage would accrue, with the considerable augmentation of their numbers if women of the description they cohabit with in India were brought with them; since I understand it is not possible to withdraw women from China.

Women willing to associate with the Chinese are of very low character, and only found among the slaves. Free women of colour consider themselves in every respect superior for, though the Chinese are free, the work they perform is that of slaves."

The experiment was a failure and in 1814 Governor Woodford, in a despatch on the subject of introducing additional labour, wrote to the Secretary of State :—

"The few Chinese that remain (about thirty) are useful as fishermen, butchers, porkfeeders, etc.; had they brought with them their wives and families and their priests, they would certainly have been of great use in supplying many articles of domestic use and comfort. But I understand that they did not show themselves to be well calculated for the fatigues of husbandry nor has their disposition led them to prefer that pursuit."

In the meantime the case of the *Fortitude* proceeded accord-

68

ing to law. In December, 1806, Hislop reported that she and her cargo

"had been condemned in the Court of the Vice-Admiralty of the Island and the sale of them has been advertised accordingly by the Principal Officer of His Majesty's Customs, to take place on the 20th day of next month."

The Indian goods in the cargo were sold and the Captain refused to take over the ship owing to "damage by the seizers." The officers, with the exception of the Chief Mate, had returned to England with the members of the crew by securing work on other ships homeward bound. When the vessel was put up for sale at £8,000, there were no bids for her and the Government bought her in at £4,150 on behalf of the East India Company. She sailed for England with the mate as captain, loaded with a cargo from Trinidad, and eventually made a profit of £2,000 for the company.

Hislop was faced from the start of his Governorship with financial difficulties for, by 1805, there was no money in the Treasury. The defence of the island, such as it was, was financed to a large extent by local inhabitants who made voluntary donations to the cost. The Home Government, appealed to time and time again, made no move to help. The general feeling in England was that very soon Trinidad would have a proper constitution and therefore it would be unwise to exercise the Royal Prerogative and allow the Governor in Council power to raise taxes for the immediate needs of the colony. The Secretary of State informed Hislop that :—

"It is extremely important that a form of Government as nearly as possible approaching to what subsists in His Majesty's other Colonies should be established without delay."

For this reason it was deemed inadvisable to govern Trinidad by Orders in Council, and there was a consequent lack of urgency in dealing with the financial problems besetting the island.

Trinidad, with the rest of the West Indian colonies, suffered from the Home Government's policy during the Anglo-American War of 1812, and from the continued application of the Navigation Laws.* Trade between the British West Indies and America

* The Navigation Act, first passed in 1651, forbade the carrying of merchandise to England or the Colonies in any but English ships manned by English crews. The Act was subsequently amplified and smuggling had to be resorted to by manufacturers and colonists.

was at a standstill and some of the islands were reduced almost to famine level.

Joseph Marryat,* Trinidad's Agent in London, wrote to Lord Castlereagh on the subject of a petition sent by the Trinidad planters, asking permission to barter sugar for American provisions and lumber. He explained that :

> "An infant Colony, like any other infant, requires fostering and indulgence at first, which may be dispensed with after it has attained a certain degree of strength and maturity."

Many of the planters, he continued, were small men who were unable to obtain credit owing to the depressed state of the market. Their products were not of the highest standard and often scarcely covered their costs when they were forced to sell sugar at £3 10s. a hogshead in London, against £20 by barter in the American market. The Order prohibiting the sale of sugar to America had caused a drop in prices of about $2.50 per hundredweight.

> "The state of distress in which the inhabitants are thus placed is really deplorable and has excited much dissatisfaction . . .
> Though I am a strenuous advocate of the Navigation Laws and am particularly prompted by my interests as a merchant to recommend the enforcement of them, yet in this instance Your Lordship will permit me to observe that necessity supersedes all laws, and that the inhabitants of Trinidad may plead the most imperious necessity in support of their present supplication."

Once more there was no response from the Home Government, but Marryat wrote to the Governor to tell him of discussions he had held with Mr. Cook of the Colonial Office and Mr. Huskisson at the Treasury. He had found that the Privy Council were determined to enforce the Navigation Laws and hoped to recompense the West Indian islands by securing for them the monopoly of the European market.

In spite of the shortage of ready cash in the island, particularly in the Treasury, defence works were continued. With the continued struggle between England and France, there was a constant fear that a surprise attack might force the surrender of the island. Picton's plan for the fortification of St. Joseph was abandoned in favour of the old Spanish proposal to turn Chaguaramas into an impregnable base similar to Cartagena and

* See pages 50 and 112.

70

Havana. The site was surveyed and preparations for its fortification were begun. The peninsula of Pointe Gourde was chosen as the Military Post and Chaguaramas Bay as the Naval Station.

In April, 1803, a military party was established at Pointe Gourde and a road had been built to the top of the hill opposite the islands of Carrera and Cronstadt (this road was for many years kept open as a warden's trace starting from Carenage Bay). No proper road had yet been built into Port of Spain. The island of Gasparee was chosen for the naval shore base and the displaced owners were granted lands in compensation at Quiacuana (Chaguanas), though their lands were held on Spanish Government grants which did not contain such an agreement.

The fortifications were built with slave labour supplied by a levy on all plantation owners, ranging from one to thirty-six slaves according to the size of the plantation. All workers were housed and fed at the Government's expense. Owners from great distances, Band d'Este and La Brea, were permitted to pay $9 per month in lieu of providing slaves.

Towards the end of the year, Governor Hislop decided that La Vigie would be a better site for permanent fortifications of the colony than Pointe Gourde. In this decision he was supported by local officers and the Council. Permission was sought from the Secretary of State to proceed with new plans. The work was encouraged by the news in May, 1804, that the French fleet was in the Caribbean and was expected to attack Trinidad. This scare made the whole island conscious of the weakness of its defences and a report shows that at the time there was hardly a substantial defence armament in the colony.

St. David's Tower (Picton's Fort, Laventille Hill)	4 cannon
La Vigie (Fort George)	2 13 inch cannon
	2 24 lb. guns
	4 10 inch cannon
	2 mortars
	2 10 inch howitzers
Fort Abercromby (Las Cuevas)	3 24 lb. guns
	4 other guns
Maceripe (Macqueripe) Bay	2 guns

Lt.-General Sir William Myers, Commander-in-Chief British Forces in the West Indies, took strong exception to a change in defence plans for the colony being made without his prior knowledge and approval. Particularly was he annoyed that a soldier

71

of Colonel Hislop's standing should have gone over his head to the higher authority of the Secretary of State. Hislop was forced to point out that besides being an Army officer, he was also Governor of Trinidad, and that whilst he meant no slight to the General, the defence of his colony must take precedence over military etiquette.

Myers at once sent Colonel Shipley, Commandant of the Royal Engineers, to Trinidad to report on the work being undertaken. The report was in terms which the Commander-in-Chief desired, stressing that Pointe Gourde should be fortified and La Vigie abandoned. Myers at once informed Hislop and instructed him to carry out the details of the report and finish the fortifications at Pointe Gourde with the utmost despatch.

In November another invasion scare occurred and in the crisis the Council of Advice agreed with Hislop in refusing labour for the work at Pointe Gourde. In a despatch to London, Hislop explained that Pointe Gourde had already cost some £24,000 and could still only boast one battery "en barbette", a block house, barracks and a hospital for one hundred men. Moreover, he explained, the site was unhealthy; there was no natural supply of water, which would involve heavy expenditure on the building of tanks. Added to this was the great disadvantage that if the enemy scaled Mount Catherine, they could command the whole of Pointe Gourde. The only way to make the site healthy would be to cut a canal through the Carenage swamp (later a canal was made and called Hart's Cut), at an estimated cost of £3,000. Against this he pointed out the advantages of La Vigie, which was known to be healthy, and which possessed a spring giving up to 8,000 gallons of fresh water a day. The cost of defence works here would be comparatively small as the site was a natural fortress, the hill behind the site being almost inaccessible. The local Military Board, reporting on the two sites, was unanimous in condemning Pointe Gourde in favour of La Vigie as the proper place for the permanent fortifications of the colony.

Hislop's independent action displeased the Commander-in-Chief, who issued orders to all serving officers in the island that they should render no assistance with any works in connection with La Vigie. The Council of Advice, in the face of a constant threat of attack, continued to support the Governor and went so far as to suggest that none of the colony's meagre funds should be permitted to be spent on the works at Pointe Gourde. Hislop, in spite of his superior officer's displeasure, continued the workings at La Vigie and by the end of the year had completed a safe communicating road to Port of Spain, with a bridge over the Mucurapo River at Boissière Village. A covering battery named after Abercromby was also completed, with two eighteen pounders 560 feet up the hillside.

The Secretary of State, realizing that the conflicting views of Hislop and Myers might lead to disaster through negative action, sanctioned the work at La Vigie on condition that the Pointe Gourde base was completed. This did not satisfy Hislop, nor did the promise of three extra companies of soldiers when they could be spared from Antigua. He was annoyed, too, by Myers' statement that the Council of Advice was incompetent to judge the military significance of the works at Pointe Gourde. He therefore sent the Attorney-General (Mr. Gloster) and the Surveyor-General (Colonel Rutherford) to Barbados for a personal interview with the Commander-in-Chief. These two delegates appeased General Myers, who finally sanctioned the stationing of troops at La Vigie and the issue of war supplies for use at the fort.

(2) *Invasion*

Early in 1805 Hislop received the news that Spain had declared war on England and that the French fleet had been sighted off St. Lucia. At any moment an attack was expected and martial law was proclaimed in the colony. All resources were concentrated at La Vigie, leaving only enough men at Pointe Gourde to man the guns. A labour force of some 750 Negroes was recruited from the estates and was used for strengthening the old batteries, building new, and erecting barracks and other buildings. These men were supplied with a week's food at the expense of their owners and lodging at the expense of the Government. For the first time in her history Trinidad raised a corps of local troops from the estate Negroes, " the Royal Trinidad Rangers ", who proved themselves as loyal and dependable as the regular West India battalions.

By mid-April news arrived that the French fleet had moved north, and martial law came to an end. The defence works were continued at as great a pace as possible, for Hislop estimated 2,000 days' labour before he could be satisfied as to the safety of the colony. To achieve his object he put a labour levy on the inhabitants of Port of Spain.

On May 19th intelligence was received that the French fleet had arrived off Martinique, accompanied by a large landing force. Martial law was once more proclaimed, batteries were

73

manned, extra labour forces mobilized, all horses, mules and carts were commandeered and a further corps of 500 pioneers was formed from the trustworthy Negroes. A Military Board was set up, consisting of the Governor, Colonel Walker, Commander of the Regular Forces, Captain Columbine, Commander of the Naval Forces and Colonel Rutherford, in command of the Militia. Plans were made for holding as many widely separated points as possible with, in the event of a withdrawal, La Vigie (regarded as well nigh impregnable and capable of withstanding a protracted siege), the final rallying point.

For over a month preparations continued with feverish haste. Then, on June 1st, came a despatch from St. Lucia reporting a fleet of twenty-eight ships to the windward of Gros Ilet and thought to be heading for Trinidad. On June 3rd tension was raised to a high pitch by a Barbadian despatch confirming the news but stating that a large British fleet was soon expected with reinforcements for the islands.

The alarm came at 2.30 a.m. on June 7th, when the North Post signal station reported that four guns had been fired out to sea to windward of the post. At daybreak a schooner had arrived at Chaguaramas with the news that the French fleet had anchored on the previous night in Courland Bay, Tobago. At 8 a.m. the North Point signalman reported sighting twelve men-of-war and ten other ships bearing down on the Bocas. He also added that the schooner *Tobago*, which had been heading for Barbados had, on sighting the fleet, altered course to the south in an effort to evade capture.

The next message reported that the fleet had passed Las Cuevas at 7 a.m. and that a brig had entered the bay. The officer in charge of Fort Abercromby had abandoned his post with all speed in the face of this enemy attack. After spiking his guns and burning the huts, he had made all possible haste over the hills to St. Joseph.

At 11 a.m. signals announced the fleet entering the Gulf of Paria. All batteries were manned and naval men and Fencibles under Captain Cribb manned the coastal guns, under whose protection the merchant ships were grounded. By 3 p.m. the fleet was in full view in the gulf and it was noted that all vessels were wearing the St. George's ensign. Correct day signals had been exchanged at Fort Abercromby and at North Post, but Hislop was far from satisfied that this was not an enemy ruse to lull the islanders into a false sense of security. There had been a recent report of a British ship being captured by an enemy vessel wearing false colours and the French had used the same trick when attacking Dominica. As the fleet approached, tension increased. Every man on the island was ready to give a good account of himself. Regulars and Militia alike were intent on repelling the enemy when, to their surprise, that same enemy turned and sailed out of sight towards the Bocas.

The next step in this attack upon Trinidad was a letter to Hislop from Sir William Myers, written on board Nelson's flagship *Victory* in Courland Bay, informing him of the arrival of the British fleet and asking information concerning the well-being of the colony. Hislop replied by reporting the arrival of the French fleet, its entry into the Gulf of Paria and its rapid leave-taking for fear it should be caught in shallow water by Nelson.

On June 9th, it became known that the British fleet, under Admiral Lord Nelson, had passed along the north coast of Trinidad. Seeing the fire at Las Cuevas, Nelson had anticipated finding the French in the gulf and had prepared for action, but on finding the gulf empty had sailed away.

Martial law was withdrawn and life in the island returned to normal. The two periods of martial law, February 26th to April 15th, and May 19th to June 9th, had cost the colony dearly. Labour and pay for officers and men totalled £10,515.

In October, Admiral Cochrane, Commander-in-Chief of the West Indies station, visited Trinidad. His views on the defence of the island coincided with those of Hislop. He condemned Pointe Gourde and was much in favour of the defence works being completed in La Vigie or, as it now became known, Fort George. Thus encouraged, Hislop sent Colonel Rutherford to London to discuss various defence schemes with the Secretary of State. These discussions resulted in estimates being passed for the establishment of 2,000 men at Fort George, complete with ordnance stores and barracks. Above the fort was established the Cumberland Battery and, half-way from the hill, the York, Princess Charlotte, Abercromby and Cambridge Batteries. To complete the permanent defences of the colony, a line of thirty-two pounders was to be mounted along the shore below the fort. The Secretary of State, much to Hislop's satisfaction, instructed that the work on Pointe Gourde should be closed down and the site abandoned.

(3) *Crisis at Home*

The threat of foreign invasion, with its consequent panic and tension, was followed at the year's end by a period of equal anxiety. In December, when all were making preparations for the Christmas festivities, the inhabitants of the colony were thrown into a state of alarm by rumours that the slaves were planning a revolt for Christmas Day.

At once the Governor called a meeting of the Council and informed members that he had in his possession evidence of plans for a widespread revolt. The object of the plot was the elimination of all the whites and free coloured peoples in the island. As the slave population was in the neighbourhood of 20,000 and the whites with the free coloured totalled only half this number, it was obvious that swift action must be taken. Orders were issued for the arrest of the leaders and a proclamation was issued assuring the public that adequate steps were being taken to secure the safety of the colony and its inhabitants.

The examination of witnesses brought to light the existence on the island of a secret society of some magnitude, which was particularly active in the districts inhabited by French settlers, especially Diego Martin, Maraval and Carenage. The slaves were organized into " Convois ", " Regiments " or " Bands ", each with a high-sounding name :— " Dreadnought Band ", "Danish Regiment" and " Monkey Corps " amongst others. Each " Band " had its own King and Queen and sundry Princes and Princesses. Certain facts about this organization had been known for some time, but it was regarded as politically harmless, as the meetings of the various " Bands " were held ostensibly for the practice of native African dancing. It was found that most of the members of the " Bands " were, in fact, innocent of blame, being ignorant of the policy of their leaders and the real intention of the meetings. The leaders had planned to rise suddenly on Christmas Day, when slaves and masters alike would be in the midst of festivities and, starting from the Cuesa Valley, to spread insurrection all over the island.

Swift action was needed. Hislop informed the Cabildo that after consultation with his Assessor, Gaspar de la Guardia, he had decided it was unwise to depend upon the slow though thoroughly competent tribunals whose many formalities might cause delay which would prove dangerous. Acting on the advice that " according to Spanish Law the Governor in Council is fully empowered to act judicially in matters of this kind ", arrests would be made and the trials would be carried out forthwith.

On December 19th, the Council tried the accused and meted out punishment to the guilty.

In a letter to the Secretary of State, Hislop stated on December 19th :—

". . . I am able now to inform Your Lordship that the Council sat on till ten o'clock last night on the trial of the four Negroes who have been chief instigators of the intended insurrection.

All were found guilty, and three of them (two styling themselves Kings and one a General in Chief) were condemned to be hanged this day at twelve o'clock. Their heads to be exposed after death on poles erected for the purpose, and their bodies to be hanged in chains on the sea side near the district where they resided.

The Council continues to sit daily for the examination of others implicated in this diabolical plot . . ."

He wrote again on January 18th, 1806 :—

". . . In addition to the three leaders who were executed on December 19th, judgment was passed yesterday on six more. The most culpable are sentenced to lose their ears, to be flogged under the gallows and then banished from the Colony for ever. Some less culpable have been sentenced to corporal punishment and to work in chains for a specified period. Those least culpable are to suffer a moderate chastisement.

I am sorry to say, there are still twenty or thirty more on whom judgment is to be passed, and among them some who are notoriously and deeply involved in this crime. One of the principal instigators is still at large and I have offered a reward of £200 to apprehend him . . ."

Shortly after the Governor had taken this action, news of the trial of, and verdict against, General Picton arrived in the colony and caused some uneasiness. If Picton was guilty in the use of Spanish Law, then it was equally illegal for the Council to have punished the offenders in the incipient slave riot under the same law. The Council decided to ascertain how far Spanish law was in force in the colony and if there was a special code for the island issued under any of its former Governors. Many experts were consulted and in the opinion of all Spanish Law was in force at the capitulation and was still in force. There was no evidence of any special code of law having been issued for Trinidad.

The Governor's swift action in stamping out the slave revolt had the desired effect in re-establishing internal peace and it

77

was not for another five years that any laws had to be passed concerning the behaviour of the Negro population. By then it had become the custom of many to walk out at night carrying heavy wooden cudgels and with these to strike out at unoffending citizens in the hopes of starting a brawl. The Cabildo, in an effort to put a stop to this public nuisance, issued an order forbidding Negroes to carry cudgels and instructing all citizens who found them in possession of such implements to hand them over to the Gaoler to be dealt with. If the offender was a free Negro, the penalty was to be one months' imprisonment; if a slave, he was to receive twenty-five lashes and his owner fined $10 for not overseeing him properly. All persons of colour were obliged to carry a lantern at night and slaves to have specially written permission stating on what business their masters had sent them out after dusk. The use of musical instruments was by this instruction forbidden in any grog shop either by day or night.

The instruction was unpopular and the Cabildo was forced to point out that the word " garrot " used in the order meant large cudgels with knots and metal ferrules and was not intended to stop any persons from carrying a " beaustick " or cane " for his convenience or as a master of fashion ".

(4) Abolition of the Slave Trade

In 1807, a new problem faced Trinidad, along with all the West Indian colonies.

The anti-slavery movement was growing in strength in England and it was clear at least as far as the British colonies were concerned that abolition of slavery would in course of time become an accomplished fact. Planters and those who had invested money in the colony were worrying about their future.

Trinidad, which had only been opened to settlers since 1783, was likely to be exceptionally hard hit, for there was already a labour shortage. Shortly before the Act to Abolish the Slave Trade came into force in 1807, an Order in Council was issued prohibiting the direct import of slaves into any colony conquered by the British. This Order, which forbade all British subjects to have any connection with the slave trade and imposed heavy penalties for investing capital in it or using British ships in the foreign slave market, was a severe blow to Trinidad, Tobago, Demerara and St. Lucia, as it put an end to the introduction of any further slaves to these colonies.

78

Canning's theory, first expressed in 1802, that Trinidad should be regarded as an "Island of Experiment", was strongly supported by many influential people in England, none of whom had any financial interests in the colony, and a pamphlet, "The Crisis in the Sugar Colonies" was published. In it the author dwelt at some length on the question of slave labour in Trinidad and suggested :—

(1) That the introduction of slave labour should be strictly forbidden.
(2) That Crown lands should only be granted on condition that they were cultivated by free Negroes from the older colonies or from Africa, who should be bound to serve their employers for a term of years at a fixed wage.
(3) That power to inflict corporal punishment should be limited.
(4) That Magistrates unconnected with the island should be appointed to see that the regulations were carried out.

To these ideas was added the suggestion that Trinidad should be the "entrepot" for British manufactured goods for export to South America and that it should be "a form of experiment on which to work out the problem of 'Negro emancipation'." Though it found plenty of support in England, the Government never regarded the proposals as entirely suitable or practicable.

When the Bill for the Abolition of the Slave Trade was read the second time in the House of Lords, petitioners against it were unable to gain a hearing. Lord Eldon, however, took up the cause of the loyal inhabitants from the French colonies who had settled in Trinidad and had been promised protection. They had purchased land and cleared it and if they were now unable to obtain labour, they would be ruined. It was thought that this, at least, represented a strong case for compensation by the Government.

Marryat, the Agent for Trinidad, was strongly in favour of putting the case for compensation before the Commons at the earliest opportunity, so that it might be accepted in principle. He was afraid that His Majesty's Ministers would try to rush the Bill through before any actual claim for compensation could be received. He wrote to the Governor on February 7th, 1807 :—

"However discouraging appearances may be I consider it my duty not to relax my endeavours to support the just claims of those whom I have the honour to represent, and shall present another Petition to the House of Commons when the Bill comes before them. By confining it more particularly to the point of compensation the House may perhaps be prevailed upon to hear evidence."

On February 19th, a Petition from Planters, Merchants, Mortgagees and others interested in the colony was placed before the House. Marryat wrote again to the Governor in Council explaining a Resolution passed by the Commons in which it was suggested that, by way of compensation, a bounty of 2s. per cwt. should be paid when the average price of sugar, excluding duty, was below 40s. per cwt. There was also to be an additional bounty of 10s. per cwt. on exported double-refined sugar when the price fell below 45s., and to encourage the consumption of rum, a duty of 2s. 6d. per gallon on all foreign spirits entering England. It was suggested that sugar should be used in the distilleries in place of wheat and barley. This last suggestion was, however, thought to be against the interests of English agriculture. The West Indian planters and merchants were dissatisfield with these measures, which they considered insufficient to give the necessary relief to the depressed state of the sugar market.

A petition from Trinidad against the Abolition of the Slave Trade was presented on February 19th, but was never heard, though the debate in the Commons went on for some hours. It was stated that if later it could be proved that anyone had been injured by the Act, claims for compensation would be considered, but that would not prevent the House from passing the Act to Abolish the Slave Trade. Those who had interests in the colonies claimed that the West Indies had been settled and cultivated under the assurance that they would always be able to obtain supplies of slaves from Africa. If this was no longer possible, then the colonies' estates could not be worked and rival nations, owning colonies where there was no ban on the slave trade, would prosper at the expense of the British. The Anti-Slave Trade supporters looked to William Wilberforce, who steadily proclaimed that the slave trade was the most criminal in which any nation could engage and therefore it should be abolished at once and for ever.

The Act was passed, received the Royal Assent on March 25th, 1806, and was put into effect as from January 1st, 1807. It prohibited the slave trade as from January 1st, 1808. It also enacted that no vessel should clear out for slaves from any port within the British Dominions after May 1st, 1808, and that no slave should be landed in the colonies after March 1st, 1808.

The labour problem remained unsolved. Some colonies had insufficient labour, others more than they could use, but as it was prohibited to remove slaves from one to another, there were cases of unemployment. The lack of understanding between those who had supported the Act and those who had opposed it ruined hundreds of families and blighted the hopes of flourishing colonies. The Abolitionists, having gained their victory, did not anticipate that emancipation would follow immediately. The planters and others expected it at once. They could not forget what had happened when the French Government had suddenly emancipated all slaves in 1794, and were naturally fearful of the future.*

(5) The Constitution and the Free Coloured Peoples

In spite of a flourishing trade the colony's revenue was insufficient to meet its expenditure, dependent as it was on Abercromby's 3½% import and export duty. Owing to the skill with which the traders avoided paying their dues and the fact that trade with the Spanish Main was free of duty, the income from that source was not enough to meet the needs of the Government. The total passing into the Colonial Treasury was entirely inadequate for the Government's commitments.

Under Picton's administration the income had been more than sufficient, but by 1806 the expenses in connection with the Government by the Commissioners and ever-growing liabilities had led to a Government debt of £4,000. For long periods Government officers went without their pay and the Colonial Treasurer reported in 1807 that he "was extremely sorry to inform the Board of Cabildo that there was not and had not been for a considerable time past the value of 5/- in the Colonial Chest."

From official papers laid before the Council of Advice at the time, it was ascertained that the colony's debt had risen to £10,866.

This state of financial affairs was repeatedly communicated to London but the Home Government was unresponsive. The basic cause of the financial troubles was constitutional rather than economic. A much more difficult problem faced the English Parliament than appeared to the inhabitants of the colony. To break the deadlock the Attorney General (Mr. Gloster) presented a case to London, asking that the Crown Law Officers should investigate the situation.

His contention was:

(1) That if the power of making laws for a conquered colony

* See p. 159.

existed in the Crown, the capitulation did not appear to restrict the exercise of it.

(2) That the cession of the island by the Treaty of Amiens did not appear to have altered that right specifically, but it might be worth enquiring whether yielding to the British nation by Treaty made any and what alteration in the King's original title of acquisition by conquest.

As far as he knew, he stated, the King had never given up any of his rights, nor had he ever taken away the designation of a conquered colony, nor had Trinidad been put on the same footing as other West Indian islands. He therefore recommended that if the Law Officers decided that the King had the right, a duty of $3\frac{1}{2}\%$ should be placed on all exports and $2\frac{1}{2}\%$ should be placed on all imports from Britain. There should also be a tax of 4% on the rental of all houses and a poll tax of 20/- on all white peoples, 30/- on all coloured peoples and 5/- on all slaves. If, however, the Law Officers decided that the King had no right to legislate and raise taxes by order of his prerogative, then a constitutional form of Government should be framed for the safety and existence of the colony. Without funds it was impossible to continue Government, to pay the salaries of officers or to pay the stipends of the Protestant and Catholic clergy.

These views were forwarded to Mr. Marryat in London to bring before His Majesty's Government. His reply held out hopes that a constitution might be granted rather than the King exercise his prerogative in the matter of taxes. He pointed out that in all matters pertaining to the colony the Governor should first officially place the facts before the Secretary of State and not appeal directly to the Government through the Agent or the Crown Officers. This had been the case when an appeal against the order prohibiting the barter of sugar with America had been forwarded and for this reason had received no reply.

After an interview with the Chancellor of the Exchequer, Marryat again wrote to the Governor stating that Trinidad's position was under review. There were many difficulties to overcome before a constitution could be approved and it seemed likely that the King might exercise his Prerogative as far as taxes were concerned.

This talk of a new constitution worried the free people of colour in the colony. After the capitulation many had left rather than take the oath of allegiance to the King of England, but those who had stayed had settled down to become good and

peaceful citizens. Governor Chacon had made an effort on behalf
of these settlers to ensure that they should continue to enjoy the
same privileges under English rule as they had in the Spanish
colony.* His efforts had not been in vain, but the free coloured
population felt they were restricted under the new Government,
as they had never been accepted socially. They were, however,
in better circumstances in Trinidad than they would have been
in any French or other English colony.

The loyalty of this section of the community had been proved
at the time of the expected slave revolt in 1806, and had been
officially noted by the Governor and by the Board of Cabildo.
Many of them were now prosperous and resented being unable
to share the privileges of the white settlers and being looked
upon officially and socially as a class apart. Regulations such as
the Cabildo's instruction on the carrying of cudgels showed that
those in authority were creating a distinction between the white
and coloured people. When it became common knowledge that
the question of a new constitution was being raised in London
and that under British law the free coloured peoples might
officially and permanently be considered as a separate group, an
address was submitted to the King. It proclaimed the loyalty of
the free coloured peoples to the Crown and pointed out that
they constituted the majority of the free people of the island and
prayed that when the constitution was granted to the colony,
their claim might be considered.

" Conscious of the rectitude of their intention and of the
faithful discharge of their duties as members of society, they
are inevitably led to serious contemplation of the situation in
which it is their fate to be placed in that society; and with
every tender and delicate consideration towards all the circumstances connected with that situation, they cannot avoid
perceiving that at a moment when the feelings and the pursuits
of their fellow colonists are ardently and actively employed in
projecting and soliciting new forms of Government and
political regulation from the Parent State (in which not only
the comfort and happiness of His Majesty's subjects of colour
are entirely overlooked, but the very existence of such a class
appears to be forgotten) it becomes their duty to employ such
means as appear to them necessary (and at the same time
consistent with the principles of order, respect and obedience
towards the Government, which they profess to act upon and
from which they will never be found deviating) to awaken
the reflection that there exists in this colony a numerous,

* See Appendix V.—Articles of Capitulation.

opulent and useful class of free subjects who are entitled to something . . ."

To this Governor Hislop replied that he would like to know what distinct objects they had in view. He hoped to force the petitioners into stating some definite claim which he could have ruled out of order and not in accordance with the colonial system. The leaders of the free coloured people were not to be caught in such a trap, and replied :—

July 7th, 1810.

" Sir,

The persons of colour charged with expressing to His Excellency the sentiments of that body have the honour to say in answer to your note, that their object (at this moment when a new system of laws is framing for the Government of this Colony) is to implore the consideration of their Sovereign towards the general interests of his coloured subjects with a view to such a moderate and consistent plan of improvement in their condition as it may appear susceptible of.

As they have always considered that any specific claims or pretensions on their part would be highly unbecoming they have never entertained or encouraged any discussion on such subjects.

We remain,
Your obedient subjects,
Desir Fabien, Wm. Vesprey,
Jno. Welsh Hobson."

Hislop having failed to procure any statement of aim or any specific complaint from the people of colour, recommended to them that they :

" . . . defer their wish of applicating the Throne until they should have just grounds for complaint, which he fully trusts they will never experience under any form of law which His Majesty may in his wisdom be pleased to determine on for the future Government of the Island."

He also gave his fullest testimony to their undeviating loyalty, peaceful and praiseworthy conduct, which justly entitled him to the confidence he had placed in them as good and faithful subjects of the King.

On the same day he laid the subject before the Council, who agreed with all he had done and recommended that a delegation of the free coloured peoples be called before the Cabildo and asked to state their aims and desires. The Governor suggested a Committee of the three senior Councillors to investigate the background of all those who had signed the petition to the King and to find out which were natural-born subjects and which were not, the latter not being eligible as British subjects to sign petitions to the Crown.

At the same meeting a coloured man, Lucas Prieur, was brought before the Council. He had, it was stated, been deported from the colony in 1803 for crimes committed thirteen years previously and was strongly suspected of the murder of Le Chevalier de Vourvires at La Roche Quarrée. He was sentenced by the Council to be confined to gaol until he could be shipped to Martinique. In less than a week he had escaped and Hislop called a special meeting of the Council at which he spoke very seriously of this episode, commenting unfavourably upon the large number of coloured people who had recently entered the colony without permission. To stop this illegal immigration instructions were issued to Commandants of Quarters and Commanders of Militia to report on the character of all the coloured people in the island.

The Committee of the Free People of Colour now submitted an explanation of their desire to petition the King. In a firm yet respectful manner they referred to the difference in tone between the Governor's recent note and the action he had caused to be taken against the character of the coloured population. Hislop's reply to the Committee was again unfavourable and he accused them of " culpable want of caution " in that they had allowed the name of Lucas Prieur to appear amongst those who had signed the original petition to the King.

A reward was offered for the apprehension of Prieur but the placards were removed from their places in the town each night, despite the most careful precautions. The free coloured peoples were credited with this nightly action and were also held responsible for Prieur's escape from gaol. The Governor therefore informed the Committee that under existing circumstances he could not give permission for them to present a petition to the King. They were, however, always at liberty to petition him or the Council. A curt note from the Committee stating that they " would wait patiently upon events " brought the episode to a close after causing much unnecessary resentment amongst those who had proved themselves to be loyal and peace-loving subjects.

Another abortive effort was made at this time to change the colony's constitution. The " English Party " set up a committee under the chairmanship of Dr. Alexander Williams to petition the British Government for a constitution similar to that granted to other West Indian colonies. Dr. Williams, who had lived in the island since the days before the capitulation was, with a few of the older Spanish, French and English settlers, quite satisfied with the regulation of the colony under Spanish law. He was of the opinion that if properly administered the laws were quite suitable for the life and progress of the island, and had little desire to change to a system about which he knew so little. The Committee proposed a scheme which, whilst consistent with the colonial system, was unlikely to be acceptable to the Home Government as it excluded the people of colour from all benefits which would accrue to the colony if it were adopted. This scheme never reached the stage of a final decision.

(6) *Governor v. Chief Justice*

In March, 1809, the Secretary of State informed the Governor that His Majesty's Government had decided it would be advisable to appoint a professional man to the office of Chief Justice and that Mr. George Smith, lately Chief Justice of Grenada, had been nominated. The Governor was instructed to explain to Mr. Nihell, who held the office, that the reason for making the change was the growing importance of the colony and not any dissatisfaction with the manner in which he had always carried out his duties. The Council of Advice was to be consulted concerning Nihell's retiring pension and the sum they recommended would have the full support of the Secretary of State.

According to his commission, Mr. Smith was appointed Chief Judge, Alcalde del Crimen, and Fiscal for the administration of justice for the Island of Trinidad, at a salary of £2,000 a year. On arrival in the colony on May 15 he gave the impression of being an able man, who understood the technicalities of Spanish law and was opposed to its abolition. Had it been abolished, the great powers with which he was vested would have been abolished too. These powers seem to have gone to his head, for his attitude from his arrival gave offence to all sections of the community. The "English Party" were particularly hostile, for they had been gradually winning the Governor over to their way of thinking and were hoping for the institution of English law in the colony in the not too distant future. Almost at once conflict between the Governor and the new Chief Justice became apparent and the resulting confusion was reminiscent of the days of the three Commissioners. Smith considered that by virtue of his office he was free from any sort of Government control, and to all intents and purposes above the law.

Governor Hislop claimed that his commission had not been changed. As Governor of the Colony he was Judge of Appeal in all criminal cases, being President of the Court of Royal Audience, as had been the case ever since the Capitulation. Smith on the other hand claimed that the Governor's position had been altered; that now that he had been appointed Chief Justice (Oidor), a regularly constituted Court of Royal Audience had been created and that the Governor, as Viceroy, was only the President of the Court. He quoted from the Law of the Indies (Law 32, Title 15, Book 2):

"The Viceroys, as President of the Royal Audiences shall have no vote in matters appertaining to justice and we commend that they do leave the administration thereof to the Oidors of the Royal Audience."

Hislop refused to accept this ruling until he should be officially appointed Viceroy. He had no intention of giving up his powers as Governor in return for a mere title. Neither Governor nor Chief Justice seem to have thought of the simple expedient of putting the matter before the Secretary of State for decision of the Home Government, so the wrangle continued.

In January, 1810, Hislop announced that he was under orders from the Commander-in-Chief West Indies to take part in an expedition against Guadelope and that, during his absence, Lt. Colonel Tolley, of the 1st West India Regiment, would administer the Government. This was the first time since the capitulation that the colony had been left in the hands of an Acting Governor, and the "English Party" saw it as a heaven sent opportunity for promoting their policy for changing the laws. However, they had reckoned without Chief Justice Smith who, within a few days of Hislop's departure, proposed and carried the following address from the Council:

"To the King's Most Excellent Majesty:
The members of Your Majesty's Council established in the Colony of Trinidad beg leave to approach Your Majesty with assurances of their inviolable attachment to Your Majesty's Sacred Person and Government, and with all humility pray
That Your Majesty will be graciously pleased not to permit any change in the existing Government of this Colony without proper steps being taken to ascertain the real sentiments and wishes of the inhabitants of this Colony on a subject so important to their happiness and welfare.
George Smith, St. H. Bégorrat, Arch. Gloster, John Nihell, John Black, Jno. Smith."

The Cabildo at the same time forwarded a similar address to the King and in retaliation the "English Party" flooded the island's newspapers with strongly worded articles against the policy of the Chief Justice. Mr. Gallagher, proprietor of the *Trinidad Weekly Courant* was promptly imprisoned on Smith's orders. When Hislop returned he strongly resented what he considered as the Chief Justice's usurpation of the powers of the Executive.

The "English Party" realized that whilst Smith remained in office their cause could not hope to flourish, let alone succeed, and determined that although he held a King's appointment, he must go. They did their best at all times to goad him into some action which the Home Government could not afford to overlook.

Smith, having circumvented the "English Party", should have been in a position to call for support from their rivals, but by his pride and temper he had made enemies throughout the community and all parties were eager for his removal from office. Thus, when Hislop returned from Guadeloupe, he was presented with an address carrying four hundred signatures, designed chiefly as a mark of respect to the returning Governor, but also as a demonstration against the Chief Justice.

Smith wrote to the Governor describing the address as " a low and malicious form of insult " and tried to explain what had happened. Hislop's reply was carefully phrased, but the contents of the letters soon became public property and at the next meeting of the Council the Chief Justice found himself the only member to vote against a petition to the King for a change in the laws of the colony.

The petition, after some delay, was passed as the "general wish of the proprietors and inhabitants of Trinidad." This, however, was not the case, for none of the inhabitants except the nominated Council of Advice were consulted. There was one phrase in the petition which was new to the island, suggesting the change "with such modification as local circumstance may require."

The question of English law for Trinidad was under discussion in London at the time. Mr. Marryat, now a Member of Parliament, took every opportunity of putting the circumstances before the House, as he was virtually the head of the "English Party". He felt that the free people of colour had dangerous desires and that the sooner Trinidad came under English law the better it would be for the colony. The Government, moved at length to action, appointed a barrister, Mr. Stephen, brother-in-law of William Wilberforce, to report to them on the multitudinous reports and petitions from the colony. This appointment must have dashed Marryat's hopes, for Stephen was known to have strong views on the rights of the slaves and the coloured peoples.

Marryat also strongly supported Hislop against the actions of the Chief Justice, of whose conduct he wrote :

"It has been marked with such intemperance that his recall appears absolutely necessary for the peace and happiness of the Colony. I have expressed my sentiments on this point without reserve to His Majesty's Ministers."

Marryat's endeavours were unrewarded. The Home Government did not give Trinidad the law and institutions which, in the eyes of many, were quite unsuited to a colony where the attitude of the white to the coloured people was so short-sighted and unjust. The King's decision on this point was communicated to Hislop in a despatch dated November 27th, 1810. Undeterred by this setback, Marryat tried once again to bring forward proposals for giving Trinidad English law. He spoke at length in the House, attacking Spanish law particularly as administered by Chief Justice Smith. Mr. Brougham in his reply vindicated the application of Spanish law in Trinidad and the motion was lost without a division.

Meanwhile the situation in Trinidad had not remained entirely quiet. The Secretary of State was continually receiving reports of cases where the Chief Justice had behaved in the most extraordinary manner, but still the Home Government had to lend him its outward support.

It was John Sanderson, an English barrister practising in Port of Spain, who brought things to a head. An acting Deputy Judge-Advocate for the Militia, he considered it his duty to call upon the Chief Justice concerning sundry minor irregularities lately perpetrated by a solicitor named Love. The Chief Justice, though he disliked Love, refused to take action and Sanderson appealed to the Governor. This enraged Smith to such an extent that he accused Sanderson of having gone from a higher to an inferior jurisdiction. On the grounds that he had accepted fees from both parties in a case pending (a grave offence under Spanish law) he issued a Court decree suspending Sanderson from his office of Deputy Judge-Advocate under penalty of sequestration of half his property by the Crown.

Sanderson once more appealed to the Governor, who placed the facts before the Council of Advice. After careful investigation the Council declared Sanderson to be not guilty of professional misconduct and the Chief Justice to have acted without sufficient evidence. The Governor on this advice annulled the Court decree of suspension and Sanderson was reinstated.

There the matter might have ended as just another case of the Chief Justice overreaching himself. Sanderson, however, elated by his victory, wrote a letter to the *Weekly Courant* accusing the Chief Justice of "malice and ignorance of the law" and incorporated in the letter the minutes of the Council meeting at which his case had been heard. He then challenged the legality of the position of the Chief Justice.

"I will not comply with it (the Commission) and consequently I set the authority he has usurped at defiance, and express my contempt of him as an unjust and dishonest man."

This direct challenge to an officially appointed officer could not be tolerated by Hislop, who sent a letter to Mr. Gallagher, calling attention to his publication of Sanderson letter :

Government House,
29.12.1810.

Mr. Gallagher,
In order to do away with an impression which might otherwise be made on some minds from an avowal which appeared in a letter signed "John Sanderson" and published in your last paper whereby an idea is attempted to be supported, grounded on certain specific Spanish Laws therein quoted, that a non-compliance with the judicial orders of the Chief Oidor would be justifiable, His Excellency the Governor in consequence feels himself bound to declare that such a doctrine can never be tolerated in this Government, nor under any pretence whatsoever can he admit of any hesitation in yielding implicit obedience to an authority proceeding out of a Commission under the Royal Sign Manual until revoked by the same; and His Excellency will therefore, in pursuance of his duty, be ever ready to accord to it every aid and assistance which may be required of him for the due maintenance thereof.

His Excellency has at the same time to express his concern and dissatisfaction at having seen the minutes of proceedings of His Majesty's Council of the 22nd instant introduced into the body of the letter, the general nature and tenor of which deviate so far from the principle of temper and moderation he on all occasions has invariably recommended, and which has consequently incurred that entire disapprobation which on any similar occasion he will deem it his duty thus publicly to avow.

By His Excellency's Command,
Thomas Walker, Secretary.

The Council also passed a resolution condemning the action taken by Sanderson. The Chief Justice, seeing an opportunity to assert his power, ordered the newspaper in which the offending letter had appeared to be recorded in the Council's minutes so that " he could punish the author for libel." He then ordered the printers, Matthew Gallagher and Thomas Palmer, to appear before him and sent a copy of all the papers concerned to the Governor with a request that he would deal with the case in his own (the Governor's) Court.

Hislop was suspicious of the Chief Justice and turned the matter over to the Council, which concluded that Chief Justice Smith was competent to deal with the case as one of contempt of court. They declared that the Governor had done all that could be expected of him by writing to the *Weekly Courant* censuring Sanderson and declaring his official support for the Chief Justice's position.

Smith would not let well alone and issued an order for the arrest of Sanderson and the sequestration of his property. Sanderson countered by claiming immunity from arrest as Deputy Judge-Advocate and at once appealed to the Governor in the Court of Royal Audience. Hislop refused to take any action without consulting his Assessor, Andres Level de Goda, an exiled Spanish lawyer from Caracas. He stated that Sanderson, as a barrister, should be accorded the rights and privileges of an Hidalgo and should not be imprisoned in the local gaol but in the Cabildo House, one of the forts or placed under house arrest in his own home. Sanderson was therefore taken to Fort George. Smith, who was becoming more and more incensed each time he did not get his own way, wrote across the order for his arrest :

"Let John Sanderson be informed that when he has any representation to make on any particular points he will do well to make it directly to this Court, which knows full well its duties in the administration of justice; for which purpose His Majesty has been graciously pleased to confer upon it full powers without subjecting it to the control of any authority within the Colony."

The Chief Justice became more annoyed when the Governor

91

decided that Sanderson should be granted his freedom on bail on the surety of his supporters.

Even his friends were alarmed at Smith's high-handedness. It was not only the " English Party " who were petitioning the Government in London to have him removed; even the merchants of Bristol laid a petition before Parliament :

> ". . . That the system of jurisprudence at present in force in the said Island (Trinidad) is wholly incompatible with its commercial relations with this country and highly prejudicial to the interests of the petitioners, and pray the House to afford them some relief in the premises either by moving His Majesty to place the said Island upon the same footing as the other British West Indian Colonies or by such other mode as to the House may seem most fitting."

When it became known that Hislop had been granted leave to return to England, the whole community became alarmed, fearing what the Chief Justice might do without the restraining influence of a Governor who knew his peculiarities. Both the Cabildo and the Council addressed the Governor, asking him not to leave before arrangements had been made for the proper administration of justice in the colony. Hislop regretted that he must leave but informed the inhabitants that General Munro was on his way to take over the administration. This assurance seems not to have satisfied the public, for the Cabildo prepared and presented an address to the Governor giving in detail the evils to which the colony was exposed by the manner in which the Chief Justice exercised the powers given him by his commission. They added that the idea of one person holding as many as three offices was repugnant to Spanish law, and passed a resolution that " the Hon. George Smith should be suspended from the execution of his office until the determination of His Majesty should be known."

The Governor and the Council realized the serious nature of this resolution and modified it by restricting the Chief Justice's authority to the appellant jurisdiction only, before forwarding Smith a copy. The receipt of this was acknowledged by a violent attack upon the resolution which ended :

> ". . . Circumstanced as I now am my public duty requires that I should repair immediately to England, and I request of His Excellency that he will order the usual pass to be signed on my giving the customary securities."

This reply was read at a meeting of the Council, which refused to accept it as a formal protest against their resolution, and issued a statement informing the public of what had taken place. The Chief Justice's reply was minuted with a note to the effect that he himself was aggravating the issue.

A second application to leave the colony was made to the Governor by Smith, but Hislop regretfully pointed out that under Spanish law only the King could give leave for the Chief Oidor to be absent from his district. This brought Smith down to earth and he realized that if he was to do any good to his cause, he must be in London before Hislop. He decided to move quickly. Without waiting for official leave, he booked a berth on a British schooner, which after clearing Port of Spain, lay in Maceripe (Macqueripe) Bay waiting for him to join.

Smith was assisted in his speedy but undignified departure by a young Anglo-Virginian, William H. Burnley, who with Mr. J. B. Littlepage, had been appointed acting Depositor-General. It would appear from a letter from Mr. Black, a member of the Council, to Marryat in London, that Burnley had with Smith's knowledge, if not connivance, been doing extremely well out of his post and was reputed to be worth half a million dollars at the time.

A lengthy dispute between Governor and Chief Justice ended with the departure of Smith, who never returned to the colony, but was later posted to Ceylon, where he eventually ended his life by his own hand.

(7) *Fire*

Hislop's governorship was not taken up entirely with wrangles over defence and authority. He had other problems to deal with.

Just before midnight on the night of March 24th, 1808, the inhabitants of Port of Spain were rudely awakened by the beating of drums and the ringing of bells. Fire, the deadly enemy of the wooden town, had broken out. In a short time, whilst the citizens were panic-stricken, the breeze had fanned the flames so that Frederick Street was enveloped. In what seemed but a few moments the fire covered an area from Henry Street on the east to Chacon Street on the west and from King's Street on the north to Queen's Street on the south. So fast did the flames spread that many had only just time to escape, and were forced to leave all their possessions behind. Mingled with the cries of the people were the squeals of the horses and mules, trapped in the town's stables. To add to the confusion was the dull roar of exploding kegs of gunpowder and barrels of rum as the flames advanced and engulfed either stores or grog-shops. So great was the glare that when the soldiers were called out at Fort George, the parade ground was as bright as day and they could clearly see the movements of sailors on the decks of ships below them in the harbour.

Efforts to extinguish the fire were hopelessly inadequate. The "pump company with water engines", aided by the civil population, the Militia and the Army, were rendered useless through lack of water. Even the levelling of streets of houses had no effect. The town was in complete confusion with the mob pillaging houses and stores. Hislop himself was early on the scene and by his personal efforts encouraged the saving of as much property as possible from the chaos.

By morning the capital was a smoking ruin.

In spite of its magnitude, only one life was lost in the fire, that of a Negro servant of Mr. Sandes, the Vendue Master, who was trapped in a house near the seat of the fire. One soldier of the 37th Grenadiers died later as the result of burns sustained when rescuing a child from a burning house.

Port of Spain was crippled. Damage to buildings alone was estimated at $3½ million, and 4,500 people were rendered homeless, the greater number of these being destitute. Merchandise, produce and personal effects destroyed amounted to another half million sterling. Though most of the provision stores and warehouses had been destroyed, the Commissary Stores and the King's Provisions were saved. Martial law was proclaimed. With careful rationing under the eye of Hislop and the Council, famine was averted, whilst ships were sent to neighbouring colonies to purchase provisions. The port was declared an "open port" for all neutral ships for some months to enable enough building materials to be brought in. The response from the other West Indian colonies was immediate and Admiral Cochrane instructed captains of ships under his command to board all vessels in West Indian waters and to divert them to Trinidad regardless of their original destination.

The cause of the fire was never established but it was surmised that it was due to the carlessness of an apothecary, Dr. Schaw, of Frederick Street. He entered an outhouse with a lighted candle and accidentally set fire to some wood shavings and straw. The flames spread so rapidly that before anything could be done a neighbouring store of nitrates and essential oils was aflame.

The town, being built of wood, with the exception of a few storehouses built by the original French settlers, was soon on fire. Hislop, in his report to England, stated :

" Of public buildings not one has been saved, Government House, the Customs House, the Hospital, the Protestant Church, the Gaol, the Town Hall and part of the Public Archives and the Treasurer's Office, all have fallen a sacrifice to the flames."

The damage was so great that it was impossible to rebuild out of private funds or from the island's Treasury. Twelve blocks were almost entirely burnt out, nine blocks partially destroyed, making a total of 455 principal houses and stores as well as four times that number of smaller types of buildings. To meet this tremendous rebuilding programme and for the alleviation of distress the Home Government voted £50,000. When General Sir Thomas Picton heard of the disaster, he returned the £4,000 which had been subscribed towards the expenses of his trial by his friends and supporters.

CHAPTER NINE

GENERAL MUNRO, 1811–13

GENERAL MUNRO arrived in Trinidad to take up his two years Governorship on September 27th, 1811. He was faced with the problems passed on from Hislop's administration. Almost as soon as he arrived he received a Memorial from the Attorney-General (Mr. Ashton Warner) backed by the advocates and solicitors in practice in the colony, asking for some arrangements to be made for the administration of justice. The situation had been left in complete disorder following the unofficial departure of the Chief Oidor. It was also asked that a copy of this Memorial setting out their difficulties should be sent to the Secretary of State. The remedies, as we shall see, were left to his successor.

During his short period of office Munro received an Order in Council for the registration of slaves in the colony. This task, which may have seemed easy to those who framed the Order in London, was difficult to put into practice. The chief obstacles in the way of obtaining an accurate return of the slave population were the difficulties involved in getting from one part of the island to another and the fact that many of the owners had introduced slaves illegally and would if possible avoid registration to save themselves from the courts and to keep their numbers low in case of the introduction of a slave tax. Munro wrote to Henry Murray, the Registrar of Slaves :

". . . Whereas having taken into my consideration the the official representation . . . of the seventeenth instant stating your utter inability to comply with that part of the Royal Ordinances of 26th March, 1812, which directs that 'when and so soon as all the original returns or schedules which shall have been delivered to the said Registrar pursuant of the said Order shall have been fairly entered and Registered as aforesaid which shall be done and completed within the term of two Calendar Months from and after the date of the first publication at Trinidad'. And I have well and minutely deliberated on the facts . . . and of the absolute necessity for the extension of time to be granted to enable you to complete the enregistration of the returns of all slaves within this Island . . . I do by these presents and in virtue of the Prerogatives, Powers, and Authorities in me vested . . . give, grant, and concede unto you . . . an extension of time from the day of the date of these presents unto the 31st day of August next ensuing . . ."

The immense task of registration was not finished when Woodford arrived to take over the Governorship.

Other problems arose from the rapid deterioration of conditions in Venezuela.* British ships and other vessels in which the merchants of Port of Spain had an interest were frequently boarded by officers of both the royalist and the insurgent camps. These ships were seized without regard for treaties of alliance or for declarations of neutrality. Munro, without any naval force at his command, was unable to make any effective answer to the merchants' plea for help. However reasonable, moral or legal the merchants' claims might be, without armed support in the Gulf of Paria it was impossible to put an end to the legalized piracy of either side in the Venezuelan conflict.

An account of the Venezuelan conflict is given in the next succeeding chapter. Munro's connection with it came about when early in January, 1813, a party of insurgents from the mainland, led by Santiago Marino, who had taken refuge on Chacachacare in an effort to escape to neutral territory and re-equip themselves, issued a Proclamation.

"Whereas the Spanish General Don Domingo Monteverde has violated the agreement with the Illustrious General Miranda on the 25th July, 1812, and whereas the amnesties granted in that solemn treaty have been replaced by the scaffold, by the prison, by persecution and sequestration and whereas the said General Miranda has been the victim of the perfidy of his adversary. Whereas the people of Venezuela are wounded almost to death. Now, therefore we, forty-five emigrants, have agreed this hacienda under the patronage of the courageous Lady Donno Concepcion Marino, united in close council and urged by sentiments of deepest patriotism and have resolved to make an expedition to Venezuela with the object of saving our ever beloved country from subordination

* The Spanish American Colonies were in open revolt against the Mother Country and were seeking independence.

to Spain and of restoring the dignity of the Nation which has been torn away by the tyrant Monteverde and his irruption.

We mutually pledge our honour as Caballeros to conquer or to die in this glorious enterprise and in faith thereof we commit ourselves to our God and to our swords.

We declare Colonel Santiago Marino to be the Supreme Chief of this expedition with full plenary powers.

Chacachacare, 11th January. 1813.

President of the Council—Santiago Marino.
Secretary—Francisco Azcue."

Where Munro's feelings lay it is impossible to state but on the appearance of the insurgents being reported he issued instructions for action to be taken. On January 14th he wrote to Lt.-Colonel Lopinot :

" Sir,

In consequence of an official notice I have received yesterday the 13th from Don Juan Gavazzo, Commandant of the Village and Coast of Guiria for His Catholic Majesty importing that a number of people of colour and vagabonds of other classes living under the protection of this Government have rendezvoused at the Island of Chacachacare with the intent of attacking the Spanish Continent by a Military expedition under the orders of St. Jago Marino, who is the principal proprietor of the Island, I have deemed it expedient for His Majesty's service to order you to go to the Island of Chacachacare and take information on this singular occurrence of which no suspicion founded has been reported to me . . . I deem it proper to order a detachment of the 1st West India Regiment to accompany you under the Command of Captain Nixon to the employed as circumstances may require.

On your arrival at Chacachacare you will immediately repair to the dwelling house of Mr. Marino and make known to him the object of your mission and should you find Mr. Gavazzo's complaint founded in any degree, you are to order immediately the persons assembled (of whatever class they may be) to disperse and, in case of resistance or insolence, you will apply to Captain Nixon for military aid to carry your orders into execution doing so with as little injury to those refractors as the case will admit; but should they quietly submit and repair each to his respective home, there is no more to be said.

It having been this day reported that the expedition (as it is called) has already proceeded to the Main in breach of the repeated orders of this Government respecting the neutrality —should you find it so and that St. Jago Marino has accompanied it—you will in this case leave his house and property in the charge of Captain Nixon and his detachment and repair immediately here with your report.

Captain Nixon of course must be there at discretion until provisions and further orders be forwarded to him."

On January 15th, Lopinot reported that he had been to Chacachacare and found no expedition nor any signs of one. Mr. Santiago Marino himself was absent but five principal persons in the island denied, untruthfully as later appeared, that any expedition had been there.

Munro then issued a Proclamation stating that the Government had no sympathy with the insurgents, was strictly neutral and banished Marino from the colony and seized his property and that of all connected with the affair.

CHAPTER TEN

VENEZUELAN INCIDENTS

ON ACCOUNT of her geographical position it was inevitable that Trinidad would be affected by any big movements in the neighbouring provinces of the Spanish Main. Socially and commercially there were many ties between the two countries. Trinidad had depended for some years on the supply of beef and other foodstuffs from Venezuela and there was a constant, if illicit, movement of political offenders between the two countries.

During the French Revolutionary and Napoleonic wars the British had done all they could to harass Spain on the high seas and through her colonies. Picton's Proclamation of 1797 had strengthened the hand of the revolutionaries or as they called themselves, the " Patriots ", who were preparing for a long struggle against the authority of Spain; he had also encouraged contraband trade between all the Spanish colonies on the Main and Trinidad.

About a month after Picton's Proclamation a plot was uncovered in Caracas, which Pedro Carbonnel, the Captain General, reported to Madrid, stating officially that he considered the cause to be :

" the prompting the conspirators received from the English Commandant (Picton) of Trinidad, who had from thence not only inundated the whole coast of Venezuela with papers both written and printed but made offers of powerful protection and of free and extended commerce for the benefit of the people of Caracas."

In July, 1818, the Council of the Indies* informed Juan Cassas, the new Captain General, that Charles IV and Ferninand VII, had abdicated in favour of Joseph Bonaparte and that Murat was now Lt.-General of Spain. This news caused

* See p. 27.

great excitement in Caracas; creoles as well as European Spaniards felt that they had been cheated; street corner meetings passed addresses of loyalty and swore revenge on the French. The Captain General was forced to take an oath of allegiance to Ferdinand and the two Commissioners who had brought the disturbing news rapidly left the colony.

The same day a British man-of-war arrived with the information that Britain and Spain were now allies against the French.

The Captain General was in an uncomfortable position. On the one hand Bonaparte might take exception if his authority was slighted. On the other, Ferdinand's supporters were strong, numerous and ever present. His indecision was reflected in the excitement of the people. The general confusion was increased by the publication of a Proclamation, said to have been issued by the Supreme Junta of Seville, head of loyalist Spain, calling on all officials in Spanish America to submit to its orders as representing the provincial authority of the rightful King. The Cabildo studied the Proclamation but could not agree as to its value. The Royalists were of the opinion that the Junta was irregular and illegal. The Captain General decided to support the Junta, by force if necessary, and in so doing caused a breach between the official Spanish Government and the colonists. All members of the community, whether Spanish or native born, resented his step and at a public meeting it was decided to set up a local Junta on the lines of that of Seville to protect the rights of Ferdinand in his colony. These proposals were presented to the Captain General in the form of an address signed by the instigators of the plan. He, fearful for the future of the colony, at once ordered the arrest of the signatories, one of whom he sent to Spain to be dealt with; others he exiled or sent to gaol while a few were released.

The Junta of Seville, which had taken over all power and authority of the deposed King, recognized the loyalty shown to the Crown of Spain by its American subjects in the New World by announcing that they would be regarded as " an integral and essential part of the Kingdom." For the first time there was to be equality between Spaniards born in South America and those born in Spain. The Spanish American colonies would in future be able to send a limited number of deputies to the Cortes of Spain.* This statement was well received as a foretaste of better things to come.

* The Assembly of the States of the Realm in Spain.

A new Captain General was now appointed, a distinguished servant of his country, both able and energetic. In normal times Vincent Emparan would have been welcomed, but there had grown up a party of influential men who, whilst desiring to remain associated with Spain, wished to be rid of the despotism of viceroys. They were staunch Royalists but resented the presence of a Viceroy and attempted once more to set up a local Junta in the name of King Ferdinand.

When news arrived that the Junta of Seville had been dissolved and that France held all Spain except Cadiz and L'Isle de Leon, it was decided to hold a demonstration against Emparan and in favour of a local Royal Junta. On Holy Thursday, when the Cabildo met under the Presidency of the Captain General, the demonstration took place and a Junta with full powers of the executive was set up. Emparan, the Auditor de Guerra and other high officials were banished from the colony. The new Junta was at once recognized by the other provinces, who hastened to follow the example of Caracas and set up Juntas of their own.

Initial contact was made with the Council of Regency which had replaced the Junta of Seville in Spain and now ruled with authority in the name of the King. The next step was to open up trade with the rest of the world, particularly with Britain, whose traders were given a preference of one quarter less tax than other nationals.

An agent, in the person of Simon Bolivar,* was sent to London to ask for protection and assistance in the event of Venezuela being attacked and to urge the British Government to use its good offices in extracting for her certain privileges from the Spanish Crown. The task was not easy, for England and Spain were allies, and though Venezuela claimed to be loyal to the interests of Ferdinand there were many signs of independence. England was unable to do more than make promises and hold out vague hopes for the future in return for trade concessions; and with these Bolivar had to be content.

The Spanish provisional Government was alarmed at the setting up of the Venezuelan Junta and particularly at the opening of the ports to world trade, which was against Spanish commercial policy. In August, 1810, the popular party were declared to be rebels and the province was treated as enemy territory and its ports blockaded. This first act of Spain against her colonies

* See Appendix XII.

had its repercussions in Trinidad, for as we have seen, there were ships of all parties in the Gulf of Paria plying between the island and the Main, and as the fortunes of war varied, so did the ability of the Royalists and the Patriots to capture one another's cargoes.

Guayana and the Orinoco Delta were held for the Royalists, the coasts from Maturin to Cape la Peña for the Patriots, and every vessel entering or leaving Port of Spain was boarded by officials of one or the other, if not of both, parties. Cargoes were often seized in complete disregard of the alliance between England and Spain. The merchants of Trinidad were so badly affected by this indiscriminate seizure that they sent a Memorial to the Governor (General Munro), pointing out that though Britain had declared herself neutral in the quarrel between Spain and her colonies, it was still the duty of the Government to protect British trade and commerce. This was a reasonable enough point, but it evoked no response and the Gulf of Paria continued to be a playground for legalized pirates.

By the end of 1812 the Venezuelan Patriots were driven underground, hostilities ceased and it seemed that the colony was now loyal. Patriot leaders had either left the country or had been captured and there was peace under the strong arm of General Monteverde, until he followed up his successes, aided and abetted by Ceveris, with ruthless and unnecessary cruelty. This gratuitous barbarity roused the people to open revolt, especially in the Cumana province, and hundreds fled into the hills rather than obey the Royalist commanders.

It was at this stage that some forty-five of the Patriots, led by Santiago Marino, gathered on the island of Chacachacare, as already related. Marino, a creole from Margarita, had friends and relations in Trinidad and had himself lived in the colony for a time and had there picked up the rudiments of soldiering whilst serving in the Militia under General Picton.

He planned to capture Guiria, a small town on the gulf coast of Venezuela, held by five hundred Royalist troops under the command of Juan Gavazzo, a naval officer. In January, 1813, his force, armed with a few old muskets, crossed the Boca Grande in canoes. On arrival at Guiria they found that Gavazzo and his men had moved inland, leaving the defences in the hands of the local militia. This opposition Marino's small force quickly overcame, and news of his victory spread through the surrounding countryside. In a short time he found himself at the head of a fighting force of nearly five thousand men armed and supplied from captured Guiria; this force he led out against Maturin on the Rio Guarapiche.

Thus the second stage of the war for Venezuelan independence started from Trinidad.

CHAPTER ELEVEN

SIR RALPH JAMES WOODFORD, 1813–28

(1) *The New Governor*

SIR RALPH JAMES WOODFORD, Second Baronet, born July 21st, 1784, was the son of Sir Ralph Woodford, sometime Resident Minister to the Hanse Towns and later Minister Extraordinary to Denmark. At the early age of twenty-nine he was appointed Governor of Trinidad, a well-educated young man of decided character and personality, who arrived in the colony on June 14th, 1813. He was entrusted with great powers by the British Government to enable him to bring about the reforms necessary, to clear away the many abuses which had followed from the experiment of the Commissioners' Government and from the disputes between the late Governor and the Chief Justice.

In his commission, his position was clearly stated. As far as possible, Spanish law was to remain in force and the powers of the Executive Government were to be vested solely in him. He was to have such rights and privileges as had been reserved to Governors under the Spanish Crown. The Courts of Civil and Criminal Justice were to continue as they had done before the capitulation and the judicial powers conferred upon Spanish Governors by virtue of their office were to be enjoyed by their English successors, with the same authority or jurisdiction, whether appellate or original which had been exercised by the Court of Royal Audiencia at Caracas. The jurisdiction of all courts was to be centred in Woodford as Governor, Commander-in-Chief and Vice-Admiral. In criminal trials he was Judge of Appeal, holding criminal jurisdiction over all cases from theft to murder. Actions concerning widows and infants were also under his care in the Causas de Cortes. He had power to appoint judges to lower courts and to deprive of their office, if he thought fit, all those who had no direct appointment from the Crown. Crown Officers he could suspend until such time as the Crown decided on its course of action. As Intendent of the Royal Domain, he was judge in all matters pertaining to Crown lands, but in civil cases the right to appeal from his decisions to the Privy Council was granted to the inhabitants.

In spite of these great powers his task was not easy, for he had at the start to put down abuses which had continued so long that they had an almost prescriptive right to exist. In executing his official functions he was bound to make enemies, but from the moment of his arrival he made it clear that he was going to govern the island justly and firmly and to find out for himself what went on in the colony. To gain this knowledge he corresponded personally with all heads of departments and brought the Government under his direct control.

At his first appearance as President of the Cabildo on June 21st he stated in his opening address that he would give his support to the Illustrious Body in carrying out its duties, but he would have no tampering with the powers of the Executive and he warned them against " mischievous discussions." He made it abundantly clear that he would brook no interference with his position and intimated in civil but quite unmistakable terms that the Illustrious Cabildo had no power to control him as Governor.

The following month Woodford met the Council for the first time and at once informed them that he had studied the accounts of the Committee appointed to oversee the expenditure of the £50,000 voted for rebuilding after the fire of 1808. It appeared from these accounts that the gaol had already cost £30,000 and was still incomplete and that at least another £24,000 was needed to finish the Protestant Church. As a result of this investigation he had stopped work on rebuilding until he received a reply from London in answer to his despatch on the subject.

At the close of the meeting Woodford informed the members that he had received a despatch from the Secretary of State referring to the differences between Governor Hislop and the Chief Justice. He was instructed to inform the Council that, after careful scrutiny of the facts, it was considered that Mr. Smith had shown " a great want of temper, discretion and tact " and it could not be recommended to His Royal Highness, the Prince Regent, that he be reinstated. The Prince Regent had agreed with the advice of his Privy Council but had added that " the same want of temper, discretion and tact was equally apparent in the members of His Majesty's Council." He therefore directed that the members " shall be removed from their seats, His Majesty having no further use for their services."

The members of the Council who had supported the Cabildo when Chief Justice Smith was suspended, many of whom sat as

Councillors under Picton, left in indignant surprise, certain that their dismissal was the work of this new young Governor. There is, however, no evidence to support this theory. For some months Woodford carried on without a Council of Advice, but before the end of the year he appointed Manuel Sorzano, a Spaniard; Laurence Nihell, an Irish settler under the Cedula of 1783; Colonel Lopinot, a French Royalist, and William H. Burnley* as his advisers.

(2) Venezuelan Insurrection

The early days of Woodford's administration were complicated by events on the Spanish Main. Trade was being ruined for Trinidad merchants by the insurrection in Venezuela. Royalists and Patriots alike were committing outrages on shipping in the Gulf of Paria, particularly the Royalists. Though by his commission Woodford was Vice-Admiral, he had no ships under his command and was only able to appeal to Sir Francis Laforey in Barbados.

" I must however entreat your kind attention to us in the very unprotected state we are in and to the daily increase of the maritime and territorial power of the insurgents on the Spanish Main whose piratical acts are extended to the seizure of boats and trading launches of the Royalists at anchor on the coasts of this Island, thus insulting the King's territory and preventing all intercourse with the inhabitants.

The temptation furnished to the slaves to obtain their freedom by desertion to the country in revolt is facilitated by the uninterrupted course of their boats in the Gulf, which has had only about ten days naval protection since my arrival. If therefore you could favour us with a small boat which could remain entirely in the Gulf . . . you would add much to my ease as well as to that of the inhabitants in general, particularly on the distant parts of the coast . . ."

Woodford was not prejudiced in his opinions on the Venezuelan struggle. He wrote to the Officer Commanding His Catholic Majesty's ship *Nuestra Senora de las Nieves* in November, 1813 :

" Sir,
It having been reported to me that the Spanish launch *Rosario* has been taken possession of by H.C.M. Vessel under your command, the said launch being under the protection of these batteries, I have, in the name of the King, my Master, the ally of H.C.M., whose Officer you are, to demand restitu-

* See p. 93.

tion of the said launch . . . and in the event of your refusal to comply with this demand, I shall take such measures as I may judge the most advisable for the insult you have committed upon King's territory."

More difficulties were provided by a constant stream of refugees who came into the colony, many of them old folk and children whom Woodford permitted to stay in the island. Others, who he realized were former citizens from British and French colonies and who had moved into Venezuela during the Napoleonic war, he hoped to turn into good citizens by giving them the protection they needed.

Though continually having to report cases of insult to British Sovereignty, and in spite of the failure of the blockade of the Venezuelan coast announced by General Munro, but never put into effect by the British fleet, Woodford did his best to conciliate both the Royalists and the Patriots, though his sympathies appeared to be with the Royalists. He wrote to the Commodore of the Royalist flotilla in the Gulf in January, 1815 :

" Sir,
    It has always been my desire to see the unfortunate revolt of the Spanish Main come to an end, and more especially that the provinces bordering on this Gulf should return to their allegiance; and with this object I have on two different occasions offered to the insurgent leader at Guiria to serve as a mediator for the return of those provinces to the Spanish Government.
    Mr. Clozier . . . has informed me of the wretched state of affairs in Guiria, of the alarm which exists there, and lastly of the serious outrages committed by the emancipated slaves who fled into the mountains, and also that the insurgent Chief, Bideau, is inclined to capitulate.
    It has occurred to me that both you and General Morales will excuse the liberty I take in entreating you to employ such measures for the possession of the Gulf as will avoid the effusion of blood, by guaranteeing his life to the said Chief and giving him a safe conduct to some other Colony . . .
    I enclose the accompanying letter for General Morales and a copy of the note I have sent to Bideau."

To General Morales.

" Sir,
    Since my arrival in these Islands in June, 1813, my most anxious desire has been to see the legitimate Government restored in the Provinces of Venezuela and the horrible

108

effusions of blood put a stop to which the Revolution has occasioned.

In this desire I was pleased to find that General Monteverde fully shared . . .

Your Excellency would excuse the liberty I take in begging of you to adopt such measures as, whilst protecting the rights of His Catholic Majesty, will at the same time stay the effusion of blood . . . I beg to congratulate Your Excellency upon the success you obtained at Maturin."

To Jean Baptiste Bideau.

Government House, Trinidad.
18.1.1813.

"The Governor of Trinidad has just learned that terms of capitulation have been offered unsuccessfully to Mr. Bideau . . . he cannot but take the present opportunity of repeating to Mr. Bideau his anxious desire to bring to an amicable end the sanguinary struggle which has so long desolated the neighbouring Continent, and he has expressed himself in the same terms to the Officer Commanding the flotilla and the General commanding His Catholic Majesty's troops, feeling convinced that they will be ready and willing to avoid the ruin of innocent persons.

Should this proposal be accepted by both parties, the Governor is prepared to send a vessal to Guiria to convey Mr. Bideau and his staff to any one of the neutral Colonies which he may name."

These appeals fell on deaf ears and when, a few months later, General Morales took Guiria, every patriot was killed by his order. Bideau himself escaped with his family and some supporters to Trinidad. Many of his party were French people of colour who had left Trinidad immediately after the capitulation and Woodford, rather than let them remain where they might easily cause trouble, gave them stores and money and chartered a ship to carry them to St. Bartholomew, a French island off the coast of St. Martin in the West Indies. He even went so far as to hold back a Royalist vessel in Port of Spain until the fugitives had a fair chance to get away. He permitted Bideau's wife and family to remain in the colony.

Woodford's action was typical of his policy, for whilst he would not allow Trinidad to become a rendezvous for conspirators, he was equally determined that he would give his protection to those whom he allowed to stay in the colony. General Morales took the strongest exception to this, and wrote to the Governor in March :

". . . All these reflexions and the faithful attachment which England has shown Spain, and which has made her her friend for ever, induces me to hope that Your Excellency will not only not admit fugitives, but that you will order to be delivered up to me those described in the annexed memorandum, the vessels and flecheras that have taken refuge in your island, and also the ex-Marquis del Toro with all his followers, including Colonel Sucre . . ."

To this Woodford replied :

". . . So long as these unfortunate persons who (to save their lives and to escape the horrors of civil war in Venezuela) in the midst of peril and in the extremity of misery and affliction, sought hospitality and security, do not by any improper conduct forfeit that right which humanity gives to them to my protection, it is not possible for me to deprive them of this asylum without express orders from His Majesty's Government to that effect; but I can assure Your Excellency that should they in any way contravene the Laws of this Colony they will be punished as they deserve . . ."

In August, 1815, Trinidad again declared herself neutral in the Venezuelan struggle in the hopes that trade regulations would be altered and that the navigation of the River Meta in Colombia, which flows into the Orinoco, would be opened. Woodford inherited Picton's ambition to make Trinidad the centre of West Indian trade. The Home Government, in an effort to encourage this, suggested that a " draw-back " should be allowed on all goods exported from Trinidad to Venezuela in launches or open boats. Woodford, not sure that this suggestion would be beneficial, referred the question to a special committee. Mr. Meany, the Inspector of Spanish Launches, giving evidence before the committee, supported the Governor. He stated that the trade with the Main was chiefly in dry goods and that the cargo purchased from various stores was already made up into convenient packages of the size and weight for transport by the pack animals of the purchasers. No bills or invoices were given or demanded, the Trinidad merchants knowing full well that the goods would be smuggled into Venezuela. If the Custom House took too official a notice of the trade, the Venezuelans would retire from it, being frightened that Spanish spies might hear of these dealings and they would be obliged to pay exorbitant duties on their cargoes. Others supported this view and the committee asked Woodford to report to the Secretary of State that, in their opinion, a " draw-back "

lands that had already been granted on lease, and that in Trinidad the Crown had not this right. He quoted particularly the case of Don Gaspar de Percin on the island of Gaspar Grande, whose lands, granted by Governor Salaverria, and taken over by Chacon for building a battery, were surveyed, appraised and paid for, although the grant had not been recorded in the Libro Becarro.* The matter had never been satisfactorily cleared up but Woodford seems to have been prepared for questions, for he replied that Marryat had mis-stated the case and he quoted from the proceedings of the Court of the Intendent of Crown Lands, giving details as to the reasons for and the values of payments made to Percin by the Government and quoted the law under which the resumption had been made. Marryat, undeterred by this defeat, brought up other cases in an effort to prove that the Government's land policy was a failure.

The whole question of land had been a thorn in the side of the Government since the capitulation, when it had been uncertain whether the island would continue to be held by the British or be returned to Spain. It had been impossible to make a Crown grant of land owing to the uncertainty of the future of the colony and there was the added difficulty that land held under Spanish law was held under conditions diametrically opposed to the English law of land tenure. The whole position had been considerably complicated by the influx of French and other settlers after the Cedula on Colonization in 1783.

As early as 1784, Chacon had had to publish a Proclamation stating :

"All colonists who had been admitted previous to the date of the publication of the Cedula should appear before the Governor and renew their oaths of allegiance, making a Report of the Lands which had been apportioned to them, and making entries thereof in the Libro Becarro, specifying particulars so as to obviate for the future all possibility of obscurity."

The penalty for failure to comply with this order was forfeiture of the right to be a colonist within the meaning of the Cedula, and forfeiture of any favours which the King of Spain might think fit in the future to confer upon the settlers of Trinidad as a body.

The following year Chacon had been forced to issue another Proclamation, pointing out the care he had taken to see that

* Libro Becarro—Book of Registration.

the Cedula of 1783 was carried out. He also referred to the trouble caused by

> " confusion, contradiction and uncertainty in which landed property was involved from the arbitrary occupation thereof by ancient Spaniards, without previous form of concession, admeasurement or demarkation of boundaries."

In order to remedy this state of affairs, orders were issued clearly stating under what terms colonists and others could hold land.

The early settlers took advantage of the Cedula of 1783, under which Spain departed from her normal colonial policy and allowed foreign settlers into Trinidad. They had settled quietly and had taken possession of their lands without causing any trouble. They were a little more active than the original Spanish settlers at first, but soon became as indolent as their predecessors. They were roused to renewed activity by the influx of political refugees from Santo Domingo and of the Republican French driven out of their original island homes by the British. Chacon's position had become difficult, not to say dangerous, when he found himself with no means of enforcing his will upon people whose political creed taught them to disobey constiutional authority as the first duty of a good Republican. He was therefore forced to let them remain in the lands which they occupied.

After the capitulation the British continued this policy of letting those in possession remain in ownership even though grants had not been confirmed or in some cases were legally forfeited. Successive Governors and Councils had raised the question of land tenure with the Home Government but it was not until 1815 that any decision was reached.

In a letter to Woodford, the Secretary of State wrote :

> ". . . In the present despatch I shall confine myself to conveying to you the instructions of His Majesty's Government with respect to the confirmation of grants of land made by your predecessors and with respect to the restrictions and limitations under which it appears to me most advisable that future grants should be made . . . I am to authorize you in cases in which any occupier or possessor of land either under Spanish or British authority shall have commenced its cultivation to confirm to him, without any restrictions as to the future cultivation of the land, all that part of the original grant which may be in actual cultivation at the time together with a further portion of land not exceeding in quantity that which has been cultivated.

The only case in which you will consider yourself at liberty to withhold the confirmation is that in which the land in question may be required for public service. Should the land so cultivated be required, it will be necessary that you should make to the occupier a grant elsewhere corresponding in value to that of which he has been deprived.

It appears also expedient to impose as the price of this confirmation a small quit rent on the land regranted . . . In making new grants of land to persons desirous of establishing themselves in the Colony you will adhere to the following regulations, viz. :

1st. You will in no case make a grant above 200 acres without specific authority from home.

2nd. You will portion the grants made by you to the means for cultivation which the person applying for it may give satisfactory evidence of possessing.

3rd. You will in all cases reserve a moderate quit rent proportionate to both the value of the land and the produce which may be raised upon it. By this means the rate of quit rent to be paid by an acre of land when in canes or provisions will bear proportion to the value of the respective crops.

4th. You will insert in all grants a special provision that land shall revert to the Crown unless a portion of it be cultivated within a limited period.

5th. You will reserve to the Crown the right to metals and minerals.

6th. You will insert such stipulation with respect to making of roads, canals and other means of communication as peculiar circumstances of the Colony may appear to require.

7th. You will annually report to me a detailed account of the grants made by you in the preceding year . . ."

Woodford issued a Proclamation to this effect in December, 1815.* Those who were unable for one reason or another to produce any evidence save occupation of their land were thrown into a panic, thinking the Proclamation the thin edge of the wedge which would separate them from their livelihood.

There was little evidence of this panic in Trinidad itself for it was impossible to hold a public meeting if the purpose was to criticize the Government, and Woodford was not a man to be taken lightly. In London, however, opposition was active through the body known as " The Committee of Landholders of Trinidad" under the leadership of Marryat.

This Committee took its case to the highest authority and

* See Appendix XIII.

spoke with some weight, as may be seen from its correspondence with the Secretary of State for the Colonies :

". . . The Committee are instructed by their legal advisers, that the new rights claimed by the Crown and enforced by Sir Ralph Woodford, upon lands held in Trinidad under Spanish Grants may be effectually resisted in a Court of Appeal, but had much rather owe the redress of that and other grievances of which the inhabitants of Trinidad and others interested in that Colony complain, to the grace and justice of His Majesty's Ministers, than to any other mode of proceeding, and with this feeling submit the present statement to their consideration."

Whilst a lengthy correspondence was carried on, the Proclamation of 1815 was modified. In consequence of the representations made to the Government, it was decided in 1816 that all lands held prior to the capitulation in 1797 were to be exempt from the annual quit rent of 5s. per quarree* no matter how defective the grant, tenure or occupation may have been.†

The Committee of Landowners was still not satisfied, complaining that the new rights claimed by the Crown destroyed the security of all private property and that a system of confiscation was being set up to which there was no end; all would be at the mercy of the Governor. Many of the proprietors, they claimed, "had possessed their land since time immemorial"; others had a just title by prescription. All had had their property guaranteed at the time of the capitulation. Sales and conveyances of land had taken place, held under these same titles, many of them under the authority of the Courts of Justice. All had been paid for and if the properties were forfeit to the Crown as being held by defective or void titles, the result would be endless litigation and confusion. In support of their complaints they stated :

1. Those grants of land under the old Spanish Laws were exempt from any qualification or restraint; in fact, the land was held "gratuitiously for ever" under the Cedula of 1783.‡
2. Under the terms of the capitulation, those who held land in Trinidad were entitled to hold them upon terms under which they originally occupied or cultivated.
3. It was not true that by the Laws of the Indies (The Colonial Laws of Spain) lands were liable to resumption by the Crown for insufficient or partial cultivation.

On these grounds they claimed that Woodford was enforcing

* 1 quarree—3 1/5 acres.
† See Appendix XIV.
‡ See Appendix I, Art. 2.

conditions contrary to the laws of Spain; that the Cedula of 1783 did away with all the laws and regulations contrary to its articles, and that Chacon's Proclamation of 1785* applied only to those who had occupied lands without any title at all, and exempted from "resumption" for partial cultivation all those who possessed them under the condition of conforming to the Cedula. All that was required from landholders under Spanish law was that they live upon their land and cultivate it for a term of four or five years. If the holder left the island before this period had elapsed, it could be granted to new settlers as it was then according to the Cedula forfeit to the Crown. This was the only way in which the land could revert to the Crown. After the probationary period had been completed, the law, they claimed, gave undisputed possession of lands to the holder, including the right to dispose of them by sale or in any way the owner desired.

The clause making it compulsory to place and keep a fixed number of Negro or other labourers on the land was another bone of contention. The Committee held that it was illegal because no such condition existed under Spanish law. It was unworkable because the abolition of the slave trade by the British Government had completely changed the labour situation in the colony. The suggestion that the Government could resume land for public service was also objected to by the Committee, as it would be a new right set up against landowners. It would place "the property of everyone in a dangerous position, making him liable to be ejected from his house and land at the pleasure of the Governor and in exchange he might be given waste land in some part of the Colony which was of no value."

Concerning the titles referred to in the Proclamation as being invalid, either on account of neglect on the part of the owners or for want of some specific declaration of the Royal pleasure, the Committee stated that according to the third article of the Cedula, all grants of land were to be registered in the Book of Registry (Libro Becarro de Publicion), but it did not make registration compulsory on the new settler nor essential to the validity of a new title. The third article was a suggestion, not a condition, and it was the duty of the Crown's officer to make the registration of lands and grants; thus no penalty could legally be imposed for an omission which was not the fault of the holder of the land. They stated that the Spanish Escribanos were notorious for their neglect in making entries in the Libro Becarro, because the original landowners regarded any effort by

* See Appendix XV.

the Escribanos to collect fees for registration as an attempt to extort money unofficially for themselves.

The most offensive portion of the Proclamation of 1815 was thought to be the clause which made all uncultivated or only partially cultivated lands liable to forfeiture to the Crown. The Committee regarded this as both arbitrary and illegal.

Woodford defended the Proclamation against the charges of the landowners with views diametrically opposed to theirs:

"That a regulation defining the boundaries of lands, or leading to an authenticated measurement of them with a neighbouring proprietor, could not be justly said to foment litigation or to weaken the security of those who advanced money upon their property. The blame of any loss sustained by the parties should not be charged upon the Government which having detected had always provided a remedy for the defect of titles; whose object was merely to enforce order and regularity in such, to regulate their enrolment and to put upon record for the information of any lender of money the interest and means of the proprietor."

He contended that by the special enactments of the Cedula of 1783 and the General Law of Spain, all lands were held on condition that they must be cultivated and also that those to whom they were granted were obliged to register the grant themselves. Whereas the Committee maintained that the existence of plans or surveys of lands in the possession of occupiers were a title equivalent to a title from the Crown, Woodford held that this was unsupported by any authority or practice. He denied that the words of the Cedula, "gratuitously for ever" barred the right of the Crown to impose quit rents or fines legally. The phrase could not be read as "unconditionally." As to the resumption of land for public service, he maintained that the right of resumption had always been possessed by the King of Spain and therefore passed to the King of England at the capitulation.

The two main points at issue were:

1. Which lands were private property at the time of the capitulation?
2. Whether the Proclamation of December 5th, 1815, interfered with the legal rights of existing landowners or was it inconsistent with or repugnant to the Spanish law so far as that law applied to Trinidad?

Woodford was anxious to settle the questions, not only for the benefit of the individual landowners but for the good of the colony as a whole. Investors were unlikely to put their money into a colony where land tenure was likely to be insecure. Since he had to administer Spanish law, he carried out the policy of Chacon. He allowed all holders of land who, through ignorance or other causes, had broken the law, to redeem their position and make it secure by the payment of fines to the Crown within a fixed period. The Committee of Landowners accused him of being tyrannical and acting in every way contrary to English justice, but Woodford used the great powers conferred upon him by the British Government firmly and tactfully to enforce his regulations for the benefit of the community as a whole.

(4) *Conditions of Slavery*

The abolition of the slave trade by the British Government in 1807 was the first step towards complete emancipation from slavery. The West Indian planters realized that this could not be far away and they rigidly opposed the fulfilment of the policy. Their opposition had been strong enough to secure the blocking of a " Slave Registration " Bill in 1815,* but two years later they were unable to stop a similar Bill being passed through Parliament in London.

In 1823 Thomas Fowell Buxton ("Elephant" Buxton), on whom the mantle of leadership fell after the retirement of Wilberforce through ill-health, brought to the notice of Parliament the condition of slaves in the West Indies. In his speech he did not cite any cases of suffering from Trinidad, and it was apparent that the worst cases occurred in colonies where English law and trial by jury were in force. As a result of the debate, the Secretary of State was instructed to open correspondence with the colonies where slavery existed. Woodford received a despatch from Earl Bathurst, especially recommending that flogging of female slaves and the carrying of whips by the drivers (overseers) be stopped. It also instructed him to warn the planters in his colony that an Order in Council would shortly be issued incorporating Buxton's proposals for the amelioration of the condition of the slaves.

Woodford placed this information before the Council and asked their opinion. They replied :

". . . relative to the motion of Mr. Buxton for the amelioration of the condition of the slaves, we are of the opinion that there can be no dissent from the principles contained in the resolution of the Honourable House."

* This Bill was designed to afford a check on slave mortality and to stop smuggling of slaves between the colonies.

They went on to point out that most of Buxton's improvements were already in existence in the colony, but whilst they agreed with Buxton in principle, there were certain points which they thought to be of doubtful value and others to be impracticable.

1. " That the slave should be attached to the Island and under certain restrictions to the soil." The advantages of this system appeared very doubtful.
2. " That a slave should be allowed to purchase his freedom a day at a time." This was considered impracticable.
3. " That Sunday should be devoted by the slaves to repose and religious instruction and that other time should be allotted to them for the cultivation of provision grounds." This was objected to unless His Majesty's Government guaranteed full compensation to the proprietors for the loss of the substitute day.

Woodford studied the reply of the Council, then brought forward a list of resolutions which he proposed sending to the Secretary of State.* These were unanimously accepted on condition that no more concessions should be expected of the slave owners. The resolutions were based chiefly on the principles of amelioration through religious instruction and compensation to owners in cases of emancipation.

William Burnley, although voting in favour of the Governor's proposal, stated that he had not altered his opposition to the measures taken by the Home Government. It was unwise to unsettle the minds of the slaves without being able to do them any good. He suggested that rather than have the proposed Order in Council, a monthly register should be made of all complaints of slave against master or master against slave. Publication should be made in the *Colonial Gazette* with full details of names, the nature of the complaints and the ruling of the judges in each case. It would then become known to the world that slaves in Trinidad were well cared for and it would act as a deterrent to any cruel master there might be in the colony. The suggestion was accepted by the Council but the question of publication was held over for further consideration and no decision was ever reached.

A few days after this Council meeting, a " social gathering " was held for the planters at Tacarigua, where the proposed Order in Council was freely discussed and criticized. Burnley was the chief speaker at this clandestine gathering and thereby earned

* See Appendix XVI.

for himself a firmly worded rebuke at the next meeting of the Council. He pleaded that he meant no disrespect to the Executive and Woodford allowed the matter to drop.

More and more, Burnley was becoming the champion of the planters' cause and expressing his views ever more forcibly. He ended one of his speeches in the Council :

". . . in conclusion I move that the draft of the proposed Order in Council be published in order that all the inhabitants of the Colony interested in its provisions may have the opportunity of expressing an opinion on it."

Woodford's reply to this was that it would only be a waste of time because the general opinion had already been expressed and that it was not necessary for him to

"consult the feelings of the inhabitants generally, it was not even incumbent upon him to consult the Board, a step which he had only taken from motives of courtesy, and a desire to obtain the benefit of their advice."

The planters became more and more apprehensive over the Order in Council and what the future held for them. The independent members of the Council, led by Burnley, had a personal interest in the slave question and they wanted to do more than just advise on a matter which so nearly affected them. Burnley himself went so far as to ask the Governor to lay before the Council copies of all the correspondence with the Secretary of State concerning the Order. Woodford refused to comply and Burnley expressed the views of the independent members :

". . . some doubt exists in the minds of members of this Board as to their possessing the privilege of giving their advice or opinions on any subject unless when called upon to do so by His Excellency.

After tentatively examining the tenour of the oath taken by members, I am of the opinion that the obligation 'to promote the good of His Majesty's affairs to the best of their ability' imposes upon them the duty of giving their advice unsolicited, upon any subject which might be considered as affecting the welfare of the Colony. In this view I may be wrong but it is important that the doubt should be set at rest as no member wishes to step beyond the limits of his official duty, whilst all are anxious to avoid the charge of neglect from ignorance of the duties which devolve upon them."

Woodford, knowing that the Home Government was considering making some changes in the form of Government in Trinidad, guardedly and without rancour replied :

"As a matter of courtesy, members of the Board may be allowed to offer their opinions and advice upon subjects not immediately brought before them, but I am not at all prepared to go so far as to say that they have such a right. I will, however, refer the matter to Lord Bathurst."

Burnley pressed the Council to ask the Government not to enforce the Order in Council until such time as the planters could send a petition to the Secretary of State, as the result of the enforcement would be the ruin of the colony and no good would be done to the slaves. Once again Woodford had to disagree with him, pointing out that he would have no powers to hold up the Order and that the draft copy had only been issued to acquaint those concerned of the coming change and not for amendment.

The planters, led by Burnley, were not questioning the Order in Council on the rights or wrongs of amelioration of the conditions of the slaves. They resented the interference of the law, knowing that in the whole of the West Indies there was no other colony where slaves were so well treated as in Trinidad. They would not have opposed making obligatory by law what had been the custom of the colony for many years, had they not seen in the Order the next step towards complete emancipation and the probable ruin of their estates.

As an institution there was no argument in favour of slavery. Though legally the slave had no rights, in Trinidad there were many privileges to which he was entitled by tradition and common usage. Medical attention, support in old age, Christmas, New Year and Easter gifts, supplies of clothing and many other comforts, were all part and parcel of the master-slave relationship in the colony. There had, of course, been individual cases of cruelty and ill usage but these the authorities punished severely. Many of the planters thought it very unfair that the Order in Council should be tried out in Trinidad, where arrangements were so much better than in the other colonies, and that when the law turned custom into obligation all kindly feeling would disappear.

Burnley and other members of the Council signed a protest against the Order, feeling it their duty to express their opposition in some concrete form. Woodford refused to accept this as a valid reason and accused Burnley of trying to embarrass the Government. He did, however, write to the Secretary of State:

"... When Your Lordship considers that persons are now for the first time forbidden to strike any female slave; that this class is allowed by all to be the most prone to give offence, and that it will become even more difficult than at present to restrain them, from the knowledge that their master cannot punish them as he was accustomed to, Your Lordship will, I think, be disposed to make some allowance for the infirmities of human nature, and at least save the family of the offender from ruin which might fall upon them in consequence of an intemperate action of his own . . . That as the Colony is made the subject of an experiment, and the planters and the proprietors of slaves are exposed to all the risks attendant upon the trial of an uncertain measure, His Majesty would be advised to afford some boon in the shape of special bounty to the produce of the Colony that may act as an encouragement to the planters to cheerfully co-operate in the measure."

The Order in Council was proclaimed on May 24th, 1824, to come into force on June 25th. Woodford forwarded copies of all correspondence, petitions, etc., to the Secretary of State and mentioned in his covering despatch the general fear of the planters that the Order would lead inevitably to emancipation, which in its turn would lead to the impossibility of cultivating estates and the ruin of many families through the forfeiture of lands to the Crown. To this despatch he received a reply:

"It is assumed that the present Order will create alarm, and depreciate the value of property in the Colony and that it will thence follow that the mortgagees will take immediate measures to sell the mortgaged estates, which under the Ordinance they can effect with a delay of only three months. Now even if the apprehensions which have been expressed by the Council were admitted to be well founded, or in other words, if it were granted that the tendency of the recent Order would be to create alarm and depreciate the value of estates, the apprehended consequence of ruinous sale would not ensue."

The planters were not deceived with fair words and promises, and though many did not consider slavery, per se, to be anything but an outrage on humanity, they felt that its existence was not their fault and that it was unfair to ask them to bear the cost of its removal. Slaves represented earned or inherited wealth. This wealth was now to be taken from them on the grounds of humanity, by a political party which was using the cause of humanity to appease the opposition in Parliament. A more cheerful and optimistic view might have been taken in Trinidad if the planter had been assured that the benevolent

Government which was taking away his living was as particular to stop all forms of brutality in its own country as in bettering the conditions of the slaves in the colonies. Whilst child labour continued in England and whilst women worked for a pittance in the coal mines, the West Indian planter felt that there was a little too much noticing the mote in one's brother's eye and not enough notice being taken of the beam in one's own.

Although he appeared high-handed in his dealings with the representatives of the planters, Woodford was well aware of their position and saw how their future was likely to be affected by the legislation which was to be introduced experimentally in the the island. In his despatches to the Secretary of State he endorsed the views expressed by Burnley and his colleagues, though in Council he followed the course of his duty in carrying out the instructions of His Majesty's Government. The effect of his despatches cannot be judged, but it was not until March, 1825, that the final Order was sent to Trinidad with instructions that it was to be rigidly enforced.* Accompanying the Order was a despatch from the Secretary of State, Earl Bathurst, which concluded :

"I cannot conclude without reminding you that there is nothing in the provisions of this Order which can give the planter any just claim for compensation. I am as ready as any man to acknowledge and maintain that the slave must be considered the property of his master. But a slave has his rights—he has a right to the protection of his master in return for his service, and the Law must secure for him that protection. There is nothing in the provisions of this Order which goes beyond the limits which this principle prescribes. In most cases they do little more than what practice has sanctioned or the law has already enjoined. The master is not deprived of the services of his slave on any day except Sunday, and it is to be hoped that no Christian master will so far forget himself as to claim indemnity for the loss of that which his religion must have taught him he ought never to require."

A further despatch brought Woodford instructions for carrying out the Order in Council and for the appointment of the proper officers to carry out the work.

"You must take care to appoint those who are most likely to fulfil the expectations of His Majesty's Government, and you will distinctly understand that it is to your exertions that

* See Appendix XVII.

His Majesty looks with confidence for overcoming that spirit of opposition which seems to have been industriously infused into the minds of many individuals from whose general character a better disposition was to have been expected."

The officers who were expected to see that the Order was carried out were the Commandants of Quarters and Woodford was instructed to remove from office any who refused to co-operate. Though they were not Government officials in the ordinary sense, the Commandants recognized the power of the Governor to remove them from their positions of trust.

It soon became apparent that many of the fears of the planters were coming to pass; the law courts were fully occupied hearing cases of slave against master and master against slave. Often key workers were missing from plantations or business houses because they were serving sentences imposed by the courts for trivial offences. Work could not be carried on efficiently and estates began to fall out of cultivation. Many who owned small shops or were engaged in making small goods and who depended on the slaves in making their livelihood were extremely hard hit by the continual interference of prison sentences with their work. The unceasing efforts of Burnley and his followers forced an order to be published in the colony giving authority to stop sales of estates which had, " owing to results of political events or occurrences of a public nature become depreciated in value ", if the court had reason to believe that depreciation would not become permanent. This order could not exceed a period of six months delay in sale at any one time nor a total of two years by the issue of successive orders. A certain amount of security was given to the planter in that there was a chance to raise additional money and the threat of immediate eviction no longer hung over his head.

(5) *Church and State*

In 1813 Roman Catholics were very much in the majority over all other religious denominations in the colony. At the capitulation the inhabitants had been guaranteed the free exercise of their religious beliefs and the Protestant faith as yet had had little time in which to make an impression. There existed the curious anomaly of the Royal Vice-Patron of the Holy Roman Catholic Church in the colony being a Protestant, for under Spanish law ecclesiastical jurisdiction within certain limits belonged to the Crown. The early English Governors of Trinidad held this unique position among colonial Governors, a position which they filled with dignity. Woodford was more conscientious than his predecessors, exercising his duties with even more care and strictness.

On great occasions, New Year and the festival of Corpus Christi, he attended High Mass at the old Catholic church, which stood on the site now known as Tamarind Square. A guard of honour would form outside the Cabildo Hall in Brunswick (now Woodford) Square to receive him as he came from Government House in his carriage drawn by four horses, accompanied by his mounted Aides-de-Camp. Members of the Council, the Board of the Cabildo and the principal public officers, all in uniform, robes of office or court dress, formed a procession behind the Governor, who carried the wand of the Perpetual Corregidor. As they moved through the streets, lined with garrison troops and the Militia, arms were presented. On arrival at the church the procession was met by the clergy, who conducted the Governor to a specially prepared Chair of State. At the Elevation of the Host, the troops presented arms and a twenty-one gun salute was fired from the Sea Fort Battery. The procession reformed after the service and marched in state to the Cabildo Hall.

In accordance with Spanish law and a Bull of Pope Julius II, final confirmation of all ecclesiastical appointments in the colony was made by the Governor. In practice an appointment would be made by the Church authorities but could not be taken up without consultation with and confirmation by the Governor. Trinidad was at the time in the Diocese of Guayana, whose bishop was represented by a Vicar-General in the colony. This was neither convenient nor in line with the political situation in the island as there were more than twenty parishes whose priests were paid from Trinidad funds. On Woodford's suggestion the question was taken up with the Home Government, who conferred with the Vicar-General and with the Vatican. After discussions between the Secretary of State and Dr. Poynter, Vicar-Apostolic of the West of England, Trinidad was separated from Guayana and like the other West Indian islands placed under its own Vicar-Apostolic. The first to hold this position was James Buckley, who took up his duties in 1820.

Dr. Buckley proved himself to be a wise, firm and excellent guide and pastor. A man of the world and a scholar, he was able to carry on his discussions with Woodford in an atmosphere of mutual respect and cordiality. Official correspondence shows that Woodford did not allow any religious differences, which might be personal, to stop him taking the utmost care of the welfare of the Roman Church.

Government House,
1.2.1814.

It having been represented to His Excellency the Governor that certain sums, to a considerable extent, have for a long period remained due to the Holy Roman Catholic Church from the heirs and executors of pious deceased persons, either on account of legacies bequeathed by them or dues to the Church for interment, the Governor and Royal Vice-Patron has been pleased to approve of the report made to him by his Ecclesiastical Judge, and all persons are hereby called upon to pay, within three months of the date hereof, into the hands of such persons as may be appointed for the purpose, the sums due by them as above-mentioned.

His Excellency has named :

Messrs. John Nihell
Aaron Jessee
Abraham Pinto
M. Sorzano
F. Salazar
J. Alcazar
F. Peschier
V. Patrice
M. Francesci,

a Committee for carrying these dispositions into effect, and they will meet, together with the Ecclesiastical Judge and Vicar, from time to time, in a convenient place, to make the necessary arrangements for pursuing the claims of the Church hereinbefore stated, and they will all assemble at the Government House on the 1st day of May next, to report to His Excellency the amount of the sums which may have been recovered or which may remain due, together with such observations and regulations as they may together judge proper to be laid before His Excellency, for the future support and due observance of the rights and privileges of the sacred trust committed to their enquiry.

By Order, P. Reinagle, Secretary.

There was in Port of Spain only one Roman Catholic Church, a wooden building in bad repair. This Woodford considered should be replaced by a larger and more permanent structure to fill the needs of a growing population. He was not able to put the work in hand at once, owing to financial difficulties, but by 1816 sufficient funds were available from subscriptions and grants from the Cabildo and from colonial funds to enable the work to be started. Plans were drawn up by Philip Reinagle, who was an architect as well as being the Governor's Secretary, and were sent to London together with plans of the other proposed new buildings. Reinagle, who did this work free of charge, was later placed in charge of all public works at a fixed salary, but owing to illness he had to be replaced by Captain Peake of the Royal Engineers before his works were completed.

On March 25th, 1816, Woodford, with the rites fitting to the occasion, laid the foundation stone of the Roman Catholic Cathedral. The building was laid out in the shape of a Latin cross, stone built with material carried from the east coast of the island. The iron framework for doors and windows came from England, accompanied by a glazier, as there was no one in the colony who could undertake this work. On more than one occasion building was held up through shipping delays and it was not until 1832 that the cathedral was consecrated.

The oldest parish church in the island was that of San José de Oruña (St. Joseph). Here was established a Hospice or Convent of the Observabatines, a branch of the Franciscan order, from which the spiritual work of the church was carried out. The old church was in a very bad state of repair and Woodford laid the foundation stone of a new and bigger building on March 18th, 1815. Three years later it was consecrated with all the pomp and ceremony due to a new church in the ancient capital of the colony.

Woodford was a frequent visitor to the ancient parish of Arima. The original church had been built during the early days of the Spanish occupation and had been dedicated to Santa Rosa de Lima, the first saint of Latin America. On the occasion of her festival, Woodford attended services in the church, which housed the earliest patronal statue in the colony.

In the Diego Martin area of the island the only place of worship was the chapel attached to the residence of the Bégorrat family.

As Governor, Woodford was also head of the Established Church of England in the colony. During his Governorship much was done to put this church, then under the jurisdiction of the Bishop of London, on its proper footing, even though its membership in the island was very small. The Reverend J. H. Clapham, originally Brigade Chaplain, ministered to all Protestants from 1797 onwards, but after twenty-five years decided to retire. Though he had not always agreed with Woodford's ideas on ecclesiastical management, nor co-operated as well as he might have done, Woodford managed to procure for him a pension of £200 a year. In a despatch confirming the appointment of his successor, the Reverend G. Cummins, the Secretary of State wrote:

". . . It is ordered by His Majesty's Government that the Governor, as His Majesty's representative, is to be considered as the Head of the Church of the United Kingdom established in the Colony, which I notify for your guidance."

In 1827, the Bishop of Barbados and the Leeward Islands was nominated to a seat in the Trinidad Council. On January 19th, at a meeting of the Council, the members present were the Governor; the Bishop of Barbados, Dr. Coleridge; the Chief Justice, Mr. Ashton Warner; the Hon. Dr. Llanos, and the Hon. F. Peschier. The chief business of the day was to consider Dr. Coleridge's plan to include Trinidad in his diocese in the same manner as other West Indian islands were already incorporated. He also suggested that a Rector of Port of Spain be appointed with the additional title of Bishop's Commissary, giving him authority over other Church of England clergymen in the colony. Other suggestions were that a curate be appointed to Trinity Church; that the rectory and lands belonging to it should be kept in repair and good order at the expense of the colony, and that where churches might be needed in the island they should be built and maintained by the Government. The Council adopted and approved the measure but would not vote on it on the grounds that the recent Order in Council had caused so much expense to the colony that it was impossible to increase its financial burdens.

The fact that this motion was paving the way for the foundation of a new State Church was completely overlooked. According to the terms of the capitulation and to Spanish law, the Roman Catholic Church was still the State Church, yet there is no record of any form of protest against Dr. Coleridge's plan from the leading Roman Catholic churchmen.

Before the fire of 1808 the church which combined the duties of Garrison chapel and Protestant Church was at the south-east corner of Brunswick Square. This had been built in 1801, the first baptism to be recorded being that of the infant daughter of Col. Balfour of the 57th Regiment; the first marriage between William Whitmore and Elizabeth Tinling. After the fire a new church was started in the middle of the square, based on a model sent from England and approximating closely to the chapel in Pentonville Prison in London. When the building was ready for its roof, the citizens of Port of Spain, who had never approved of the plan, protested that the square had originally been granted for the use of the public as a place of recreation and that it was illegal to build there. They petitioned the Governor, who condemned the plan as being entirely unsuited for a church in the tropics. The Protestant community raised enough money to remove the new church and to restore the square for its original purpose. The foundation stone of the new Trinity Church was laid by Woodford at the south side of the square on May 30th, 1816. The new plans were drawn up by Philip Reinagle.

A party of workmen came from England to help with the building of the new church, some of the stone for which came from the Hollington quarries in Staffordshire. Though the outside was finished in 1818 (the porch carries an inscription AN. DNI. 1818 REGNI—R—GEORG II—TERTII—58), the church was not ready for consecration until 1823 owing to delays caused by lack of funds. It was over the consecration that Woodford and Clapham, the rector, had their major disagreement, Woodford insisting that the consecration should take place on Trinity Sunday and Clapham equally insisting that, as there was no Bishop available, it would have to be postponed until a later date. Woodford had his way and actually went so far as to draw up a form of service to be used.

At 10.30 a.m. on May 25th, 1823, the day of the consecration, the Illustrious Cabildo met formally and proceeded to the church. The Members of H.M. Council were drawn up on the left and Public Officers on the right of the entrance awaiting the arrival of the Governor and the clergy. The Governor, His Excellency Sir Ralph Woodford, arrived shortly after 11.30 in his State Coach, preceded by outriders and escorted by a detachment of the Trinidad Light Dragoons. He was accompanied by the Rev. J. H. Clapham, the Rev. David Evans, Garrison Chaplain, and the Rev. George Cummins. A procession was then formed and was received at the West Door by Church officials and Church-wardens. The service lasted until 2 p.m. when the Royal Standard was flown on the Tower.

Woodford was very generous to the new church. He presented a chalice, paten and flagon, a sufficient supply of fair linen, fifty-nine Bibles and prayer books and a copy of *Macklin's Bible in seven volumes*. He also gave complete uniforms for the Beadles and went so far as to provide a clock and a peal of six bells. The bells he was unable to hear, for though they were mounted with wheels and ropes, there was no one in the colony who could ring a peal. Later a Mr. Fuller and six others who "felt inclined to learn the art of ringing" and who had gone to the expense of purchasing a set of sixteen handbells and "expected a ringing tutor from England", came forward with proposals for organized bell-ringing. In spite of this, Woodford was destined never to hear his bells ring, for the great earthquake of September 20th, 1825, damaged the church and the tower had to be rebuilt, the bells not being rehung for some years.

Woodford also tried to establish a properly trained choir, but owing to the expense of obtaining an organist who could teach boys to sing, the project was dropped and the alternative suggestion, that the Garrison Band Master be lent to the church, was not taken up. Another experiment, that of lighting the church with gas made with pitch from La Brea, proved unsuccesful as more smoke than light was generated.

The internal organization of the Church was very different from that of today. The pulpit was in the place where Woodford's memorial now stands. The Governor's pew over the north door was reached by a " truly great staircase."

" On great occasions, Sir Ralph required the attendance of his whole staff of officials, in full dress, in his pew beside him, regardless of their religious views."

On ordinary Sundays he occupied his private pew in the north-east corner "modestly curtained". Over the altar hung a large picture, painted and presented by Mariana Birch whose father was a Colonel in the Garrison. There were four large pews in the centre of the church reserved for the Council, the Cabildo, the Garrison and strangers. In all there was accommodation for 380 white people, 120 coloured and at the west end there was a roped off space for slaves. Only 112 seats in the church were free, the remainder being rented. Pew rents appear to have been very hard to collect, as it is recorded that one churchwarden proposed that the list of defaulters be posted in the Intendent's Court as a necessary measure to force people to pay their dues.

Wesleyan Methodism was introduced into Trinidad from Grenada by the Reverend G. Talboys in 1810. There was opposition to it at first as members of the Roman Communion and followers of the Church of England held that the preaching and administration of the sacraments by the missionaries were contrary to accepted practice. These differences were overcome as time went on, and in March, 1826, Henry Gloster, Protector of Slaves and Syndic Procurator of the Illustrious Cabildo, laid the foundation stone of the Hanover Wesleyan Church. In nine months the new church was opened by the Reverend S. P. Wooley and tradition has it that much of the work was performed by slaves.

In March, 1828, the Right Reverend Dr. Buckley fell ill and a few days later died at his residence in Cumberland Street at the age of 58. His passing was mourned by people of all colours and creeds in the colony. His mortal remains lay in state in the Cabildo Hall, attended by the Alquazil Mayor and two clergy, from early morning until 4.30 p.m. A great procession then followed him to his grave, Governor Woodford in a long black cloak and attended by train-bearers and accompanied by all the officials of the colony being chief mourner.

(6) *Opening up the Island and Negro Immigration*

When Woodford arrived in the colony he could not fail to notice the bad state of the few roads which the island possessed. Almost at once he wrote to Mr. Maingot, the Surveyor-General, reminding him of his duties and instructing him to carry out the necessary repairs before the wet season set in. Later Woodford suggested that repairing of roads by local labour should be replaced by a turnpike system; this met with opposition from the estate owners and was allowed to lapse.

With energy unusual in a Governor, Woodford visited many distant parts of his territory. In an effort to make his report on the colony one of his own findings, rather than the confused reports of his officials, he visited many places to which no Governor had ever before penetrated. His suggestions for development and improvement were far-reaching, involving the opening up of the interior with new roads. This, he was convinced, would be of great economic benefit to the colony even if money had to be borrowed for the initial work. The Secretary of State, after reading Woodford's report, granted permission for the construction of a coast road from Matura to Mayaro, with travellers' rest houses at intervals along it. The Indian track between Arima and the L'Ebranche River was to be reopened and a Custom House established at Mayaro. It was easier and quicker to trade with Tobago through Mayaro than by transporting produce overland to Port of Spain and thence by sea to the smaller islands.

A further development, made on the recommendation of Mr.

Mitchell, Commandant of North Naparima, was the expending of £72 on cutting a trace five yards wide and five miles long from Savanna Grande to the Ortoire River. On this trace estates for the production of ground provisions and canes were to be laid out. Yet another innovation was the arrival of the steamer *Woodford* to ply out of Port of Spain and connect the north and south of the island by a regular service.

From the Commandants of Quarters, Woodford called for reports on their districts with details of the soil, water supplies, timber and facilities for road making. Surveys were made and notices published stating the Government's intention of making fresh grants of land. It was hoped that these grants might be taken up by white soldiers disbanded after the Battle of Waterloo. Woodford was instructed by the Home Government to make available for them lands suitable for growing cocoa, coffee, cotton and ground provisions. Other lands were to be provided for stock farms for which Woodford was to arrange to import cattle from the Spanish Main. All lands were to be granted on the condition that a certain number of white persons were employed as labourers. The scheme fell through in spite of the grants being of 100 acres, because it was impossible to induce Europeans to settle in a country whose climate they firmly believed to be deadly.

Labour was the chief problem of the West Indian colonies. Efforts to supply the need from Europe had failed and the only answer seemed to be the constant and continued introduction of slave labour from Africa. This was opposed by all who were determined to see the end of slavery at all costs, but was supported by the planters who, since the abolition of the slave trade, had found it increasingly difficult to maintain existing estates and virtually impossible to open new ones.

In 1818, Woodford asked his Council for suggestions for attracting labour to the colony. The new Chief Justice, John Biggs, favoured adding an inducement to English ex-soldiers by granting them lands already cleared and prepared at Government expense. This policy was considered too risky and experimental. Mr. Nihell suggested obtaining Negroes from Africa on a ten years indenture. This was not considered practicable; though the African was robust, it would waste both the planters' and the Government's time to teach him what he had to do. Manuel Sorzano, a Spanish Royalist, opposed any suggestion of free labour from the Main on the grounds that the peasants there were politically unreliable, but he considered that by increasing the communications of the island and by reducing the cost of the necessities of life, a steady flow of immigrants to the colony could be created. Colonel Lopinot, a Frenchman of the old régime, was certain that the abolition of slavery would bring ruin to the island. William Burnley, the Anglo-American, stated that if Trinidad could increase its labouring population sufficiently, it could supply the rest of the West Indian islands with cattle, rice and corn. He supported Sorzano's opposition to the introduction of South American peons as he felt that they were a dangerous and objectionable class of person. He concluded his speech :

" Upon serious reflection I am fully convinced that from Asia alone is to be derived the population we require."

His conclusion was not put into practice for another thirty years, nor were any of the Council's suggestions acted upon.

Some progress was made with the introduction of immigrants into the colony, for in 1815 a party of 50 American Negroes arrived in the wet season. These were free Negroes who had served in the British forces during the American war of 1812-1814. All wished to settle on the land rather than be apprenticed to any particular trade. They and the party which followed them a year later (34 men, 15 women and 17 children) were taken under the wing of the Government, which was determined that they should have every chance to make a good life for themselves in Trinidad. Initial expenses were paid from the Colonial Chest and later refunded by the Home Government. A Superintendent was appointed to look after their needs, tools were provided and they were carefully watched over for the first six months of their stay. With them they brought rice seed from California and their attempt to grow it is the first on record in the colony. They were finally settled on lands in the Princes Town area, where descendants of these " Americans " are still to be found in the Company villages, farming lands inherited from their ancestors.

The " Americans " were not the only ex-soldiers who settled in Trinidad. In 1819 a settlement was formed in the Arima area towards the east coast. This was for free Negroes who had served in the British West Indian forces during the war against Napoleon* and were now being disbanded. Five years after their foundation Woodford visited the district and

* These West Indian forces had consisted of white regulars, local Militia and several corps of black troops. Regiments comprised 1st, 2nd and 3rd West India Regiments and Royal Yorkshire Rangers.

found the children to be strong and healthy, but he doubted if there were enough women present to ensure the complete success of the enterprise. He pressed for the cutting of new roads, for extensions to the settlement had carried it some seven miles towards the east coast and the safe harbour of Manzanilla was their only real means of communication with the rest of the island. One site which had been settled by the Regiments had been abandoned early. This on the banks of the Caroni River had been found to be too unhealthy.

In 1825, Woodford was able to report that the settlements were progressing satisfactorily in spite of difficulties in obtaining civil and medical superintendents. He hoped that within a twelvemonth all would be well and that the cost of the experiment would not have exceeded the grant made by the Treasury in London for the purpose. He suggested that women should be brought from Sierra Leone and cared for by Government until such time as they could be disposed of to men who could support them, then

> "the settlers would be happy and the settlements would become nurseries of a young and free population."

Nothing came of the suggestion at the time.

(7) Health in Trinidad

In the days before the capitulation it was forbidden to practise medicine or surgery in the colony without a licence from the Medical Board. Picton, on assuming the Governorship, had reconstituted the Board and Hislop had renewed its life. Woodford, however, found that owing to lack of Government support the Board had been unable to stop many persons from practising medicine without the necessary licence.* By a Proclamation of December 20th, 1820† he re-established the Board on its original basis as it had been before the capitulation.

> "We order that the Protomedicos shall not give licences in the Indies to any Physician, Surgeon, Apothecary, Barber, Veterinary Practitioner or others who practise the faculty of Medicine and Surgery unless they shall appear personally before them to be examined and shall be found able and competent to use and exercise the same and the Protomedicos may demand on account of a licence and visit of an Apothecary's shop a fee not exceeding three times as much as are required and taken by the Protomedicos of the Kingdom of Castile, Law 6th 1579."

* See Appendix XVIII.
† See Appendix XIX.

137

"We command that no person whatsoever shall be allowed in the Indies to practise Medicine or Surgery unless they shall have the degrees and licences of the Protomedico which are provided by the laws and in consequence legitimate certificates. And we order the Fiscals of Our Audiencias to ask in this respect what they shall think fit and the neglect of the said Officers in the execution and enforcement of the several provisions of the law will be a charge in the Residencia against the same. And this will be executed in Towns of the Spaniards and not in those wherein the Indians live. Libro 5. Titule 16. Law 4th 1648."

Early in 1814, Bartholomew Portel, Alcaldes of the First Election, reported on the increasing number of lepers wandering about Port of Spain. Woodford, who had already been considering the problem, instructed the Surveyor General to carry out a survey of the island of Monos with a view to erection of a Lazaretto. The Surveyor's report stated that the number of inhabitants who would have to be compensated for the loss of houses or lands would cause such an extraordinary expense to the Government as to make the experiment impossible. The other islands of the Bocas were tried but were too heavily populated to make Government action practicable. For the time being the plan for a Lazaretto had to be abandoned though Woodford kept it in mind. There were some seventy known lepers at this time who had to find what accommodation they could, as the health services were unable to deal with them.

Malaria, yellow fever and smallpox were the chief troubles of the medical profession and of the Governor. In 1819 an epidemic of smallpox broke out on the mainland and spread to Trinidad. All the inhabitants of the colony were ordered to be vaccinated as a preventative precaution. A Public Vaccinator was appointed to see that this order was efficiently carried out and a penalty of £100 currency was imposed on all who neglected to have their slaves and families vaccinated.

Hospital accommodation at the time of Woodford's arrival was at its lowest ebb. The hospital in Port of Spain, an old Poui-wood structure, had been destroyed by the fire of 1808, and only temporary housing for the sick existed. To help create funds for a new building a tax was imposed on all legacies.

(8) *Militia and Defence*

The Trinidad Militia had originally been formed by Governor Picton to assist the Military in keeping peace and order in the colony. It had served its purpose and had shown its readiness for duty on all occasions. By the time of Woodford's arrival there was a noticeable lack of interest in its activities. Added to this, the new Governor found that there were very many people living in the colony who were receiving protection and all the benefits of the law, yet were evading their military duty. By a Proclamation in 1814, Woodford reorganized the whole of the Militia and ordered that

" Every Male Resident in this Island being White, Coloured, and Free persons, and now residing therein, from the age of Fifteen to Fifty-Five do give in their names."

The strength rose to 3,000 officers and men, divided between

1 Regiment of Light Dragoons
1 Regiment of Hussars
3 Regiments of Infantry
1 Brigade of Artillery
3 Corps of Mounted Chasseurs, in 8 sections
2 Battalions of Sea Fencibles.

During the month of December, each year, martial law was declared, and all officers and men were obliged to wear uniform and to perform the duties of a garrison, including drills and parades. Civil courts were closed and all crimes and misdemeanours were dealt with by the Military. The period of martial law was also one of festivity, for over Christmas military balls and suppers were held every evening. At the time, duelling was the popular method of settling old scores and Woodford was determined to stamp out this custom, which he regarded as wasteful and degrading to the colony. By regarding the carrying, sending or accepting of a challenge as an offence, and by imposing heavy penalties, he managed to check and eventually put a stop to it.

The regular Army, whom the Militia were to assist, was based on the " citadel " at La Vigie (Fort George). As early as 1810 this " citadel " was reported to be in a bad state of repair and in urgent need of attention, but no funds were available for building work of this nature.

A difference of opinion had arisen between the Army authorities and the Government of Trinidad over the unfinished fortifications at Pointe Gourde (Chaguaramas), which had been abandoned in 1809. Captain Yorke, then " stationary engineer " in Trinidad, had wished to remove the materials for the completion of a new Ordnance Depot at Cocorite. He had applied direct to

139

Major-General Johnstone at his Headquarters in Barbados and received permission to go ahead with his plans. The unfinished works at Pointe Gourde were to be handed over to the Ordnance Department and final adjustments of price were to be made in London between the Treasury and the Master General of Ordnance.

When it was discovered that these arrangements had been made without consultation with the local Government, Governor Munro had at once ordered that no steps be taken until the position had been clarified by H. E. Sir George Beckwith, Commander-in-Chief in Barbados.

The whole matter was still under discussion in 1814 when Woodford received a despatch from the Secretary of State asking for the claims of the colony against the Board of Ordnance. In reply, he stated that owing to the fire of 1808 all relevant documents had been destroyed and that he was unable to forward any account for expenses. He could, however, quote Governor Hislop as stating that by 1805 Pointe Gourde had already cost £24,000 and at that time Fort George had not been started. As far as he was able to ascertain at the time of writing there was an outstanding debt of about £768. As the officers of the Ordnance had proceeded with the removal of buildings from Pointe Gourde without any reference to the Trinidad Government, he had concluded that the whole matter had been taken out of his hands. The valuation of the buildings had not been made in accordance with their value in their original position but as it had been found convenient for the engineers to transport them. In his opinion it would have been better to leave the buildings for a much needed lazaretto.

For the first year of his administration Woodford had to combat the hostility of Major-General Clay in command of the regular forces in the island. Being jealous of the civil Governor, Clay refused to co-operate and support the Governor in measures for the defence of the colony. Twice in 1814 he refused to allow Woodford to use troops to support the Militia and police in cases of trespass on British territory by Venezuelans. He withdrew his men from their positions as guards over prisoners outside the gaol and constantly caused trouble for both Woodford and the Chief Justice by his insistence that all military personnel were outside the scope of the civil law, even when they offended against it. One of Woodford's minor causes of irritation was Clay's refusal to fire a salute from the sea fort after the reading of the peace signed with France. He was, however, eventually removed and replaced by Major-General Crocker, who proved more co-operative.

In 1824, the foundation stone of a new military barracks was laid at St. James. Most of the material for the construction came from the Maraval Valley and occasioned an action between the Government and Jean Boissière over damage to the latter's sugar estate at Champs Elysées caused by the removal of so much stone. The barracks took three years to build and were completed at a cost of about £80,000.

(9) *Rebuilding Port of Spain*

By the time that Woodford became Governor of Trinidad little had been done in the building scheme initiated by Governor Hislop. Much money had been spent and there was little to show for it. Wooden houses had been built with complete disregard for the safety or sanitary regulations and the new Governor was forced to instruct the Commissary of Population, who was also the Surveyor General, to enforce the law more strictly. A general tidying up took place. Owners of empty lots were made to enclose their ground and grow some useful crop on it. In 1814 a Proclamation was issued informing all citizens that they must clean the streets outside their houses and lots every Wednesday morning and Saturday evening on pain of a fine of $2.00 for the first offence, to be doubled on each subsequent occasion.

By law each householder was responsible for paving the road outside his property. Since the fire there had been much evasion of this responsibility and Woodford was forced to take action. With the Surveyor General, he arranged houses in blocks and paved the pathways at the initial expense of the Cabildo, assessing the owners and extracting the money later. With the memory of the fire still vivid in their minds, they ordered the Alcaldes de Barrio to see that casks of water were kept outside each house during the dry season.

In 1816 steps were taken to improve the appearance of the capital. Woodford employed a German botanist, resident in the colony, to plant trees in Brunswick and Marine Squares. The former, now Woodford Square, was almost in the middle of town; tradition had it that two rival tribes of Indians had once fought a great battle here and before the capitulation it was known as the " Place des Armes."

Marine Square, " Calla Marina ", was a low lying beach in Spanish times, with water coming up to the position of the present buildings on the southern side. A short distance from the shore, which was dotted with huts and shanties, was the small island housing the fort and connected to the mainland by a draw-bridge and causeway. The square had never been properly laid out and was used by the Militia for parades. To the west was a large area of waste land, the Ariapita Estate, on which Government buildings were eventually erected, and beyond this was the busy district of "Corbeau Town." The corbeaux flourished as the chief scavengers of the island and were pro-tected by law.

To beautify the squares Woodford obtained rare and beautiful trees from Venezuela and the other West Indian islands. In Brunswick Square pitch from La Brea was used in an unsuccess-ful effort to smother the weeds. In all these improvements Wood-ford took a keen personal interest, rising early in the morning to ride round the town criticizing and encouraging all that was going on. In his wide-brimmed hat he became known as "Gouverneur chapeau paille."

The northern boundary of the town ran along what is now Oxford Street, Newtown being thick, uncultivated bush, a favourite resort for local sportsmen.

As the Public Offices were all destroyed in the fire, temporary accommodation had to be found for the employees in premises on the corner of St. James' Street (now Frederick Street) and Duke Street. For a rent of 25 joes ($200) per month paid to Mr. A. D. Clarke, the Secretariat, the Treasury, and the Sur-veyor General's offices were housed.

In 1814, Woodford asked the Home Government for authority to purchase land on which to build permanent Government Offices. Approval was given in 1818 when the financial position of the colony had improved, but the Treasury in London made it quite clear that they could no longer provide pecuniary assis-tance, and that no new buildings should be started until the Protestant Church was almost completed. The Government of Trinidad were able to save themselves certain expenses by tak-ing over the Artillery Depot in Brunswick Square when the Ordnance Department moved to its new building at Cocorite.

The Post Office, which handled only incoming mail and out-going overseas mail, was situated in the private residence of Richard Galway. After 1815 his widow continued the work from 13a Frederick Street. This was no expense to the local Govern-ment as it came directly under the Postmaster General in London.

In an attempt to improve the amenities of Port of Spain,

Woodford went deeply into the question of its water supply. Even when on leave in London he wrote to Colonel Young, administering the Government in his absence, asking for particulars upon which estimates for a new supply could be based. Robert Eccles & Co. had already provided some figures but Woodford was not sure that they were the best obtainable. He asked for plans to be forwarded and a report on the work carried out in pipe laying and the erection of the necessary buildings. He suggested that the scheme should be paid for by the Cabildo pledging their income to pay the principal and interest if the Secretary of State proved willing. Meanwhile a Proclamation was issued in April, 1821, prohibiting the washing of clothes in any river so that the purity of the colony's water supply might be safeguarded.

(10) *The Official Residence*

On arrival in the colony, Woodford used the semi-official Governor's residence on Belmont Hill* as his home. He reported to the Secretary of State that it was in need of extensive repair, even though much had been spent on it already. He added that owing to the poor state of the colony's finances, it was not possible to spend more. The residence did not belong to the Government but was on land that was the subject of a lengthy law suit and an offer made by Woodford of £1,500 to clear the suit was rejected.

It appeared that the property, about 41 acres of land, on the spur of the Laventille Hills and known as Belmont Hill, had been owned successively by several Spanish settlers who had come to Trinidad in 1780 with Mons. Rivire on the persuasion of St. Laurent. In 1781 it had been sold to Francis Pascal Soler (also known as Pascal Dubac) by Donna Ynges Hopsdale and had been resold almost immediately to a merchant named Edward Barry. In 1785 Barry made application for title to the property, which had been surveyed by Mr. Juillet, but the necessary official procedure had not been complied with and a deed was never issued. The grant was never made but Barry was not disturbed in his occupancy. In the same year the law suit by Barry and Dawson his partner began and continued into the next century. By 1808 the case was still unfinished and the property was in the hands of the Court, which placed Don Gaspar de la Guardia at Belmont Hill as its trustee and guardian. The estate was valued at £400 for the 41 acres and the several wooden buildings upon it. When Colonel Fullarton arrived as First Com-

* Now site of the new Hilton Hotel.

143

missioner for the colony, he rented Belmont for $100 a month and used it as his country residence when not occupying the town house at 29 Brunswick Square.* Hislop too decided to use Belmont as his country seat. After the fire it became the official residence of the Governor. He described it as being little more than a hut, neither wind nor rain proof and the whole in a decaying condition. As Port of Spain was extending to the north he found the situation quite convenient and decided to rebuild the house. The Council appointed a committtee of two to investigate the title to the property as it was clear that Hislop was prepared to buy the whole estate if it was free of embarrassment. The Courts had as yet come to no conclusion on the title and the property had to continue to be rented.

Munro, who followed Hislop, also made Belmont Hill his official home.

Woodford, after his failure to purchase the property with his first bid, claimed that it was unalienated and therefore had reverted to the Crown, and he instructed the Attorney General to make out an order for its resumption. The agent of Edward Barry represented to the Court that they had been in possession for twenty-nine years and that for nine of these the Crown itself had paid them rent. This was countered by the Attorney General with the assertion that twenty-nine years did not give a prescriptive right to ownership which, according to Spanish law, necessitated possession for forty years. The Chief Justice, John Biggs, gave as his opinion that the Barrys had a good and valid title to the property. The Attorney General appealed to the Court of the Intendent of Crown Lands. This being Woodford's own Court, the decision of the Chief Justice was reversed and it was ruled that the Barrys had no legal right to the property, which reverted to the Crown. The Barrys then took the case to the Lords of the Privy Council in London, where Marryat, the former Agent for Trinidad, acted for them.

On the advice of the Secretary of State, Woodford put his case in the hands of the Treasury Solicitors and agreed to abide by their decision. He was advised that a good case could not be made out for the Crown owing to the length of undisputed possession and to the recognition of that possession by the Trinidad Government, which had repeatedly paid rent for the property. If the Government wanted the site, then it would be best for them to buy out all claims for as low a figure as possible.

On this, Woodford offered £6,000 currency (about £4,000

* This house was on the site of the present Deanery.

144

sterling) for the property free of encumbrances. William Burnley, acting as local agent for the Barrys, countered with a demand for £9,000. This the Government refused and started to remove all its buildings and improvements. Edward Barry, the heir to the estate, compromised and accepted £5,175 sterling as a full discharge of all claims and rights.

In 1819 the Government took possession, but Woodford did not stay long. Since 1815, when it looked as though the Government would lose its case for Belmont Hill, he had been casting around to find a better site.

He advised the Secretary of State that a house and lands known as Champs Elysées, in Maraval Valley, conveniently near the citadel of Fort George, would be suitable and asked for permission to negotiate. The property had a large amount of land, worn out by over-cultivation and suitable only for pasture. Here he proposed to build a new house with materials available on the estate, as it was in a healthy position and had a good supply of fresh water. The owner was asking $76,000, but Woodford was sure that he could purchase it for $45,000, spread over four years.

This estate of some 670 acres had been obtained by Roume de St. Laurent from the Spanish Government in 1779 for his mother, Madame de Charras, the former Rose de Gannes de la Chancellerie. Later it had been enlarged and some $33,000 had been spent on its development. It passed then to Thomas Maturin, Chevalier de Gannes, who administered the property, and François de Gannes, his brother in Grenada. The estate had not prospered and Marryat had been instructed to put Champs Elysées up for sale in London in 1803. No satisfactory offers were received by the owners and money had to be borrowed on mortgages from Jean and Elias Boissière.

Woodford could easily have purchased the estate had not his available funds been used in settling Negro ex-soldiers in the colony. Being unable to obtain a grant from the Home Government he had to let the opportunity pass and Jean Boissière, pressing his claims against the owners, became the sole proprietor in 1817.

In the same year Woodford tried once more to find a good site for an official residence and opened negotiations with the heirs of Henri Peschier for an estate in St. Anns. The Board of Cabildo strongly supported the purchase and though £7,682 was asked, it was eventually agreed to pay £6,000 over a period of years. The deed of conveyance (No. 1219 of 1817) was executed on August 18th and two parcels of land known as Paradise Estate or Paradise Farm were transferred. The boundaries of the property were :

North by the lands of Montelambert.
South by the public roads to Maraval and
St. Anns respectively.
East by St. Anns Road and St. Anns River.
West by the public road to Maraval and
by lands of Mr. Morrison.

The heirs of Henri Peschier reserved from this sale the "mill rollers etc." and a piece of ground in which the family ancestors were buried, 6,000 feet square or half a quarree in size. The Cabildo ordered that the heirs be notified that the burying ground as reserved must be enclosed and kept in order at the expense of the family.

In 1819, the heirs of the Abbé de Laquarée and Mark René, Baron de Montelambert, sold to the Cabildo a parcel of land lying to the north of the Paradise Estate known as Hollandais, for £1,661, spread over three years. This land was enclosed by the Cabildo and appears to be that portion which is the frontage of the Botanic Gardens and the present site of Government House.

In 1820 the Cabildo ordered that both parcels of the estate were to be transferred to the Colonial Government on the terms of their purchase and the transaction was brought to an end in 1825.

Of the 232 acres, 2 roods and 23 perches, which had been taken over, 199 were laid out as the Queen's Park as pasture for the cattle of Port of Spain. There was a loss of certain lands to the public by the enclosure of some pasture in front of the building that became Government House. Later more land was lost in the creation of the Pitch Walk around the Grand Savannah as it was called. The chief use of the land was for pasture and pleasure and there is a record of a race meeting being held on the Queen's Park as early as 1828.

Woodford described his new official residence as inadequate, but better than anything in the past. He wrote :

"I do not offer it as a specimen of taste in architecture or of convenience in arrangement or design for there was originally not any of either, nor would the cost contemplated admit of such consideration."

He described the work as "rough and substantial" and spent

146

some £4,790 on reconstruction. Much of this was done with the timbers etc. of the old out-buildings from Belmont Hill which, after Woodford had moved into his new quarters, was used as the official residence of the Chief Justice.

The work carried out by Woodford in reconstruction must have been fairly substantial for the house continued in use until the fire of 1867.

Woodford's keen interest in beautifying Port of Spain was shown in his laying out of a Botanic Garden in front of the new residence in 1820, and his appointment of Mr. David Lockhart as the first curator. Lockhart was sent several times to St. Vincent, where the first Botanic Garden in the West Indies had been established, and to South America to procure plants and trees for the new Gardens. Woodford himself was always on the lookout for new flowering trees and shrubs and for other plants which might be used in starting new industries in the island. He was especially interested in the introduction of nutmeg trees and spices.

(11) *The Outlying Districts*
(a) *Indian Settlements*

The native Indian settlements* at Toco, Siparia, Savanna Grande and Arima had been set up under the Spanish Law of the Indies, which decreed that special protection should be given to the Indians of the New World. The case for these Indians was presented by the Dominican missionaries, of whom the best known was Bartolome de las Casas, the Apostle of the Indies. He it was who was indirectly responsible for the introduction of African slaves into the New World. So keenly did he strive to protect the Indians that he advocated a policy for introducing

* *Aboriginal Indians.*

Between 1600 and 1800, the aboriginal Indians had begun to die out, and their arts became lost. In 1783, the Indian population was 2,000. By 1797 there were about 1,000. At the present time there appear to be hardly any left. Traces of them can be observed in place names,, which indicate where they had settlements—Arima, Aricagua, Arouca, Carapichaima, Chacachacare, Guaracare and Tamana. De Verteuil, in his miscellany *Trinidad,* states that in 1856, " the 30th August is still a holiday, but bears quite a different character. People still crowd to the village from different parts of the island but there are no more Indians, neither are their oblations seen adorning the churches; their sports and their dances have passed away with the actors therein, and, in their stead, quadrilles, waltzes, races and blind hookey are the present amusements of the village."

Today at Arima there are still people who claim to be Caribs, who celebrate every August when the Queen of the Caribs is crowned, but in comparison with the pure blooded Caribs of Dominica there is evidence of an addition of Negro and Spanish blood.

147

the powerfully built African as a stronger and better fitted cultivator of the land rather than driving the more puny Indian on the plantations.

All settlements set up for the Indian population had a similiar plan. By law no individual Indian could own any property, but each separate community had its own Cabildo and a Corregidor appointed by the Governor. A priest was supplied to give religious instruction and the Indians were expected to give their labour for upkeep and cleaning of both church and presbytery. If they refused the priest had power only to inflict moral punishment.

Woodford took a keen interest in the well-being of the few remaining native Indians under his care and never failed to attend the Santa Rosa festival at Arima. On this day the Indians celebrated the festival of its patron saint. A " King and Queen ", usually a young couple, were chosen and the whole population dressed up in the brightest of colours. After a thanksgiving service in the church, specially decorated with local produce, the crowd proceeded to the Casa Real (the Royal House) to pay their respects to the Corregidor, who gave the signal for the carnival to begin. Palm beer was consumed, games were played, dancing took place, and amongst the main features of the day were archery competitions. People came from all over the island to attend with the Governor, to see the bright and amusing festival and to watch the natives of the island enjoying themselves. Before leaving Woodford awarded prizes to the children who had earned them by good behaviour or by progress in the settlement school.

(b) San Fernando de Naparima

This town was planned as far back as 1786, when a grant of land made to Isidore Vialos included a reservation for building a town near to the sea. The grant was never officially confirmed and Vialos parted with his property to Jean Baptiste Jaillet, the owner of Mon Chagrin Estate before the capitulation. Jaillet, either in ignorance of the reserved portion or through plain sharp practice, divided the original grant into small lots and sold to any who wished to buy. Many of the lots were sold and by 1792 the town of San Fernando had come into being under the encouraging eye of Governor Chacon.

The centre of the town's life was the Plaza San Carlos, where stood the market; there was also a church, a presbytery and a cemetery as well as a rest house for visitors. The four main streets were St. Vincent, Chacon, Penitence and Quenca Streets.

The Spanish Government out of necessity had condoned the irregular sales by Jaillet and treated them as occupancies. But after the capitulation any sale or transfer that took place without the knowledge and sanction of the Intendent of Crown Lands was held to be null and void. Many such transactions took place but it was not until after May 1st, 1818, when a fire of unknown origin completely destroyed the town, that any action was taken.

In September, the Commandant of North Naparima reported to the Cabildo that there was difficulty in defining the boundaries of the town and that many landholders had very obscure tenancies. The question came before the Council who recommended to the Governor that the Crown should be satisfied to retain the "King's fifty paces" (fifty yards inland from high water mark), and that the other occupied land be left in the hands of its holders. To this Woodford agreed and the new San Fernando was built on the site originally chosen by the last of the Spanish Governors.

(12) *Death of the Governor*

On March 29th, 1828, three days after the funeral of Dr. Buckley, Woodford, who had not been in the best of health for some time, informed the Council that he was taking a short cruise aboard H.M.S. *Slaney*. He added that Capt. Capadose, senior military officer in the colony, would administer the Government in his absence.

The strain of his work was beginning to tell and he needed a rest. Dr. Buckley's death had been a great blow, as the friendship between the two had been very real and close. But though he was in poor health, he was eager to recuperate and return fit and well to his task. When he sailed on April 1st, he was in good spirits.

On July 23rd, a rumour ran through Port of Spain that the Governor was dead. No one really believed it, but a few days later the news was confirmed in a letter to the Acting Governor from Robert Snell, Captain of H.M. Packet, *Duke of York*, dated May 19th.

The letter stated that Woodford had embarked in the *Duke of York* at Jamaica, a very sick man, a change of climate having been ordered as the only hope for complete recovery from his illness. He had gradually become worse and had passed peacefully away on May 16th. His faithful servant, Benjamin Coombs, who had accompanied him from England to Trinidad, had never left his bedside and was with him to the last. The letter continued :

"From the high and noble character of the deceased, and his well earned popularity in Trinidad and at the request of his faithful servant, I enclosed his respected remains in a cask of spirits in the hope of being able to forward it to that Island where he was so loved and to that Church built under his immediate eye; but the extreme heat of the climate has prevented me from having this melancholy pleasure of shewing my respect for the inhabitants of Trinidad, but not until the Official Report of my Surgeon that five of my crew were ill from the effluvia of the corpse did I this day reluctantly commit it to the deep . . ."

As soon as the news of the Governor's death had been confirmed, memorial services were held in all the churches of the colony. A meeting was called in Port of Spain to find some permanent way in which the feelings of the inhabitants could best be expressed. Owing to the bad feeling between the " English Party " and the old settlers, such names as Farfan, de Creny, Mayan, Guiseppi, Cipriani, de Gannes and de Verteuil were not amongst the thirty-one signatures of those responsible for the meeting. Had there not been this ill-feeling, the leaders of the old French and Spanish families would certainly have joined with the other planters and merchants who wished to pay their respects to the late Governor who had shown them such friendliness in the past.

The meeting was well attended. Judge Johnstone took the Chair and alluded to the sad event which led to the calling of the meeting. After the opening remarks, in which he referred to the enlightened policy which had marked Woodford's term of office, unprecedented in length amongst British Governors of the colony, he continued :

"These facts, Gentlemen, force themselves upon your attention in the state and character of your Revenue, in the appearance and efficiency of your Militia; in the security of peace and property, in the establishment and order of your tribunals; in the regular and open administration of Justice; in the formation, cleanliness and condition of the streets, buildings and markets of your metropolis; in the solid establishment and improvement of your High Roads; in the regulation and maintenance of your Public Prison; in the institution of your Public Schools; in the structure and decorum of your Churches—all silent witnesses far more impressive than would be the feeble utterances of my tongue . . .

". . . I need scarcely tell you, Gentlemen, that our gratitude and respect as husbands and fathers are due to our lamented Governor for the high moral character and consideration which by his sound example and refined conduct, both public and private, he raised for and bequeathed to this Colony.

I cannot doubt that the sense of that gratitude and that respect will be expressed in terms and in a manner suited to the excellence of him whose loss we deplore . . ."

The meeting was also addressed by Mr. Fuller, who proposed resolutions of appreciation for the virtues and talents of the late Governor. A subscription list was opened for the erection of a suitable monument in his memory, to which £1,500 was subscribed before the meeting broke up.

As a mark of respect and expression of public feeling all public offices were closed for a week, except for the most urgent business.

A committee, appointed by the subscribers to the Memorial Fund, decided to place a monument in each of the prinicipal churches in Port of Spain. In Trinity Church, a full sized, semi-recumbent figure was executed in marble by the famous sculptor, Chantrey. Beneath the figure was inscribed

TO THE MEMORY OF

SIR RALPH JAMES WOODFORD

For fifteen years Governor of this Colony,
and Founder of this Church, who was born
on 21st July, 1784, and died the 16th
May, 1828.

THE INHABITANTS OF TRINIDAD

Deeply sensible of the substantial benefits
Which his long administration of the Government conferred
upon the Colony
And of the irreparable loss which they sustained by his death,
Have caused this monument to be erected,
As a lasting memorial to his many public and private virtues,
And of their respect and gratitude.

A smaller monument consisting of his bust " en medallion " can be seen in the Lady Chapel of the Roman Catholic Cathedral, which was still unfinished at his death.

The *Naval and Military Gazette* of September, 1828, in a brief sketch of Woodford, wrote :

"He had been many years Governor of Trinidad in which peculiarly difficult and important post his conduct gained him the confidence of the inhabitants and the respect of all those whose concerns brought them to the Island. The ardently expressed gratitude of his unfortunate countrymen who were cast upon his generous compassion by storms and other disasters during the struggles of the South American cause (which their gallantry aspired to join) has yet more established his character in the light of a true British Governor, and his name as such will long be remembered on that coast with reverence and affection . . ."

When Woodford had arrived in the colony in 1813, it was badly in need of a strong man who could deal firmly with political, economic and social problems. Fifteen years later the effects of his firmness were patent. Trade was good, roads and communications had been improved, new estates and settlements had been opened up, new churches had been built and schools firmly established on a proper footing. The Militia was a well-disciplined body and the public offices were functioning efficiently. He had, in fact, laid foundations upon which the future of Trinidad could be built.

His strong personality made his detractors accuse him of being haughty and proud, but those who worked with him and knew him described him as being courteous and well-bred. His portrait, painted by Sir Thomas Lawrence, depicts him as a dignified and handsome man.* In private life he was kind and friendly, but knew when to be severe. As Governor of the colony he demanded to be treated with the dignity due to his office, and when this was forgotten he had no compunction in administering a stern rebuke. He obviously enjoyed a certain amount of pomp and splendour but from official rather than personal pride.

Following Naval and Military Governors as the first civilian to hold the post, his approach differed from that of his predecessors. He aimed to produce a civil administration rather than a disciplined organization. That he succeeded is shown by the state of the colony at his death, and by the way in which Governors who possessed neither his skill nor his personality were able to introduce difficult changes in the life and economy of the colony in the years which followed.

* This portrait is still hanging in the Council Chamber of the Red House.

CHAPTER TWELVE

MAJOR GENERAL SIR LEWIS GRANT, 1829-33

(1) *The Transition*

WHEN WOODFORD left the colony on April 1st, 1828, Major
J. V. Capadose of the 1st West India Regiment undertook the
administration of the Government. Within three weeks Lt.-
Colonel Sir Charles Felix Smith arrived to take up command
of the regular forces in the island and by virtue of his position
to relieve Capadose of the administration.

As soon as Woodford's death was officially confirmed, Sir
Charles Smith claimed to be Governor of Trinidad and called
upon William Burnley, the senior member of the Cabildo, to
administer the necessary oaths. Burnley refused on the grounds
that all that was necessary had been done when Smith took the
oath as Administrator and there was no precedent for confirming him as Governor. Smith, rather than be disappointed in his
ambition, approached Mr. Fuller, the Attorney-General, with
such insistence that under protest he complied. The main reason
for Smith's desire to become the Governor in name as well as
in practice was that once the oaths had been administered he
would be free from military control and have more personal
power.

One of his first acts was to rent a furnished house in Port of
Spain, claiming that the official residence was unfit for human
habitation whilst repairs were being carried out. It was unfortunate that he had to pay his own rent as both the Trinidad
and the Home Governments were reluctant to pay his expenses.

Smith's glory was short lived, for early in July Colonel James
A. Farquharson, of the 25th Regiment (the King's Own
Borderers), arrived from Demerara. He was officially appointed
to act as Governor until His Majesty appointed a permanent
holder of the post. Smith did not easily give up his position
and appealed to the Secretary of State for support, only to be
told that His Majesty's Government considered that he had no
claim to the office he desired to fill.

A little under a year later, Major General Sir Lewis Grant, recently Governor of the Bahamas, was appointed as Governor of Trinidad and on March 10th, 1829, was sworn in.

(2) The Land Question

During his period as Acting Governor, Farquharson received the report of a Commission which had been set up by the House of Commons before Woodford's death. On the suggestion of Mr. Hume, the Commission was to " Inquire into the condition of the West Indian Colonies." In November, 1823, three Members, Henry Maddock, Fortunatus Dwarris and Jabez Henry were appointed under Royal Warrant to enquire amongst other things into :

1. The Administration of Civil and Criminal Justice.
2. The expediency of maintaining the Spanish Law or substituting for it the Law of England so far as the same might be applicable to the circumstances of the Colony.
3. The land question.

They informed the public of Trinidad that :

". . . In regard to that part of the King's Warrant which related to the change of laws, the Commissioners think it necessary to observe, that in their instructions from Earl Bathurst, H.M. Secretary of State for the Colonial Department, it is observed that it does not involve the question of convening a Legislative Assembly in Trinidad, and that upon this subject there is not the slightest reason to anticipate any departure from His Majesty's determination, which has already been expressed in the most explicit terms."

The " English Party " resented this statement of policy. In the hope of gaining public support they called a public meeting under the Chairmanship of Mr. Cadett. To this assembly they invited all slave owners who, without regard to politics, wanted to prove to the Commission that the Order in Council would ruin the colony. William Burnley and St. Hilaire de Bégorrat were the chief speakers, the latter objecting to the introduction of English law without a change of constitution, stating :

". . . if that were to take place, I should feel considerable alarm as to the security in their properties of those proprietors in the Colony who are of foreign descent."

The meeting proceeded to elect a committee to further its interests.

The uneasiness felt for the future by the " English Party "

and the independent planters in turn disturbed the colonists of foreign extraction. They feared that those who were persistently advocating a change in the constitution might become the dominant party in the island, and under the guise of patriotism would strike at property and religion. The Commission was able to reassure them as to the safety of their religious practices and made several suggestions for changes in the judiciary and in the administration of the colony.

Acting on the report of the Commission, which was reduced to two members when Jabez Henry died on the return journey, the Secretary of State wrote to Woodford. This despatch was received by the Acting Governor, Farquharson :

"In the history of this controversy (the Land Question) which Mr. Dwarris has placed at the head of his Report, is to be found a complete justification of the measures you adopted so far as your own personal responsibility may be in question.

The successive Proclamations of December, 1815, November, 1816, and of 1st December, 1818, were approved by H.M. Government.* The general policy of these measures, if considered without reference to the difficulty of carrying them into execution, could hardly be disputed, and upon this subject the opinion of Mr. Dwarris appears entirely to coincide with your own. It is therefore gratifying to me to be able to state that the objections which have been made to the steps adopted by you in respect to the Grants in question are reduced to a legal controversy in which neither the soundness of your judgment nor the uprightness of your conduct are impeached."

The report endeavoured to make the question of land tenure clear. On the grounds that records and title deeds may have been lost or destroyed in the fire of 1808, it recommended that the Crown give landholders the benefit of any doubt and follow the principle of Spanish law under which lands were not resumed by the Crown if they had once been surveyed by the holder. This would benefit many of the poorer settlers who had failed to register their grants on account of high fees.

Persons who had proof neither of grant nor survey, and who possessed lands, were divided into two classes :

1. Those whose possession had been continuous from time immemorial.
2. Those who possessed land but could not produce evidence of more than forty years occupancy.

* See page 114 et seq.—Land Policy.

From the purely legal point of view the report saw the weakness in this division, but its authors were unable to offer any solution to the problem of sustaining claims. The experts in Spanish law were unable to agree. Possession from time immemorial seemed to be accepted as a principle, save that it was hard to prove such possession in a colony which had until comparatively recently been an unoccupied wilderness. In theory the rights of the Crown were absolute and universal before colonization began. The lawyers were also unable to agree that the period of forty years was a prescriptive period against the Crown.

The Secretary of State was unwilling to act upon the abstract question of law without the advantage of further inquiry and professional assistance. He was:

> "not disposed to rest the decisions of these claims merely upon the legal title of the claimants. Whatever may be the absolute rule of law, it is obvious that justice and sound policy require that persons who have long entered the possession of property should be maintained in that possession unless when the disturbance of them would be compensated by some public advantage of great moment. The most recent of the Titles in question must now have continued for thirty years, and after such a lapse of time they could not be disputed without much greater injury both public and private than would be sustained by the confiscation of them. Under these circumstances I am commanded by His Majesty to signify to you his pleasure that the several Proclamations of December, 1815, November, 1816, December, 1818, and May, 1823,* be revoked, and you will issue a Proclamation in His Majesty's name for that purpose."

Though this sounded a simple answer to the problem, it failed to provide any regulations for confirming grants the deeds of which had been lost or destroyed, nor did it mention land which had been granted upon special terms or under specified conditions. The Secretary of State went on to suggest that a general registration of all lands in the island should be made, to prevent any further controversy over the titles of the occupiers and to define the unceded territory belonging to the Crown. The Governor and Council were to be given complete discretion in organizing this registration, which, though to be rapid and effectual, was to be carried out as cheaply as possible. To this end the fees for registration were to be kept low.

* This Order extended the time within which petitions for confirmation of lands held under the Spanish Sovereign could be submitted.

Owners wishing to extend their holdings were to be encouraged and were to be subject to a nominal quit rent as an acknowledgement that their lands were held from the Crown. Those who had no title but that of possession might, when they registered their holding, pay a quit rent not exceeding that normally imposed on grants direct from British Governors. It was to be clearly understood by all concerned that owners accepting these terms might, if they preferred, rest on the registration of their claims rather than on the payment of quit rent. All landholders would thus be equal in the right of their holding, either under old or new grants.

The Secretary of State concluded his despatch by stating:

"Upon this part of the subject I cannot however furnish you with any instructions until I shall have learnt whether in your judgment any valid objections would arise to making compensation to those parties in the mode pointed out by Mr. Dwarris."

Opinions on the despatch varied. Some held that in it the Home Government had condemned Woodford's land policy. Others held that though the Proclamations had been revoked and resumption by the Crown had been discontinued, yet, by enforcing the registration of land and by granting titles, the Government were supporting what Woodford had always tried to do.

Farquharson, who inherited the problem, laid the despatch before the Council and pointed out the difficulties he could see in enforcing its instructions.

1. It would be impossible to compile a register of old Spanish grants owing to the bad state of existing documents, spoiled by insect damage and damp during the course of years.

2. The checking of lands to which there were no title deeds would necessitate the heavy expense of a full-scale survey.

3. By revoking the old Proclamations some sections of land resumed by the Crown and regranted would be liable to be claimed by the original owners to the great loss of the present occupiers.

After thirteen years of agitation, correspondence and ill-feeling, the land policy of Trinidad was back as it had been before Woodford issued his first Proclamation in 1815, and those which followed in 1816, 1818 and 1823. All were revoked and there remained no evidence that any policy for the future had been agreed.*

(3) *Slavery*

On March 18th, 1829, a despatch was received from England concerning the disabilities suffered by people of African birth or descent.

". . . It is hereby Ordered, That every Law, Ordinance or Proclamation . . . in force within His Majesty's said Island of Trinidad, whereby His Majesty's Subjects of African Birth or Descent, being of Free Condition, are subjected to any disability, Civil or Military, to which His Majesty's Subjects of European Birth or Descent are not subject, shall be, and the same and each of them are and is for ever repealed, abolished and annulled."

This document added fuel to the fire of irritation already kindled in the hearts of the many colonists who regarded Emancipation as the next and inevitable step towards their complete destruction. In England the anti-slavery movement† was daily increasing in strength. Leading citizens were making and publishing speeches in which the West Indian planters were treated with scorn and represented as cruel monsters perpetually intent upon devising methods of torment for their slaves. The British public, unable to hear of the actual conditions in Trinidad, were being taught and were coming to believe that slaves in the West Indies worked all day in chains, driven by overseers of great physical strength armed with rawhide whips.

The planters' position, put at its very lowest, was that from a purely economic point of view, a person paying a high price for any creature was unlikely to batter it to death at the earliest possible moment or to maim it and render it unserviceable. There were, of course, isolated cases of cruelty in the colony but these were dealt with by the authorities. The picture painted by the eloquent anti-slavery speakers, of the whole of the West Indies a great sugar-cane patch, peopled by maimed and wounded Negroes groaning under the weight of chains and shrinking from the ever-falling lash of the overseer's whip, may have been true of other colonies, but not of Trinidad.

There is no doubt whatever that the supporters of the anti-slavery movement acted as they did from the best of motives, but

* See page 114 et seq. and pages 219 and 278.—Land Policy.
† The Anti-slavery Society was founded in 1823.

they allowed themselves to be carried away by their zeal for reform. They worked themselves into a frenzy in the name of religion and humanity, and vented their wrath against planters as a whole, regardless of the fact that they were often their own friends or relatives. The chief offence of the planter was that he had legally become possessed of slaves, under a system which had been introduced into the colony long before he was born, in order to foster the commercial interests of the class of persons who now decided that for philanthropic reasons he was to be ruined.

The abolitionists claimed that slavery was an evil to be removed at all costs and as speedily as possible. In theory this commendable object could have been achieved by a single act of the supreme authority. In fact the difficulty was in devising a way by which a body of slaves could with safety and profit to themselves, and to their former owners, be converted overnight into free people. Historically there was no real precedent for such an action and any legislature undertaking it was bound to be faced with endless difficulties.* In one stroke there would come about a complete reversal of habits, ways of thought and modes of life, all of which had grown up over several centuries. The change from a system based on the right of a few to command the services of the many, to a system where the former master and the slave, who had but the slightest idea of liberty and the responsibilities of free people, were to be equal, was a task not to be undertaken lightly. The eloquence of Wilberforce and Brougham and the articles of Jeffrey, Stephen and Clarkson, swept the people of England along with them. They only saw that in the colonies there was a great wrong which must be righted. The planter from the West Indies had neither the time nor the aptitude to present his case in the best light and his efforts to make his position clear were ridiculed and sneered at.

Governor Grant was fortunate in that the Order in Council of 1824, though not popular in the colony, had been put into operation with the minimum of friction by his predecessor. The situation had not got out of hand in Trinidad as it had in other colonies, but firmness and tact were needed in handling both planters and Negroes. The serious slave risings in Demerara and Barbados were examples of what could happen as the result of mismanagement and a vacillating policy by the Government.†

* There were examples of what could happen when emancipation was given suddenly as in the French colonies, where many slave owners were brutally done to death.
† See Appendix XX.

159

Trinidad, being in the same geographical location as the other colonies, suffered through having to share their reputation for cruelty and lawlessness, though no actual outbreaks of violence were reported from the island. All West Indian planters were treated in the same manner—brought down to the level of the lowest. When all was finally settled, many prosperous families had been swept away or reduced to a state of penury, their estates having passed into other hands. As the new owners often left these estates to strange managers under an attorney, the effect was rarely beneficial to the estate slaves.

Under the provisions of an Order in Council of November 5th, 1831 (The Code Noir), any slave owner who ill-treated his slaves was liable to prosecution at the suit of the Attorney-General in the newly-established Criminal Court. This procedure was extremely unpopular with the planters as many of the cases which came before the Chief Justice and his two Assessors (the Governor's Assessor and one of the two Alcaldes of the Cabildo) were merely frivolous.

In May, 1832, the case of Rex v. Vesprey came before the court. The defendant was charged with having switched a certain female slave for gross impertinence and sundry rude gestures. The Alcalde, Mr. Frederick Brown, rose from his seat and addressed the court:

" I have attentively read the depositions in this prosecution —perhaps the word persecution would be more applicable. Criminality, it appears to me, attaches more to the audacious slaves population, instigated and encouraged as they are by this mode of frittering away the time of this Court, of the Court of Criminal Enquiry, of witnesses and (a matter of far more consideration) all to the great detriment of their owners' interests, whose authority they are made to defy, and whose ruin they are made to attempt, not to mention the extraordinary expense fixed thereby on this impoverished country. It is to be regretted that those whose official appointments compel the exhibition of so much zeal and alacrity on one side, are exempt from the responsibility of their proceedings in such cases as the present may occasion.

I respect everyone who does his duty conscientiously, and observe, that as I attach blame to none, I feel myself entitled to an equal claim to justice in declaring that I shall never be made a tool to injure the inhabitants of this conquered Colony and shall therefore quit this Bench without a vote on the present occasion, as I shall do on every future similar case that may appear before me. In thus saying and acting I beg to state to my colleagues that no disrespect is meant to them."

Mr. Brown then bowed and left the court. The other Alcalde, Mr. Bushe, was sent for to complete the numbers, but the Registrar returned to state that he was engaged on urgent business and was unable to attend. The court was forced to adjourn.

The *Port of Spain Gazette* commented favourably on the situation under the heading of "A Noble Act", and the Chief Justice, unable to ascertain the author, retaliated by refusing to insert any further court advertisements in the paper. Governor Grant called an emergency meeting of the Council and stated his views on the action of the Alcaldes and the very serious consequences which might arise from their behaviour in nullifying a Court of Justice in the colony.

The "Code Noir", published in November, 1831, was not proclaimed in the colony until early the following year, but was met with a protest from the slave owners on the grounds that its enforcement would mean the ruin of the planter and trouble with the slaves. This protest was framed at a meeting under the Chairmanship of Robert Neilson, an unofficial member of the Council. Burnley, who was about to leave for England, was chosen as the meeting's delegate on the question of the emancipation of the slaves.

The majority of the clauses of the Order dealt with the relation between master and slave, many of them being in the opinion of the planters impossible to put into operation without causing great distress to the island as a whole. Another protest meeting was held under the Chairmanship of Samuel Samuel, at which the chief speaker was the rising young barrister, Edward Jackson. He complained that the Secretary of State's despatches implied that the West Indian colonists were incapable of conducting their own affairs, and he dealt at length with the treatment of slaves and the anticipated emancipation. On this point a formal protest was signed by :

"Capitulants, Proprietors, Planters, Merchants and others possessing or being interested in property, in Estates, and in Slaves in the Island of Trinidad."

Copies were forwarded to the Agent in London, Joseph Marryat,* who was instructed to present it in the right quarters. He was authorized to request some members of the House of Lords, if possible the Earl of Eldon or the Duke of Wellington, to present the petition. He was also to canvas the support of other members of the House who were well versed in colonial

* Son of Joseph Marryat, senior, the former Agent in London.

affairs or who " have distinguished themselves as lovers of justice and protection of property ".

A copy was also to be presented in the House of Commons; for this the support of the Marquis of Chandos, Sir Robert Peel and Mr. Hume, was expressly desired.

In the colony itself, a deputation of twenty-seven was appointed to wait upon the Governor to make a protest against the clauses in the Order restricting the hours of labour for slaves, and fixing the days on which they were to work in their gardens. The delegation was to make a strong point of the ruinous condition into which the colony would fall if the Order was implemented. Governor Grant refused to receive the deputation.

In his speech, Jackson had proposed that the committee should be strengthened by the inclusion of new members. An attempt was made to enlist the support and sympathy of the free coloured proprietors, with whom under normal conditions the white owners would never openly have associated. To these overtures the free coloured proprietors replied through the *Gazette* :

" Sir,
By the *Port of Spain Gazette* of the 18th instant, we are informed that at a Public Meeting of the inhabitants of this town held on the 6th, we were nominated members of the ' Trinidad Standing Committee '.

Our occupations in the country have prevented us from taking an earlier opportunity to acquaint you that we cannot, consistently with our line of conduct which we have prescribed for ourselves, accept the honour which the meeting has been pleased to confer upon us.

It will at all times afford us pleasure to co-operate with you in every measure in which you may consider our humble assistance useful to the general interests of the community of which we are members . . .

We have the honour to be, Sir,
Your very obedient servants,
Noly Beaubrun
P. R. George Bertete
T. R. Crosbie
J. V. Navet."

The free coloured proprietors had no desire to become involved in anything which might prejudice their position, for they were growing in wealth and were beginning to be considered a powerful body of respectable people. They had not forgotten the treatment they had received from Governor Hislop nor were they fully satisfied with the current trend of policy, for they could not fail to notice that in every attempt to alter any part of the constitution, there was no mention of their future position. They held firmly to the 12th Article of Capitulation* as their constitutional anchor and had no desire to join any political demonstration which might alter their standing. Their refusal to join the Trinidad Standing Committe was accepted and George Reid, the Secretary, wrote :

" Gentlemen,
    I duly received your communication of January 27th addressed to Mr. Scott, and laid the same before the Committee.
    In reply I am directed to state, that the members of the Board are well aware that the enactments contained in the Order in Council of March 18th, 1829, by removing all civil and military disabilities from His Majesty's subjects of free condition, but of African descent, have placed those persons in a more advantageous position than they could ever hope to attain under the protection of any other Government, and that consequently the injury which will result from the operation of the Slave Code of November, 1831, may not in their estimation counter-balance the advantages they derive from that political boon.
    The Committee therefore fully appreciate the sentiments which guide your request, have directed me to withdraw your names from the list of members of the Board; and in the same spirit of good will which directed your nomination have desired me to express the satisfaction they experience in knowing that every benefit which may follow their exertions, must be equally shared by every class of His Majesty's subjects."

Though there was considerable perturbation in Trinidad over the Order in Council, there was no outbreak of violence. The Port of Spain Gazette was filled with articles and letters on the burning topic of the day. Exaggerated reports of violence in the other colonies were included and the general tenor of the correspondence reflected the strong feelings of the planters.† Open discord was not far away. The situation might easily have got out of hand.
    The rival newspaper, the Royal Gazette, made an effort to give Trinidad an unbiased and unexaggerated view of the events of the day. It became the organ of the Anti-Slavery Party and the supporter of the old " English Party " in an effort to gain

* See Appendix V.
† See Appendix XXI.

control of local affairs at the expense of the "foreigners" and the Roman Catholics.

The anti-slavery party in England did not help to make relations between master and slave easy. In speeches up and down the country and in the House of Commons, they influenced the public against the slave owners of the fifteen colonies. In May, 1832, Fowell Buxton stated as a positive fact that the number of stripes inflicted with the cart whip in the West Indies exceeded two millions yearly. He ended his speech by saying :

> " It is true that in chartered Colonies no record of punishment is kept, but I have got the fact by comparing the population and the number of stripes inflicted in the Colony of Demerara, which is a Crown Colony, and which of course kept a record, with the population of other Colonies, assuming the same ration of punishment, though it was probably much greater in those Colonies where the punishments were not recorded. Taking Demerara, which is a meliorated Colony as a criterion, the general condition of the slaves throughout the West Indies may be judged of."

The slave owners of Trinidad strongly resented any comparison between themselves and the owners in Demerara. They had always prided themselves on their good treatment of slaves under the law originally laid down by the Spanish Government. Demerara on the other hand had a reputation for notorious cruelty and had inherited the traditions and customs of the Dutch, who were amongst the most brutal slave owners in the world.

The Trinidad slave owner considered himself as a special case, for under the Cedula of 1783, when foreigners were allowed to settle, they were encouraged to bring slaves. The greater number of slaves, the greater the grant of land.* This policy had been continued after the capitulation. The owners felt that by fighting against change to the bitter end they might achieve some compromise which would allow for the economic running of their estates. The effects of this continuous fight with the Government were felt by the slaves themselves, who regarded their owners as waging a perpetual war for their possession. The younger slaves grew up in an atmosphere of distrust and even hate for the slave owner.

William Burnley, as delegate from Trinidad, joined forces in London with Joseph Marryat, son of the late Agent, and Member of Parliament for Sandwich. Marryat was the unpaid and

* See Appendix I.

164

officially unrecognized Agent for Trinidad but was always willing
to turn his hand to anything that would benefit the colony in
which his family had large estates. With Burnley, he tried to
persuade the Government that there should be some alteration
in the Order in Council, at least as far as Trinidad was concerned. A committee was set up in the House of Commons to
consider a Bill designed to afford some relief to the Crown
Colonies in which the Order of 1831 had been adopted and
£75,000 was asked for this purpose. There was much opposition
to this measure and Marryat, in an effort to put Trinidad in the
most favourable position, read a letter stating that the Order
was working well in the colony and that in his opinion the
planters and owners were entitled to some relief for the losses
they had sustained through their loyalty to it.

The reaction to the report on the debate when it reached
Trinidad was most marked. Marryat was accused of " treachery "
and " trying to purchase himself a baronetcy ". He defended himself against these charges in a letter addressed to the Trinidad
Committee and at a general meeting under the Chairmanship
of Mr. Fuller it was suggested that no decision should be taken
until Burnley should send a full report on what had taken place.
A lengthy motion proposed by Mr. Murray and seconded by
Edward Jackson ended :

> " That with the full knowledge and conviction of the mis-
> chievous and destructive effects which the Order in Council
> has already produced, and a deep sense of the total ruin of
> all property which must attend the enforcement of all its
> clauses, this meeting is of the opinion that Mr. Marryat cannot,
> with safety to the public or satisfaction to himself, continue to
> act as Agent of a community which considers its very existence
> as dependent on the rejection, or at least the modification of
> this obnoxious measure; but that as Mr. Marryat, in his
> communications to the Committee, has stated that his speeches
> are misrepresented in the newspapers, and as further informa-
> tion on this subject may be shortly expected both from our
> Deputy, Mr. Burnley, and from Mr. Marryat himself, this
> Meeting deems it expedient to postpone, until the public
> meeting on December 6th next, their consideration of Mr.
> Marryat's offer to resign his trust as honorary Agent of
> Trinidad."

Before this motion could be put to the meeting, Mr. Waller
supported by Mr. Lake, proposed an amendment :

> " That this meeting, viewing with alarm the line of conduct

adopted by Joseph Marryat, Esq., M.P., on the occasions referred to, do accept his resignation as our Agent, and that the same be communicated to that gentleman with as little delay as possible."

The amendment was carried by a large majority and before the meeting closed, William Burnley was nominated as the colony's Agent.

Under the law which had abolished the slave trade (1807), it was forbidden to transfer a slave from one British possession to another. This was considered a great handicap to Trinidad where labour was scarce and the introduction of " foreign " slaves was the only way of keeping up manpower. After Woodford's death, the law had been largely disregarded and there was a considerable traffic in domestic slaves from Barbados. There was a shortage of trained domestics in Trinidad and it was generally believed that Barbadians were better servants than Trinidadians. Planters, merchants and professional men brought Barbadian slaves and entered them in the colony on certificates issued by the Collector of Customs and the Registrar of Slaves. In his triennial return to the Secretary of State, the Registrar reported the names of all new arrivals in the colony. The slaves were more often than not sold at a good price as trained domestics. That this was taking place was well known to the Government, for the Crown sometimes benefited by levying on the slaves or by selling them at the order of the court.

A great stir was caused when, on February 3rd, 1832, a Proclamation was issued :

" Whereas it hath been represented to Us that divers persons have been imported into Our Island of Trinidad from Our other possessions in the West Indies, in violation of the laws for the abolition of the Slave Trade, and that persons so imported are now holden in slavery in Our said Island of Trinidad, and that the persons engaged in effecting such importations, or some of those persons, engaged therein in ignorance of the provisions of the law in that behalf . . .

Now We do hereby make known to all whom it may concern, that We have strictly charged and enjoined Our trusty and well-beloved Lewis Grant . . . and all Judges, Justices and all other Our officers . . . forthwith to adopt all legal and necessary means for procuring to Us the persons so illegally imported . . ."

The Proclamation gave two months grace for all who were prepared to grant manumission to illegally held slaves, and was signed by Philip Dotin Souper, Colonial Secretary.

At once a public meeting was called and a committee set up to wait upon the Governor with the facts and figures on the importation of slaves since January, 1825. Grant suggested that a Memorial be drawn up so that he could give formal answers to the owners' questions. A lengthy correspondence took place between the Governor, the Attorney-General and the Committee, as the Collector of Customs refused to give certain details which were deemed necessary for the completion of the Memorial.

Meanwhile action had to be taken by the Government. They had already taken a large number of Barbadian slaves from their masters and were keeping them at public expense. After six months the Attorney-General decided to deal with the first 144 out of a total of nearly 600 cases. From these he obtained nineteen convictions, all by default. Many owners failed to appear, many because they were too poor to do so. The remaining cases were adjourned or never reached court.

In November the Attorney-General started once more and it was known that he was about to take a firm stand and apply the letter of the law in all cases. Events were not so happy for him as he had hoped, for on the Sunday evening, before the court opened, all the relevant papers disappeared. These papers were kept in a press in an old house on Lower Prince Street and were not under any form of guard. The only resident in the building was an old free Barbadian Negro, formerly belonging to one of the Alquazils of the court. This man was permitted to make use of a small room in the yard. On the Sunday evening he noticed that the door of the main building was open and on looking inside he discovered that the press had been rifled. He at once reported the matter to the Registrar and was promptly placed in gaol on suspicion.

On Monday morning a few of the missing documents were discovered scattered about Shine's pasture outside the town but there was no evidence to show how they got there.

An extraordinary development took place on the Tuesday. At midday, the Acting Attorney-General, the Chief of Police, and several of the Alquazils, called at the house of Mr. Porter and Mr. Wilson, merchants trading as the firm of Robert Neilson and Co., and without a warrant carried out a search of the premises. Both Porter and Wilson were most indignant when they discovered that one of their servants had been taken for questioning by the police. They went at once to the Attorney-General's office and found that not only was their servant being questioned but that they themselves were both under suspicion of being concerned with the missing documents. Having expressed their views in the most forceful language, they took their servant home with them.

At this point the Attorney-General seems completely to have lost his head. He sent for the Governor, went himself to fetch the Chief Justice and instructed the Chief of Police to take out a warrant for the arrest of Porter and Wilson. The party of high officials was joined by the Registrar of Slaves and all the Alquazils of the court. Rumours were flying around Port of Spain. It was even whispered that the Militia had been called out. When the Chief of Police arrived at the house to make the arrest, he found a large audience gathered to witness the act. The crowd, however, were denied any excitement, for after the production of the warrant there was a long argument which ended when the two suspects offered bail for their appearance in court the following morning at eleven o'clock.

On Wednesday they arrived at the court accompanied by a large party of planters, merchants and professional men as well as an interested and inquisitive crowd of sightseers. The Attorney-General sent a message from his apartments above the court stating that he was prepared to accept the bail and there the matter rested.

No further evidence was produced concerning the missing papers, nor has any since come to light, but the general feeling in the colony was that some person or persons of high standing in the community were involved. None of the officials had enhanced his popularity with the public by this incident; none were popular before and the method of handling the problem of the missing documents did nothing to endear an already unpopular Government to its critical subjects.

Letters and articles in the Press, speeches at meetings and conversation in private, all turned against the Government, the enforcement of the Slave Code and the changes in the administration of the colony. Governor Grant, never popular with the majority of the colonists, had the unenviable task of administering two much resisted and much resented policies.

(4) *Constitutional Changes*

Before Woodford's death it had become known that the Home Government had decided to make some alterations in the constitution of the colony. The changes envisaged were not divulged and there was widespread speculation. In November, 1830, at a meeting of planters, merchants and proprietors in the home of Robert Neilson, it was decided to appoint a committee to correspond with the West Indian Party in London and to appoint Joseph Marryat as Honorary Agent for the Trinidad colonists. Marryat was not destined to hold this position for long, for his unpopularity after his speech on the Order in Council forced his resignation two years later.

The duty of the Committee was to watch over the interests of the colonists, to communicate with the Governor on points which they deemed to be of vital interest to the life of the colony and to convey copies of resolutions passed at meetings to the right departments.

Over the expected constitutional changes the committee corresponded with the Governor and with London and on June 1st, 1831, a letter appeared in the *Port of Spain Gazette* from the Secretary of State, acknowledging a letter from the committee and stating :

" I am directed by Lord Goderich to apprise you, and you will be at liberty to communicate the information to any other persons who may be interested in the subject, that arrangements are in progress, and will possibly be completed within a very short time, for carrying into effect the greater part of those changes which appear to be necessary in the Political and Judicial Constitution of Trinidad. It is intended to create a Council of Government selected partly from the Public Officers and partly from the principal proprietors of the Colony. To the Governor, acting with the advice of that Council will be given authority to make all necessary laws.

It will be required that accounts of Revenue and Expenditure should be published once in each half-year for general information. A republication of all Laws of the Colony will be among the first duties of the Governor. The Courts of Audience and Appeal will be abolished. The number of Judges in the Court of First Instance will be reduced and that tribunal will henceforth be holden by professional Judges only and by professional Judges and Assessors in criminal cases. The Judges will be remunerated exclusively by salaries; they will receive no fees, nor exercise any patronage over the Officers of their Courts. It will be among the first duties of the Judges to establish such Rules of Procedure as may most effectually abridge the delay, and such Tables of Fees as may properly diminish the expense, of litigation. Various amendments of the General Laws of the Island will be recommended to the early attention of the Governor and Council."

This statement gave rise to much speculation and discontent.

The majority thought the concessions small, but many felt that in a community of so many mixed races, the division of the Governor's responsibility might lead to awkward situations. Unfortunately the changes were announced at a time when the colonists were interested chiefly in their own personal troubles. Convinced that the implementation of the Order in Council would bring them to ruin, they were unable to raise much enthusiasm for the welfare and government of the colony in the distant future.

On December 27th, 1831, His Majesty's Council in the Island of Trinidad, as it had been since 1801, met for the last time. Those present were His Excellency, the Governor, Sir Lewis Grant, the Acting Chief Justice, Mr. L. H. Johnson, Dr. Llanos, Messrs. F. Peschier, H. Murray, A. Gomez, and J. Peschier. After the minutes of the last meeting had been read and confirmed, His Excellency addressed the Council :

" Gentlemen, I have called the Council together today for the purpose of communicating that I have in my possession a new form of Government, which His Majesty has been pleased to adopt for this Colony."

He then explained that the existing Council would be dissolved and that a new one would be formed forthwith. The duties of the new Council would no longer be purely advisory. It would have legislative functions and authority. It would be composed of public officers and nominees selected by the Crown from amongst the inhabitants, the former to take precedence. The Order under which the changes were made was read to the members and the names of the new Council were announced :

Official Members :	His Excellency the Governor
	The Chief Justice
	The Colonial Secretary
	The Colonial Treasurer
	The Attorney-General
	The Collector of Customs
	The Protector of Slaves
Non-Official or	William H. Burnley
Nominated	Dr. Llanos
Members :	F. Peschier
	H. Murray
	J. Peschier
	R. Neilson.

From 1797–1801, the Governor, who was also Commander-in-Chief, had had absolute power in the colony. If he needed advice he asked a Council of his own choosing, not one imposed on him either locally or by London. In 1801, Picton had had instructions to form a Council of Advice, but he was not compelled to accept its suggestions, nor were the members permitted to vote on any subject. The responsibility of government rested entirely upon the shoulders of the Governor who, after listening to the advice of his Council, used his own judgment and was himself responsible for good or bad policy.

Under the system of the Governor's individual responsibility, the colony had prospered, though there was a certain amount of dissatisfaction amongst those who were not chosen as advisers, particularly those who measured their importance by financial rather than intellectual standards. With all its faults the system had proved its worth, for the Governor could shelter behind no one and the Council had no control over him. Decisions were his alone.

The new system changed the picture. Trinidad was to remain a Crown Colony, which meant there would be no elected representatives of the people on the Council and that the island would be ruled through the Colonial Office in London. But, and this was important, the Governor would be able to shelter behind the Council if mistakes were made and the responsibility for bad policy and administration would be divided. Though the Governor would no longer be able to act in an absolutely arbitrary manner, he would still be able to force his policy on the Council, as he would have the support of the official members and if necessary his own casting vote. There were to be no additions to the political liberties of the people of Trinidad but there was created an instrument which, if it fell into the hands of unscrupulous people, could lead to a more despotic form of government than in the days when the Governor carried the whole responsibility for the colony's administration. In July, 1832, Governor Grant informed the Council that His Majesty had decided to fix the Chief Justice's salary at £2,000 per year and had appointed two Puisne Judges at £1,000 a year. He had already managed to arrange for his own salary to be fixed at £5,000. In 1830, he had seen that the West Indian troubles were undermining confidence in the financial market and had commuted his fees and fixed salary, which amounted to £6,000 a year, for the lower sum, which was guaranteed by the Cabildo.

Grant also informed the Council that the office of Criminal

Enquiry had been abolished at the instance of the Home Government and that the Attorney General would in future take over its functions.

A Committee was appointed to look into certain other important items in which His Majesty's Government were interested:

1. The amendment of the Law concerning Ganancias, under which all rights of a married woman to share in all property brought by her into the family common stock, or purchased by her husband, or herself during marriage, were regarded as a co-partnership into which every child of the marriage entered at birth.
2. The liability of infants to be arrested for debt.
3. The law on inheritance.
4. The legal period of majority.
5. The introduction of some procedure analogous to writs of Habeas Corpus.
6. The abolition of the office of Depositor-General and the adoption of the English system of arbitration.

This was almost the last time that Dr. Llanos served on the Council for, soon after his appointment, Burnley astonished the colony by challenging the legality of his nomination on the grounds that he was an alien. Llanos was, in fact, a Spanish Royalist, who had come to Trinidad in 1810 from Caracas, where he had been practising in the courts at the outbreak of the Venezuelan insurrection. On arrival he had been granted a licence to practise in Trinidad by Governor Munro and had earned the esteem and respect of all. Woodford had appointed him to a seat on the Council in 1823, and he had served continually without any complaint as to his nationality.

As the matter was raised officially by Burnley, Grant had to refer it to the Secretary of State for an official ruling. An answer was received in August, 1832:

" I have received your despatch dated 24th March respecting the objections made by Mr. Burnley to the qualifications of Dr. Llanos to act as a member of the Legislative Council at Trinidad.

It appears to me that the objection to Dr. Llanos admits of no answer; that he is an alien is not disputed; and the legal inference is plain, that he is not competent to hold such a trust as that of a member of a Legislative Body within His Majesty's dominions.

The answer ' that he has already filled various offices equally incompatible with his character as an alien ' proves only that the Law was negligently administered.

Much as I regret the loss of the services of Dr. Llanos, it is impossible for me to resist such an objection at present, when distinctly brought under my notice."

This decision of the Secretary of State, though legal, caused offence to all settlers of foreign birth and the *Port of Spain Gazette* was full of letters and articles attacking the Government's policy. "Alien", writing in August, stated :

"Sir,
We have perused with interest the article contained in your valuable paper of the 18th instant concerning Dr. Llanos, and your judicious observations on the subject . . .
Since the conquest of the island in 1797, the portion of His Majesty's subjects of late stigmatized by the name of "Aliens" had enjoyed the protection of the British Government to the same extent as either British born subjects or the Capitulants. This system originated with Picton, the pride of Great Britain, Picton the true British soldier who paid for his military honours with his blood and who died on the field of battle, crowned in glory! He gave to foreigners every encouragement. The same system was acted upon by Governors Hislop, Munro, Sir Ralph Woodford, and the late Acting Governor, Sir Charles Smith . . .
The British Government certainly had the right not to have received aliens, or to have imposed such restrictions as might have been deemed proper; but they were received unconditionally, and for thirty-five years the legality of the measure was not brought into question; to impose, after such a lapse of time, conditions evidently not contemplated at first sight, would be a breach of national faith. . . ."

The crux of the matter was that Dr. Llanos had served on the Council of Advice only in the days when the Governors were permitted to choose whom they would for this function. Now the Council was a legislative body and no matter what his services or reputation, no alien was allowed to serve. Grant should have realized this and submitted the list of his nominees for official approval before making his choice public.

Dr. Llanos resigned and was succeeded by Mr. Roxborough, and for the first time in its history the Council was composed entirely of Protestants. It was unfortunate that this should have been brought about by the resignation of Dr. Llanos, for it tended to create bad feeling amongst the settlers and was regarded as a deliberate threat by the Government against all aliens. There grew up a hostility against all things English which had never existed before. The "English Party", seeking its own ends, made use of this bad feeling at a time when ruin was practically staring the island in the face. Much more could have been achieved for the colony's future had it been possible to forget the racial and religious differences and for all parties to concentrate on the economic and financial problems that faced Government and citizen alike.

As it was, many of the foreigners were gravely alarmed at the course of events and a Memorial was sent through the Governor to the Secretary of State. The reply was reassuring.

" Sir,

I have received your despatch (No. 47) of the 2nd ultimo, enclosing a Memorial addressed to myself by certain foreign Inhabitants of Trinidad, in which the Memorialists protest and remonstrate against confiscation of their property with which they have conceived themselves to have been threatened by the British Government.

You will lose no time in informing the Memorialists, that no such intention as they ascribe to His Majesty's Government has ever been entertained; and you will add that I have received His Majesty's commands to convey to them the assurance that nothing could be further from His Majesty's purpose and feelings, than that any unnecessary distinction should be made between the right of his protection inherited by his British-born subjects in Trinidad, and that acquired by those foreigners who have taken up their permanent abode in the Colony and identified themselves with its interests. The Memorialists may be satisfied that His Majesty is animated with the same desire to establish the security and promote the prosperity of all classes of the inhabitants of Trinidad."

The minds of the " aliens " were set at rest, but Grant was tactless in publishing the despatch as for general information rather than communicating its contents informally and thus missed an opportunity of bringing the British and the foreigners firmly together.

Another change introduced into the Government of the colony concerned the position of the higher public officers. The Secretary of State, in a despatch in May, 1831, stated :

" No claim to compensation for loss of Office can be considered to arise in the case of any Public Officer who shall have engaged himself in trade or agriculture during the period of his services. Henceforth, every person entering Public Service in Trinidad must be previously divested of property in plantations within the Colony, or in agricultural slaves, wheresoever situated; and every judicial and legal officer of the Crown, except the judicial assessors in the Criminal Court, must, although not now taking Office for the first time in the Colony, divest themselves of such property above mentioned within two years of the date of your receipt of this despatch."

The timing of this change was unfortunate, and the natural reaction was that the inhabitants of the colony felt more insecure than before. Whether Government policy was right or wrong Trinidad saw a future in which the chief officers would have no stake in the colony except their wage cheque. They would, in fact, be more foreign to the island than the " aliens " and might introduce legislation from personal motives and from expediency rather than with consideration for the well-being of the colony as a whole. Up to this time the Council and officers had been almost without exception men with an interest in the island, who even if working for their own advancement also worked for the good of the colony. Now it appeared that this would be changed and the colony would be in the hands of a public service almost inevitably recruited from outside.

The new constitutional changes were on the whole unpopular, and combining with the unpopularity of the Slave Laws encouraged hostility and bitterness amongst the inhabitants. There was room for dissatisfaction, for the Court Assessors were not functioning in the way that had been hoped. Speeches, articles and letters showed the feelings that were rife in the colony so noticeably that even in London the critical situation was noted. The outcome was a lengthy letter to the Governor, published in the *Port of Spain Gazette,* addressed from London by the Secretary of State, in which new proposals were made for the organization of the courts dealing with slave problems.*

(5) *The Cocoa Planters*

In January, 1829, a full report on the cocoa industry showed that the combination of bad harvests and low prices for both cocoa and coffee was responsible for great suffering and poverty amongst the planters and that many estates in the Arima district of the island had been abandoned. The following year, the industry going from bad to worse, a meeting was called to discuss measures for improvement and the setting up of a board for the inspection of cacao. The Chairman, Antonio Gomez of La Pastora Estate, Santa Cruz Valley, with the other members signed a memorandum addressed to the Governor, asking for his help.

* See Appendix XXII.

175

The bad weather had led to such bad crops that the merchants, on behalf of the planters, asked Government for a postponement of six months in the paying of the slave taxes.* Times were indeed hard. The merchants were petitioning the Government that the recently repealed system of passports or exit permits should be re-enacted, so many people were leaving the colony without paying their just debts. The Governor, in his report to the Secretary of State, mentioned the difficulties of the times, particularly in the capital, where many houses were for sale, their owners being unable to afford the taxes due. In the hopes of a more prosperous future, applications were being received for extension of time for tax payment. Meanwhile both revenue and population were on the decline. In 1827, revenue was £50,000 from a population of 42,692. In 1830 it had dropped to £43,196 and the population to 41,873.

In 1832, the leading cocoa planters held another meeting under the chairmanship of Don Antonio Faustino de Leon, and a committee of five eminent planters—José Francisco Farfan, Faustino de Leon, José Maria Hernandez, Celestin Dancla and St. Hilaire de Bégorrat, were appointed to draw up a petition to the Governor. The members of the committee were knowledgeable in the industry and were citizens of long standing, all being Capitulants, and their petition was supported by the necessary documents.†

In it they described the state of the cocoa industry during recent years, the difficulties which the proprietor had to face and overcome from the fall in prices and from the imposition of the Order in Council. The petition was presented personally to Governor Grant by Mr. Bégorrat in June, 1832, but it was not until the following October that Grant addressed the committee :

"In reference to the Petition of the Cocoa Planters of the 5th of May, 1832, I deem it most expedient that an enquiry should be made into the actual condition of this class of persons, their past and present circumstances, the objects of their wishes to be specified, and a remedy to be suggested. The report should be summary, and should contain facts and practical suggestions. Mr. Bégorrat having consented to take part in the Inquiry, Mr. Joseph Basanta will be so good as to consult with Mr. Bégorrat in carrying the inquiry into effect, and when completed and passed to the Governor, it will be forwarded by first opportunity thereafter, if it should come to him three days before sailing of Mail-boat. It would be well

* An annual tax of $1 per year per slave owned.
† See Appendix XXIII.

176

the report should be summary, and contain facts and practical suggestions and nothing speculative."

A special Committee was at once set up to comply with Grant's wishes and to produce a report. The different cocoa growing districts were to be represented and eight members were chosen. There is no record of the result.

(6) *The Churches*

There was growing demand throughout the colony for more clergy of all denominations. The Vicar-General, Father de Goff, asked Governor Grant for an increase in the stipends of all his parish priests, who were doing valuable work in ministering to the people of town and country alike. He also stressed the need for additional priests as the burden being carried was more than sufficient for the few he had. He was supported in his plea by the Rt. Rev. D. MacDonnell, Bishop of Olympus, and lately Vicar-Apostolic in the Danish and British West Indies, who had been appointed to succeed Dr. Buckley in Trinidad.

Churches were being built in spite of the difficulties in raising funds. In San Juan, under the guidance of Father Alfonso, a committee headed by Mr. L. Lapeyrouse and Mr. Juan de la Forest corresponded with the Governor on the details of finance for the new church to be dedicated to St. John the Baptist, finally opened in 1832. At Carenage, the Cipriani family had given land to the church and a building was in the process of erection. In Port of Spain great efforts were made to raise funds for the completion of the cathedral which in 1829 still needed a roof. It was completed and consecrated in 1832.

The Church of England was stressing the need for its permanent establishment in the colony and its maintenance out of public funds. More clergy were needed as well as schoolmasters and mistresses throughout the island. There was a special need for another clergyman to work in the Carapichaima district amongst the slaves. Repairs were needed on Trinity Church, whose tower had been damaged in the earthquake of 1825 and had had to be redesigned as a spire.

The Wesleyan Methodists, led by their minister, Mr. Fiddler, also pressed the Government for permission to extend their work, particularly amongst the plantation slaves.

(7) *Finance*

When Governor Grant was on leave in England, Sir Charles Smith (Acting Governor) uncovered a deficiency in the finances of the colony.

Since the days of the capitulation the office of Colonial Treasurer in Trinidad had been entirely different from similar posts in the other colonies. The Government had been continually in debt to the Treasury since 1808, and the colony's assets were represented by notes of hand payable on demand. These notes the Treasurer negotiated with the merchants when he received them and when money was needed for Government purposes he negotiated more notes for the amount of cash required. The most peculiar feature was that the Treasurer was allowed to speculate on his own behalf with any notes he held.

Whilst the trade of the colony was good and Government expenditure small, this practice seems to have worked satisfactorily but, as circumstances changed and expenditure grew, it became increasingly necessary to budget for the future. Sir Charles Smith decided to review the financial position of the colony and gave instructions for a full report on the monies available in the Public Chest (Colonial Treasury).

The result of this enquiry was the finding of a deficiency of £16,000. A committee was set up to examine the books kept by Mr. St. Hill, the Treasurer. After careful scrutiny they reported that as far as they could find out, no regular books had been kept since 1819 and that the total deficit was more than £20,000.

Proceedings were taken against St. Hill in the Court of the Intendent, where it was declared that he owed the Crown the sum of £15,322. The whole of this sum was refunded and no further charge was laid against the Treasurer for fraud or dishonesty. He had taken advantage of a system which he had found to be existing and had become more and more involved in bad speculations. Though there were no further charges and the colony suffered no financial loss, St. Hill was deprived of his office as Treasurer.

Owing to the weak financial position of the colony, the Government offices were housed in very inadequate quarters and public works were held up. Reinagle, Pilkington and Bridgens were all eager to create new buildings but progress was of necessity slow. When Antonio Gomez, Chairman of the Roman Catholic Committee, approached the Governor for funds to complete the roof of the cathedral in 1829, the most he could get was a grant of £500.

The Treasury building itself was in a very bad state of repair. The old building in Brunswick Square, where most of the other Government offices were housed, was so bad that the upper rooms could not be used on account of the weakness of the floors. The lower floor was considered safe but the Government archives were suffering badly from damp, insects and rodents.

There was no money for building but the Government had perpetually to find extra funds for emergencies. In August, 1831, a disastrous hurricane struck Barbados, causing unparalleled loss to the colony. Crops, public and private buildings, sugar mills and nearly all the colony's store of provisions were destroyed and aid had to be sent from Trinidad for fear that famine would cause a high death roll. When the news first reached the island, some speculators formed a ring to buy up all the provisions available, hoping to profit by the advanced prices that Barbadians in their half starved condition would be prepared to pay. Sir Charles Smith placed an embargo on all ships in the harbour and called upon the Council to provide enough money to send sufficient supplies to the sister colony.

(8) The Militia

Christmas, 1832, held little promise of gaiety. Though martial law was proclaimed for the usual month and balls, suppers and parties were arranged, the prevailing gloom cast by the difficulties of the planters overshadowed the season. The Order in Council and the expected emancipation of the slaves hung like a dark cloud over the festive season.

If Government policy was unpopular, so were its chief administrators. Governor Grant was known as a weak character, continually given to changing his mind and the new Chief Justice, George Scotland, was finding it very difficult to fill the shoes of his predecessor, Ashton Warner. Warner, who had died at the end of 1830, had been so popular in the colony that as a mark of appreciation for his twelve years as Chief Justice the inhabitants had petitioned the Governor for a pension to be provided for his wife and children.

Even in the Militia there was evidence that Christmas was not going to be a joyful season. The crack regiment, the Artillery, commanded by Colonel Nielson, was in a state of ferment. Nielson was one of the bitterest opponents of the Order in Council. He had taken a very active part in all the protests against the Government policy and had been particularly vehement over the question of the Barbadian slaves. One of the officers under his command was Young Anderson, the editor of the *Royal Gazette* (later known as the *Observer*), who was a well known supporter of the Government and the cause of the " Saints ",* a man who had made many enemies amongst both

* The nickname given to the Anti-Slavery Party.

the white and the free coloured peoples in the colony. The feeling of his brother officers towards Anderson was patent long before the period of martial law was proclaimed, but during the month tension mounted until in February it reached a head. Nielson received a letter from his officers in which they stated that they refused to meet Captain Anderson on the parade ground. He took no action on receipt of this letter or subsequently, when his officers marched off parade in a body on the arrival of Anderson. However he did report the matter to Governor Grant who, though he approved of Anderson, his paper and his politics, took no further interest in what had happened.

Though incidents such as this were unfortunate in that they kept the colony divided into opposing factions, they still afforded some entertainment. E. L. Joseph, the author of *The History of Trinidad,* used this and other incidents in his musical farce " Martial Law in Trinidad ", which he produced later in the year on the stage at Orange Grove, near the site of the present Colonial Hospital.

Early in 1833, it became known that Sir Lewis Grant would soon be leaving the colony and that His Excellency Sir George Fitzgerald Hill, lately Lieutenant-Governor of St. Vincent, would succeed him. Hill arrived on board H.M.S. *Despatch* on April 14th, but did not assume office until the 22nd, when Governor Grant departed.

CHAPTER THIRTEEN

LT.-GOVERNOR SIR GEORGE FITZGERALD HILL,
1833-39

(1) Initial Problems

The New Governor was an Irishman, who was married to a daughter of the well known Irish family of Beresford. He had at one time been the member for Derry in Grattan's Parliament and had held the office of Clerk to the Irish House of Commons. In April, 1833, he assumed duties as Lieutenant-Governor of Trinidad instead of Governor. There appears to be no explanation for this change of title. All his predecessors were Governors, and no alterations were made to the procedure by which he governed or to the instructions which he received direct from the Secretary of State for the Colonies in London.

On the day he was sworn in Governor Hill's troubles began. He was handed a Militia Order dated April 20th, describing the incident which had taken place amongst the officers of the Artillery Regiment the previous February. He was surprised to find that no action had been taken and that nothing had been said to him by Governor Grant during the week in which they had been in the island together. Hill regarded the Militia as the backbone of the colony's defence and the standby in all cases where there was a breach of law and order (he had been a Colonel in the Londonderry Militia himself) and depended upon the Artillery Regiment to be an example of good discipline to the rest of the corps. Action had to be taken. Whilst considering the best way to handle the situation, Captain Anderson called upon him to complain of the behaviour of his brother officers. The Governor sent him away with an instruction to submit all complaints in writing.

Through the Deputy Adjutant General he then received a letter from Colonel Nielson, enclosing documents excusing the behaviour of his officers and asking for a military enquiry into the conduct of Captain Anderson.

In a quandary, Hill found it difficult to arrive at a satisfac-

181

tory conclusion. To hold a military enquiry, which was his instinctive wish, would be to reopen the controversy. He contented himself with expressing his displeasure with Colonel Nielson for failing to take the necessary disciplinary action against his officers for behaving in a manner unsuited to the discipline of the Militia. It was obvious that politics were mixed up with the running of the Corps and that Anderson as editor of the *Royal Gazette* was engaged in matters which might lead to further trouble in his regiment, so to settle the matter once and for all, Hill appointed Anderson to the staff of the Deputy Adjutant-General and left his reproof of Colonel Nielson on record.

Another immediate problem was the attitude of the general public towards the Chief Justice, George Scotland. He was thoroughly unpopular in the colony after the way in which he had handled the cases of the Barbadian slaves. Politically he was known to favour the abolitionists and was also accused of avarice and of nepotism. He had indeed broken the old Spanish laws when he appointed his son as Escribano (Clerk) of the Supreme Court, for the law forbade the appointment of any relatives of judges holding office and had fixed a minimum age for officers. Young George Scotland was not only the judge's son but was also under age for his post.

The *Port of Spain Gazette*, owned by Mr. Drinan, edited by Mr. Stewart and published by James Mills, had already fallen foul of the Chief Justice; because of its articles and letters, it had been stopped from advertising the court notices but now its attacks earned two writs for libel. These cases were to be heard before Mr. Wylie, the Acting Attorney-General, who was known to hold the same political views as the Chief Justice, and there was much ill-feeling and scepticism. Fortunately Mr. Rothery, the newly appointed Attorney-General, arrived in time to act as judge.

On the morning of the trial the court was packed but it was found necessary to postpone the hearing as the Court House had been entered overnight and a safe containing £200 in gold, as well as the relevant papers, had been carried off. The Governor, the Attorney-General and the Chief of Police, started an investigation in the middle of which Father Patrick Smith,* parish priest of Port of Spain, entered with the missing £200. Though pressed by the Governor for information, he refused to divulge names, saying that all he knew was under seal of the confessional.

* See p. 225.

Many years later, after the deaths of the perpetrators, the details of the episode were made known to the public; all taking part were friends of the accused and sworn enemies of Chief Justice Scotland. In an effort to annoy him and to help their friends, they had broken into the Court House, which was comparatively easy as it was only an old wooden building, and had removed the safe to Shine's pasture outside the town. On opening the safe they were horrified to discover that they had not only the papers but also £200 in gold. The papers they had burned, and acting on the advice of a friend, had sought the good offices of Father Smith in the return of the money.

The stealing of the papers caused some delay but, as they were only copies, the trial took place later and the defendants lost their case. The costs amounted to £1,200 currency which they were unable to pay. As individuals they were all sold up but even then there was still a deficiency and Stewart and Mills were thrown into gaol. For a time the editorials of the *Port of Spain Gazette* were dated from No. 1 Clarence Street, where the gaol was then situated.

Chief Justice Scotland had won a paltry victory which did nothing to improve relations between him and the inhabitants of the island.

(2) *Emancipation*—1834

On July 18th, 1834, the Committee of Inhabitants in Trinidad wrote through its Chairman, Edward Jackson, to the Governor. They wished to know as soon as possible what measures His Majesty's Ministers were proposing for carrying out the Secretary of State's resolutions concerning the emancipation of the slaves. The English newspapers led them to believe that great importance was attached to the co-operation of the colonial planters, considered essential to the smooth working of the scheme, and they, as planters, wondered what was expected of them.

Jackson pointed out that a general meeting of the inhabitants, which included all the principal merchants and planters in the colony, had been convened for eleven o'clock the following morning. He stated that he would consider it a favour if he could "without impropriety or inconvenience" be given information which he could pass on to his Committee at the meeting.

Governor Hill answered the letter immediately :

"Assure yourself and those gentlemen on whose part you have made this application, that I will always respectfully receive and candidly reply to their communications on the concerns of this important and interesting Colony. In the present instance I do not possess the means of giving the information to the extent required.

I commence however, by directing your attention to an authentic copy (enclosed) of the Resolutions which have been passed by the House of Commons.

In reply to your second query—the nature of the co-operation required, and the terms on which it is expected—I have to announce His Majesty's confident hope that his faithful subjects of Trinidad will now approach this question with the dispassionate seriousness due to the immense interests at stake; that they will deliberately estimate the progress and present state of public opinion as bearing on this subject, and as regarding the extinction of slavery as inevitable; and that therefore they will unite in the zealous prosecution of this great design to a successful issue. They can most usefully by conciliatory explanations to the slaves prepare their minds for the intended change, and can exert themselves by friendly means to dispel any illusions under which the Negroes may be found to labour, as to what is to be the real nature of their own condition. Like all the rest of His Majesty's subjects, they will be required to earn, and must earn, the food they are to eat, by industry, and entitle themselves to protection by sub-ordination to the laws.

On your question of the terms on which co-operation is expected from the Colonial proprietors, supposing it to refer to the grant of money, I refer you to the 4th resolution; and I have to state that it is proposed for the distribution of it, that a Body shall be constituted, armed with judicial powers for adjusting the claims between the different Colonies and between the different proprietors in the same Colony, to a participation of it.

I have thus endeavoured, as far as my communications enable me, to impart to you all the information you have asked for, and

have the honour to be,

Sir,

Your obedient and humble servant,

G. F. Hill.

This letter gave no new information to the Committee, but aggrieved the meeting by suggesting that its members should assist in maintaining law and order, as in their opinion any breaches of the peace which took place would be entirely due to the anti-slavery policy of the Government.

The day of emancipation was fast approaching, but it was to be by stages that full freedom was to be gained. The slaves understood that on the great day they would receive their freedom and had made it clear that after midnight on July 31st, they would do no more work for their masters. Orders in Council, Ordinances and Proclamations, which had been published for their benefit were explained to them but were laughed at or rejected. The apprenticeship scheme by which complete freedom was withheld for a matter of six years did not appeal to them. They could not see that the enforced delay of six years in the case of field workers and four years for domestics could be of any advantage to them. They had made up their minds to reject the scheme and were convinced that the King had given them their freedom and that their masters and the Government had invented the scheme to trick them out of their rights. They claimed that the masters were " dam tief " and the Governor " old rogue " and that the King was not such a fool as to buy them half free when he could well afford their complete freedom.

Under the scheme slaves were to continue to work for their masters as apprentices. Though hours of labour were strictly limited, corporal punishment could be inflicted for failure to do the necessary amount of work. Masters were compelled to supply food and clothing to their apprentices and to grant freedom at once to all children under six years of age for whose moral and religious instruction arrangements were to be made. To prevent the Act being abused, the planter magistrates were replaced by stipendiary magistrates from England, who were obliged to submit regular reports on the progress of their districts.

A sum of £20,000,000 was voted as compensation to slave owners.* All claims to this sum were to be adjusted locally by a judicial body.

The apprentice system was dispensed with entirely in some colonies as it soon became clear that its practical application was very far from easy.

The Special Justices who were to arrive from England to oversee the carrying out of the provisions of the Abolition Act were late in arriving. Governor Hill was forced to make alternative arrangements. He divided the island into nine districts and appointed the most respectable inhabitant in each area as Superintendent Special Justice, with a large number of Special Justices under him. The numbers were kept high, ninety-two in all, so that nobody would have to give too much time to the task. Instructions were sent to all Superintendents, to Special Justices,

* £1,039,119 was allocated to Trinidad.

and to the Commandants of Quarters. As a precaution, Hill decided to have the Militia on duty as a special guard in Port of Spain on August 1st. Members of the Royal and Loyal Regiment volunteered in sufficient numbers and were ordered to be at their posts by 6.00 p.m. on July 31st. Colonel Hardy in command of the regular troops at St. James's Barracks was kept informed of all military dispositions and movements.

Friday, August 1st, 1834, morally the greatest day in the history of the British West Indies, dawned and 850,000 slaves legally became free men.

From the surrounding country hundreds of the new free swarmed into Port of Spain and crowds gathered round the Government offices long before the Governor and officials arrived. The two Special Justices sent from England, Captains Hay and McKenzie, arrived just in time to see that all was done according to the plans of the Home Government. They, with the Governor, explained the new conditions carefully; that obedience was still due to masters and that there were serious penalties for riotous behaviour. The crowd took no notice of what was said and became abusive and defiant. More and more people were packing the town and with every fresh arrival the mob became more rowdy and abusive. As a safety measure the Governor called out the Militia, and in a very short time, the Town Corps turned out to a man. Colonel Hardy was asked to send a company of regulars from the 19th Regiment to ease what looked like becoming an ugly situation, but to Hill's annoyance, he supplied only 30 extra men. Throughout the day the crowds continued to grow and it became obvious that they had no intention of returning to their estates. In the evening when Hill returned to Government House, he was met with abuse on all sides and it was not until after dark that the Negroes showed any disposition to leave town. The Militia, Cavalry, Artillery and Infantry patrolled the streets all night as a precaution against any sudden outbreak of vandalism.

Saturday saw even larger crowds, more defiant than before, and when Hill tried to persuade them to return home, he was laughed at and hooted for his pains. When he toured the Militia pickets, he was accompanied by a shouting mob behaving in the most outrageous manner. At this moment when it looked as though the crowd might get entirely out of hand, Colonel Hardy withdrew his extra guard and left the work of keeping order to the Militia whilst the regulars were at liberty to wander round the town.

Several arrests had to be made owing to bad behaviour and in the afternoon the special Magistrates sat to try the prisoners. Seventeen of the ringleaders were condemned to stripes and hard labour. At 5 o'clock they were sent to gaol under a Cavalry escort. It was hoped that this might impress upon the mob that stern measures would be taken, but it only excited them the more. A great crowd followed the escort, swearing that they would all rather die than go working for their masters again.

From a platform outside the Government offices, Captain Hay read the clause from the Order in Council, declaring that an assembly of more than three apprentices was a riot if it continued for more than ten minutes after notice had been given and a flag displayed. This warning was read out both in English and French and the flag of the Loyal Battalion of the Militia displayed. No notice was taken by the crowd and after twenty minutes the order was given to the Cavalry and two Picket Guards of Infantry to clear the streets. The charge was made under the supervision of the Special Magistrates and the mob fled.

The inhabitants of Port of Spain were thoroughly alarmed by the position in which they found themselves and urgently requested the Governor to declare a state of martial law, as they had no confidence in the workings of the Council. Two days of continual deliberation had not removed the mob and there was a rumour that the Negroes from the outlying parts of the island were assembling for a march on the capital. The Government was in a position of complete embarrassment, for the Negroes, though provocative and clamorous, had kept within the law in so far as not one had been found armed with a cutlass or even a " beau-stick ". There had been no reports of drunkenness, robbery or personal violence.

On Sunday the Special Magistrates, the public officers and the leading citizens of all classes once more petitioned the Governor to declare martial law, but without result. On Monday morning the magistrates tried and sentenced some sixty prisoners, thirty to be publicly flogged and the remainder to hard labour for offences against the Order in Council. Tension reached its height. Colonel Hardy seriously considered calling out his regular troops, and the Militia remained under arms throughout the night preceding the carrying out of the punishment.

At 8.00 a.m. on Tuesday morning, the condemned men underwent their punishment, some at the Royal Gaol and others in

Marine Square. The crowd, which was expected to be very hostile, was neither so large nor so unruly as on previous days and there was no trouble over the infliction of the punishments.

Thanks to the good sense and energy of Captain Burns of the 19th Regiment, who was in command of the regulars and the Militia and was also a Special Justice for the area, the reports of Emancipation Day in the Naparima district were all of peaceful behaviour. Trinidad could say that emancipation became a fact without any real crisis, without recourse to warlike methods and with a minimum of disturbance.

(3) *Immigration*

The British West Indies, particularly Trinidad and British Guiana, adopted a bounty system for immigrant labour. Under this system, captains of visiting vessels received a bounty for each labourer they introduced into the colony, no matter from what country he came. As a result, immigrants arrived in Trinidad from Madeira and the Azores, Malta, France, Germany and the United States, as well as from other West Indian islands of Barbados, Grenada and Antigua. This system was not really successful as often the immigrants were not of the type most needed and there were opportunities for fraud, many of the immigrants being introduced several times. Though the plan was costly, there were comparatively few immigrants compared with the numbers needed.

Governor Hill, in a despatch of July 20th, 1834, reported to London the arrival of the British schooner *Watchful* from Fayal in the Azores, with forty-four men on board engaged as indentured labourers on the land for three years at $6.00 per month. Planters regarded them as a valuable acquisition and wanted more, and he asked the Colonial Office if there were any objections to continuing immigration on these lines.

His despatch crossed one from London asking for his views on European immigrants in Trinidad and he wrote in November explaining the position. A further party of twenty-nine men, seven women and ten children had already arrived and on September 30th another thirty-two men, eight women and three children had reached the colony. Mr. Seale, an English merchant in Fayal, was responsible for arrangements with the planters and was prepared to send a party of 100 persons. Hill suggested that it ought to be possible to introduce an equal number of males and females and thus ensure the growth of a white, rather than a black, population in the colony.

188

Low wages in the Azores were creating the desire for the people to emigrate and Hill hoped that their coming would bring down local wages. These stood at 2s. 6d. sterling for three days, enough to keep a Negro for fifteen, and this, it was found, did not encourage work. Hill was not sure how the additional inter-mixture of population would affect society but thought it would necessitate some changes in legislation. So far the Portuguese had not been really tested by the climate and it remained to be seen how they would react to tropical conditions. The first party to arrive had been put to work on an estate at Las Cuevas and many had died.

The following year two petitions were addressed to the Governor by the Portuguese.

The first stated that the petitioners were subjects of the Crown of Portugal who had been in the colony for ten months. They and many others had been induced to come to Trinidad by "evil disposed persons" under false pretences. They had left their native country of Fayal to become agricultural labourers in Trinidad. Only one-third of those who came were still alive, the others "having fallen victims to the unhealthiness of the climate, or to the cruelties of the system of slavery to which we, with the unfortunate blacks, have been submitted." The con-solation of their religion had been denied to the sick and dying and the dead had no Christian burial. They prayed His Ex-cellency to " collect the few Portuguese labourers yet in existence in the colony and that you will humanely relieve their immediate and pressing necessities, particularly those of the poor and help-less orphans, and that you will cause them to be transported back to their own country."

The second petition was from Josef da Costa, who stated that he had sailed from Fayal on October 31st, 1834, and had, with twenty-seven others, landed clandestinely on the north coast of Trinidad before reporting to the Customs. At the place of their disembarkation there were already nine of their countrymen, four of whom had since died without medical or spiritual attention. He had moved to the estate of Mr. Graham at Chaguanas, where he and others worked for two months in the fields with the Negroes. Many fell sick, including da Costa and his wife, but through the kindness of Mr. Graham, they were taken to the Marie Ursula's Hospital in the capital, where his wife had died. He then worked for a Mr. Lock, who treated him so badly that he left the estate and came to town, where he was starving and in great misery, and he prayed that his case might be looked into.

The Portuguese experiment had not succeeded as Hill had hoped and the colony was still unable to solve its labour problem.

Other free immigrants at this time were African subjects who were found aboard ships engaged in the slave trade off the Guinea coast and were confiscated by the British Navy, which was maintaining costly patrols in the area. Some of these men joined the coloured troops under the British flag whilst others were sent to the different colonies as free labourers.

By the end of 1838, Hill reported to London on the labour shortage. Immigrants were badly needed and planters were offering three bits* a day as pay with salt fish, a house, provision grounds and medical attention in an effort to get enough hands to bring in the sugar crop.

The Council in November passed the following resolution, which was to apply to those coming to Trinidad from the other West Indian islands, the British Possessions in North America, but not to those coming from Africa :

1st. That in the opinion of the Board of this Colony the quantity of labour available for the purpose of raising and manufacturing the staple articles of produce is not sufficient to maintain the cultivation already established and to give employment to the fixed capital already invested in buildings and machinery and that therefore unless effective measures are immediately adopted and promptly executed, a large amount of existing capital will be lost and the prosperity of the Colony materially and permanently injured.

2nd. That it is therefore necessary and expedient to provide at public expense such means of giving facility to immigration as may secure to the Colony a sufficient number of labourers accustomed to agriculture and inured to labour in a tropical climate.

3rd. That for this purpose His Excellency the Lt.-Governor be requested and authorized to establish, in such places as he may think fit, proper persons as Agents for the purpose of facilitating the immigration of agricultural labourers to this Colony and to grant all such Agents an allowance in lieu of salary, twelve shillings sterling for each effective field labourer of good character as may be sent by them to this Colony and that such Agents be authorized to make arrangements and contracts for the passage of such emigrants to this Colony at reasonable

* Three bits—30 cents or 3 shillings.

rates to be defrayed in conjunction with the Agents' allowance at public expense on their arrival.

4th. That an Immigration Office be established in this Colony under the charge of an Officer to be appointed by His Excellency the Lt.-Governor and it shall be the duty of such officers to receive all such immigrants on their arrival to provide for their immediate subsistence and comfort and for their location under such rules and regulations as may be established by the Governor in Council for that purpose provided that no such regulations shall in any manner affect the free choice of such immigrants as to the person by whom and the places where they are to be employed nor in any manner restrain them from hiring their services to the best advantage.

5th. That an Ordinance be forthwith prepared for the purpose of carrying the measures recommended in these resolutions into immediate operation and that His Excellency be requested to instruct the Attorney-General to introduce such Ordinance.

The Ordinance was prepared later in the month (November, 1838), introduced by Edward Jackson, the Acting Attorney-General and was passed by the Council. By it the immigrant was guaranteed free passage and free choice of where he would work. It was hoped that if labourers would immigrate and the labour already in the colony would remain static on the sugar estates, there would be an increase in the quantity of sugar produced and a consequent rise in revenue. Hill doubted this, as he realized that the Negroes were still suspicious of their former masters and preferred to move about the island from one estate to another. As two days' pay was sufficient to keep a Negro for a week, they were encouraged in what he called " their natural disposition to sloth and repose." He hoped that the competition of immigrant labour would eventually cure this habit in the Negro workers.

The Council accepted the idea of a bounty for all female immigrants in the hopes that they might induce families to stay in the colony and thus increase the labour force for forthcoming generations. They also insisted that Negroes and immigrants alike should have complete freedom of movement, even if it meant leaving the island for, unless this was granted, the Negro would still feel that he had not yet attained his freedom and would remain a hostile and unwilling worker.

Governor Hill ended his report to the Secretary of State on immigration :

191

". . . with respect to the admissibility of charging the expenses to the Public Treasury, it seems justified by the provision of the law that the Immigrant arrives here unfettered by restriction, therefore private individuals could not be expected to incur the expense of bringing agricultural labourers into the Colony, who might after arrival refuse to be employed for those who had supplied their maintenance and passage money."

(4) *Apprenticeship*

On the anniversary of the Emancipation in 1835, many of the inhabitants feared that there would be a repetition of the behaviour of the previous year but the day passed uneventfully and the *Port of Spain Gazette* reported :

" The first year of absolute freedom, of civil equality in the eyes of the law for all classes of the population has just passed away—the great measure of Emancipation has had a year's trial, and whatever may have been its results elsewhere, truth compels us to state that Trinidad has less reason to complain of the working of the new system of free labour than many of the neighbouring colonies. This we say advisedly and without hesitation. The natural fertility of our soil, and the very favourable weather for manufacturing sugar during the whole of the last crop, partly accounted for this; but much of it, no doubt, is to be attributed to the improved and improving habits of the labouring population. Occasional complaints there have been, however, of the conduct of the labourers— of their unsteadiness—their disregard of engagements—their roving habits—their propensity for intoxication—and these complaints were well merited, it cannot be denied—in many instances, but after all, looking at the results, we think that the condition of the island and its future prospects may be contemplated without fear or dismay. Contrasted with other Colonies, there is room rather for congratulation and satisfaction. We look forward, too, with some confidence, to more settled habits on the part of the labourers, for as they advance in the paths of civilization, the more will they become acquainted with duties and obligations, and be sensible that it is by sober and steady habits alone that they can improve their condition and render themselves comfortable if not independent. The great truth that it is by labour alone—continuous and unremitting labour—that the great majority of mankind obtain the means of subsistence, will surely, though perhaps slowly, make itself felt by the most dissipated and improvident amongst them. The old notion that freedom meant merely a cessation from labour, generally maintained as we believe it was by those upon whom the first year of freedom has just closed, is, we have heard, obliterated from their minds forever . . .

The employers too, we hope, have not been idle spectators of the progress of events during the period we have named; have not been heedless witnesses of the cause that may have retarded or assisted their manufacturing operations. Their conduct, so far as we are acquainted with it, has been generally entitled to great praise, for it requires no ordinary discretion to descend becomingly from superiority to equality—the superiority of the free man to the slave, or, what is little better, the apprentice.

The great majority of the labourers are well disposed and industrious, and these we think should be encouraged by every means within the power of the proprietors. One of these means would be found in the simple plan of renting to them their houses and grounds at a fair valuation. This would ensure from them more regular attention to their duties and would moreover act as a check on the dissolute and idle vagabonds who, to the great annoyance of the peaceable and honest, infest almost every estate in the Colony."

These hopes were never fully realized, but the article demonstrates that there was reason to expect that with good management and forbearance the labourers might work as free men where they had previously worked as slaves. One of the prime causes of the failure of the new system was the fact that the labourers did not wish to work, but this was not the only cause of trouble to the planters during the years following Emancipation. In 1836 a circular was sent to all Governors of colonies by the Secretary of State:

" Sir,
The accounts which I have received from time to time of the conduct and industry of the apprentices appear to prove that cultivation may be possibly carried on in the West Indies as long as apprenticeship lasts, and afford much encouragement to hope that full and complete emancipation will be attended with beneficial results both to the employers and to the labouring population.

It must not be forgotten that the conditions under which society has hitherto existed will, on the expiration of the apprenticeship, undergo an essential change. During slavery, labour could be compelled to go wherever it promised most profit to the employer; under the new system it will find its way wherever it promises most profit to the labourer. If, therefore, we are to keep up the cultivation of the staple productions, we must make it the immediate and apparent interest of the Negro population to employ their labour in raising them.

There is reason to apprehend that at the termination of apprenticeship this will not be the case. Where there is land enough to yield an abundant subsistence to the whole population in return for slight labour, they will probably have no sufficient inducement to prefer the more toilsome existence of a regular labourer, whatsoever may be its remote advantages, or even its immediate gains. Should things be left to their natural course, labour would not be attracted to the cultivation of exportable produce . . . The depreciation which would take place in property, and the rude state into which society would fall back in the meantime make it desirable to adopt measures to check this apparently natural course.

How far it may be possible to check it effectually, it is not easy to determine. But by diminishing the facilities for obtaining land, it may certainly be impeded . . . It is of great importance in the meantime that the evil should not be aggravated by the inconsiderate neglect, or incautious distribution of those lands which are at the disposal of the Crown.

In order to prevent this, it will be necessary to prevent the occupation of any Crown lands by persons not possessing a proprietary title to them; and to fix such a price upon all Crown lands as may place them out of the reach of persons without capital . . .

In new countries, where the whole unoccupied territory belongs to the Crown, and settlers are continually flowing in, it is possible, by fixing the price of fresh land so high as to place it above the reach of the poorest class of settlers, to keep the labour market in the most prosperous state from the beginning . . .

This policy has of late years been pursued with very good results in our North American and Australian Colonies; and there is no doubt that it may be applied with advantage in the West Indies also . . . I have therefore to request that you will take the matter into your earliest consideration, and then submit to me in detail the arrangements which you may recommend as best calculated to carry the views of His Majesty's Government into effect in the Colony under your care.

One general regulation, however, I am prepared immediately to enforce—that in future no Crown land shall be disposed of to private individuals otherwise than by public sale, a minimum price being fixed . . .

The object is not to force the cultivation of the present staples by depriving the Negroes of every other source of subsistence; but merely to condense and keep together the population in such a manner that it may always contain a due proportion of labourers. When that is the case the most profitable produce will always afford the highest wages, and the highest wages will always draw the largest supply of labour. The minimum price of land therefore should be high enough to leave a considerable portion of the population unable to buy it until they have saved some capital out of the wages of their industry; and at the same time low enough to encourage such savings by making the possession of land a reasonable object of ambition to all . . .

In many cases serious difficulties will occur in securing unsold lands for the future from the intrusion of usurpers and squatters. You will not omit to notice the nature and extent of these difficulties in the Colony under your care, and the measures by which they may be most conveniently overcome.

I have further to request that your communication on this subject may be accompanied by the best information which you can obtain as to the extent and value of the Crown lands under your Government, and the proportion of them which is already occupied by persons without legal title.

I have the honour to be, Sir,
Your most obedient servant,
Glenelg."

Governor Hill did nothing to help the Home Government in overcoming the difficulties with which they were faced. He sent no information as requested, but in October, 1838, an Order was issued making "squatting"* a punishable offence. The Order was not effective for it contained a clause limiting the authority of magistrates to cases where the squatter had been in possession for less than a year. For many years the Commandants of Quarters had by custom given written permits for free peoples to occupy pieces of Crown land. They were loosely worded documents containing no clause as to limits of occupation. The holders of these permits considered themselves entitled to any section of Crown land they liked and frequently cleared a site of valuable timber before moving on to another patch and doing the same again. No surveys were made of these holdings and it was impossible for the magistrates to discover who were squatters and who were not. If there had been undisturbed possession, though unauthorized, for more than a year, the magistrate had no jurisdiction and an action for ejectment could only be brought in the Supreme Court, a lengthy and expensive process. The Order became a dead letter and squatting on Crown lands continued

* Occupation of lands by persons with no proprietary rights to them.

195

unabated.* Many squatters, though breaking the law, were leading busy lives and developing good estates and in some cases even paying land taxes. As squatters they were liable to ejection and it was not for many years that their position was made secure, when it was decided that " owners " who had cleared lands and brought them under cultivation should be able to obtain legalized possession.

Lord Glenelg's reference to the success of the apprenticeship scheme was a little premature for it soon proved to be almost unworkable. It was little better than the slavery which the Negroes had suffered before and the British Government passed a resolution to end the scheme in 1838. The colonial Legislatures, without any external pressure, reduced the period of apprenticeship to two years, some abolishing it altogether. Antigua and Bermuda had both rejected it. In Trinidad the planters were at first reluctant to do this and in June, 1838, the Council, after three meetings, issued a Proclamation securing for apprentices :

One day a week for themselves—a Saturday, so that they could attend market.

Limitation of daily labour to nine hours between 6 a.m. and 7 p.m., with time allowed for meals.

The continuation of all privileges, indulgences and allowances which had been established by law or custom for three years before the Abolition Act.

An hour a day for mothers to suckle children under twelve months.

A reduction of working hours for mothers of more than three children and a grant of one dollar a year for each child.

Governor Hill felt that apprenticeship should be abolished as soon as possible and on July 25th he asked Dr. Jean Baptiste Phillipe,† the first coloured member of the Council, to propose a resolution to that effect. The motion was seconded by Charles Warner, cousin of the Acting Colonial Secretary, and was passed with little opposition. The Rules of Procedure were suspended and the Ordinance went through all its stages in a single day so that the public could be informed that it would come into force on August 1st.

Emancipation, which had theoretically been granted to the slaves in 1834, became a reality in 1838.

The abolition of the apprenticeship system made it imperative

* See p. 219.

† Author of *The Free Mulatto*, an address to Lord Bathurst on the claim of the coloured population, 1824, reprinted in Trinidad by Allen & Blondel, 1882. See also Appendix XXV.

that there should be a change in the magistracy so that those who had achieved their freedom should be enabled to forget the old days as soon as possible. If they were to be dealt with by persons who had previously handled their cases in court, they would always be suspicious. The new magistrates, it was considered, should all be able to speak French, as eight of the previously appointed officials had had to use their police sergeants as interpreters.

Hill, in his report to the Secretary of State, enclosed copies of other Ordinances passed, including one to regulate the duties between masters and servants. This gave power to either party to end agreements entered into by one month's notice, it being felt that long contracts were not advisable. He ended his despatch :

> " Already considerable progress has been made on many of the Sugar Estates in settling terms on which Labourers have actually commenced work; the wages generally are eight dollars per month and three pounds and a half of salt fish per week, with house and cultivatable ground.
>
> The labourers have left some of the estates and proposed to work on others; this has occurred where as apprentices they had experienced harsh treatment.
>
> On a few estates where the Proprietor had published an offer of twelve dollars a month to Negroes from Grenada and St. Vincent, his labourers refuse to work for him for less. This cannot last and I contemplate with great satisfaction the obvious conviction of the labourer that he must earn his bread. If the measure of Abrogation had not been carried, confusion and disorder would have ensued to an extent that might have ended and I think would have ended in very serious violence against which, however, I was prepared, but thank Providence the affair has ended otherwise.
>
> My attention and more active efforts towards the improvement of Trinidad may now be employed."

(5) *Mutiny at St. Joseph*

The mortality rate in British forces stationed in the West Indies was so high that during the eighteenth and nineteenth centuries the Home Government raised a number of Negro regiments for this service. In 1795 Governors were instructed to lay before their Legislatures a proposal to raise five such regiments of five hundred men each under white officers, as well as to arrange to keep the local Militia in good order.

During the American War of Independence, a number of slaves had been formed into the " Carolina Corps " who, in

197

return for their loyalty, were sent to Jamaica to settle on the land. The Jamaican Government objected strongly to having in the colony large numbers of free Negroes, all of whom were ex-soldiers, and who had been fighting successfully against their previous masters. This objection was maintained by all the other British islands and the Home Government was forced to keep them in the Army and send them in 1783 to Grenada under the Leeward Islands command, where they formed "The Black Corps of Dragoons, Pioneers and Artificers" and later distinguished themselves in expeditions against Martinique, St. Lucia and Guadeloupe.

A further Negro regiment, "Malcolm's Rangers", was raised in 1795, but was eventually combined with the "Black Corps of Dragoons" or "Carolina Corps" to form Major General Whyte's "Regiment of Foot", later known as the 1st West India Regiment. This regiment won battle honours at Guadeloupe and Martinique and earned a great name at New Orleans, Honduras, Sierra Leone and Ashanti. It continued in being until 1925, wearing until the last the Zouave uniform especially requested by Queen Victoria.*

In 1837 a detachment of the regiment was stationed at St. Joseph and amongst its recruits was Daaga, an African Chief, who was a giant, standing six feet six inches without shoes. As the adopted son of the childless king of an African tribe, he had often made war in his own country against the Yorubas, selling his prisoners to the slave traders who brought many of them to Trinidad. He himself was captured by the traders after being tricked aboard one of their vessels and had been shipped in chains to Brazil. During the journey the slaver was captured by a patrolling British cruiser and Daaga was taken to Sierra Leone. Here, with other able-bodied men, he was drafted into the West India Regiment and sent to Trinidad, where he was baptized into the Christian faith and given the name of Donald Stewart. This stalwart and ill-favoured giant was unable to distinguish between the Portuguese who had captured him and the British who had saved him from slavery; he had been tricked of his heritage and his chieftainship and he wanted revenge.

At the full moon in June, 1837, he led a mutiny of some 280 recruits. Shouting their war cries, they set fire to the barracks, seized arms and tried to overwhelm the garrison, their intention being to overcome all opposition and then to march back to Guinea. Their geography was as faulty as their competence with

* The Jamaica Military Band still wear this uniform.

firearms and the mutineers were soon overwhelmed, captured and court-martialled. Daaga or Donald Stewart and two of his followers were shot.

(6) *Communications*

Spain had never been in very close contact with her colony. At times only once in every twenty years did a ship pass between Trinidad and the Mother Country. It was not until after the capitulation that anything like a regular service of packet boats connected the island with her new owners. This, like all sailing ship services, was unreliable owing to the vagaries of the weather. In 1837 a regular fortnightly steamer service between Trinidad and Falmouth was opened.

(7) *Financial Trickery*

Soon after the St. Joseph mutiny, the inhabitants of the colony were disturbed by news of defalcation by the Colonial Treasurer, Major Ford. As there were no banks it was the custom to allow merchants to use any surplus funds from the Treasury for trading purposes. Due notice was usually given before the inspection of the Treasury vaults so that Ford always had time to replace any sums that had been borrowed. In 1836, a Government Committee arrived to make their inspection without giving the usual notice and Ford was caught with the vault nearly empty. Being a resourceful man, he set the Committee to work counting and checking £1,500 of silver threepenny and three-halfpenny pieces whilst he rapidly rounded up his friends and hauled baskets of doubloons* through the back window to make up his deficiency.

This narrow escape from detection did not seem to worry Ford. The next day he had money out on loan and was doing a little speculation of his own. Suspicion must have been aroused in official circles for another inspection was made and Ford could not replace the money in time. A serious deficit was discovered with the result that Ford lost his position and was imprisoned as a debtor to the Crown. He was released at the end of the year when his sureties paid £4,000 into the Treasury. This did not cover the monies lost but it was realized that as there was no likelihood of any more forthcoming, it served no useful purpose to continue to detain Ford.

This blatant roguery helped focus attention on the confused state of the colony's finances and on the inexplicable disappearance of the accumulated Legacy Duty money which had been set

* See Appendix XXIV—Currency.

aside for building a hospital. To appease the public, a committee comprised of John Losh, Charles Warner and B. Parkhurst, offered a prize of £25 sterling for the best plan for a Colonial Hospital. Nothing came of this except the opening of temporary accommodation in the premises of Dr. Cadett in Cambridge Street.

(8) *Education and the Churches*

In 1835 the Home Government made a grant of £25,000 to the Church of England for building school houses in the West Indies. This grant was shared by the Church Missionary Society, the Society for the Propagation of the Gospel, the Society for the Conversion of the Negroes, the London Missionary Society and the British and Foreign Bible Society. To this was added a further sum of £160,000, which had originally been left by Lady Mico in 1666 for the redemption of "poore Christian slaves." The bequest had originally been intended to buy the freedom of slaves captured by the Bey of Algiers, but when the Mediterranean had been cleared of pirates, this use had passed out of existence. On Fowell Buxton's suggestion the money was used in conjunction with a Government grant of £17,000 a year for five years and Mico Charity schools were opened in Trinidad,* Demerara, the Bahamas and St. Lucia in 1837. Mico Training Institutes were also opened in Jamaica and Antigua.

In 1836 the religious Order of St. Joseph opened a school for " young ladies ", now St. Joseph's Convent, the first secondary school for girls in the colony. Under the Reverend Mother Marie de la Croix it was opened at the house of Madame La Cadre in St. James Street.

There were only two places of worship in Port of Spain that were not Roman Catholic at this time, the Wesleyan Chapel and Trinity Church, where the Rev. George Cummins was rector and Rural Dean. In 1823 he had succeeded the Rev. J. H. Clapham, who died in 1835, having served the Protestant community since 1797, first as Brigade Chaplain and later as rector.† Cummins was assisted by the Rev. David Evans, who had followed Clapham as Chaplain to the Forces stationed at the barracks, and by a younger curate.

There was an ever-increasing number of Scots in the colony, who felt the need for a Presbyterian form of worship. On August 1st, 1836, they held a meeting under the chairmanship of Mr. Roxburgh and decided :

* Port of Spain and Manzanilla.
† See p. 130.

1. That there being a numerous and respectable body of individuals resident in this Island who profess the form of worship of the Established Church of Scotland, and who contribute largely to the revenues of the Colony, this Meeting is of opinion that they are entitled to claim from Government the same privileges, with regard to the establishment and endowment of places of worship of their persuasion, as are already enjoyed by their brethren of the Church of England and of the Roman Catholic Church.

2. That Presbyterian Churches, in connection with the Established Church of Scotland, having been erected in British Guiana and Grenada, to which ministers have been appointed whose stipends are paid out of the public revenues of these Colonies, there is every reason to hope that the British Government, on proper representation being made, will be induced to sanction the extension of the same advantages to this Colony; more especially at this time of particular crises, when an anxious desire exists on their part to promote the moral and religious instruction of our labouring population.

3. That a wide field exists in Trinidad for the labours of Presbyterian Ministers without interfering with the flocks of either Protestant or Catholic Clergymen already beneficed; as there is only one Protestant Episcopal Church and one Methodist Chapel in the whole Island, which being both situated in Port of Spain, the Protestant inhabitants in the remote country districts are destitute of religious instruction, while several extensive and populous quarters are entirely without places of Christian worship of any denomination whatsoever.

4. This meeting cordially concurs in the sentiments expressed in the first Resolution agreed to by the individuals who assembled on the first instant; viz. : " That it is expedient and highly desirable that an Association be formed for the purpose of furthering the establishment of Presbyterian places of worship in this island "; and that this meeting do form itself into such Association, to be denominated " The Trinidad Presbyterian Association ", and which all persons friendly to its object are invited to join.

5. That Joseph Graham, Esq., be elected President of this Association, Thomas Roxburgh, Esq., Vice-President, William Cross and John Ramsay, Esq., Joint Secretaries and Treasurers; and that Colonel Hamilton, Dr. Anderson, John Lamont, Henry Graham, John Losh, Jas. Taylor, Robert Dennistoun, Alexander M'Alister, Robert Gray, Alexander Gray, Anthony Cumming, Alexander Jack, and David Hutchinson, Esqs., do form, with the Office Bearers,

a Committee of Management, with the power to add to their number; one Office Bearer and two other members to form a quorum.

6. That the Committee be instructed to prepare a Memorial to be presented to the Honourable Board of Council, praying that the stipend of a Presbyterian Minister be included in the estimates for 1834; also a Memorial to the Secretary of State for the Colonies, praying that part of the funds expected to be placed at the disposal of Government, for religious purposes in the West Indian Colonies, may be appropriated to the building and endowment of Presbyterian places of worship in Trinidad; and further, to adopt such measures for furthering the objects of the Association, as to the said Committee may appear from time to time expedient.

7. That a subscription of Twenty Shillings ($2.00), to constitute a fund for defraying incidental expenses, be paid to the Treasurers by each member joining the Association.

The foundation stone of Greyfriars Church was laid on April 10th, 1837, on a site bought from the Cabildo for £300, and on January 21st the following year the Rev. Alexander Kennedy declared the church open for public worship. Kennedy was supported by funds from Greyfriars Church, Glasgow, as well as by his new congregation.

During the interim between the first meeting of the Association and the opening of the church, the old theatre in Cambridge Street was used for worship. This building afterwards was used as a hospital.

(9) *Notes*

Under Ordinance No. 4 of 1835, the Police Force of Port of Spain was re-established in a more effective manner, but this did not mean that the gaol was more efficiently organized. Its condition and that of other prisons in the West Indian colonies was shocking. As the local Legislatures were unwilling to make any alterations and frequent adverse reports were being made by missionaries, the Home Government passed an Act of 1838 for the better government of prisons in the West Indies and removed control of these institutions from the Legislative bodies.

At the end of 1834, Governor Hill reported to the Secretary of State that he had been asked by the Captain of an American vessel for permission to fish for whales in the Gulf of Paria. He stated that whilst he had been unable to refuse permission, he had laid down certain conditions which made it almost impossible for the vessel to carry on a whaling business. These conditions were necessary as the inhabitants of Trinidad had for some years had "profitable employment" from the whales which lived in the gulf waters.

(10) *The Finger of Death*

In 1836, three eminent members of the colony's society died. Each had in his way much to do with the creation of Trinidad and its fundamental shaping.

Gaudin de Hervy de Soter, though never very prominent in political matters, was the son of the Royalist leader, Colonel de Soter, who had distinguished himself in the struggle between Royalists and Republicans in Martinique. With his father, he had come to Trinidad as a member of Sir Ralph Abercromby's personal staff and had served well at the time of capitulation. He settled in the island and died on September 30th on his estate, "Frederick" in the Quarter of Caroni.

Mr. Black, a native of County Antrim, had left his native Ireland for Grenada when Lord McCarthy was administering it for the British. There he had risen to the rank of Colonel of the St. George's Militia, and had become a member of the Council by 1777. After the capture of the island in 1784 he had migrated to Trinidad and had played a prominent part in the affairs of State during the time of the administration by the Commission. He was eighty-three years of age at the time of his death.

The third death of 1836 was that of Lady Hill, wife of the Governor, which occurred at Government House on November 2nd. At her own request she was buried in the grounds of Government House.

In January, 1839, the Attorney-General, Mr. Rothery, passed away. The Governor nominated the Solicitor-General, Edward Jackson, to act until the wishes of Government could be ascertained, and Charles Warner was made acting Solicitor-General. Warner was the son of Colonel Edward Warner, owner of the Woodford Dale Estate at Savanna Grande, a direct descendant of Sir Thomas Warner who, in 1626, had founded the British settlement in St. Kitts.

On March 8th of the same year, after a short illness, Sir George Fitzgerald Hill, Lt.-Governor of Trinidad, died at Government House at the age of seventy-seven, the first Governor to die in the colony. He was buried in the grounds of Government House at St. Ann's beside Lady Hill.

Though Sir George Hill's administration had been severely

criticized by many of the inhabitants of the island, he was acknowledged to work with the best of intentions and no one ever doubted his integrity. He had been impartial and honest. Feeling in the colony at the time of his arrival had been very confused, and he had had the task of handling the emancipation of slaves and the abolition of the apprenticeship scheme, both of which he had dealt with tactfully. He was easy of access to all and had the reputation of having more real friends in the colony than any previous Governor.

CHAPTER FOURTEEN

COLONEL SIR HENRY MACLEOD, 1840–46

(1) *The Governorship*

ON MARCH 9th, 1839, the day following the funeral of
Governor Hill, Colonel John Alexander Mein, of the 74th Regiment, was sworn in as Acting Lt.-Governor of Trinidad.

A despatch dated May 20th from London announced that Sir
Evan Murray MacGregor of Barbados had been appointed
Governor-General of all the British West Indian Colonies to the
south of the 14th latitude north. The Lt.-Governors of Trinidad,
British Guiana and St. Lucia, continued to correspond with
and to receive instructions directly from the Secretary of State
as they had done in the days of the full Governors. The new
Governor-General was normally to visit the smaller colonies only
on instruction from the Secretary of State or at the request of
the Lt.-Governors concerned. The position of the Governors of
Trinidad was hardly altered but the despatch started rumours
that there was to be a new form of Government for the colony.

On May 29th, Sir Evan MacGregor arrived in the colony. A
special meeting of the Council was called to receive him and to
be present whilst he took the oath as Governor-General of
Trinidad. He was received with the rites due to his rank, a guard
of honour from the 74th Regiment being in attendance. Sir
Evan's instructions and commissions were read by the Clerk, the
oaths were administered by the Attorney-General, and each
member of the Council was sworn separately. A note of discord
was struck when Mr. Darracot refused to take the oath. He was
immediately suspended and replaced by a nominee of the
Governor-General. Sir Evan then addressed the Council and
took the opportunity of referring to the greatness of Sir Ralph
Woodford and the benefits of his administration.

The new Governor-General left the same evening and Colonel
Mein continued as Acting Lt.-Governor. It never became known
why there had been any change nor what was the purpose of
Sir Evan's visit, for when Sir Henry MacLeod arrived in April,

1840, he was sworn in as Governor and Commander-in-Chief of the Colony.

(2) *Immigration*

(a) *Europeans, Africans and Americans*

At the first meeting of the Council over which Colonel Mein presided, William Burnley raised the question of immigration. " An Ordinance for facilitating the immigration into this Colony of labourers accustomed and inured to labour in a tropical climate " had been passed the previous November, but had proved unsuccessful. Failure was due to its restricting the field of immigrants. The other colonies had no spare labour and their Governments resented the idea of Trinidad trying to entice what labour they had by offering high wages. Burnley suggested that the Ordinance be amended to allow immigrants from Malta, Sierra Leone and free Negroes from the southern states of America.* He had heard that there were slave owners in America who were willing to emancipate their slaves if they were sure that they would find good homes and a chance to better themselves.

A new Ordinance was drawn up on these lines, submitted to London for the Royal Assent, and duly proclaimed on December 24th, 1839.

Meanwhile, Colonel Mein had been in correspondence with Sir Evan MacGregor in Barbados on this subject. In January of 1840 he wrote enclosing a copy of the Ordinance and stating :

> ". . . There is only one modification under which the Immigration Law has thus been put in force upon which, in publishing, I felt called upon to exercise any particular discretion. I allude to the measure enjoined by the Order in Council for providing that an equality of sexes should be as much as possible ensured in our operations under the Immigration Ordinance.
>
> Your Excellency will observe that the restriction which I have in consequence felt bound to prescribe in this matter is that the passage of immigrants under the Ordinance shall be paid for in proportion of five males to four females.
>
> In support of this part of my Proclamation, I have only to give Your Excellency two reasons on which I grounded it.
>
> The first was that the chances and risk of life in this climate, and more particularly amongst the class of labourers whose resort here it is our object to encourage, are greatly against the male.
>
> The second and more important reason is that in Port of

* See Appendix XXVIII.

Spain and its suburbs, there is a population according to the last census, of 6,781 females to 4,912 males; and that in the country the proportion of inhabitants is even greater in favour of the female sex.

Another provision of the Royal Order in Council pronounces it to be expedient that Agents to be appointed under the Immigration Ordinance should be appointed, removed and controlled by the authority of the Executive Government solely.

In accordance with this decision, I beg leave to acquaint Your Excellency that I have appointed Mr. R. T. Buchanan to be Agent in New York, and Mr. Hinto at Philadelphia . . ."

Shortly after his arrival Governor MacLeod wrote to the Secretary of State concerning the condition of the European immigrants into Trinidad, asking for Government support in putting an end to indiscriminate emigration by European peoples.*

Later he explained the major difficulties involved in the introduction of free labour in the colony.

1. Proprietors needed labour to keep up production and to increase production of staple goods by extending cultivation.
2. Introduction of free labour meant that eventually the labourers would look forward to owning their own property.
3. Sugar estates would be too expensive for purchase by these people. They would have to cultivate cacao or other crops on smaller allotments.

His suggestions for overcoming these difficulties were :

1. That Crown property should be divided into allotments of suitable size and granted to individuals on fair terms.
2. Roads in different parts of the island should be opened up as the smallholders would depend on good communications.
3. Scattered settlements should not be allowed and where they already existed should be tactfully removed by granting fresh lands on a commutable quit rent system.
4. Villages of free Negroes from America should be established at intervals along the lines of communication.
5. Owing to there being no laws of naturalization in the colony, the possession of land should be for a stated period and be followed by the full possession of British citizenship.

These suggestions, he felt, would mean a steady flow of the right type of immigrants and thus would overcome the labour shortage and develop the resources of the colony. He ended his despatch by stating that the free Negroes who had recently arrived from America† were a most valuable acquisition. They

* See Appendix XXVI.
† See Appendix XXVIII.

spoke English and would spread the customs and language of the Mother Country, they were industrious, were of correct moral conduct and held strong religious views which would be, he was sure, an example for others to follow.

In May, 1841, MacLeod sent his report on the first immigrants from Sierra Leone under the latest Proclamation :

" I am happy to report that these people arrived in good health, after a passage of twenty-eight days, and I was rejoiced to find them much more advanced in every way than I had expected—all speaking good English and many able to read and write . . .

I have seldom met persons more alive to their own interests, but I have recommended them to hire themselves in bodies of eight or ten—for, besides thus diminishing the feeling of strangers, always more or less felt in a new country, it gives them a sort of mutual protection.

Sixteen of these immigrants are Kroomen, vastly superior in appearance and bearing to the other races. They generally confine their labour to the shipping, but the high wages and other advantages on the estates have tempted even these to take that employment, but I do not look to their remaining at that work, and their return to their usual occupation will be of great value to the shipping ports.

We must not look upon these people as settlers, but, if this Island answers their expectations, they tell me, great numbers of their Countrymen will come. They perfectly understand the facility afforded them of returning to their native country by working their passage via England, and they are all, I believe, expert seamen. We shall thus establish a constant communication with Africa."

By June the Stipendary Magistrates' report showed a general improvement in the state of the colony and the condition and character of the inhabitants. The system of smallholdings was extending, though with some detriment to the labour problems of the sugar estates of the south, but San Fernando was being supplied with its necessary provisions as a result. Schools and churches were being opened in different areas of the colony, the Government bearing half the cost of construction. The sugar crop was good and, with the promise of favourable weather and more satisfactory immigrants, the next year's crop was expected to be better. Internal trade had increased through hucksters and small retail shops; revenue from imports had risen £3,000 in a single year.

The two major complaints against labourers were those of drunkenness and roving. These were confined almost entirely to immigrants from other West Indian islands. To overcome these habits the Governor suggested that money allowances should be made in lieu of a rum ration and that more should be done in the way of establishing villages and renting land, as a local interest could better be created by the tenure of property. The wages paid in 1841 throughout the colony were 2s. 1d. sterling per day, with allowance for house, land, salt, provisions and rum.

Two further Proclamations on the subject of immigration were received from London. One in 1841 stated that one-third of all immigrants must be female. The other in 1842 informed the Governor that in future Her Majesty's Government would control immigration from the west coast of Africa to Jamaica, British Guiana and Trinidad. The s.s. *Senator* (360 tons) had been chartered by the Land and Emigration Commissioners to collect Africans wishing to settle in Trinidad. The estimated expense of £4,726 19s. 0d. was to be refunded by the Trinidad Government to London. An Ordinance, signed by Arthur White, the Colonial Secretary, was at once issued, empowering the Colonial Treasurer to pay the Home Government a sum not exceeding £14,000 per year for the carriage of the immigrants.

William Burnley, as a member of the Council, and Chairman of the newly formed " Immigration and Agricultural Society " and one of the largest landowners in the colony, had his finger on the pulse of the island's economic life. His frequent visits to America, Canada and England kept him in touch with the latest developments amongst emigrants. In 1839 he tried to persuade some of the free Negroes in Nova Scotia and New Brunswick,* who were a charge upon the community, to come to Trinidad. Unfortunately they had lived so long on public charity that they were not interested in the idea of working in the colony.

In America there were some half a million free people of African descent, many at a reasonably high standard of civilization. They felt insecure socially and politically and, being unable to return to Africa, looked to the West Indies for improved living conditions. Burnley was anxious to encourage their movement to Trinidad as he considered their influence on the local free Negroes would be beneficial and their knowledge of cotton and tobacco of great benefit to trade. He also advocated that Africans

* Negroes who had escaped from slavery in the Southern States.

209

liberated from captured slave ships should be sent to the colony rather than disposed of in foreign territories.

Two years later, when in London (No. 6 Bryanston Square), Burnley wrote to the Secretary of State reporting that already over 1,000 free Negroes had emigrated from America and that on the whole the experiment was proving a success. He asked that the regulations fixing the proportion of males to females should be rescinded and left to the discretion of the Governor, that all persons of African descent coming to the colony should be given British citizenship and that the duties on salted provisions from America should be reduced.

There were many difficulties to overcome in bringing free coloured peoples from America. Burnley, writing to his wife, complained that the Colonial Office would only allow passages to be paid in pairs, "which they laugh at here and call the cock and hen system". There were also many Americans who did not approve of so many labourers leaving for Trinidad and spread tales amongst the intending emigrants that they would be fed entirely on monkeys, lizards and parrots.

His chartered vessel, the *William*, arrived in the colony with a full complement of immigrants who were all placed on the Perseverance Estate at Guapo. He brought with him also two young men, Burley and Mayo, who were well versed in tobacco cultivation. He wrote home in February:

> "Emancipation has increased the security of property ultimately but in the meantime one-half of the white people are utterly ignorant how to manage the changed circumstances, so that some properties are doing well, and some wretchedly badly. Perseverance amongst the number; so I must without delay make a change; the same with Mon Plaisir at La Brea."

He was worried about the state of the colony and his opinion of the Governor was:

> "Sir Henry MacLeod is an attentive man of business, and keeps our body (the Council) to their work. But like all British Governors he is infected with jealousy, and we are not likely to be very thick together; in fact, I am considered too great for a subject, but I am unfortunately also independent, so that I shall go my own way without requiring his assistance."

Later he says that he was:

> ". . . on very cool and distant terms with the Governor."

Burnley had been back in the colony for two months and had received no invitation to Government House.

He reports the Solicitor-General, Edward Jackson, as saying that the Chief Justice was not popular :

". . . hated by everybody, and not even on very good terms with himself."

Burnley was also worried about his own estates and their management and decided to replace any of his managers whom he found unreliable. Orange Grove at Tacarigua was in excellent condition, but not his other properties. The Orange Grove estate was of some 2,266 acres and was shared with his manager, Lionel Lee, and valued in 1837 at £20,000, Burnley's share being £15,000. Though prices were rising profits were falling, as his crop results show :

Crop results from 1835–1840.

Crop	Hogsheads of sugar	Price per 100 lbs.	Profit
1835	399	23/1¾	£6,798
1836	354	29/5¼	6,688
1837	276	25/9¾	4,088
1838	332	26/3½	3,313
1839	312	28/9	3,971
1840	300	37/10½	3,433

(b) *The Immigration and Agricultural Society*

Shortly after the death of Governor Hill, a public meeting was held under the chairmanship of Mr. James Lamont to consider the necessity of encouraging immigration. Burnley spoke on the difficulties which faced the colony since " the former slave was now the master and he who was once master was now the slave." Though surrounded by " the elements of superabundance " he feared that the black and white population would fall together unless the labour problems of the colony were put right.

" I will now entreat your attention to a most important subject. Never allow yourselves to countenance anything like vexatious legislation as applied to the labouring classes . . . I believe the labouring classes perfectly able to take care of themselves. There is also another subject on which some gentlemen, I am afraid, may at first be disposed to differ from me—I allude to the acquisition of lands by that class. At the present moment no doubt we cannot afford to lose a single individual labouring for wages, but it is always bad policy to legislate for the moment . . . I will set my face most strenuously against their fraudulent occupation of the Crown lands, or of any land which does not belong to them; but the acquisition of land in fair purchase by the most saving among them would be an ultimate boon to the Colony . . . All that I wish to impress upon you at the present is, not to attempt to throw any obstacles in the way of that which God and Nature seem to have intended, namely to render the Island of Trinidad a little terrestrial Paradise for the African race. When that conviction shall be firmly established in the minds of Africans scattered abroad, I will not exchange an estate in Trinidad for any three in another Colony; and as to the admission of slave-grown sugar into the British market, if it cannot, with a happy and numerous population, beat the slave-owner out of the European market, I have formed a false and mistaken idea of the fertility of the soil of Trinidad."

After further speeches and resolutions, William Burnley was appointed first Chairman of the Immigration and Agricultural Society.

The Society drew up a report on conditions in Trinidad which they forwarded to London for comment and asked for answers to certain questions :

1. Whether the maximum expenditure to be incurred by the Colonial Treasury for immigration should be fixed?
2. Whether encouragement should be given to immigration from places in Africa outside British Dominions?
3. Whether publicity should not be given to the dangers incurred by European immigrants, especially from France and Germany?
4. Whether the law against " squatting " may not require amending?
5. Whether we may not have been doing harm instead of good by the extent to which gratuitous education has been accorded to the children of Negroes and whether, therefore, the gradual reduction of the Education Grant is to be regretted?

James Stephen, commenting on the questions from the Colonial Land and Emigration Office to the Secretary of State, stated that the advocates of slavery had grossly misunderstood and misrepresented the real character of the Negro race and that in spite of a falling off of profits, there was an all round improvement in the material comforts and the moral and intellectual state of the people. Society was on the whole in a healthy and improving state. In fact, the abolition had borne fruit earlier and more abundantly than the originators of the measure had anticipated. He felt that the advantages of immigration were over-rated as every imported labourer increased the amount of

212

labour needed, for he at once became a consumer who had to be supplied. Houses, clothing, food and many other things, in which he had formerly not been interested, would now become necessities and there would be an increased demand for builders, tailors, market gardeners and others. Under these terms immigration would cause a rise, rather than a fall, in wages. Attempts to increase the population by the artificial means of immigration would mean engaging in a struggle against one of the fundamental laws of human society. It was only by the natural increase of the species that Trinidad or any other country could secure a proper balance between capital and labour, and could secure the maximum profit compatible with the general prosperity of the labourers.

The Secretary of State replied to the five questions of the Society:

1. A maximum charge ought certainly to be fixed; or such an alteration in the Ordinance made as would enable the Governor annually to apportion the charge to be incurred to the probable state of the Island's finances. I think this subject ought to be brought without delay under Sir H. MacLeod's notice, although there is no immediate pressure upon the revenue ...

2. I do not think it would be safe to allow this; I should be disposed at the same time to afford facilities for the introduction of Africans into our African dependencies, at least Sierra Leone and the Gambia, with a view to re-emigration from thence; and I am strongly of the opinion that such a measure is not at variance with the real interests of the liberated Africans.

3. Sufficient publicity may be given by laying papers before Parliament. The attention of the Emigration Commissioners might, however, be called to the subject with a view to discouraging British emigration.

4. I would wish to know whether there are any specific amendments of the Ordinance which are suggested either in the Resolution of the Committee or the evidence thereof, and if so to refer them to Sir H. MacLeod for his opinion.

5. I see no reason to think that the time has not yet arrived, when we may safely and advantageously commence a gradual reduction of the aid given for Education, and know the labouring population in this respect were upon their own resources, which are ample.

(c) *The East Indians*

The introduction of East Indians into the island of Mauritius

213

had proved a success and in 1842 the Trinidad Government favoured a similar policy if permission could be obtained from the Home Government. All other schemes had failed to produce either the numbers or the quality of persons required to work in the island. The following year, the Secretary of State, realizing the parlous condition of labour in the colonies, asked the Governor-General of India to reconsider the four-year-old prohibition of East Indian emigration to the West Indies.* A Protector of Immigrants was appointed in India and negotiations were entered into to permit emigration to British Guiana, Jamaica and Trinidad, on the understanding that return passages should be provided for all who emigrated.

In July, 1844, the Secretary of State allowed up to 1,000 emigrants to leave India; and this number was increased to 2,500 on condition that the local Legislatures would provide the necessary funds. The cost was estimated at £15 per person plus a return passage at the end of five years. Owing to the increase in numbers, Agents were appointed in both Calcutta and Madras.

Ordinances were immediately passed by the Trinidad Government, making arrangements for the raising of a loan of £250,000 and allowing for the repatriation of immigrants.

Governor MacLeod sent copies of the Ordinances home, together with a list of wages fixed by the Immigration and Agricultural Society, which represented the planters.† He stated that none of the papers he had received from London gave him any guidance on the situation and he could give no guarantee that the scale of wages would continue as high as it was starting. Trinidad and British Guiana were the two most interested colonies and would go to great lengths to secure the capital already invested in them and they were more likely therefore to offer higher premiums. At the same time it might be necessary to instigate some emergency legislation if labour became too plentiful. He ended his despatch :

" It might be for Your Lordship's consideration, therefore, whether it might not be advisable to direct, that should the rate of wages fall considerably below those stipulated to the particular parties at first leaving India—perhaps it might be proper to fix a minimum rate—and that if the Coolies should on that account wish to return before the five years were com-

* This prohibition had been caused by outcry against ill-treatment and unsatisfactory conditions of the first East Indians to reach Georgetown in 1838.
† See Appendix XXVII.

pleted, then the Government out of the money provided for Immigration purposes should defray the expenses of their passage back."

The first East Indian immigrants arrived in Trinidad on May 3rd, 1845, on board the *Fatel Rozack*, in number about 219. From the start the experiment seemed doomed to failure for the immigrants had been recruited from the bazaars and streets of Calcutta and were unaccustomed to agricultural work. There were complaints from both employers and employees.

The scheme had not even the full support of the island. In July a Memorial was forwarded to Governor MacLeod protesting against East Indian immigration and stating that the Memorialists had seen statements in the papers of a proposal for a loan of £250,000 to be raised on the security of the Colonial Government for the express purpose of securing East Indian immigrants. They quoted an advertisement published by the Immigration and Agricultural Society :

"That it is the opinion of the Society that it is expedient that an immediate reduction should take place in the money expenditure on sugar plantations throughout the Colony, and that it is evident that the existing rates of salaries and wages hitherto paid to Managers, Overseers, Mechanics and Labourers, are far beyond the means which sugar cultivation can possibly afford; and it is therefore urgently recommended to resident proprietors and attorneys of those who are absent to be prepared to make reductions as aforesaid on such a scale as will tend to meet the impending difficulty of foreign competition in the British Market."

This, with the intended loan would create, the Memorialists were certain, an organization of a closed union of sugar planters with full power to cut salaries without opposition and to flood the labour market with East Indians. They pointed out that the revenue of the colony was insufficient to pay the colonial expenses without additional burdens on the taxpayers and that to pay the interest and to establish a sinking fund to repay the principal of such a large debt as that contemplated would require additional taxation. The managers, overseers, mechanics and labourers, as well as the store and shopkeepers and the general inhabitants of the colony would have less money to pay increased burdens. Incomes would go down and taxes would rise and the result would be fewer respectable immigrants to the colony from the other islands, Sierra Leone and America. They foresaw the day when the East Indians would want to return to their native land, where living would be cheaper, and when the creoles of the colony might even consider moving to the Spanish American colonies, which were becoming more prosperous and peaceful. These colonies were only a short distance from Trinidad and possessed virgin soil and every type of climate and were looking for immigrants.

The Memorialists also accused the Society of being interested purely in immigration and having forsaken agriculture. No longer were they seeking any alternative to the labour problem than that of immigration. They had not issued any theories or practical guidance on greater use of animal or mechanical power in agriculture.

" If the plough was used as in the equally wild countries of Canada and the United States, the present extent of cultivation might be doubled with the same number of hands, and salaries and wages remaining the same."

Wages, the Memorialists felt, were if anything too low rather than too high, being hardly sufficient to supply the necessities and conveniences of life in an intemperate climate. They suggested that though the experiment in Demerara with the East Indians had proved a success, immigration into Trinidad should only be permitted on condition that it did not involve the colony in debt or increased taxation. Trinidad, under a good Government, should flourish, as she was rich in natural advantages and resources, though some alteration in the sugar duties would help her economic advance.

A reference was then made to the communications of the colony, which were in a deplorable condition. Development depended upon good and new roads and the Memorialists suggested that money be borrowed for their upkeep and construction rather than for immigrants. Tolls should be established at certain points and should be moderate so that road users and those who benefited from their construction would pay in proportion to their use. Eventually, as the colony prospered, the tolls would repay the interest and capital costs. It might be that American road contractors would be attracted to the island. They would be more capable than the East Indians and less costly.

This Memorial was signed by Thomas Hinde, supported by 140 other signatories.

East Indian immigration was suspended by the India Government until 1849, as mortality on the long sea voyage was high in the small and badly ventilated ships.

216

(d) Eastern settlements

Colonel Mein had suggested in 1841 to the Home Government that owing to inefficiency the settlements of discharged soldiers in the Manzanilla area should be abandoned. Governor Mac-Leod, in consultation with Mr. Bishop, the Commissary-General, and after a personal tour, advised against this policy on the grounds of injustice to the soldiers and harm to the colony.

The problem was not one of an easy solution. The settlements were important to the colony as the best means of opening up communications with the east of the island. The original establishment had been good but Woodford's plans had not been properly executed. Roads had been allowed to deteriorate, only being repaired when they became completely impassable. The general lines of communication had been forsaken, with the result that much money had been spent to little purpose. The Government had failed in its duty to the discharged soldiers. No longer were there superintendents and medical officers, or efficient officials; good houses had fallen into disrepair and a lack of interest by energetic officers had led to a similar apathy on the part of the settlers. Some had continued to cultivate their lands under Government patronage. Others had moved to other parts of the island.

MacLeod considered that it would be unjust to penalize the industrious on account of the idle. He wished to reopen communications with Port of Spain so that produce could be brought to the capital by the shortest route. He asked for permission to use part of the accumulated pension fund (amounting to about £8,000) for this purpose, estimating that £3,000 would cover the cost of moving the Superintendent's house and the school and would cover initial repair work on the roads and bridges. The fund available was created by saving the pensions (2½d. per day) allowed for discharged soldiers. Those who received Government lands were not paid their pension. Those who left the settlements forfeited their land but received their pension. Once MacLeod had re-established the settlements, and opened up communications and thereby raised the value of land in the area, he proposed paying all pensioners their daily pay and treating them as ordinary inhabitants of the colony, responsible for making their own way in the world.

To bear out his views, he enclosed to London a letter addressed to himself by the Reverend J. H. Hamilton, Minister at Tacarigua, describing a tour of the eastern settlements of the island

and containing a memorandum on suggested improvements which should be carried out in the district.*

In a letter dated March 24th, 1842, the Secretary of State replied :

". . . I have to consider whether it is probable that the future maintenance and encouragement of the settlements will be attended with results which their founder, Sir Ralph Woodford, and every other Governor has failed to bring about.

I do not see any reason to conclude that the ill condition of these settlements is owing to neglect.

The respective Governors have in their turn made attempts at improving the state of the settlements, but their attempts have failed and they have left the settlements in such a state as to be the subject of complaint by their successors . . .

A few hundreds of Africans were located in an isolated situation, not indeed very remote from civilized society, if distance only be considered, but so difficult of access that the distance, such as it was, became a bar to communication and the problem was to instruct and superintend them and keep them well ordered and industrious . . .

You consider the road to have been neglected, and you propose a large expenditure for its repair . . .

Sir Ralph Woodford had intended that the road should be kept in repair by the settlers paid out of the fund.

The settlers could not be induced to do the work, and then the alternative was adopted of giving them a vessel for conveyance of their produce along the shore; and the enormous proportion which the cost of conveyance bears to the value of the produce shows a forced and artificial state of things.

If the road continues impracticable, the superintendence, medical care and moral and religious instruction of the settlers must be attended with great difficulty . . .

The reliance must be upon the resident officers. But it is seldom desirable that educated persons should be induced, even if they can be induced, to separate themselves from civilized society . . .

The circumstances of the Colony since the Abolition of Slavery appear to tend both naturally and usefully towards the dispersion of such settlements as are remote from plantations and towns.

The high price of labour and the activity which prevails in the populous parts of the Island must draw the best men away from such settlements, and many appear to have left accordingly, and are probably employed elsewhere to better account both for themselves and for the community.

* See Appendix XXIX.

Upon the whole, therefore, I am unable to concur in the expediency of the course which you recommend in regard to these settlements ...

The specific conclusions to which I have come with the concurrence of the Lords Commissioners of the Treasury, and on which I have to request that you will act, are as follows:

1. The obligations into which the Government has entered with the disbanded soldiers must of course be fulfilled ... you will be guided in this matter by the decisions of the Lords of the Treasury ...

2. These obligations will be held to be no longer in force in the case of those who have deserted the settlements and who shall fail to return to them after three months' public notice to that effect.

3. To those who shall have remained constantly at the locations, the pension of 2½d. per diem shall be paid; the land they occupy shall remain in their possession and the schools shall be maintained; but nothing more shall be undertaken with a view to encourage the settlers to remain; and the establishment for the superintendence of the settlers shall be broken up as soon as can be done without injustice to the parties employed in the service.

4. After a lapse of three months from the issue of a public notice to the effect that desertion of the settlement for a period of two months or for periods which, in the course of a year, shall amount to two months, shall exclude the person so deserting from the right to return to the location or to receive the pension ...."

(3) Land

(a) Squatters

Lt.-Colonel Charles Chichester, who undertook the administration of the Government during the absence on leave of Governor MacLeod, was faced with the problem of ejection of squatters on Crown and other lands. Many difficulties had been found in the execution of the Proclamation of March 30th, 1838,* by which squatters were to be summarily ejected. In four years only eleven cases had been brought before the magistrates. There were a number of causes for such a small number of prosecutions. These Chichester pointed out to the Secretary of State:

1. All cases had to be taken before the magistrate before the offender had been in possession for a year.

2. The extreme difficulty in detecting the squatter in the thinly populated mountainous and wooded areas of the island.

* See p. 195.

3. The natural reluctance of others to tell the authorities of any persons seen on Crown lands.

4. Absentee landlords could keep no real check on their distant estates and unless the Attorney or the Agent produced the squatter in court, no one else could prosecute.

5. Many estate owners did not know the exact boundaries of their lands; until a survey was made they did not realize that they had squatters on their property.

6. Many private owners turned a blind eye to squatters, and in some cases charged them a nominal rent, and made use of their labour during busy seasons.

Because of these difficulties the law had been almost a dead letter since its inception. Chichester and his law officers had tried to devise some means of dealing with offenders, but as investigations proceeded the difficulties appeared more and more insurmountable. He therefore asked for some revision in the methods for stopping squatting.

The Secretary of State could only suggest greater vigilance and activity by the Surveyor-General and his staff until a new Order in Council should be produced.

Had squatting only taken place on Crown lands, then the whole responsibility would have been on the shoulders of the Surveyor-General, but his hands were tied when it came to dealing with the squatter on private lands, for no one but the owner could proceed against the offender.

The Secretary of State had given consideration to requiring at least five years occupancy as a squatter's proof of possession but thought it would be unfair and would cause hardship, particularly in cases where squatters had been tolerated for several years and had improved the property on which they had set up their abode. The longer the period of occupancy, the more difficult became the ejectment. The shorter the period, the more vigilant the authorities would have to be. The Secretary of State ended his despatch :

" Upon the whole therefore I do not at present perceive that any new provisions of law can be devised which would offer better prospect of preventing the practice of squatting; but I wish you to make every effort in your power to give effect to the existing laws in conformity with the views I have explained to you; and if in the course of these efforts it should appear that any improvement of the law which has not yet occurred to us can be safely adopted, I shall be happy to consider your suggestion to that effect.

In the meantime it may be desirable that you should issue a

Proclamation enjoining in the name of Her Majesty's Government a more strict observance of the existing law against squatting."

(b) *Survey*

Early in 1841, the Governor-General of the Windward Islands recommended a survey of the dependencies under his jurisdiction. This suggestion was placed before the Trinidad Council and Messrs. William Burnley, James Walker, Charles Warner, T. B. Wylly and John Losh were appointed a Committee to enquire into the matter and report back.

The Committee reported that they considered the benefits of a survey would not compensate for the expenses involved. The proportion of Crown lands to private property in Trinidad was much higher than in any other of the colonies and the returns from lands unofficially appropriated would be insignificant. The nature of the terrain, mountainous and densely wooded, would mean great expense in carrying out the survey and the quick growth of the vegetation would necessitate frequent surveys unless a great additional expense were incurred in the erection of permanent landmarks. They recommended that partial surveys should be made in areas where there was known to be a doubt about boundaries.

It had been suggested that this survey should be made on the same lines as those used by Captain Dawson in New Zealand, involving dividing the land into sections. This was felt by the Committee to be impracticable as owing to labour costs and to the alluvial quality of the soil, very few people lived in the interior. The coastal districts were preferred or areas where a community of settlers could combine to make the necessary roads. The Committee considered that it would be a better plan to find the best natural level for roads and when they were constructed to divide the adjoining lands into allotments for sale. This would provide one permanent boundary of the holding and would save the Crown having to make reservations for communications in their leases.

Over the question of the size of allotments, the Home Government had suggested that 40 acres should be the minimum. With this the Committee was unable to agree, as they thought that such a small parcel of land would too easily come within the reach of persons who were required by the colony as labourers. They suggested that the minimum should be 100 quarrees (320 acres) and that 200 quarrees should be considered the minimum for a sugar estate. Of the 208,379 acres recorded as belonging to private owners, 150,000 were not under cultivation and would be available for sale in small parcels at a price similar to that being asked for Crown lands.* Crown lands should not be disposed of until the labouring population warranted it by a sufficient increase. The balance between land and labour must be most carefully watched if the security and prosperity of the colony were to be maintained. The Committee therefore suggested that the Governor should apply to the Secretary of State for the establishment of a Land and Immigration Fund, as in South Australia, upon the security of which funds could be raised to meet all expenses of immigration and to furnish a pool from which inevitable surveys of the colony could be paid.

(4) Education

After emancipation the educational needs of the colony became very obvious. The Mico Charity School in Port of Spain, a school for boys organized by the Cabildo and a few denominational schools were all that were available for the needs of the ever-growing population.

Early in 1840, the Bishop of Barbados, in whose diocese Trinidad lay, announced in a letter to Governor MacLeod that he was about to ask for Government assistance to support seven additional schools. A few days later the Roman Catholic Bishop asked for support for four schools which had already been opened and were staffed by some of his priests. The Wesleyans were also known to be preparing to make a request for support for their schools and it looked as though other denominations would be doing the same in the near future. The need was great but MacLeod was not satisfied that education was being developed in the right way :

> " I regret to observe that it appears to originate more in a spirit of rivalry or jealousy than to be regulated by any sound principle."

No sooner did one denomination open a school than others followed their example, without any serious consideration of the needs of the district and then all called upon the Government for help in maintenance, regardless of the number of pupils, which might range from five to fifty. MacLeod considered that the time had come for the formulation of some kind of educational policy in the colony, the current system being too haphazard and the Government having no means of ascertaining that grants were being spent to the best advantage.

* See p. 278.

One of the major difficulties in education was that of religion. The majority of the inhabitants were Roman Catholics, yet the owners of most of the property in the colony were British Protestants. Combined with this was the problem of the immigrants and the different languages spoken in the island and also the scattered nature of the settlements, many being far from the centres of population. He wished to devise a scheme whereby the rudiments of education could be extended to all, one which would gradually introduce the English language to all people.

The Home Government was very much in favour of some form of progressive means of providing instruction for the whole population regardless of religion. It had been suggested that the Mico Charity could help the colony substantially, but here a difficulty arose, for the Charity's trustees insisted upon the Bible being used as a school text book. The Bishop of Olympus had personally agreed to its use but had warned MacLeod that under no circumstances would many of his priests tolerate the use of the Bible as a school book.

The Governor asked the Secretary of State to let him have copies of the principles upon which the National School Board of Education for Ireland worked, in the hope that this might form the foundation for education in Trinidad. If this were the case he was prepared to form a Board of Education :

" In the appointment of such a board, of which I should be the head, I should take care that every Church and class of religion should be duly represented; and in its formation the Bishop of Olympus assures me that he and his Clergy will give their most ready and hearty concurrence.

In the meantime, I shall make it perfectly understood that all grants of money made for the erection or maintenance of schools shall be subject to revision."

In a later despatch to the Secretary of State, MacLeod once more stressed the need of some unified plan for education and pointed out Trinidad's unique position amongst British colonies owing to its very mixed population. The immigration of peoples from so many scattered nations as well as the differences of religion made it imperative that there should be some system in the colony. Education, he stressed, should be under Government control and should be accessible to all nationalities and religious groups. This would ensure that in future generations the English language would be understood by all the inhabitants, two-thirds of whom were still speaking French or Spanish. It

223

was necessary that peoples living under British rule and claiming the benefits of British citizenship should at least be able to read the laws by which they were governed. There was a constant demand from the churches for more grants from the Government, which already paid half the salaries for teachers, and there appeared to be no reason why these demands would not be constant and ever-increasing.

In January, 1842, the Secretary of State replied:

". . . The question of education, embarrassing in any of the Colonies, is surrounded in Trinidad by peculiar difficulties, arising out of language and of religion . . . As to the former point of difference, I think it is quite clear that it should be a leading object with the Government to encourage by every means in their power the diffusion of the English language; and it would not appear unreasonable to require instruction in that language should be made a *sine qua non* in every school applying for aid from public funds. Differences of religion present a more formidable obstacle; and some regulations appear obviously desirable to prevent the establishment of three or four schools set up for the mere purpose of rivalry, by different denominations, all claiming and all receiving the aid of Government, in a district the population of which could be abundantly supplied by a single school. On the other hand I much doubt the possibility of laying down and adhering to a rule, in such a society, of withholding all aid from all schools which shall not be conducted according to a single scheme laid down by Government. The system introduced into Ireland was founded upon necessity arising out of circumstances in some degree analagous to those you describe and was intended to communicate to children of all denominations religious education without shocking the prejudices of those who dissented from the Church of England, or introducing doctrines at variance with the opinions of the Church. But, although schools upon this principle have rapidly multiplied in Ireland, the system has met with decided opposition from various quarters and especially from the clergy of the Church of England; and I fear it must be admitted that in a few instances has affected that combined education which was one of its main objects, but different schools, taking their colour from their respective local superintendents, have become for the most part exclusively Roman Catholic, or Presbyterian or Church of England, the latter being comparatively a very small number. Now this is not the effect I am desirous of producing in Trinidad . . . such a system might be productive of great good in Trinidad, I am afraid that it would be hardly justifiable to calculate upon such a contingency . . . In conformity, however, with your wish . . . I have given directions for supplying you with the principal rules and regulations under which the Irish system is carried on, and a copy of the scripture books which have been prepared for general use in their schools . . . You will endeavour to ascertain by private and personal enquiry how far the clergy of the various denominations might be expected to co-operate in such a scheme, and I will await with much anxiety your report upon this interesting question. Should the result be such as I am afraid we must anticipate, it will be necessary to take steps for restricting within reasonable limits the liability of the Government to be called upon to aid in the establishment of schools of an exclusive character; and perhaps no better course could be pursued than that which is adopted in this country of taking an annual grant to a limited amount in aid of education, and receiving through certain authorized channels applications for participation in the grant, delegating to a Committee of the Privy Council the examination separately of the merits of each particular application and laying down at the same time certain indispensable conditions with reference to the amount of local contribution, the number of scholars anticipated, right of Government inspection and other points to which it is now unnecessary to advert. In the absence of any general system under the superintendence of the Government, I see no other mode likely to be productive of equal advantages with that I have thus generally indicated . . ."

Whether the Governor made a report or not is not recorded. Certainly no change of any consequence was made until the passing of the Education Ordinance of 1851 in the time of Lord Harris.

(5) *The Churches*
   (a) *The Roman Catholic Church**
In November, 1841, Dr. Patrick Smith,† Bishop of Agna, drew the attention of the Council to an embarrassment under which he had been labouring for some time. Between 1833 and 1841 the Roman Catholic population had increased from 12,900 to 23,160, and the Bishop had on account of the numbers requiring instruction appointed a fourth curate and was paying him out of his own stipend. More priests were necessary. The Bishop and five others could not conveniently administer to his flock. As the stipends were small—£130 per annum—the Bishop had to provide his curates with board and lodging to keep them in a town where rents, provisions, clothes and servants were very

* See Appendix XXXII and p. 250.   † See p. 182.

expensive. Church fees had not increased with the population; prior to emancipation, masters had paid promptly for services to their slaves. Now that the slave was free, he expected the same benefits from his church but did not pay for them. The church could not refuse its ministrations. The Bishop quoted the medical profession to support his argument. Doctors were finding it difficult to collect their fees from the newly freed population. Expenses had risen, not only in living but in the Cathedral itself. A clerk, choristers and accolytes had to be paid. The latter had been increased in number in a desire to have " Public Divine Service performed in a becoming and attractive manner." Even the cost of washing and supplying vestments and other church ornaments had increased and very little was left from the fees when expenses had been paid. There was no fixed rate for fees and no means of forcing their payment if the party concerned did not pay. They were regarded as debts of honour.

Many of the new immigrants were Roman Catholics, especially those from Grenada and Carriacou, and as the Government was encouraging immigration, the Bishop hoped that it would also encourage the spiritual welfare of the immigrants after they had arrived in the colony. He pointed out that he had drawn no stipend when he was out of the colony on church business, that he was supporting a superannuated priest who had served in the colony for twelve years and that he himself had, during his stay in Port of Spain, given hospitality to all visiting priests from abroad and from the rural areas. He had discharged his duties to his parishioners and had worked in harmony with Christians of other denominations. He was asking now only for a grant of £130 a year for an additional curate and a slight increase in his own stipend, as Curé of Port of Spain and Vicar-General of the island.

Governor MacLeod forwarded this petition to London and suggested the payment of two extra curates. The Secretary of State replied that this was an ecclesiastical question and not one with which he could properly interfere.

When there was a proposed change in the stipends of the Church of England clergy, MacLeod suggested that there should be a rise in the stipends of the Roman Catholics so that all were on an equality, thus raising the amount needed by the church from £3,496 to £4,100 per year.*

(b) *The Church of England*

Members of the Church of England, though the largest

* See p. 293.

226

property owners, were numerically in the minority, and except in the Tacarigua area, the 10,000 members were scattered widely throughout the colony. This made it difficult in certain areas to assemble a large enough congregation to warrant the building of a church. In 1842 the establishment of the Church of England consisted of :

Port of Spain—
    1 Curate (£600 per year paid by the Colony)
    1 Assistant Curate (£450 per year, £250 from the colony, £200 from Bishop of Barbados)
Tacarigua—
    1 Curate paid as Assistant Curate in Port of Spain
Couva—
    1 Curate similarly paid
Chaguanas—
    Nobody appointed.

In addition there were two German clergy appointed by the Church Missionary Society, one at Savanna Grande, an old Indian mission station. Here there was no church, the school-house being used for services. The other German was at San Fernando, which had two churches, one in town and the other on the outskirts of the district at Oropouche. These two Germans were men of indefatigable zeal but one found some difficulty in making himself understood when preaching. The Bishop of Barbados had offered to take both into the establishment of the church and had recently appointed another German as assistant Curate in Port of Spain.

After a visit to Barbados, Cummins asked Governor MacLeod if the Trinidad Government would be prepared to pay part of the stipend of an Archdeacon of Trinidad. MacLeod was in favour of this, and in recommending a grant of £500 a year to the Secretary of State, pointed out that Cummins obviously expected the post and that while he was an excellent man with many years' service to his credit, what was really needed was " a native Englishman of talent and power as a preacher." He was sincerely interested in the church in Trinidad and pointed out that unless a good appointment was made, there was grave danger of a falling off by the congregation, who would go either to the Scottish church or to the Wesleyans. He suggested :

1. The institution of six parishes for ecclesiastical purposes. A rector to be appointed to each parish at a stipend of £350 except in the case of Port of Spain where the rector should

continue at £600. Each rector to be assigned a house and 30 acres of glebe land.

2. Attached to each rector there should be a curate with a stipend of £150, and where assistant curates were needed, they should receive £100.

3. Parish clerks and sextons should be attached to each parish, with a salary of £20 16s. 8d. per year.

Total Expenditure	£		
Archdeacon	500		
Rector of Port of Spain	600		
Clerk at Port of Spain	60		
5 Rectors	1750		
6 Curates	900		
3 Assistant Curates	300		
5 Clerks and 5 Sextons	208	6	8
	£4318	6	8

The Secretary of State was unwilling to give his consent without further information, particularly as the whole question of the Establishment of the Church of England in Trinidad was being discussed. He was dissatisfied with the way in which the clergy were being paid. The Bishop of Barbados received funds from two separate sources—a Parliamentary grant and grants from religious organizations in England. The former was a fixed sum, the latter liable to reduction or complete withdrawal. These sums the Bishop pooled and used to assist the clergy's stipends, and he proposed to allow £525 per year towards costs in Trinidad. The Secretary of State considered that the two funds should be kept separate so that in event of a reduction by the voluntary sources, the clergy would not suffer, being paid chiefly by the Parliamentary grant.

On December 17th, 1844, an Ordinance defining the establishment of the Church of England in the West Indies was passed, much to the displeasure of the Roman Catholics in Trinidad, who petitioned the Governor:

". . . Your Lordship's Memorialists beg most respectfully to represent against the passing of the said Ordinance. Two petitions signed by more than two thousand Inhabitants of the Colony, of all creeds, were presented to Her Majesty's Council of Government without effect . . .

Your Memorialists would earnestly beg to impress upon Your Lordship the fact that Her Majesty's Council of Government in this Island possesses but a single member professing the religious faith of the great majority of the people. That from the manner in which it is constituted it had no pretensions to a representative character, or to the confidence of the people, in religious subjects at least, all its members with the single exception we have mentioned being of the Church which this Ordinance, in effect, establishes and renders dominant and ascendant; and who, however estimable in other respects are, from education and connections, naturally biased in favour of the religion to which they belong.

Your Memorialists also respectfully submit that the case of Jamaica which is said to have formed the precedent on which this Ordinance is founded, is not applicable to this Island, and affords no ground for a similar enactment here, insomuch as the circumstances . . . are not only dissimilar but totally different. Jamaica with a population of over 300,000 souls does not number more than 8,000 Roman Catholics, while Trinidad with a population of over 60,000 contains by the best calculation within power to make, more than 55,000 not professing the religion of the Church of England . . . Jamaica besides has a representative Government which Trinidad has not, and we presume also that Your Lordship is officially aware of the unceasing strife which has been produced in the Colony by what is called Ecclesiastical Law.

We also humbly submit to Your Lordship that the Ordinance hereinbefore mentioned, while it is obnoxious to the religious feelings of more than five-sixths of the inhabitants of this Colony, is also highly impolitic and inexpedient as increasing, and threatening to increase still more by its operation in future, the taxes on all and every article of importation, including the very necessities of life, to support the establishment of a Church to which less than a sixth part of the inhabitants—that is the tax payers—belong."

(c) *Other Churches*

In September, 1846, a ship arrived from Madeira with 179 men, women and children aboard. These were not Portuguese immigrants in the usual sense. They were refugees, victims of their faith and suffering for being a small Protestant minority in a Catholic community. In Trinidad they founded, and themselves built, the Portuguese Church, now St. Ann's Church of Scotland, and were led by their minister, William Hepburn, who had worked amongst them in Madeira. Hepburn did not long survive and was succeeded by the Reverend Arsenio da Silva, who had been ordained by the Presbytery of Trinidad in Greyfriars Church in January, 1847. The congregation of the church grew rapidly and by 1848 there were 700 members.

An abortive effort at missionary work was made in 1842 by

the American Church. A mission was opened at Iere Village but ill-health took such a toll of the missionaries that eventually the work had to be abandoned. Of five men sent out from the United States in the first two years, two died and were buried in the colony, and two had to return home through ill-health. In 1851, the last survivor succumbed and had to return home.

The London Baptists began work in Trinidad in 1843 when the Reverend George Cowen, of the London Baptist Mission, recently Superintendent of the Mico Charity School, opened a mission in a small house in Corbeau Town, Port of Spain. His work prospered and new quarters had to be taken and lands held by the Mico Charity were purchased.

(6) *Legal Changes*
(a) *The Illustrious Cabildo*

In 1840 a great change was made in the function and format of the Board of the Illustrious Cabildo.* This body, which had functioned from the early days of the Spanish occupation of the colony, had been reduced from the Board that controlled all settlers to a municipal body responsible only for Port of Spain and now it was to become the Town Council.

In origin it was an annually self-elected body of twelve persons presided over by the Governor, who had the power, as Corregidor, to veto any of its decisions. The two senior members, the first and second Alcaldes, were magistrates; the remaining ten Regidors, two of them perpetual, had the duty of inspecting markets, taking care of the streets and superintending the hospitals, etc. To the Cabildo were attached twelve junior officers, Alquazils, divided amongst the several barrios and the harbour to assist in the performance of its duties. The powers of the Cabildo had been great. The Courts of the Alcaldes had tried all petty offences and the Board had by its by-laws regulated the day to day life of the community.

As time went on the Cabildo had become more and more inefficient. Its rulings and those of its courts had been questioned and had not always been upheld by the Executive. Members were reluctant to serve and half-hearted in their efforts, attendance at meetings was irregular and there was no proper enforcement of any procedure. This inefficiency had led to a slacking off in the performance of duties by the officers of the Board and the Governor in Council was obliged to take over the policing of the town, its scavenging and a considerable part of the Board's funds.

* See Appendix X.

Governor MacLeod, at his first meeting with the Cabildo, informed members that a reorganization would have to take place and that he proposed, as far as circumstances would permit, to make the Board the equivalent of an English Town Council. The Cabildo agreed with his suggestions and on June 1st, 1840, the Council passed the necessary Ordinance :

" Enacted by the Governor of the Island of Trinidad by and with the advice and consent of the Council thereof, for regulating the powers and Constitution and settling the mode of election of the members of the Corporate Body called The Illustrious Cabildo of the Town of Port of Spain and changing the name thereof to that of The Town Council of Port of Spain."

The Ordinance* allowed for the election annually of four Councillors from a total of twelve members (3).† All males over the age of twenty-one years who owned or rented property to the value of $200 and could speak and understand English, were entitled to become Burgesses (4). It stated the qualifications necessary in Councillors (9) and insisted upon the oath of allegiance being taken by them (14). Regulations for the duties of the Council and its procedure (17) were laid down in the Ordinance, as were in section 24 the boundaries of the town :

North : The line of the north side of Barrack Street.
South : The sea.
East : The Dry River.
West : The west side of Richmond Street extended to the eastern boundary of the Tranquillity Estate and the Tragarete Road and including Corbeau Town.

The suburbs were also defined in a following section.
The Chief Justice, Mr. Scotland, objected to certain clauses in the Ordinance.

1. Placing so high a figure as $200 for qualification as a Burgess. MacLeod answered this by stating that he had contemplated a lower figure but had found that many people of position in the town would not exercise their franchise if the field was too widely opened. The experiment on a small scale had created 872 votes. This could easily be enlarged at a later date.
2. Allowing other than British subjects to exercise a vote.

* See Appendix XXX.
† Numbers in brackets refer to the sections of the Ordinance.

MacLeod stated that he was determined to make Trinidad a British Colony in feeling as well as in fact. The people of British descent were in a small minority compared with those of French and Spanish descent; it would be unfair to give such a few the privilege of a vote to the exclusion of all other classes. The fact that they had to be able to speak and understand English showed the anglicizing tendency of the law.

3. Confusion would arise from giving the franchise to a part occupier of a building so long as he was paying rent of $200 per annum. Governor MacLeod did not anticipate any serious trouble from this cause.

4. It was a serious matter to leave more than £500 in the hands of the Town Clerk and the Treasurer. MacLeod pointed out that all expenditure of funds must be submitted to the Governor for approval. Clause 16 of the Ordinance provided that the Treasurer had to find such surety as would satisfy the Council and the Governor. To make any further restrictions he thought would be ungracious and would mean that the Government financial officers would be burdened by constant requests from the Town Treasurer.

In ending his despatch to the Secretary of State, Governor MacLeod wrote :

"I submit the measure, therefore, to Your Lordship in full confidence that it will deserve your approbation. The necessity for some change in the Municipal Government of the Town has been admitted on all hands . . . whilst Your Lordship will find that strict attention has been paid to the caution so strenuously impressed by Lord Glenelg of not permitting any Corporate authority on an elective system to come into operation except with full power on the part of the Executive Government to control and check it."

Ordinances amending that of June, 1840, were passed in December, 1840; April, 1844, and August, 1853. This last Ordinance, a lengthy document of 98 sections, greatly amplified the original Ordinance. Governor MacLeod had taken the first and necessary step in bringing the municipal working of Port of Spain into line with the rest of the British Empire.

(b) Constitutional Squabbles

In the first fifty years of British occupation of the colony no direct representation had been granted to the people. They still had no voice in the enactments of the Legislature for the government of the island. In September, 1845, a petition was presented to the Queen, asking for representative institutions but was not granted. Undeterred by this rebuff, a public meeting was held in Mr. Jobity's Theatre, to see if there was anything else that could be done to obtain some sort of government that would give the people a chance of expressing their views and having them implemented. Mr. Samuel Samuel took the chair and Mr. Savary acted as secretary. Two resolutions were passed :

1. That the system of Government at present existing in this Colony, excluding as it does all popular control, is injurious to the best interests of its inhabitants, and is, therefore, a cause of general dissatisfaction and a grievance.
2. That if Her Majesty's Ministers adhere to their late determination to refuse us a British Constitution, such as exists in other of Her Majesty's Colonies, this meeting is disposed gratefully to receive any other form of constitution which may secure to all Her Majesty's subjects equal rights and privileges; which may grant a regional legislative authority to enact, alter, or repeal such laws as local circumstances may render necessary; and which above all may give us some efficient control over the public taxation and expenditure; without which essential privileges, we hold that Trial by Jury, and the introduction of British laws, cannot alone, notwithstanding the advantages attending them, satisfy the reasonable desires of the inhabitants or compensate for the deprivation of those invaluable rights, which as British subjects, we claim and ought to enjoy.

Amidst loud cheers an amendment by Mr. Cumming was proposed and carried :

"That an humble petition be presented to Her Most Gracious Majesty the Queen, praying for a House of Assembly, elected by the people, and based upon the principles of the British Constitution."

A committee was appointed to carry into effect the amended resolution. Two petitions were drawn up, one to the Queen and another to the House of Commons, but neither was granted.

(7) *Industry*
(a) *Sugar*
After the abolition of slavery and of the apprenticeship scheme, the Trinidad Government was forced to assist and protect its planters. Machinery and agricultural implements were admitted into the colony duty free, houses and buildings for

the manufacture of sugar were made free of tax, and the stealing of canes made punishable by imprisonment and heavy fines.

The major difficulty of the planter remained the shortage of labour. This restricted the large planter and prevented the small man from extending his cultivation. Though immigrants were arriving, very few of them wished to become agriculturists. To be a shopkeeper or a mechanic was considered superior to being a labourer on the land.

In addition to the problem of labour, the planters had to meet foreign competition and heavy duties and taxes on sugar. As early as 1734 the Committee of Trade and Plantation in England reported that Dutch, French and Portuguese sugar was imported into England at a much cheaper cost than British West Indian sugar. They gave as the reasons, high navigational charges, heavy duties on imports and high cost of production. Their recommendation that direct and unrestricted exports of sugar should be permitted to countries south of Cape Finisterre was embodied in the Sugar Act of 1739, but it did not have the desired effect.

Slave labour was uneconomic because unintelligent. The introduction of new operations in production was difficult owing to the inability of many slaves to assimilate new ideas. Even on the best estates it was impossible to guarantee more than two-thirds of the total labour available owing to sickness, punishment and the high rate of mortality. The slave population did not increase naturally as the gang system was used too largely. The extravagence of the planters was a by-word, but even worse for the trade was absenteeism. Proprietors who lived away from their estates had no sense of responsibility for them and were satisfied so long as the money came in.

The wars with Napoleon did not help the sugar trade. Sugar duties went up as high as 27s. 6d. per cwt. The capture of enemy ships carrying sugar cargo increased the difficulties too, for the cargoes were taken to England as prizes and the sugar sold on the open market. The strict imposition of the Navigation Act, which stopped trade with America, also depressed the West Indian sugar trade, and the application by Napoleon of the Berlin Decree which were followed by the British Orders in Council so restricted the re-export of sugar from England that the resultant glut forced prices down.

The West Indies suffered from sugar having too great a place in their agricultural economy. When prices were high, sugar completely predominated the islands and when there was a set-back, there was no alternative crop to bring in any return. In this Trinidad was better placed than most of the colonies, for she was developing her cacao industry.

The growing Free Trade Party in England and the distillers, who wanted cheap sugar, suggested that unrestricted sugar should be admitted from the East Indies because the West Indian supply was insufficient. In the enquiry which followed this suggestion, it was satisfactorily proved that the West Indian supply was more than sufficient.

As Britain changed from an agricultural to an industrial nation, the repercussions on the West Indies were very noticeable. Britain was searching for more profitable markets than the islands. The Monroe Doctrine of the United States had restricted British expansion in the Americas and had reduced the importance of the West Indian colonies. The unexploited larger colonies of Australia, Canada and South Africa offered many more opportunities for extended trade than the West Indies, which were thought to be showing signs of becoming exhausted.

Specific duties on sugar had been introduced by the Commonwealth Government which had laid a tax of 1s. 6d. per cwt. on raw sugar and 5s. on refined. These taxes, levied for revenue purposes, had been changed as the years went by. The increase to 27s. 6d. per cwt., during the French wars brought a protest from the West Indian planters in 1806-7, but it was overruled. Foreign sugars had to pay the ordinary tax as well as a high differential duty.

In 1841, Lord Melbourne's Ministry assumed that the British West Indies could not supply the needs of the British home consumption and proposed to reduce the duties on foreign sugar from 63s. to 36s. per cwt. and to levy a colonial duty of 27s. Protests poured in from the colonies concerned, merchants and shippers pointing out that with the abolition of slavery they had already had their principal source of income taken away, and that other countries where sugar was still grown by slave labour were able to undersell sugar grown by free labour in spite of the differential duty. The question was debated in the Commons for eight days and eventually the measure was dropped.

Sir Robert Peel, speaking for the Opposition in the debate, upheld the free-grown sugar against the Government but when he formed a new Government on the fall of Melbourne, he reduced the duty on British sugar by 10s. to 14s. per cwt. and that on foreign free-grown sugar to 23s. 4d. A quantity of

235

slave-grown sugar was also admitted at a reduced rate as a result of treaties with countries which still had slave colonies. This reduction in duties led to an increased demand for sugar, so that the revenue was compensated and temporarily the planter was satisfied, but the Free Trade Party was not satisfied and in 1846 an Equalizing Act was passed. This allowed for annual reductions in the duty on foreign free-grown sugar and proportionately larger reductions on foreign slave-grown sugar until 1851, when it would enter England at the same rate as free-grown sugar. Duty distinction between British and foreign grown sugar actually ended on July 5th, 1854, the original decision that equalization should be effected by 1851 having been reconsidered in 1848. While concessions then made included the reduction of the duties on colonial rum, and the use of sugar in British distilleries, which had been prohibited, was permitted, planters objected that Parliament had refused them permission to keep the slaves, who were the mainstay of the colonial sugar industry, yet was planning to encourage nations which still allowed slaves in their colonies. The immediate result was that slave-grown sugar increased and the London market was flooded. In 1847 the differential duty was only £7 per ton and nearly 25,000 tons of slave-grown sugar were deposited in London, compared with none the previous year. The market was glutted and the price fell down from £18 to £10 per ton. Sugar estates in the West Indies changed hands at nominal figures. A Government inquiry into the coffee and sugar plantations, which took place under Lord Russell's Government in 1848, showed that there had been a large increase in the cost of production of muscovado sugar and that there had been grave capital losses on estates. Between 1832 and 1848 no fewer than 140 West Indian sugar estates had to be abandoned.

(b) *Cacao*

Cacao growers suffered from the same disadvantages as the sugar planters after emancipation and the abandonment of the apprenticeship system. Labour and agricultural problems were many. Trinidad was, however, fortunate in that it had a well formed cacao industry as a subsidiary to sugar. The growing of provisions for local consumption was still only a small part of the island economy. Most of the requirements of the population were filled by imported goods from the South American mainland.

Cacao planting was an old-established industry of the island, dating back well before the capitulation and the planters were a numerous class which included many of the oldest inhabitants of the colony, whose industry affected the whole economy of the island. Their holdings were smaller than those of the sugar planters, which required a larger outlay of capital if the production of sugar, molasses and rum were to be a success, but their difficulties were sufficient for them to send to the Governor in 1840 asking for assistance.

The Memorialists pointed out that cacao had once been a lucrative business in the colony but that now the cost of production was higher than the price paid for the goods produced. Between 1821 and 1824 cacao sold for $13 to $19 a fanega (110 lbs.) and over 3,500,000 lbs. were exported, which had meant an income to the colonial revenue of £57,851 sterling. By 1841 half the trees had been abandoned and the export had fallen to 2,500,000 lbs., with a consequent fall of revenue to £40,000. The number of cacao estates under cultivation was rapidly decreasing.

The two main causes of the lowering of prices were blamed on political dissension in Spain, the chief consumer, and the arbitrary restrictions enforced in that country. The Memorialists felt that it was the duty of the statesmen who controlled the destiny of Britain and Spain to remove the barriers which prevented their prosperity, especially as new commercial treaties were about to be signed between the two countries. By an Order in Council in 1828, the only imports to Trinidad of Spanish goods had to be in ships of Spanish register. By this Trinidad received per year a few head of cattle from Puerto Rico. If Trinidad exported cacao to Spain in British ships, the duty was $23 per fanega, nearly three times Trinidad's selling price. If the cacao were carried in a Spanish vessel, the duty was $15 per fanega. The only alternative was to ship to Puerto Rico or Cuba, bond the goods and then reship in Spanish vessels and pay a duty of $5 per fanega. This system had two great disadvantages :

1. British ships were excluded from the cacao trade.
2. As regards Spanish shipping, the owners or charterer of a ship going to Trinidad for cacao was obliged to obtain an outward cargo freight for the free port of St. Thomas, a market often glutted and open to competition of trade under all flags. After landing cargo, the vessel must proceed to Trinidad in ballast to load cacao, then instead of clearing for home, must retraverse the Caribbean Sea, to land, bond and reship cargo at Puerto Rico, and then clear

237

for Spain, from these more distant ports, in order to obtain the low duty rates, a tedious, expensive and vexatious proceeding, injurious to commerce of both nations.

The Memorialists pointed out that the object of the restrictions, namely the encouragement of British shipping, was not being attained so far as articles of Spanish production were concerned. The expectation that Spanish goods required by the colonies would be handled by British merchants or by Spanish ships re-shipping in England had not been fulfilled. Only the better class wines reached Trinidad in this manner. The bulk of imports came by way of St. Thomas. Goods were carried there by Spanish merchants, purchased by colonial traders, and only made the last part of the journey in coasting vessels of British registra-tion. These vessels seldom carried a cargo of more than fifty tons and were not manned by crews suitable for the British Navy.

". . . The Memorialists therefore humbly express their hope and prayer that Her Majesty will instruct Her Minister for the Foreign Department that in the negotiations preceding the new Commercial Treaty about to be entered into between Her Majesty and Her August Ally, Dona Isabella, Queen of Spain, the propriety of reducing the present heavy duties on cacao imported into Spain from the British Colonies, be urged . . . The Memorialists review with very great regret the preference for some time past by the Lords of the Treasury to foreign (slave) grown cacao for Her Majesty's Army and Navy, instead of Trinidad cacao at as reasonable a price if the superior quality be considered.
The Memorialists call attention to the advantages to them-selves and to their fellow subjects in the Mother Country were cacao to be more generally used in Britain. It has long been pronounced a wholesome and nutritive beverage by the leading physicians and is one of the very fine substitutes offered to the philanthropist in his effort to lessen the number of victims of excessive indulgence in alcoholic liquors . . . The Memorialists suggest that chocolate or cacao paste produced on British Plantations should be imported into the British Dominions at the same rate of duty as cacao from these Colonies . . . There is sufficient land suitable to the cacao tree to enable its cultivation to be increased fifty-fold, if need be, so that the wants of Her Majesty's subjects may be supplied to any extent and they may be rendered independent of the arrogant and distant Country which now supplies them with their principal beverage . . ."

This petition, dated July 11th, 1840, was signed by more than two hundred and fifty residents of Trinidad.

(8) *Rebuilding*

The laws passed and Proclamations issued with the purpose of making Port of Spain a well ordered town were so frequently broken or overlooked that the town was not only becoming unsightly but also a fire trap. In 1839 the matter was brought to the notice of the Council and a new Ordinance to restrict building was suggested. The Attorney-General was willing to incorporate any suggestions from the members but was not prepared to go so far as to forbid the erection of wooden buildings. This, he considered, would operate harshly against the lower orders. The question was not pressed as most of the members were personally interested in property and the matter was dropped.

Steps were taken towards the erection of new public buildings in and around the town. At Tacarigua, William Burnley gave a portion of his Orange Grove estate for the building of St. Mary's Church, the foundation stone of which was laid in 1842, and a year later it was consecrated for the use of the Church of England population in the district. Another church built at this time was All Saints at Newtown, facing the Queen's Park Savannah. It was consecrated by Bishop Parry of Barbados in 1845. The following year St. Joseph's Convent Chapel was erected.

The Government itself started building. In February, 1844, the foundation stone of the new Government offices was laid in Brunswick Square by Governor MacLeod. The building, designed by Robert Bridgens, head of the Public Works Department, consisted of two blocks connected by a double archway. The northerly block contained rooms for the Governor, the Colonial Secretary and the Council Chamber. These were all upstairs and below them were the offices of the Sub-Intendent of Crown Lands and the Survey Department. In the other block were two Courts of Justice and the Judges' chambers. Below these were the offices of the Registrar and Marshal. The building was finally opened after an impressive service in Trinity Church, by the new Governor, Lord Harris, in 1848.

Another move made by the Government was taking over the Army Ordnance Depot at Cocorite. This building, over which Woodford had had so much trouble with the Military, was purchased by the Governor and converted into a Leper Settlement.

In San Fernando too the Government carried on its construction work, the new wharf being opened in 1842. Here also the

Church of Notre Dame de Bon Secours was built and opened under the guidance of Father Griffin.

San Fernando was assuming a new importance in the island and in 1846, in recognition of this, a Town Council was established under the presidency of Robert Ffloyd.

(9) *Notes*

Trial by jury was first introduced into Trinidad in 1842.

Ice, which is now considered to be a necessity throughout the colony, was first imported to Port of Spain in 1844.

On April 20th, 1847, the first postage stamp to be issued in any British colony appeared in Trinidad. This was the "Lady MacLeod" stamp, a private issue with Government permission for postage between Port of Spain and San Fernando. Its value was five cents but the stamps were obtainable in blocks of one hundred at $4.00.

The first Portuguese shop in the colony was opened in 1848.

Sir Henry MacLeod retired as Governor in 1846.

CHAPTER FIFTEEN

LORD HARRIS AND VICE-ADMIRAL SIR CHARLES ELLIOTT, 1846–57

(1) *Immigration*
(a) *East Indians*

IN 1846, 1,556 East Indians and 5,468 other nationals, including West Indians, emigrated to the colony, but this rate of entry was insufficient to meet its needs. Soon after his arrival, Lord Harris was presented with a Memorandum from the planters, asking him to ensure additional immigration from India. This he forwarded to the Secretary of State with a covering despatch:

> "I have been called upon this year to represent to Your Lordship the increasing complaint on the part of the Planters for want of labour, more particularly towards the end of the crop season. I find it generally considered that but for continued and persevering industry of the immigrants the crops could not have been taken off and that a large proportion would have been sacrificed, for the Creole labourers left the estates and could not be induced to return to work. The Memorialists express themselves, in consequence, desirous of procuring such a supply as will ensure them from total loss of these valuable people should they insist upon returning to their own country. They all express a desire to return to their own country at the end of five years. This is greatly to be regretted for even supposing a better selection would be made now than on former occasions, yet it would be long before newcomers could be either acclimatized or become proficient in the labour required of them. I believe that a supply of Indian labourers would be of great advantage for all sugar estates in the island and would probably prevent some from being abandoned, which without such assistance could not be carried on."

It began to look as though the solution of the labour problem by immigrant Indians was doomed to the same failure as the previous scheme. Complaints were constantly being made by the Indians and by their employers and in 1849 and 1851, immigration was suspended. The Home Parliament was still very sensitive over emancipation and its results and the strong suspicion that immigrants were facing virtual slavery in the West Indies was voiced by Fowell Buxton. No amount of denial was sufficient to obliterate this idea. Lord Brougham went so far as to describe the Order in Council for the introduction of Indians in Demerara as the " establishment of what would become a slave trade."

The Anti-Slavery Society carried on an unceasing campaign against the system of indentured labour and charges were laid against the Governor and Attorney-General. In a Memorial to the Secretary of State, Lord Harris was accused of being a virtual slave owner :

" The immigrants are neither slaves nor convicts. They enter the colonies as free men, but the Legislative Bodies of Demerara and Trinidad, assisted by Government functionaries, some of whom are interested in plantation property as are the Governor, Attorney-General and High Sheriff of Demerara, and others by family connections, as are the Governor and Attorney-General of Trinidad, avoiding a direct enactment of a system of slavery, take advantage of the ignorance and helplessness of the immigrants to pass laws of a complicated character, the practical operation of which is to reduce them to a servile condition but little removed from slavery; the facts in proof of this are too many and too palpable to be overlooked or set aside."

To this Lord Harris replied :

" By my marriage I am in no way directly or indirectly interested in plantation property and am only so far connected with those who are, that Lady Harris' brother-in-law is the proprietor of some estates. These notions are promulgated by a portion of the Press in this island, which are a disgrace to the community, indifferent or worse to religion, socially licentious, libellous in attack on character, generally incorrect, frequently false in its statement of fact, and endeavouring by every means in its power to foment and increase animosity of caste and colour. Without in any way compromising myself as to what will be the ultimate result of this enterprise, I do not hesitate to assert positively that without immigrants the sugar production must be, I might say would ere this have been, abandoned."

The planters were insistent on the necessity of more immigrants, pressing for 1,000 in 1850 and the same number again

242

in 1852. That so many Indians desired to return home at the expiration of their indenture caused labour shortage and the Secretary of State suggested that an option should be given them to commute their return either for the value of their passage in land or for free passages for their wives and children to join them in the colony, together with a grant of half an acre. Some of the immigrants availed themselves of this offer and a system of village settlements was established. This did not stop nearly 1,000 leaving the island in three years. Those who stayed were unfortunately not always the best or the most capable Indians.

When immigration reopened in 1852, the type of immigrant improved. A new Order in Council introduced several safeguards, including the presence of a Protector of Immigrants in the Legislative Councils of the colonies concerned. Terms of indenture were strictly laid down, ample provision was made for food, lodging, wages, medical attention and return passages. The return of so many of the immigrants affected the finances of the colony. Later, in 1865, when repatriation reached its peak, the *British Trident* sailed for India with over £12,000 sterling in cash on board. To counteract this alarming loss of sterling, Crown lands were offered to immigrants and a large East Indian community gradually came into being, supplemented by those who, finding conditions better in Trinidad, returned from India. From 1851 to 1917 there was a continuous stream of East Indians entering Trinidad and Demerara.

(b) *Chinese*

In 1853 the Governments of Trinidad, Demerara and Jamaica requested that Chinese labour be introduced into the West Indies.

The *Australia* sailed from Amoy for Trinidad at the end of 1852 with about four hundred immigrants; complete lack of interpreters and the inability of the newcomers to speak any English made their early settlement difficult. They and the immigrants from Canton, who arrived on board the *Clarendon* at the end of April, were settled however before the rainy season began. The third vessel to arrive, the *Lady Flora Hastings* from Fukien, came late in July and brought with her many opium smokers who were a constant source of trouble on the estates. Once again the mistake of 1806 was made. There were no women amongst the immigrants. It was not until 1862 that the *Wanta* from Hong Kong included, amongst her 450 immigrants, 115

243

women shipped as wives. These women did not create a good impression in the colony.

Very few of the early Chinese immigrants repaid the money advanced to them in China and in 1861 the British Government, who were bearing the cost of immigration, decided that in future this cost must be borne by the colonies receiving immigrants. In 1866 the British and Chinese Governments agreed that the payment of return passages should be compulsory. On the grounds of expense the planters gave up the use of Chinese labour.

(c) *Portuguese*

A terrible famine in Madeira in 1846 forced many of the inhabitants to seek a fresh life in the New World. They were not interested in agriculture and of those who settled in the West Indian colonies many turned to petty commerce, which had hitherto been regarded as the particular field of the Negroes. In St. Vincent and British Guiana anti-Portuguese riots took place, but Trinidad was saved from this trouble as a large number of the immigrants moved on to the United States.

Portuguese immigration gradually declined in importance as owners did not require this type of indentured labour, and was eventually superseded by the sufficiently large numbers of East Indians entering the colony.

(d) *Emigration*

In 1852 and 1853 three parties of Trinidadians left the colony to settle in Venezuela. They left in good spirits under the direction of Mr. Numa Dessourses, professing themselves happy to leave and confident that their new settlement at Nunancia would be a success. All might have been well had arrangements been made with the Venezuelan Government for the initial imports of provisions and other necessities to be free of duty. The failure to do this meant the complete failure of the settlement, and forced the return of the emigrants penniless and in a miserable condition.

(2) *Communications*

The growing trade between Great Britain and the West Indies necessitated an improved packet service. In 1810 mail for the Indies was collected at the G.P.O., London, on the second Wednesday of each month and forwarded via Surinam, Berbice and Demerara, and was returned by way of Barbados. By 1837 this service had become a regular fortnightly steam packet run between Falmouth and the West Indian ports and later was taken over by the Royal Mail Steam Packet Company, who used St. George's, Grenada, as their coaling station and headquarters in the archipelago. The first of their vessels to reach Trinidad with mail was the *Tweed*, on January 10th, 1842.

Internal communications of the island were constantly being improved. The Wardens of the counties were made responsible for the upkeep of bridges and roads in their districts. Under Ordinance 14 of 1854, a Central Road Board was established, with a Secretary paid £500 per annum as Inspector of Roads and Bridges.

Sir Charles Elliott was keenly interested in internal communications; it was during his Governorship that the proposal to cut a canal between the Oropouche and Caroni Rivers was first considered. This 88,000 feet cut was to be carried out by convict labour at a cost of $123,000. Elliott left the colony before any decision was made and the project was dropped. He did, however, stay long enough to see two of his schemes carried through. The two-mile lagoon road across the Grand Lagoon of Oropouche connected the Naparimas with the southern districts of the island and was begun in 1853. Hart's Cut, a 2,000 feet canal, fifteen feet wide, and four feet deep, across the isthmus of Chaguaramas, was opened in May, 1856. Hart, the Superintendent of Prisons, proposed the scheme and provided labour for the operation, which he personally supervized. The cut was a great asset to fishermen and the inhabitants of the island, who were saved the long and often difficult pull round Pointe Gourde. In 1865 the cut was deepened by three feet and widened by ten feet and a wall breastwork some 200 feet long built out at the eastern entrance.*

Another suggestion for the improvement of the island's communications was that for a railway, in 1847. It was proposed to run the track from Chaguaramas through Port of Spain to the south of the island. A very extensive survey of the area was made but the Government, strenuously supported by William Burnley, was unwilling to co-operate.

William Eccles, a Scottish sugar planter, who was keenly interested in the development of the south of the island, was the first person to introduce any sort of railway system into Trinidad. All trade between the south and the north of the colony was carried on by sea as the road communications were too bad for traffic. The Wards of North and South Naparima and Savannah

---

* After nearly 100 years the cut was filled in when the north-western end of the island was leased to the United States.

Grande exported large quantities of rum, molasses and sugar from Cipero Creek and the San Fernando wharf. To facilitate transport, Eccles cut a light railway track through a hill and connected San Fernando with the Creek.* At Cipero Creek he erected cranes for loading and unloading ships and a warehouse for storing sugar. He established a saw mill and an engine repair shop and a slipway for repairing and cleaning local steamers. It was largely due to his enterprise that the San Fernando jetty was built. To accommodate the people from Pointe-a-Pierre and Savonetta, he established a station at Sandy Bay. Another at Felicity Hall saved the people of Carapichaima a tiresome journey to Couva to meet the steamer's boat.

(3) Births, Deaths and Marriages

On Good Friday, 1848, there died in Trinidad one of her oldest and most respected colonists, Paul Giuseppi, at his home, Valsayn, where the Articles of Capitulation had been signed some fifty years before. A native of Corsica, he had come to Trinidad as a young man at the time when the French took his native island from Genoa. Though he had not played a prominent part in the politics of the island, he had held the trusted position of Tenient Mayor of St. Joseph under both Hislop and Woodford.

Another early settler to pass away in the same year was Dr. Francisco Llanos, a learned Spanish lawyer, at the age of seventy-one, for many years a member of the Council of Advice and a personal friend and admirer of Governor Woodford.

The year 1850 saw something then unique in the annals of the colony. On April 16th, Lord Harris, Governor and Commander-in-Chief of Trinidad, married Sarah, the younger daughter of the Archdeacon of Trinidad and Mrs. Cummins. The whole colony gave itself to a day of rejoicing. The honeymoon was spent at Caledonia.† The following year saw the birth of the Hon. C. W. G. Harris, later to become Lord Harris of cricket fame. In 1852, a daughter, Charlotte, was born, but early the following year Lady Harris died in Barbados.

In 1850 William Hardin Burnley died and was buried in Lapeyrouse Cemetery. He had wielded great influence in the colony, even though he was not a Trinidadian. His family originally came from England but had settled in Virginia, where before the War of Independence they had been wealthy land-owners. His father had been forced to leave America for London

* Known as the Cipero Tramway.
† See Appendix XXXIV.

246

as a result of the war. William Hardin Burnley was born in New York in 1780. He was educated in England while his father was an underwriter at Lloyds of London. His education appears not to have fitted him for any profession, but he had money to invest and he took up residence in Trinidad in 1802. He had married Charlotte Brown, daughter of a Port of Spain merchant, a member of an old family from Carnoustie in Scotland. For many years he was a prominent leader of the planters and a member of the old Council of Advice and the new Legislative Council. He it was who first suggested that the solution to Trinidad's labour problems could best be solved by immigration from the East.

The probate of Burnley's will showed a personal estate of £94,296 in American securities and several estates in the colony: Orange Grove, £8,000; Phoenix Park, £6,000; Providence and Petersfield, £3,000 each; Endeavour and Perseverance, £2,000 each, and Windsor Park abandoned. He also held shares in and mortgages on Forres Park, St. Clair, Union Hall, Bonaventure, Concordia, Barataria, Nelson and Mon Repos, bringing the total value of his estate up to £149,855. After deduction of debts and small legacies, the total of £122,679 was divided between his widow in England and his two sons.

In May, 1852, Dr. Patrick Smith, first Archbishop of Port of Spain, died. He was much loved by all and his funeral was attended by the Governor and all Government officials, accompanied by the Band of the 39th Regiment from the Garrison.

(4) *Buildings*

The Roman Catholic Church of Notre Dame de Bon Secours was consecrated in San Fernando on May 29th, 1849, by the Bishop and was visited the day following by Lord Harris, who had travelled down from Port of Spain by ship. He was greeted by a seventeen gun salute from the Artillery and the day was rounded off by fireworks.

Lord Harris's building projects were not on a large scale. The gaol (built in 1812) was extended and he gave and had erected a drinking fountain on the Eastern Main Road just outside Port of Spain, a most welcome gift to both man and beast. It is still known as the Governor's Spoon, and is a land mark.

During Elliott's Governorship there was more to show in the way of structural progress. The Port of Spain waterworks at Maraval were opened in 1854. The foundation stone of the Colonial Hospital was laid at Orange Grove in 1855, the site of the old military barracks. Lewis Samuel, a Trinidadian, was both architect and contractor for this work as he had been for the new bonded warehouse on South Quay in 1852. Samuel was a busy man. In 1855 he started work on the San Fernando Colonial Hospital and completed a lunatic asylum at Belmont in 1856, which was considered most up-to-date and accommodated 40 patients.

(5) Survey

On February 8th, 1850, the Earl of Dundonald, Admiral and Commander-in-Chief, America and West Indies Station, anchored off Port of Spain in H.M.S. *Scourge*. He made his official visit to Lord Harris and afterwards described Government House as badly situated and much too low for a warm climate. Two days later he sailed for Maracas Bay to inspect the timber which he reported to be of excellent quality for ship-building. After a night off Maracas he returned through the Bocas bound for La Brea to see the Pitch Lake. In his notes he describes it as circular, some three miles in circumference and 99 acres in area. In some parts there were islands covered with plant life and here and there pools and rivulets of water. The face of the lake changed daily so that

" Where there had been an islet one day, the next presented a pool of water . . . Various attempts have heretofore been made to apply the Bitumen to useful purposes, but without success as we may judge from the total abandonment of those trials and expectations which for a brief period induced its shipment to England with a view to its application to the pavements of London and other cities. All excavation has consequently ceased and so low is the estimation in which the Bitumen is held, that the duty of embarkation is only one half-penny a ton."

In an effort to put the bitumen to some useful purpose, he experimented with it in the boiler fires of H.M.S. *Scourge*. By withdrawing some of the fire-bars and nearly filling the pit with ashes, he created a good draught. Bitumen was then thrown on the fires, where it melted and burned fiercely. The experiments proved to his satisfaction that a judicious mixture of two parts bitumen and one part coal would produce the best results. In an hour eight measures coal (about one hundredweight) and double the quantity of bitumen produced seven revolutions of the paddle wheels per minute or 4½ knots without sails. This experiment was made with the use of only eight of the *Scourge's* fires instead of the full twelve and the total consumption was little more than half the quantity of fuel usually consumed. He was convinced by further experiments in the Gulf of Paria that even in the most primitive fires bitumen had at least half the heating power of coal. He took Lord Harris for a cruise round the island to demonstrate the possibilities of the new fuel.

Dundonald described the Governor as a man

"who not only takes a profound interest in promoting the prosperity of the Island under his authority, but has been furthering the advancement of whatever may prove generally useful."

From February 23rd to 27th he toured the island with the Governor and returned to La Brea for further experiments. In his report Dundonald stated:

"Geologists may be curious to learn if any evidence has presented itself of the probable source whence the Bitumen of Trinidad has originated; although a decisive judgment cannot be formed from the fact I am about to mention, yet it seems to be in confirmation of the generally received opinion that the Bitumen is the expressed juice of forests of timber amassed and fermented under circumstances which the mind has difficulty in conceiving. On a precipitous bank of clay washed by the sea the top of which is covered by exuded Bitumen, not emanating from the lake, I found on cutting down the precipice a horizontal bed four feet in thickness, resembling a seam of coal; perfectly defined in its limits though formed of all kinds of branches and leaves . . . Being anxious to ascertain the existence of the mass of lignite, which I inferred must be at a greater depth, I commenced to bore, but by reason of the tenacity of the clay, the rods did not sufficiently clear the passage and were finally arrested at a depth of 60 feet under the bed of ligneous substance before mentioned.

. . . probably put the British Government . . . in possession of the most abundant mass of anthracite in the world; a substance which might be supplied to our steam vessels in that quarter, at less than one fourth the cost of coal; thus securing for defence and commerce, the exclusive steam navigation of these seas during a period of war.

The plains of Trinidad have a fertile soil which simply by clearing the ground is capable of being rendered the most productive in the West Indian Islands for the growth of sugar or whatever can be cultivated in a climate, the most uniform in its temperature, the most congenial to tropical plants and free from the evils of hurricanes and from all impediments to vegetation. I am confident that if the hands of His Excellency were not bound by restrictions and routine, the progress of Trinidad would soon verify this opinion."

It was largely due to the experiments of Lord Dundonald that interest in Trinidad bitumen was revived and that the Pitch Lake was opened up as a commercial enterprise.

A geological survey of the island was started in 1856 by J. G. Sawkins and G. P. Wall, appointed by the Government at £300 per year and £1 per day expenses. The task was not completed until 1858, when they handed over to Government their large collection of geological specimens. These were housed in one of the Government offices for many years but have since disappeared. The report, which was extensive and comprehensive, was published in book form in 1860. Part One was a report on the geology of Trinidad. It was regarded as a standard work on the geology of the island.

(6) *Churches*

(a) *The Roman Catholic Church*

Trinidad started its life in the See of Santo Domingo. When certain of the islands became British, a change was made and the Catholic islands came under the jurisdiction of the Catholic Bishop of London, whose Vicar-General in the West Indies was the Abbe Planquais. Trinidad was not included with the other islands and was considered to be within the jurisdiction of British Guiana. On capitulation the political situation made Trinidad's position difficult and as a result of Woodford's efforts, the Diocese of Port of Spain was created in 1820 and Dr. James Buckley was consecrated Bishop of Olympus and first Vicar Apostolic, with jurisdiction over Trinidad and the Lesser Antilles. After the death of Dr. Buckley in 1828, Dr. Daniel MacDonnell became the second Vicar Apostolic.* The population of the colony increased so rapidly that in 1837 Dr. Patrick Smith was appointed as Coadjutor Bishop of Agna and was consecrated at Port of Spain to assist in the work of the Roman Church in the British West Indies. In 1839 British Guiana was raised to a Vicarate Apostolic and its first Bishop, Dr. Haynes, consecrated Bishop of Oriense. On the death of Dr. MacDonnell, Dr. Smith became the third Vicar Apostolic and later, in April, 1850, the first Archbishop of Port of Spain, with jurisdiction over St. Lucia, St. Vincent and Grenada as well as Trinidad and Tobago. It was he who consecrated the first Bishop of Roseau of Dominica

* See Appendix XXXII.

in the Port of Spain Cathedral within a week of himself being made Archbishop.

In August of 1851 the Jubilee celebrations of the Roman Catholic Church took place. For a fortnight processions and services were held all over the island, culminating in a gigantic meeting on Mount Calvary, addressed by Fr. Christopher. On August 20th, as a large cross was being erected on the Mount, a thunderstorm took place and the cross was struck by lightning and split in two.

When Dr. Smith died in 1852 he was succeeded by Mgr. Spaccapietra as second Archbishop. He worked hard for his flock, founding and building out of his own pocket the Hospice of St. Vincent de Paul. He suffered much at the hands of the Government, particularly the Attorney-General, as he was not a British subject. In 1859 he resigned from the colony and later became Archbishop of Smyrna. Whilst he was in Trinidad he dedicated Mount Calvary Chapel in Port of Spain, a chapel in which the whole Roman Catholic community showed great interest. Bodu reports:

"... gentlemen digging sand in the Dry River, which was conveyed by ladies and children in boxes, baskets and other suitable receptacles."

On the road to the Chapel were bas-reliefs representing the Stations of the Cross, the work of Fabriche of Lyons. During Lent this road was a constant object of pilgrimage for the faithful.

(b) *Church of England*

In March, 1848, Dr. Parry, Bishop of Barbados, officiated at the first Ordinations in Trinity Church. William T. Webb, Joseph Peschier and Charles Wood were made Deacons. The first two were students from Codrington College, Barbados. Peschier was licensed as assistant curate at St. Michael's Church (Diego Martin) and Wood as Catechist and officiating minister in the Parish of St. Bartholomew (Mayaro), especially to minister to the disbanded African soldiers.

This was one of the few occasions on which the Bishop was able to gather his clergy together to deliver his Charge.

(c) *Wesleyan Methodists*

In 1850, a temperance meeting, the first in the colony, was held under the chairmanship of a Mr. Cleaver in the Hanover Wesleyan Church. It was well attended and successful in that between thirty and forty persons signed the pledge of total abstinence.

(d) Baptists

On March 14th, 1854, the Baptist Church of St. John in Pembroke Street was officially opened. The church had taken only four months to build and had cost the congregation $5,000, for the Baptists, like the Presbyterians, declined State aid and contributed generously to support their church. In October, 1856, the Reverend J. H. Gamble began his ministry in Port of Spain.

(7) Education

In 1846, education in Trinidad was at a lower standard than in any other of the British West Indian colonies. The Mico Charity schools, the Cabildo School and a few denominational or private schools were striving desperately to cope with the educational needs of an ever-growing population. Lord Harris, soon after his arrival, suggested that an Ordinance be drawn up to establish a system of general education throughout the colony, but it was not until 1851 that any real move was made. The two major difficulties were still religion and race. At length a system was evolved by which Lord Harris hoped to satisfy the aspirations of all classes of society and at the same time to convince the various religious bodies that no attempt was to be made by Government to subvert their children or to give any particular church undue predominance. The fundamental principles of the new Ordinance were :

1. That no religious instruction whatever was to be imparted in the schools.
2. Under no circumstances were schoolmasters to give religious instruction.
3. Religious instruction of the children was to be committed to their respective Pastors on a day set apart for the purpose in each week. This instruction was to be given in churches or other appointed places. On the day of religious instruction the school would be closed.
4. Instruction in schools was to be in English, and it was to be of such a character as not to offend the religious susceptibilities of the inhabitants of the Colony.
5. School expenses were to be met by local rates.
6. The entire management and control of the schools, the appointment and dismissal of teachers, the determination of the course of instruction and of the books to be used, were vested in a Board of Education.

In each ward there was to be a school where education for boys and girls was to be completely free, the costs being borne by local rates. This did not include infants. Though there was a certain amount of opposition from those who advocated daily religious instruction rather than weekly, the Ordinance did provide an answer to the difficult religious problems and went a long way towards making organized education acceptable in the country districts.

In the capital a Model Training School for Teachers was established and in 1852 all schools, both private and public, came under the supervision of school inspectors of the newly formed Board of Education.

(8) Internal Organization
(a) Wardens

In 1849 arrangements were made for the internal reorganization of the colony. The old Spanish Quarters, Barrios and Parishes, were no longer able to function properly. Under a new Ordinance, the island was divided into northern and southern districts. A line was drawn from Manzanilla Point along the course of the L'Ebranche River, thence westwards along the crest of the central range of hills to Mount Tamana; there it turned west-south-west to Montserrat and finally due west to the Gulf of Paria south of Point Savonetta. These two main districts were divided again into four counties.

North:	St. George	South:	Mayaro
	Caroni		Nariva
	St. David		St. Patrick
	St. Andrew		Victoria

A further subdivision was then made, each county being cut into two smaller districts and each district into wards, which varied in size according to population.

In 1854 an Ordinance was passed to regulate the employment of Wardens and to define their duties. These included the collection of taxes, the overseering of all roads and bridges, the supervision of all Crown timber and the issue of permits for its felling and removal and the keeping of records of all marriages in their wards. Later an Ordinance was passed permitting Wardens to perform marriages.

In 1853, in response to a petition from the Town Councillors, a new constitution based on the principles of the English Municipal Corporations Act was granted to Port of Spain. Under Ordinance No. 10, 1853, "Regulation of Municipal Corporations in the Island ", the name Town Council was changed to Borough Council and the first meeting was held under the chairmanship of Dr. Louis A. A. de Verteuil, at which James Kavanagh was appointed Mayor.

San Fernando was included in this Ordinance and the President of the Town Council (founded in 1846) Dr. Robert Johnson, continued in office as Mayor of the new Borough. In the following year a new Town Hall was built in the Borough and its prosperity was increased by the building of a stone jetty in the harbour.

(b) Police

The Police force of the colony had a good reputation and carried out its duties efficiently. It was not confined entirely to normal police duties. The postal arrangements in both Port of Spain and San Fernando came under its jurisdiction and the constables were also the island's postmen. When police duties became too onerous, the force was supported by the Garrison stationed at St. James's Barracks.

In 1849 much indignation was caused in the capital when it became known that an Ordinance was being considered under which all persons confined in the Royal Gaol would have their heads shaved after the manner of common criminals, even though they might be incarcerated for debt or some other civil offence. On Saturday, September 29th, notices appeared all over town convening a public meeting on the following Monday, October 1st, at a house in Almond Walk. So many attended that it soon became obvious that the house would prove too small to hold the numbers who wished to be present. The butchers, who had gone on strike to attend, suggested an adjournment to the empty Eastern Market. There a deputation of Messrs. Dessources, Radix, Scott, Louis Rostant and Hobson was appointed to wait upon the Governor. The deputation was accompanied to the Government buildings by an excited crowd.

Lord Harris received the deputation and agreed that further consideration would be given to the Ordinance and that their views would be noted. The Attorney-General addressed the crowd and passed on the Governor's assurance. This, however, did not appease the people and when one man who persisted in standing too closely behind the Governor's chair in the Council Chamber was arrested, riot broke out and stones were thrown at the windows. The police were unable to restore order or control the mob and a detachment of Regulars from the 88th Regiment stationed at St. James' Barracks was sent for. The Riot Act was read without effect and the order given to fire. Three persons killed and four injured, several arrests were made and the ringleaders were given terms of imprisonment. By order of the Governor they were all, with the execption of one man, released in the following July, and the shaving proposal was withdrawn.

(c) Customs

Until 1826 the Imperial Customs officers had collected all duties imposed on commercial transactions, together with fees paid by vessels entering or leaving West Indian ports, and paid them over to their respective Colonial Treasuries. From this date onwards the Commissioners of the Treasury in Great Britain had authorized the officers to retain their salaries before passing the balance over to the colonies. This raised an outcry amongst Colonial Governments, for all considered that these British Customs officers should be paid from home. Led by Barbados, the West Indian colonies objected to having to provide any portion of the Customs officers' salaries, but by 1832 the Lords of the Treasury insisted that individual colonies should pass laws imposing tonnage duties on all shipping using their ports, in case the 10% of all Imperial Customs duties which Britain was prepared to grant should not cover the salaries required.

In Trinidad a Collector of Customs was appointed by the local Government of 1850 at a salary of £800 per annum to be paid by the local Government, and this arrangement lasted for six years, when it was decided that the post should be joined to that of Receiver-General of the colony.

(9) Trade and Commerce

A great incentive to the trade and commerce of the colony was the foundation by Royal Charter in 1836 of the Colonial Bank, with a capital of £20,000,000, and headquarters in London. The establishment of a branch in Port of Spain was welcomed by planters and merchants.

In 1840 the West Indian Bank also came into being. Four years later it had to close its doors and leave the banking business of the colony to the Colonial Bank.

Trade was also helped by a revision by the Home Government in 1845 of the various acts which covered colonial commerce. This new Act aimed, not at raising revenue, but at protecting the trade of the Mother Country. Under it " free ports " were established in the British West Indian and North American territories; through these the colonists were permitted to carry on foreign trade under certain restrictions: war materials were forbidden as were coffee, sugar, molasses and rum not refined in England, this to protect the interests of the colonies. The Act was followed a year later by another which gave the Colonial Legislatures the right to reduce or repeal any duties imposed by the Act of the previous year, but it was laid down that no modification was to come into operation until proclaimed in all the colonies.

It was in 1849 however that the colonies really got their freedom to trade, for it was then that the Navigation Laws which had governed Britain's home and colonial trade were repealed after nearly 200 years' existence. For the first time, unrestricted trade was established in the West Indies.

(10) *Notes*

In 1849 for the first time two Trinidadians were raised to major positions in the colony. William Knox became Chief Justice and Louis Cipriani, Registrar.

The Corresponding Committee of the Royal Society of Arts in 1852 sent various exhibits to be put on show in London. Two committees under the Chairmanship of C. W. Warner, the Attorney-General, aided by H. Cruger, in charge of the Botanic Gardens, gained three prize awards for fibres, cacao and starches. Other prize winners from Trinidad were Mr. Wall, geological maps; Dr. Basanta and Dr. Mitchell, cotton; Mr. Devenish, woods; an exhibit of drugs from Trinidad was also commended.

Though horse racing on the Savannah was recorded as early as 1828, meetings were not held regularly until 1853, when one meeting was held under the patronage of Lord Harris during the Christmas holidays. The following year a stand was built and since then meetings have been held continuously and the number per year increased.

For some years the people of Trinidad had been supplied with their reading matter by the Trinidad Library Association, a body of private citizens who circulated books amongst their friends. In 1851, Judge Knox, supported by Lord Harris, founded a public library, one of the first to be established in the British Empire. The building in Chacon Street was opened at an appropriate time, for Lord Harris was making a great effort to establish a system of general education in the colony. He sponsored an Ordinance to provide an annual income of £300 towards the upkeep of the library and he gave many of his own books for public use.

Knox and others gave valuable volumes and books in English, French and Spanish were available to the public for a small annual subscription. By 1855 the library owned some 8,000 volumes and many early volumes of local newspapers.

In 1851 the first regular issues of stamps were made in the colony in 1d., 4d., 6d., and 1/- denominations, and the Post Office, having moved from Frederick Street to Abercromby and King's Streets, finally settled in St. Vincent Street.

Frequent attempts were made to enforce the sanitary regulations of the colony but in spite of these efforts Asiatic cholera swept the island in 1854. The disease was brought in by ships from South America and about 4,000 of the population died. So great was the death rate in Port of Spain that it was impossible to provide individual burials. Most of the victims were buried in communal graves formed by opening up long trenches.

Lord Harris left Trinidad in 1854 to take up an appointment in India. He had been a well liked and energetic Governor, noted for his unflagging work on behalf of the planter and peasant alike. Soon after his departure a statue by Behrens was placed behind the Governor's chair in the Council Chamber and his portrait by Feuré was hung with those of the other Governors in the Town Hall.*

In 1856 an American schooner, the *Silver Key,* came to Trinidad equipped with diving apparatus to try to recover Spanish Treasure said to have been on the sea bed since Admiral Apodoca had scuttled his fleet in 1797. All the expedition managed to find were Spanish guns, two of which were bought by Governor Elliott for $500 and placed outside the Government buildings in Port of Spain.

The same year saw the end of privateering, a feature of West Indian life since the earliest days. The Declaration of Paris, signed by several European powers at the end of the Crimean War, provided amongst other things for the abolition of letters of marque.

* Destroyed in a fire.

CHAPTER SIXTEEN

GOVERNOR KEATE TO GOVERNOR IRVING, 1857–80

(1) *Industry*

(a) *Oil*

Between 1857 and 1859 the Merrimac Company made the first attempts to find oil in Trinidad. The first bore was abandoned at 150 feet but the second struck oil at 160. The project was given up, however, as litigation and sickness combined with the discovery of large and fairly easily accessible oil deposits in the United States made further efforts appear uneconomic.

In 1867 renewed efforts were made by the Trinidad Petroleum Company at La Brea and by the Pariah Company on the Aripero Estate near San Fernando. Both projects suffered from lack of funds and equipment and were abandoned after the first drilling in spite of Captain Darwent's enthusiasm. Three years later some huntsmen found oil seeps in the Guayaguayare-Mayaro district and took the samples to the Warden. These samples were sent to London for analysis but were reported to be of such fine quality that the chemists regarded them as artificial.

(b) *Sugar*

The passing of the Equalizing Act of 1846 had left the West Indian sugar planters with a very strong sense of grievance. Their products had to face competition from foreign slave-grown sugar in the home market. As time passed and other countries abolished slavery—French colonies, 1848, United States and Dutch colonies, 1863, Puerto Rico, 1873—the effects of competition were reduced but new difficulties arose. In France the sugar beet industry, which had been started by Napoleon and later abandoned, was revived. Cultivation of beet was taken up in Belgium, Russia, Hungary and Holland. In these countries the industry was helped by a system of bounties ranging from £1 to £5 per ton, with home markets protected against foreign sugar by high tariffs. The foreign grower was able to sell his surplus in British markets below cost and force down the world price whilst the British producer was excluded from the foreign market. Attempts were made by the West Indian interests to bring about the abolition of the bounty system but without success.

(c) General

For the improvement of trade in the island an extension of the Port of Spain wharf opened in 1860. A temporary railway was laid down for the transport of materials whilst the work was in progress.

An abortive effort in banking started in 1864, when the London and Colonial Bank opened on April 1st. Before the end of the year it was amalgamated with the British American Exchange Bank as the International Bank Ltd. In 1865 it issued the first notes, but its life was short, and on January 1st, 1866, it closed its doors.

The year 1869 saw the introduction of income tax in the colony, five pence in the pound on all income over £100 from whatever source. Government officials who earned more than the minimum required had their tax deducted from their salary each month. A refund was allowed on life insurance premiums. This tax was withdrawn after only one year in operation.

(d) Agriculture

The Government pastures at St. Ann's and Belmont came under the care of the Curator of the Botanic Gardens and were for the use of the general public. A small monthly fee was charged to anyone who wished to pasture cattle there. Little or nothing was done by the Government to improve cattle until the Government Farm and Dairy was opened in St. Clair with two cows in 1879. The main purpose of the farm was not the improvement of stocks but supplying pure milk at reasonable cost to the Colonial Hospital. Under Mr. White, a practical farmer and veterinary surgeon, short-horned cattle and later Indian Zebus were introduced and at a public sale each year surplus stock was sold off. In 1879, the Government Stock Farm was opened at Valsayn, where the capitulation had been signed.

(2) Education

(a) The Keenan Report

Lord Harris had realized the importance of local management for schools in the colony. He had intended to make the local school boards responsible for the selection of schoolmasters, the choice of books and the course of study. He had not favoured an entirely secular education as had his predecessor, Sir Henry

MacLeod, but had wished to combine religious instruction with the secular, under the direction of the Minister of the majority group in the district. He had not been able to have his own way entirely and his plans had not been developed by the Board of education or by many of the teachers.

By 1866, when the Hon. Arthur Hamilton Gordon (later Baron Stanmore) became Governor, the system of ward schools had broken down and Archbishop Gonin presented a petition praying for its complete abolition and the substitution of denominational education. This petition was strongly supported by the Roman Catholic laity and with other similar petitions was forwarded to the Secretary of State. Three years later a Commission was appointed to enquire into the alleged lack of religious instruction for children attending ward schools. Mr. Patrick Keenan, the special commissioner, was " to make a diligent and full enquiry into the state of public education whether secular or religious."

He arrived in the colony in February, 1869, and in July presented his report. Among his suggestions were :

1. That a set of books suitable to the colony, with descriptions of the natural phenomena etc., should be compiled.
2. That the appointment of mistresses be made with a special view to the teaching of needlework.
3. That to each school there should be attached a workshop and a school garden for the boys to be taught carpentry and agriculture.
4. That the boys' and girls' model schools should be abolished and also the normal school in Port of Spain.
5. That a system of monitorship be started as an effective means of providing qualified teachers for the future.
6. That exclusive State management should be abolished, and responsible local management introduced.
7. That religious instruction be imparted in the schoolroom.
8. That the system of payment by results be applied to teachers.
9. That the Board of Education be abolished and replaced by a new Board of 12 members, 6 Roman Catholics and 6 Protestants.
10. That coolies be given an opportunity of participating in the advantages of the public system of education.

On the question of secondary education, Keenan pointed out that at the Queen's Collegiate School, which had been opened in 1859, " projected, managed and supported by the State," children of public officers received a most excellent education, paid for by the taxes of the people. It was a great boon to the public servants of the colony but he doubted whether their interests were of primary and paramount consideration.

The report proved conclusively that the secular system had failed to produce the results anticipated. It did not condemn so much the system as the Board of Education. Infant schools, evening schools, lending libraries, industrial instruction and the teaching of sciences that aid mechanical and industrial delevopment were all to have been established. Books specially adapted for the colony were to have been provided for every pupil. Little had been done to fulfil any of these provisions, the Board having disregarded its instructions.

The Governor in a despatch (6.4.1870) to the Legislative Council said :

> " After 18 years of trial, under the ablest men in the colony, that results of the existing system should be such as these, is the most emphatic condemnation of its adaptability to the wants and wishes of the Island, and the Governor has slowly and reluctantly arrived at the conviction that it stands in need of immediate and considerable reform."

There was a little opposition to reform though in some quarters feeling ran high, but in April, 1870, the Governor was able to report :

> " Since I last wrote your Lordship on this subject the attempted agitation against the new scheme of education may be said to have died away altogether.

On April 27th, 1870, the new Education Ordinance became law (No. 6 of 1870). It provided :

1. That notwithstanding the relative proportion of numbers of the Board professing different religions, the executive committee which, subject only to a formal revision of the Board, exercised all powers of the Board, should be composed of 8 members, 4 of whom were to be elected by the Roman Catholic members and 4 by the Protestants.
2. That two classes of schools of Primary Education be established —
    (a) Government schools maintained entirely from public funds of the colony.
    (b) Assisted schools established by local managers and entitled to receive aid from the public funds of the colony.
3. That Government schools be discontinued where assisted schools should be established and conducted to the satisfaction of the Board.

4. That the remuneration of the teachers of all schools of primary instruction should be on the principle of ascertained results; one part of the salary being fixed according to the class of certificate held by the teacher from the Education Board, a second part being a capitation grant in proportion to the educational results, and a third part being a capitation grant in proportion to the attendance of pupils at school.

5. Local managers were to be held responsible for a portion of the teachers' remuneration and for other expenses of the school under their management.

The main changes were the introduction of a system of local management and the removal of the proscription on religious teaching.

(b) Government aided schools

Governor Gordon left Trinidad before he was able to make his Ordinance workable. Only one school had been opened under the system of aid to the denominational schools, this by the Roman Catholic Church. In 1871 the Governor, Longden, reported that a second school had been opened by the Canadian Mission under the management of a committee in San Fernando. This school was intended for the education of East Indian children.

In 1875 an appeal was made to the Governor, Sir Henry Irving, for aid to assisted schools. An Ordinance was passed to provide sums for each pupil who passed the Inspector's Annual Examination—in Standards 1 and 2, £1; 3 and 4, £1 5s. od.; 5 and 6, £1 10s. od. There were no fees to be paid for education in the ward schools but some of the assisted schools could make a charge of a fee approved by the Board of Education.

This system appeared unfair and, in response to appeals, an Ordinance was passed in 1875 under which fees had to be paid in all primary schools. Assisted schools were permitted a proportion of free students.

From 1875 the number of assisted schools increased rapidly. By 1878 there were 35 assisted schools and 47 ward schools. Ten years later there were 76 assisted and 65 ward schools.

(c) Secondary Schools

The two secondary schools in the island were the Queen's Collegiate School and the College of the Immaculate Conception. The former was founded in 1859 during Governor Keate's administration on the model of the Queen's Colleges in Ireland. It opened in Abercromby Street and was "Projected and managed by the State." The latter, now known as St. Mary's College, was established in Clarence Street (now Frederick Street) in 1863 and conducted by the Fathers of the Congregation of the Holy Ghost and supported by the Roman Catholics of the colony.

An Ordinance was passed in 1870 for the establishment of the Queen's Royal College in place of the Queen's Collegiate School. The Ordinance provided that the management should be vested in the Governor and a Council of not more than 12 members, that the College should include a Normal School for the training of teachers for the primary schools, and that schools of secondary education be affiliated to the Royal College and entitled to aid from public funds. Such aid was to include :

1. A fixed salary for the principal or head of each school.
2. A capitation grant for each pupil over 9 years of age who should have received a certificate from the principal of the Royal College, he having given, during the preceding 12 months, such number of attendances at the Royal College as the Council of the College should determine.
3. A capitation grant on the results of the annual examinations at the Royal College of pupils of such school.
4. A premium on the entrance of each pupil of such school as a student of the College.

Provision was also made for free admission of boys from primary schools who qualified by examination, the numbers to be determined by the Council. Sons of deceased public servants were also offered free places and four exhibitions of £150 each were created.

The Ordinance became law on April 28th and on June 3rd, 1870, Sir Arthur Gordon in his speech at the opening ceremony said :

"We are met here today to inaugurate the Royal College, an institution in which the benefits of a sound education, I trust, will be secured to Protestant and Roman Catholic alike, without the slightest compromise to their respective principles. The Queen's Collegiate School of which this College is in some sort an outgrowth and development, was founded with the same object, but successful as it has been in other respects, it cannot be said to have altogether attained this. St. Mary's College was founded by private enterprise with a different view and to meet the wants of those who objected to the

Collegiate School. It has long been felt that the existence of two Colleges, one the smaller almost entirely without State aid, the other the larger, wholly without State aid, was objectionable and that the whole question of secondary education presented a most difficult problem. Some saw its solution in the withdrawal of all State aid from higher education; others in the establishment by the State of two distinct denominational colleges. I have elsewhere explained the reason why I consider both these suggestions faulty, and their probable effect bad; the one being certain to check and discourage superior education; the other likely to substitute inefficiency for efficient teaching and a small exclusive school for a wide national institution . . ."

With reference to St. Mary's College, he continued :

"I rejoice because not as yet being affiliated or in any way officially connected with the Royal College, their presence is a spontaneous evidence of their goodwill and kindly feeling, and the spirit in which they have been disposed to meet the efforts made to consult their feelings in the arrangements of this institution, a spirit yet further evinced by the fact that the Superior has informed me that he is about voluntarily to alter the course of study pursued at St. Mary's College so as more nearly to assimilate it to that pursued here. I rejoice because in their presence I hail a sign that the affiliation, which is, I believe, desired by the great body of the Roman Catholic community of this Island, and to which it has been shown that no insuperable religious obstacle exists, will take place at no more distant day than necessary to secure approval—that naturally requisite approval—of ecclesiastical authority elsewhere.

I rejoice at their presence, because it enables me before company to express my high sense of the courage and liberality which have maintained their College for years past without any aid whatever from the State, and in spite of manifold obstacles and discouragements, have caused it to increase its numbers and efficiency. I rejoice at their presence because I desire to see every youth in Trinidad of every race, without difference to their respective creeds, brought together on all possible occasions, whether for recreation or work; because I wish to see them engaged in friendly rivalry in their studies now, as they will hereafter be in the world, which I desire them to enter, not as strangers to each other but as friends and fellow citizens."

Besides these schools there were under the Education Officers many excellent private schools and such institutions as the Public

Library, the Ambulance Society and the Pharmaceutical Society.

(d) *Canadian Mission Schools for Indians*

Early in 1869, the Reverend John Morton proposed to Sir Arthur Gordon a scheme for the education of East Indian children, to be entirely dependent on Government finance. The matter was raised before the Legislative Council by the Governor, who said :

> " The present system of education has failed to produce the anticipated fruits . . . hardly an Indian child has attended a ward school, whilst the small number of the children of these immigrants who are receiving any education are almost exclusively to be found in private schools of the strictest denominational character and uninspected by the State."

He considered that the failure of the colony in overcoming the problem of educating the East Indian was due to the inactivity of the Board of Education, the inefficiency of many of the teachers and lack of supervision and local interest.

A committee was set up to consider what terms the Government should offer to those wishing to open schools for East Indian children. No satisfactory policy was produced by the members and the Chairman, Mr. Henry Mitchell (Agent-General for Immigrants) and the Reverend John Morton, the Secretary, called on the Governor. As a result of Morton's personal enthusiasm, the Board of Education was petitioned to open a trial school with Government aid in San Fernando. In 1871 the first school for East Indian children was opened in Cipero. Government aid amounted to £175 per year for a teacher; $5.50 as result fee paid for every child who showed reasonable progress in the annual examinations and a 50 cents capitation fee per quarter for every child who had recorded thirty attendances. Under these conditions it was possible for the school to make a small profit towards the rent of £200 per year for which the Mission was responsible.

Four hours' teaching per day had to be devoted to the study of secular subjects. Outside this complete freedom of religious instruction was permitted. The planters of the south supported the new educational plan and by 1874 twelve schools were open, ten supported entirely by planters, one by the Mission itself and one by Government. The number increased until in 1899 there were 16 schools under Morton's direction, 14 of which received Government support.

(3) The Constitution

(a) Résumé

The constitution of Trinidad had never been entirely acceptable to the inhabitants of the colony. The Home Government had consistently refused to grant any form of representative government on the grounds that the free people of colour far outnumbered the whites and they were considered to be politically unreliable. The majority of the free people of colour resented the establishment of a Government which excluded them from political rights and privileges. They felt that it was hardly consistent with the Articles of Capitulation* by which their privileges were to be secured and their situation not permitted to deteriorate from that which they had enjoyed under the Spanish Government.

The Secretary of State, in a despatch of 27th November, 1810 on the subject of the mixed Trinidadian population had stated :

> " Wholly ignorant of the British Constitution and unaccustomed to any form of Government which may have any analogy to it, in the case of Trinidad therefore, amongst the most numerous class of white inhabitants there can be no material prejudices either of education or habit, in favour of such a system (i.e. representative government), and the partial and exclusive principles on which it is proposed by the white inhabitants to be founded whereby the largest proportion of the free inhabitants are to be excluded from all participation in its privileges, appears to defeat the object of it and to constitute in point of justice, and upon the very principles of the system itself, a decided and insuperable objection against it."

It was necessary for the Home Government to retain control of the colonies if it were to pass any beneficial legislation to supplement the abolition of the slave trade.

> " It is essential for their purpose that in a new colony the Crown should not divest itself of its power of legislation and that neither the Crown nor Parliament should be subject to the embarrassment which, on such an occasion, might arise from the conflicting views of the Imperial Parliament and of a subordinate legislature. Under these circumstances you may consider it as a point determined that it is not advisable to establish within the Island of Trinidad any independent internal Legislature."

It was as a result of the Royal Commission of Legal Enquiry

* See Appendix V.

266

in 1823, that the first Legislature was established in the colony in 1831. The Commission reported that

"It appeared to be the unanimous feeling of all classes of the inhabitants that no change which did not at the same time confer on them the benefit of a reasonable control over the taxation and expenditure of the Colony, would be regarded as a boon from H.M. Government sufficient to satisfy their wants."

At the time when the peoples of Trinidad were expecting some sort of representation, the Imperial Government was having many difficulties with other colonies where Houses of Assembly had been established. In 1831 the slave-owning colonies were fighting against expected emancipation and it was largely due to the unrepresentative character of Trinidad's Council that the measures were passed with the minimum of trouble. The Secretary of State, writing to the Governor, explained his reasons for refusing to grant the request for representation :

". . . the benefits resulting from the election by the proprietary body in every country, of the popular branch of the legislature, are too familiar to require notice, and are so universally admitted as to preclude all controversy on the abstract principle; that principle is however wholly inapplicable to a state of society in which a very large majority of the people are in a state of domestic slavery, and in which those people who are in a free condition are separated from each other by the indelible distinction of European and African birth or parentage . . . As society is at present constituted in the Island, H.M. Ministers will abstain from advising the introduction of a representative Assembly and popular elections."

The new Council was constituted under the Presidency of the Governor with six official members, the Chief Justice, the Colonial Secretary, the Colonial Treasurer, the Attorney-General, the Protector of Slaves and the Collector of Customs. The unofficial members were selected from amongst the leading proprietors of the colony and were six in number. Each member of the Council had one vote, the Governor also having a casting vote. At the same time a small Executive Council was appointed; the Governor as President, the Colonial Secretary, the Attorney-General and the Colonial Treasurer. This body was to work in an advisory capacity.

The appointment of the Council was not approved by the free inhabitants, who were seeking greater control over the government of the colony. The planters and merchants petitioned Parliament, complaining that though they were paying the taxes, they had no say in the spending of the Island's income. The Secretary of State replied :

> "Theirs is a society in which the great mass of the people to be governed are slaves, and their proposal is that the laws should be made by a body composed of and elected by slave proprietors. Bringing this plan to the test . . . it is to be enquired how such a scheme would provide for that identity of interest which they rightly think ought to subsist, between the legislator and the subject . . . Society in Trinidad is divided into castes as strongly marked as those of Hindustan, nor can any man, who has but an ordinary knowledge of the history and general character of mankind, doubt what must be the effect of such distinctions when, in addition to their other privileges, the superior race are entrusted with a legislative over the inferior."

The policy of Crown Colony Government was reaffirmed in 1851 by the Secretary of State, Sir John Pilkington, in a despatch to the Governor of British Guiana on the control of the Crown over the proceedings of the Legislature :

> ". . . instead of being inconsistent with free representative institutions, it is in reality the only means by which it is possible to impart the benefit of them to a community of which the population at large is ignorant and barbarous, the institutions of the Mother Country become a substitute for local representative institutions and the Crown, whilst exercising this control, is in itself controlled by Parliament."

Governor Grant's commission (1831) gave him the power "with the advice and consent" of the Council of Government

> "to make and enact, ordain and establish laws for order, peace and good government of the Island."

No Ordinance could be put into effect until the King's pleasure had been made known and instructions sent to the Governor. They did not interfere with the government of the colony as much as might be supposed, for certain Ordinances were exempt from this delay. The raising of money for the annual revenue was permitted and Ordinances "in which the delay incident to a previous communication to Us would be productive of serious injury or inconvenience."

In these cases the Governor, with the advice of the Council, could fix the date for the enforcement of an Ordinance, but was obliged to report his action to the Secretary of State as soon as possible. Laws made by the Governor in Council came into force as from the date of the Governor's assent, but remained subject to disallowance, repeal or amendment.

Until 1848 Spanish law remained in force and all Ordinances which had not received the Royal Assent within two years of publication ceased to be effective. The Crown, though granting the colony certain rights, did not give up its own power to legislate. The constitution granted to Trinidad in 1831 differed from those of the other West Indian colonies but gradually became the system for Crown Colonial Government in the area.

(b) *Expansion*

In 1862 the Secretary of State sanctioned the addition of two unofficial members to the Legislative Council on the understanding that should the unofficial members vote as a party and render the official vote ineffective, two more official members would be appointed. The unofficial members had annoyed Governor Keate by moving resolutions which he considered came exclusively under the care of the Executive. His views provoked the disagreement of the Chief Justice, who on two occasions voted against the Governor, who appealed to the Secretary of State for a ruling. The Secretary of State replied that the obligation of the official members was not a subject for a distinct definition by the Secretary of State but rather for a discreet exercise of judgment by the official members in construing for themselves an imperfect obligation. If any question arose in the Council from which an official member understandably wished to stand aside he would most probably be permitted to do so after having given an explanation to the Governor. At the same time an official member could not be allowed to sit in the Legislative Council whose conscience did not allow him to give the Governor such a measure of support, whatever that might be, as practically should be found necessary for carrying on the Government of the colony . . . The right of declaring an opinion, which is not obligatory on the Government, is important as imposing a wholesome responsibility on the Government without necessarily impeding its action. I cannot doubt that the Council is legally possessed of this right.

In 1868 the Duke of Buckingham, then Secretary of State, defined more definitely the duties of the legislators.

The Governor, in his executive and legislative capacities, was obliged to obey the orders of the Secretary of State, whatever his own view might be. The same course was incumbent upon the official members of the Council. Any person whose seat on the Council was inseparable from his office was under an obligation to resign if his conscience did not permit him to give such a measure of support as was necessary for the continuation of Government business in the Legislative Council. Official members holding seats by virtue of nomination were expected to give a general and effective support to the Government and on failure might be requested to resign. Nominated non-official members were expected to co-operate with the Government on any question unless there were strong and well-substantiated reasons for not doing so. They were permitted to be their own judges on the strength of the reasons.

The emancipation of the slaves had restarted constitutional development. The majority of the Negroes were backward in intelligence and education and it was patently impossible for them to be given representative equality with the white and free coloured population of the colony. To give the white and free coloured people even limited rights under a representative form of government would have aroused the ill-feeling of the Negroes. The Crown Colony system solved the problem by vesting political power in the Governor acting on behalf of the Crown, an imperial authority to safeguard the interests of all sections of the community.

(4) *Religion.*
(a) *The Baptist Missions to the Company Villages*
The Baptist Mission to the Negroes of the Company Villages was inspired by an Anglo-Canadian lady who was instrumental in bringing the Reverend Mr. Cowen to Trinidad in 1843. Mr. and Mrs. Cowen were appointed to Savanna Grande two years later. Here they worked amongst the disbanded American Negro soldiers who had settled in the area with their families, each on a grant of about five quarrees of land. Most of these families had been baptized before they came to Trinidad and they welcomed the Cowens and helped to build a Mission House about four miles from the villages. The timber and roofing were supplied by the people, the nails by the Mission.

In spite of Mr. Cowen's hard work, transport and communication difficulties made progress very slow. On his arrival as Baptist Minister at Port of Spain in 1856 the Reverend J. H. Gamble assisted in the Mission's work.

1st Company Village

This was situated at Matilda Boundary at Mount Kelvin where a school and chapel flourished well at first, on land bought by Cowen. The Baptist Mission was not the first to start and end here. The Church of England had built a church and maintained a minister for twenty years in the village and another church in the neighbouring hamlet of Mara Nambre. The Roman Catholics had established a Mission for the Indians (Arawaks) in the early days of the colony's history. More recently the Wesleyans had opened a chapel in the neighbourhood. The people to whom the Baptists ministered were of mixed Negro, East Indian and Spanish stock and numbered about 1,500, scattered over a large area. Gamble, at the end of eighteen months, was forced to admit defeat and to dispose of the buildings in the village to pay for repair of the main Mission House.

2nd Company Village

This village never came into existence. Rumour has it that the settlers were lost at sea on their way from America to Trinidad.

3rd Company Village

This was at Mount Pleasant, where the inhabitants with little or no help built their own chapel. The people were for the most part hunters and were considered to be rough and uncouth persons who had their chief use only when there was a shortage of food. Their pastor, David Richardson, had a congregation of some sixty in his chapel as well as a well-attended ward school at Indian Walk.

4th Company Village

This village at Montserrat or Sherringville was most difficult of access in the wet season. Cowen had purchased land here and built a chapel but met with little success. He was followed by a native brother, Charles Webb, but the Mission work suffered a severe setback in 1863 when a bush fire suddenly flared up at night and consumed the chapel. The following year the crops were bad and it took a long time to build a new chapel.

These people were descendants of the Negroes who came from America, who purchased their land from the Mission for a nominal sum in 1857. They lived apart from their neighbours, not having made much progress towards civilization. They were for the most part hunters. An Ordinance was passed by which their lands came under the jurisdiction of the Warden, roads were taken over, and house and land tax were imposed to defray expenses. This brought the village into line with the other villages in the island.

5th Company Village

The chapel here was presided over by Brother Hamilton, locally known as Brother Will. He had arrived in Trinidad in 1816 and worked on till 1860. He was followed by Brother Carr from the Bahamas, who ministered to a flock of twenty Africans who had originally been slaves but had joined the army and came to Trinidad after being disbanded.

6th Company Village

Here Brother Samuel Cooper presided over a chapel of forty-five members.

The six chapels, connected with the London Baptist Mission, were all within a radius of ten miles, and did much to hold together the settlers. Had communications been better, three chapels would have been sufficient to meet the needs of the area.

(b) The Presbyterian Church

The Presbytery of Trinidad consisted of a branch of the United Presbyterian Church of Scotland under the Reverends G. Lambert, G. Brodie and W. Dickson, and also St. Ann's Church (Free Church of Scotland) under the Reverend A. Vieira.

In 1864, the Reverend John Morton, a Canadian, visited Trinidad whilst convalescing from diphtheria and spent much of his time on the sugar estates in the south of the island. Here he became deeply interested in the thousands of East Indians working as indentured labourers. On his return to Philadelphia, he suggested to the Secretary of the Board of Foreign Missions of the United Church of the U.S.A. that they should abandon their mission to Negroes at Iere Village and open a mission to East Indians. The old mission had very few followers. Its work had been interrupted and the Baptist Church in San Fernando had for long provided a minister. The property was also in poor condition. The American Church agreed to hand it over to the Presbyterian Church of Trinidad if they would carry on the work. The Presbyterians were urged to apply to the Church in Scotland for a missionary towards whose support William F. Burnley and George Turnbull, both of Glasgow and proprietors of sugar estates in Trinidad, offered £200 per year.

An appeal was made to Scotland to provide missionaries. In

272

1867 Morton himself volunteered for the post and the Canadian Mission was set up to work among the natives of India who had been brought out by the Government as indentured labourers on the colony's sugar estates.

Morton arrived in Trinidad in 1868 and lived for a time in San Fernando at the Scotch Church whilst the buildings at Iere Village were being repaired.* The centre of operations was later moved to Princes Town, then known as the Mission. From then on this work was almost entirely supported by the Canadian Presbyterian Church and in 1870 a new centre was opened in San Fernando under the Reverend K. J. Grant, and another at Couva in 1874.

(c) *The Roman Catholic Church*

A marble altar erected in the Cathedral by public subscription was consecrated on February 1st, 1857, by Archbishop Spaccapietra, who had himself given generously towards the cost. In 1862 Archbishop English, who had only arrived the previous year, died whilst visiting Grenada and was buried in Trinidad with all due ceremony.

A little chapel was built at Carenage and dedicated to Our Lady of the Sea at the end of 1876. This chapel, which is known as St. Peter's, was built of stone carried to the site by the men and women of L'Anse Powa and the actual building work was carried out by local fishermen under the direction of the parish priest, Abbé Antoine Poujade.

In 1880 a spacious fifty-room presbytery was added to the Cathedral premises and consecrated on February 2nd.

(d) *Hosein*

The festival of Hosein, as celebrated in Trinidad, dates back to the Islamic War of Succession to the Caliphate of Arabia in the seventh century. Husayan (Husein) was a grandson of the Prophet Mohammed by his son-in-law, Ali. Hassan, his elder brother, was poisoned in the dynastic struggle and Husayan himself betrayed and killed in the Battle of Kirbela in 680. It was said that his enemies celebrated their victory by dragging his head through the streets. The martyrdom of Husayan, who reputedly led a most holy life, is celebrated by the Shittite Moslems each year in the month of Murharran, which falls between October and November in the western calendar. It marks the beginning of the Islamic New Year.

* The American Church considered reviving work at Iere and on handing over to the Trinidad Presbytery contributed towards the repair.

In 1863 Queen Victoria granted permission for Hosein to be observed in the colony so long as there were Indian residents.

During the first tens days of the month, orthodox Moslems throughout the world lament the death of the martyred brothers. On the appearance of the twelveth moon of the year, work starts on the building of the " Tadjahs ". These bamboo and coloured paper replicas of the tomb of Husayan are extremely costly to make. Several families co-operate to build a " Tadjah ", working long hours after the day's work is over, great secrecy being kept before the " Tadjah " is seen by the public. Throughout the building period drums (Tassas) are beaten each night. At the same time two " moons ", large semi-circular head-dresses, are made, each standing up to five feet above the wearer's head and weighing in the neighbourhood of 170 lbs. One is red to represent the murder of Husayan, the other blue to symbolize the poisoning of Hassan.

On the night of the seventh day before the end of the twelveth moon, the " Tadjah " and " moons " are brought out into public view, but just before this is done, men, women and children make their gifts, prayers are offered and the " Tadjah " is blessed. That night a flag is raised to mark the beginning of the ceremony and at the sound of a gong at midnight the " Tadjahs " are wheeled through the streets. Led by the specially trained moon dancers, who take turns to dance under the great head-dresses, and by the constantly beating drums and followed by women and children singing appropriate songs, a prescribed route is followed. Dancers and drummers are continually relieved so that there is never stillness or silence.

" Gatka " or stick fighting is also practised at these ceremonies and dancing the fire rod. The former is a cross between fencing and single-stick, the latter dancing twirling a twelve foot pole with flaming rags secured to either end.

On the second day of the festival an afternoon parade takes place and in the evening of the third day the " Tadjahs " are thrown into the river or the sea and the festival ends with a feast for the poor of the district.

(5) *Sport and Pleasure*

(a) *Carnival*

Carnival or " Mardi Gras " was by Ordinance of 1849 celebrated on the Monday and Tuesday preceding Ash Wednesday. Previously it had been spread over a much longer period. In 1868 a further Ordinance was passed, restricting Carnival procedure and laying down certain police regulations for the masqueraders. These were aimed chiefly at the growing rowdiness of the celebrations and particular note was made of the Canboulay or torchlight processions.

These processions had their origin in the days of slavery. When a sugar cane fire started, the slaves from neighbouring estates were summoned to help to put it out by the blowing of conch shells and the cracking of the overseers' whips. In the original French, burning canes were known as " cannes brulées "; this became corrupted in the patois to " canboulay " and came to denote a torchlight procession. After emancipation Canboulay became a symbol of freedom and it was the custom to hold processions on August 1st each year. Later the date of this parade was altered to coincide with the first night of Carnival, of which it became the main feature.

(b) *The Royal Visit*

On January 7th, 1880, H.M.S. *Bacchante* arrived in Port of Spain, bearing as passengers the two sons of H.R.H. the Prince of Wales, Prince Albert and Prince George (later King George V). They were the guests of Governor Irving at St. Ann's and were lavishly entertained during their short stay. A magnificent ball at Coblentz House, with the Hon. Leon Agostini as their host, and a luncheon with Mr. Hypolite Borde at the La Pastora Estate in Santa Cruz Valley, were but part of their programme. This included a visit to the south of the island, where they visited the Mission, which was renamed Princes Town in honour of their visit. Throughout their short stay they were given a wonderful reception as they went through the countryside, Prince Albert in a coach and Prince George following on horseback.

(6) *Internal Organization*
(a) *Post Office*

In 1859 Anthony Trollope was sent to the West Indies to make a survey of the Colonial Post Offices for the Home Government. In his report he emphasized that the time had come for the Postmaster-General to give up control of local post offices and hand them over to their respective Governments. In 1860 the report was implemented with the proviso that the new authorities should not charge more than 6d. per half ounce for letters, this being the same charge as in Britain. Of this 6d., one penny was to be returned to the colony concerned, one penny to be taken as British inland rate and the remainder to the trans-Atlantic rate. From the monies received by the colony the local postmasters were to provide their own offices and pay their staff.

Incidental to Trollope's visit was his book, *The West Indies and the Spanish Main,* published by Chapman and Hall of London in 1860.

(b) *Police*

The foundation stone of the Police Barracks in St. Vincent Street was laid in 1870 on the site of the old wooden barracks of the 1st West India Regiment. This large building, comprising quarters for officers and men, an armoury and a court room, took six years to complete. Built in Italian Gothic style of limestone from the Piccadilly quarry at Laventille on the outskirts of the town, it stood four square round its parade ground and cost £90,000. In it were also included quarters for the volunteer fire brigade and its few paid members.

In 1870 the Police Band was organized by L. M. Frazer and by its regular public appearances fast became one of the features of Trinidad entertainment.

In the court room the Stipendiary Magistrate of Port of Spain sat daily to administer justice. He was supported by a staff of interpreters, for as yet English was not the common language of the many different races of the colony. It was not a rare thing to see the oath being taken by Mohammedans on the Koran, by Hindus over a brass or copper vessel (lota) filled with clear water in place of water from the Ganges.

(c) *Railways*

The idea of a railway in Trinidad was first seriously raised in 1847, but received no support from the Legislative Council. Mr. Eccles's light railways had functioned for some years in the south of the island but it was not until 1876 that any further steps were taken. On August 31st of that year the first sixteen-mile section of the Trinidad Railway was opened between the capital and Arima. This was followed four years later by a further stretch between St. Joseph and Couva, some eighteen miles distant, and four and a half miles on to Claxton Bay in 1881.

The first trip was made to Arima appropriately enough on the occasion of the Feast of Santa Rosa. The only complaints were that the station was too far from the town and the journey on foot between the two was too hot and wearisome.

(7) Buildings and Land
(a) Buildings

Normally houses in Trinidad were built entirely of wood and were a constant source of danger through fire. There had been attempts to make it illegal to build in anything but stone but these had been rejected. In 1868 the Masonic Hall of the Philanthropic Lodge was destroyed by fire after only fifteen years of existence and an Ordinance was passed to prevent the erection of more wooden buildings.

The previous year the "rough and substantial" house at St. Ann's, rebuilt by Governor Woodford, had been destroyed by fire. Monies were voted to build a new Governor's residence but Governor Manners-Sutton, careful over financial commitments, delayed progress and it was not until July, 1873, that the foundation stone was laid. The building was completed in 1876 and was first occupied by Governor Irving. Mr. Fergusson designed the house on the Indian plan, with lofty rooms and with private apartments at the head of a handsome staircase. At a cost of £44,360, it was built of local limestone, the doors and other wooden fittings being of mahogany from the Crown lands.

The cottage standing behind the residence, made famous by Governor Gordon's visitor, Charles Kingsley, who there wrote *At Last or Christmas in the West Indies* was demolished some ten years later.

In 1861 Prince Alfred, second son of Queen Victoria, was expected to visit the West Indian islands and an invitation was sent by the Governor and Council asking him to include Trinidad in his itinerary. It was realized that the colony had no building suitable for entertaining the Royal visitor and plans were drawn up by Lt. F. A. Le Messuruer (Acting Superintendent of Public Works) and Mr. S. Devenish, for a new building. The site chosen was the little savannah near Queen's Savannah and work began on February 10th. Time was short as it had to be ready for the Prince's arrival in the following month and work was carried on by day and night. Bricks were brought from the ruins of the Government's house on Belmont Hill. All was in vain. The building was never to be used by the Prince, as his visit to the colony was postponed owing to an outbreak of smallpox in the island. A visit was promised for December and the Council made arrangements to make the building "more substantial and durable", than had at first been intended. The people were well prepared to greet their Prince. Triumphal arches were erected in the streets, houses and places of business were decorated, and stands were put up so that they might see the Royal landing. Once again the colony was doomed to disappointment. Owing to the death of his father, the Prince Consort, the young Prince had to cancel his visit and it was not until 1880 that Royalty made use of the new building. The two young Princes Albert and George attended a performance of "Elijah" in the Prince's Building on January 11th.

Though it had not fulfilled its original purpose, the building was of value to the community. It was frequently used for public concerts and from 1871 onwards it housed the Queen's Royal College, whose premises at the corner of Harris Square and Oxford Street had become too small.

Charles Kingsley wrote of the Prince's Building:

"One may be allowed to regret that the exuberant loyalty of the citizens of Port of Spain has somewhat defaced one end at least of their savannah; for in the expectation of a visit from the Duke of Edinburgh, they erected for his reception a pile of brick, of which the best that can be hoped is that though it holds a really large and stately ballroom the authorities will hide it as quickly as possible with a ring of Palmistes, Casuarinas, Sandboxes and every quick growing tree!"

(b) *Land Policy**

In 1868 Governor Gordon realized that the land policy of the colony was inequitable and brought about certain important changes in the law.

The sale of Crown lands† had been virtually stopped by the prohibitive prices at which they were sold. This had been the deliberate policy of the Government to ensure that immigrants should become and remain agricultural labourers. A new generation of Negroes and immigrants had grown up since the adoption of this policy, men who were prepared to work for reasonable wages but who preferred their own holding which they were prepared to cultivate for the benefit of their families. On the other hand, to check East Indian immigrants leaving the colony on the expiration of their indentures, grants of Crown lands were continually being made in lieu of a return passage. The policy was patently restrictive, outmoded and unfair to other immigrants and the Negroes.‡

By the Ordinance of 1868 the price of Crown lands was

---

* See pp. 114/21, 154/7. Land Question.
† See p. 194 et seq.
‡ See p. 243.

reduced. An upset price was fixed; £1 per acre for the best lands and 10s. per acre for the soft lagoon lands. This enabled the small man to become a landowner and meant that more people living in the colony could feel that they had a stake in its well-being. At the same time the Ordinance invited the squatters to make their position legal by the purchase of their lands at a similar price. This put an end to the old problem of how to deal with families who for years had had no legal claim to the lands they had developed.

In 1875 a further improvement in the land policy was introduced by an Ordinance equalizing the land tax on all lands whether occupied or unoccupied.

(8) *Deaths*

On August 24th, 1859, the following notice appeared in a Port of Spain newspaper:

> "The death of Mr. Eccles may be regarded as a public calamity, and the country has suffered a loss, the extent of which it is impossible to estimate."

William Eccles, a native of Scotland, had arrived in Trinidad in 1840 to join his father on his sugar estate in the south of the island. His interest in the development of the island, particularly the Naparimas, had provided the colony with its first railway, and he had also been the moving spirit behind the establishment of the Coolie Orphan Home in 1857. In the courtyard of the Home a fountain was erected to his memory.

In 1867 Dr. Antoine Leotaud died in Port of Spain at the age of fifty-three. Of French extraction, he had been educated in France and had not taken up the practice of surgery in Trinidad until 1839. His hobby was ornithology and his collection of native birds was unique. His *Les Oiseaux de la Trinidad*, published by public subscription, became the standard work on the subject.

The year 1869 saw the deaths of four well-known figures in the political and social life of the colony. In March Monseigneur Farfan, a member of one of the oldest families in the island passed away at his residence in St. Joseph at the age of seventy-one.

In September Chief Justice Knox died. He was the first creole to fill the office of Chief Justice and was accorded a state funeral in Port of Spain. A marble bust was placed in the Hall of Justice as a memorial to his long and faithful service to the land of his birth. Archdeacon Cummins, for many years a leader in Church circles, died in October, mourned by all for the active part he had played in the development of education in the colony. In his turn he was followed by Daniel Hart, Keeper of the Royal Gaol. A versatile man who had held many posts in the service of the colony, he had acted on occasion as Marshal, Inspector of Police and as a magistrate. It was he who organized the building of Hart's Cut at Chaguaramas and also produced a book on Trinidad which was published in 1868.

(9) *Notes*

On March 7th, 1850, at about 11.30 p.m., the sleeping population of Port of Spain was awakened by the ringing of church bells and the blowing of hooters. The Crown and Anchor Hotel, situated above a store on the west side of Marine Square, had caught fire. Detachments from the 72nd Regiment and the 2nd West India Regiment were quickly on the scene with the garrison fire engine. Little could be done as the water supply was completely inadequate. A few wells in the neighbourhood were soon pumped dry. It was two days before the fire was put out, by which time it had caused damage estimated at £12,000. The disaster led to the reorganization of the fire brigade and the purchase of more up-to-date equipment. By 1859 the brigade was under the command of the Harbourmaster.

In 1857 Governor Keate opened the Coolie Orphan Home at Tacarigua. It owed its establishment largely to the enthusiasm of William Eccles and was founded to maintain and instruct the orphans of East Indian immigrants; children only being admitted on the recommendation of the Agent-General of Immigrants. Support came from the Government, from voluntary subscriptions and from the earnings of the inmates.

In November, 1876, the orphanage became an industrial school for children of all races. Under the Ordinance :

"any child found begging or receiving alms, or wandering and not having home or settled place of abode, or proper guardian or visible means of subsistence, or frequenting the company of reputed thieves, may be sent by Stipendiary Justices of the Peace to an industrial school."

Lord Harris was not the only Governor to marry in the colony. On September 11th, 1860, Governor Keate married Miss Jemima Murray, the daughter of a doctor practising in the island.

On July 10th, 1863, a severe earth tremor was felt in the island. Much damage was done to property, particularly to the Roman Catholic and Anglican Cathedrals.

In 1870 the first telegraph message was sent in the colony from St. Joseph to Port of Spain.* The following year the s.s. *Dacie* brought the telegraph cable to Macqueripe Bay and linked Trinidad for the first time with the rest of the world. That innovation had a great effect on trade in the colony, enabling orders for goods from home to be fulfilled more rapidly than ever before. Trading arrangements were also improved in the port when the Government steam dredger began operations in the harbour in 1871. In the same year a stern wheel steamer, the *San Fernando,* was launched in the colony. She was eventually sold for use on the Orinoco and was running until 1889.

In 1871, Dr. Crane was appointed to the new post of Surgeon-General to the colony and in 1875 the Government Medical Service was started.

It was in 1878 that street lighting first appeared in Port of Spain. Emmanuel Cipriani was responsible for the capital being lighted with kerosene lamps.

During September of the same year a hurricane did considerable damage to property in the town. The Post Office and the Colonial Bank were badly damaged, trees in the public squares were uprooted and lighters and small craft in the harbour were wrecked.

The Pioneer Soap Factory, the first in the colony, was opened by Charles Hales and the Chamber of Commerce was founded in 1879. At the end of the year the toll gate at St. Joseph's Road, long unpopular with the planters from the south, was abolished.

* The West Indian and Panama Telegraph Company operated this service. See p. 300.

CHAPTER SEVENTEEN

GOVERNOR FREELING TO GOVERNOR JERNINGHAM, 1880–1900

(1) *Industry*

    (a) *Sugar*

BRITAIN'S INSISTENCE on free trade led to continued difficulties for her sugar producing colonies. At the Paris Conference of 1876–77 the Continental countries agreed to reduce their bounties on beet sugar if Britain would agree to exclude all bounty-fed sugar from her markets. This involved the imposition of a countervailing duty on all bounty-fed sugar and the offer was refused.

The West Indian planter held that owing to bounties the price of sugar was reduced by £5 per ton. Representations were made to the Home Government and in 1880 a Select Committee of the House of Commons was set up to consider the question. The planters asked the Committee to recommend that all sugar which had received a bounty should be subject to an equal countervailing duty in Britain and thus enable West Indian sugar to compete on equal terms in the home market. Of a committee of seventeen, the proposal was accepted by fifteen but no action was taken.

The finances of the sugar colonies were all the time becoming more and more depressed and in 1883 a Royal Commission was set up to enquire into the public debts, revenue, expenditure and the liabilities of the colonies affected. All interested in West Indian sugar pressed for the abolition of the bounty system and the imposition of countervailing duties.

The Board of Trade, in an official memorandum, held that it was not so much the bounty system which was affecting prices as the enormous increase in world production. Cheap sugar, however obtained, was a benefit to the consumer and the British Government did not feel able to extract duties on sugar imports from other countries. Any such duties would be strongly opposed by the brewers, jam makers and the confectionery trade.

A suggestion was made that the West Indies might enter into a federation with Canada and thereby ensure through her protected markets a reasonable sale for sugar. This was investigated by the Home Government, which suggested various obstacles to the plan.

1. Canada might not be prepared to assume responsibility for loans already made to the West Indian Colonies and already guaranteed by the Home Government.
2. Canada might not be prepared to take over the public debt of the Colonies.
3. Assuming that Canadian tariffs were adopted, funds must be found for an increased Customs Department in the Colonies to check inevitable smuggling.
4. Was Canada prepared to assume that her manufacturers would obtain a monopoly of the West Indian markets?
5. The export of British goods to Canada and the West Indies had been increasing, to the latter particularly sugar machinery and plant. Could Canada check this by her own manufactures?
6. If the West Indian Colonies adopted the Canadian tariffs, there would be a general price rise and the benefit of increased sugar prices would be lost.
7. Federation was not needed to ensure the sale of West Indian sugar in Canada or of Canadian salt fish and lumber in the West Indies. This could be accomplished by reduction or abolition of Customs duties.

The idea of federation with Canada was shelved but a suggestion was put forward that the West Indies enter into reciprocity treaties with the United States or even be ceded to the States. The reply of the Home Government to these suggestions was :

" Undoubtedly the United States are a more natural market for the West Indian Colonies than Europe but Great Britain is not prepared to make special arrangements between the United States and the West Indies. The Government admit that the position of the West Indies is one of such great difficulty that the Government should not stick at trifles with a view to help and relieve them; and of course the day is gone when Great Britain would seek to retain any colony which desired to claim independence, or transfer its allegiance to another Power."

Trinidad, in an effort to gain some of the American market, revised her tariffs to meet the requirements of the McKinley

Tariff Act of 1890. This Act placed sugar on the free list if the countries exporting it to the States were not discriminating against American products by imposing heavy duties on imports. Unfortunately little was gained by this policy as America still gave a bounty of two cents per pound to home producers of raw sugar.

Continued complaints from West Indian planters led to the appointment in 1896 of a Royal Commission of Enquiry. This, under the chairmanship of Sir Henry Norman, collected data in London, the West Indies and the United States. By August of the following year, the Commission's report was presented.

The report blamed the depressed state of the West Indian sugar industry on the fact that 53% of the produce from the islands was sugar. In all the West Indian colonies, with the exception of Grenada, which no longer produced sugar for export, the industry was threatened by bounty-fed beet sugar, which in total satisfied 60% of the world's demands. There was a hope that the United States, having repealed the McKinley Act and imposed countervailing duties on bounty-fed sugar, might increase its demand for the West Indian product. Unfortunately improved methods of production and new inventions in sugar machinery were decreasing production costs, especially in the beet areas, where new varieties of beet with a higher sugar content were continually being introduced. Another factor which depressed the industry was the extension of beet growing to Egypt and Argentina.

The probable results of the failure of the industry were dealt with in the report. Sugar, it was stated, could not be replaced in most of the colonies. Its disappearance would mean unemployment, loss of revenue and a fall in the standard of living. Barbados, St. Vincent, Antigua, St. Christopher, Nevis, Montserrat and St. Lucia would suffer most. British Guiana would be badly hit and Dominca was already reduced to one-sixth of its former output. Trinidad and Jamaica could depend on other industries and Grenada had already stopped export. To counteract the disaster of the failure of the industry, the report made several suggestions.

1. The abolition of the bounty system must be aimed at as it was impossible to suggest countervailing duties on export bounties.
2. New industries must be established in the Colonies to replace sugar.
3. A system of peasant proprietors should be introduced and

the Imperial Government should at its own expense set up a department of economic botany. Schools should be attached to the various Botanic stations to instruct the peasants in systems of agriculture. Training for other industries on a limited scale should be included in the scheme.

4. A fruit trade should be established in the Colonies and steam communications with New York should be subsidized.

To deal with the immediate situation and to ease the burdens of the West Indies, the Commission stressed the need for cheap and frequent communications between the islands. Grenada, St. Vincent, Barbados and Trinidad should be connected by a regular subsidized steamer service. This should be extended to St. Lucia and the Leeward Islands when necessary. Banking facilities in the colonies, particularly in the smaller islands, should be extended and when necessary the Government should assist financially after careful checking.

The Commission felt that they could not recommend a general federation of the British West Indies but suggested that the Governments of the Windward Islands and Barbados should be combined and could perhaps include Dominica and the Leeward group. A combined Civil Service for the whole of the West Indies was not considered to be of vital importance.

It was thought to be unlikely that any new industry could replace sugar in Barbados, St. Christopher and Antigua, and it was not anticipated that Trinidad and Jamaica would require special assistance. Grenada could share with the Home Government in the cost of a Botanic Department. A consulting officer should be appointed for Trinidad, Jamaica and British Guiana, and towards the cost of experimenting a grant of £1,000 should be made and a further £1,000 should be provided for prizes for successful cultivators and to help elementary schools to teach agriculture. Higher schools should be further subsidized for instruction in scientific agriculture at the rate of £2,600 per annum.

Special remedies unanimously agreed were :

1. The settlement of the labouring population on small plots as peasant proprietors.
2. The establishment of minor agricultural industries and the improvement of small proprietors' methods of cultivation.
3. The improvement of means of communication between the small islands.

4. The encouragement of the fruit trade to New York and later to London.
5. A loan from the Imperial Government for the establishment of " central " factories in Barbados.
6. That the subject of emigration from distressed areas should be discussed by the Governments concerned.

The sugar market became more depressed in 1897–98 through the formation of cartels in Germany and Austria, which increased bounties. Continental producers were able to sell at high prices in their own protected markets and to undercut West Indian sugar in the British and foreign markets. America (1897) and India (1898) imposed countervailing duties equal to the amount of the bounty but England refused and remained the dumping ground for continental beet sugar. Canada, in 1898, granted a 25% reduction on British West Indian sugar and increased this to $33\frac{1}{3}$%, but the American market, with its countervailing duty, was more popular with the producers.

The British Government at once began to give effect to recommendations of the 1896 Commission. Mr. Joseph Chamberlain, Secretary of State for the Colonies, announced in 1898 that a new West Indian Department of Agriculture would be established under the guidance of Dr. Daniel Morris (Assistant Curator at Kew Gardens). An immediate grant of £4,500 was made for the initial expenses and a further £17,500 was to be spread over ten years. The colonies affected by the new department were to share a grant of a further £250,000.

The first West Indian Agricultural Conference was held in Barbados in 1899 and Dr. Morris explained the two main objects of his department.

1. To restore the sugar industry to a position where it could be carried on at a profit.
2. To encourage the development of other industries in the Colonies whose conditions were favourable.

The first of these objects was all but impossible to achieve, as it was not until 1903 that sugar bounties were abolished on the recommendation of the Brussels Conference.

In an effort to improve the inter-island communications, an agreement was signed in 1900 between the Canadian Government and Messrs. Pickford and Black, for a fortnightly steamship service alternately from St. John and Halifax to the West Indies. A yearly subsidy of £27,000, shared between the British and Canadian Governments, was included in the five year contract. The Imperial Government followed this by entering into a contract with Sir Alfred Jones, who for a subsidy of £40,000 per year (shared by the Jamaica and Imperial Governments) undertook to transport 20,000 bunches of bananas fortnightly from Jamaica to England. This company eventually came under the control of the United Fruit Company.

(b) *Oil*

In 1893 interest in oil was aroused once more in Trinidad. New oil fields were being opened up in other parts of the world, and locally Mr. Stollmeyer had made successful experiments in running a steamer on lignite and pitch. It is suggested that Mr. Lee Lum, who had estates in the Guayaguayare area, remembered samples found by huntsmen in 1819 and took fresh ones to Mr. Randolf Rust in Port of Spain. The report on these samples was favourable and Rust immediately started a search for oil in the south-east of the island. It was not until 1901 that he was able to find capital to back him. The Walkerville Whisky Company founded the Walkerville Company of Canada, and sent Dr. Ellis, a geologist, to the island. The No. 1 well was sunk at Guayaguayare and produced three hundred barrels, enough to encourage further drilling. Ten more wells were sunk without striking oil and by 1907, the Walkerville Company withdrew, leaving Rust to continue to raise funds for companies until 1924.

(c) *General*

In 1886, a public meeting, under the chairmanship of Mr. D. V. Benson, was held at Port of Spain to consider the formation of a Joint Stock Company for the cultivation of ramie (*Boehmeria nivea*) for fibre. The meeting was well attended and a company formed. A Mr. Emmanuel, experienced in ramie cultivation in both Algeria and Venezuela, was called in as consultant. Cultivation started at Orange Field, Carapichaima. This venture did not last for any great length of time.

Three other industries which were founded in the same year were short-lived. An ice factory at La Basse, opened by Messrs. Meston, showed great promise under the direction of Mr. Williams. When Williams left there were so many breakdowns with the American equipment that the factory had to close and send all the machinery back to its makers.

The Crown Colonial Soap Company was successful in the hands of an enterprising Venezuelan, Regulo Machado, but when it became a joint stock company it proved a failure. The piano factory started in Port of Spain by Mr. H. Strong, was doomed to failure from the start.

In September, 1887, an important debate took place on the asphalt concession. In spite of much opposition, the Government accepted the terms of the British-American Corporation and granted a 21-year lease with a minimum royalty of £10,000 per annum for exclusive rights to take pitch from the lake.

The following year Greyfriars Church started a Penny Savings Bank, the first in the colony. This example in the encouragement of thrift was quickly followed by other religious bodies.

(d) *Agriculture*

By 1890 control of agriculture was in the hands of eleven district Agricultural Boards, each under the chairmanship of the Warden. On March 2nd Governor Robertson informed the Wardens that he had decided to form a Central Agricultural Board. The first meeting was held on April 16th, at which the Governor was elected President, Mr. H. Fowler (Colonial Secretary) and Mr. L. A. A. de Verteuil, Vice-Presidents, the Wardens and the Superintendent of the Botanic Gardens ex-officio members, and Professor P. McCarthy (Government Analyst) Secretary. The object of the Board was :

" the agricultural development of this fertile island either in regard to existing or subsidiary interests."

To attain its object the Board was prepared to assist the District Boards in every way possible and to deal with any suggestions from individuals which might prove beneficial to the island.

An Agricultural Society was founded during the administration of Governor Broome and incorporated by licence on July 30th, 1891. Its objects were the encouragement of all things connected with agriculture and the printing and circulation of papers of agricultural interest. The Government made a grant of £400 per annum to assist this object in 1894, and increased it by £200 per annum in 1896.

Mr. J. H. Hart, Superintendent of the Botanic Gardens, established a section for economic and scientific work on part of the old St. Clair pasture in 1898, and laid a firm foundation for progress in the future. In 1897 the Government purchased the River Estate in Diego Martin and the following year started a

Botanic Garden and Government Farm in Tobago. In 1900 the St. Augustine Estate was purchased for experimental agricultural work.

(2) *Education*

The system of " Grants in Aid " to denominational schools was far from satisfactory. More than half the colony's schools were assisted and the managers all felt that to have to rely on the results of an annual examination made budgeting too difficult. There were too many circumstances over which neither they nor the teachers had any control. The Canadian Mission schools suffered most from this system.

Governor Robertson stated :

"Considering how much the Indians have done to develop the resources of the colony, the provision of educational advantages for their children is a duty which the Government and their employers owe them and from which there is no escape."

The assisted schools in the south were finding things very hard. The sugar market was at its worst and the planters were no longer able to bear the burden of estate schools. It became evident that the Government must accept more responsibility for education. In 1890 a new Education Ordinance was passed, under which the Government increased the proportion of its aid. It now undertook to pay $\frac{3}{4}$ of the teachers' salaries, the cost of buildings and school furniture and, where buildings were rented, $\frac{3}{4}$ of the rent. School fees were to remain compulsory, with the exception of those for children of indentured labourers and the very poor. For these the Government undertook to pay fees to the school managers. Another great improvement was the clause in the Ordinance which required teachers to possess certificates. Those already teaching were given five years in which to qualify. Provision was also made for the maintenance of training schools for teachers for all types of schools. Particular stress was laid on educating East Indian children, as the immigrants numbered over 70,000, or about one-third of the total population.

Under the Ordinance (No. 17 of 1890) the Board of Education was reformed to consist of eight members, with the Governor as President. Two members had to be Legislative Councillors, four to be persons " professing the Roman Catholic religion " and " four not so professing." They were to be responsible for the development of elementary education, for exempting certain children from payment of fees, and for the provision of travel

K   289

passes on the railway for such as needed them. In their hands lay the future training programme of the colony's teachers and the establishment and control of a superannuation fund.

With the new system came the end of the Normal School connected with Queen's Royal College and the abolition of free admission of the children of public servants.

The growing population and the enthusiasm of the various denominations for education led to a steep rise in the number of asssisted schools. Between 1890 and 1897, 18 new schools were opened, bringing the total in the colony to 158. Government schools during the same period dropped in number from 56 to 52. The cost of education was continually rising. In 1889 the cost varied between 38/- and 45/- per child and in 1897 the total cost had increased by £1,140 over the total for the previous year. Compulsory education and the establishment of night schools were being considered and the combination of these two items were certain to raise the colony's education bill still higher.

The period 1901–02 saw further changes in primary education. After a long struggle school fees were abolished and the Government had to make up the loss of revenue to the assisted schools by paying the whole of the teachers' salaries. There was a certain recompense in that grants made to existing schools for buildings and furniture were reduced. Schools established after 1902 received only the teachers' pay in full from the Government.

The system of assisted schools had been of great benefit to the colony, for though the Government had provided ward schools, the churches followed the population, building schools in new settlements as the need arose. Until 1902 the churches also helped to secure maximum attendance of pupils at their schools so that they could profit by the maximum Government assistance. The Canadian Mission had as early as 1894 taken advantage of the 1890 Ordinance and opened a Presbyterian Training College for teachers in San Fernando.

(3) The Constitution

In 1886 the non-official members of the Legislative Council complained that they had little or no control over the expenditure of the colony. As a result of this complaint a Finance Committee was set up. This committee consisted of the Colonial Secretary, the Auditor-General, the Director of Public Works and all the non-official members of the Council. It's duty was to examine every item of proposed expenditure before it was laid before the Legislative Council and its recommendations were laid before the Governor. This system gave the members a more vital interest in the workings of the colony but did not in any way weaken official control over expenditure, as the Governor could recommend to the Secretary of State the disallowance of any vote even if unanimously agreed by the non-official members.

The composition of the Council was changed in 1889 so that members were chosen from the different counties into which the colony was divided. In 1898 the Secretary of State ordered that the appointment of non-official members must depend entirely upon their fitness to fill the position and not upon residential qualifications. Tobago was exempted from this rule. That island was not constituted a ward of Trinidad until 1899.*

The number of members was also raised, from twenty-one to twenty-two—eleven officials, including the Governor and eleven unofficial members. The Governor's casting vote gave the officials a majority of one. The Council remained entirely a nominated body until 1924.

In 1892 the Port of Spain Borough Council, led by Henry Alcazar, demanded " nothing less than Jamaica was granted in 1884."

The Jamaican constitution of this date had provided for nine official members and nine elected members in the Legislative Council. Only two officials were appointed at first, thus giving the elected members a majority of seven.

In 1895 an Ordinance of November 25th provided that the fourteen parishes of the island should each constitute an electoral district and return one member to the Council. Only four nominated members were appointed, but the Governor had authority to appoint ten more and with his own vote create an official majority. It was not until 1899, when the elected members continued to oppose a Tariff Bill, the passing of which was urgent to the financial state of the colony, that the Governor exercised his powers. Following this the Secretary of State directed that the numbers of nominated members be kept at full strength to ensure the Government's working majority when necessary.

A deputation was sent from Trinidad to see the Secretary of State, but he refused to give way and ordered that the question be laid before the Legislative Council. In December, 1894, the aged Dr. de Verteuil introduced a motion for reform and was supported by the Attorney-General. The motion was lost by twelve votes to six. An important factor in the debate was East

* See p. 317.

Indian immigration. It was realized by all that if the motion were carried, immigration was doomed.

Further progress was held up by an unfortnate quarrel between the Colonial Government and the Port of Spain Borough Council. The Council sent a deputation to the Governor demanding relief from certain charges levied by Government in respect of vaccination, poor relief and education. Though certain progress was made, Mr. Chamberlain submitted counter proposals in the form of an ultimatum. In the event of non-acceptance, the Governor was instructed to introduce an Ordinance abolishing the municipality and putting the administration of the town in the hands of a commission. The Council was divided on the acceptance of this ultimatum and at an election held in November, 1898, John Rapsey, of the "no surrender" party, was elected Mayor in place of Henry Alcazar. After two special meetings a resolution was passed calling on the Secretary of State not to abolish the municipality before he had received a petition from the Council. No notice was taken of this resolution, which was cabled to London, and Governor Jermingham abolished the Borough Council and appointed four Commissioners, who held office from 1899 to 1907.

In 1888 Arima, one of the oldest towns in the island and the third most important in the colony, was created a Royal Borough. It was the first and only town in the British West Indies to have this honour conferred upon it. The first Mayor of the newly created Royal Borough was Charles Pamphile Lopez.

(4) Churches
(a) Canadian Mission

The work started by John Morton continued to thrive. In 1881 a new centre was opened at Tunapuna and later one at Couva. In 1886, when a station was opened at St. Joseph, the total number of schools for East Indians reached forty-two, with an enrolled membership of nearly two thousand pupils. The teachers were mostly locally taught and trained but were supplemented by several trained lady teachers from Canada. To help with the work, grants were received from the Mission in Canada and certain sums were raised by the East Indians themselves.

(b) Church of England

The Church of England, which had become the established church of the colony in spite of strong opposition from the more numerous Roman Catholics in 1844, was faced with disestablishment when the Gladstone Ministry came into office in

England in 1868. It was decided to withdraw British grants to the Church of England in the West Indies, with the exception of Barbados. The Ordinance published in 1844* under which Trinidad was divided into parishes and emoluments were fixed for the clergy, had also enacted that

"All laws, ordinances, common and ecclesiastical which were then used and enforced in England should be accepted, esteemed and taken to be in full force and virtue within the Island."

This was repealed in 1870 and from then on all Christian denominations became entitled to a proportionate share of the ecclesiastical funds.

In 1872 Trinidad was detached from the Diocese of Barbados to form a separate diocese under Bishop Rawle.

(c) Other denominations

The foundation stone of the chapel in Tranquillity was laid by Governor Robertson on March 18th, 1886.

In 1887 the Salvation Army began its work in the colony.

(d) Hosein

The Hosein processions, though primarily conducted as religious ceremonials, occasionally got out of hand and the inhabitants not taking part frequently suffered much inconvenience. In 1884 a Proclamation was issued to the East Indians of Naparima that their processions would not be allowed to pass through San Fernando. To ensure its enforcement the approaches to the town were guarded by armed soldiers and police. This did not deter the participants in the procession, who insisted on their usual procedure. The crowd got out of hand when stopped and the Riot Act had to be read. It became necessary to open fire and twelve people were killed and eighty injured. After this incident the Hosein processions were restricted to the savannahs of the various estates in the area and the processions were no longer permitted in town.

(5) Sport and Pleasure
(a) Carnival

By 1881 the Canboulay at Carnival was becoming a menace to the safety of the town and Captain Baker, who had been appointed Commandant of Police some four years earlier extinguished the torches as a fire precaution.

The police force consisted largely of Barbadians and was un-

* See Appendix XXXI and p. 228.

popular with the majority of the people in the colony. Shortly before the 1881 Carnival certain trouble makers accused Baker of wantonly interfering with the ancient customs and rites of the people and placarded the town with notices.

"News to Trinidadians. Captain Baker demanded from our just and noble Governor, Sir Sanford Freeling, his authority to prevent the night of Canboulay, but our Excellency refused."

Baker took no notice of these placards nor did he report them to the Governor who, when he was informed, sent a message to Baker stating that nothing must be done about the torches without his personal authority. The message never reached Baker, who issued instructions to the police. On Sunday night 150 men were on duty, prepared to see that no torches were carried. When they tried to carry out their instructions to extinguish the torches, rioting and fighting broke out and thirty-eight of their number were injured, eight seriously. Twenty-one of the mob were arrested and committed for trial.

Early on the Monday morning, Baker reported to the Governor and suggested that regular soldiers from St. James Barracks be brought into town in case of emergency. Fifty men from the 4th Regiment were moved down to Police Headquarters and forty-three local residents were enrolled as special constables. The Mayor had meanwhile called a special meeting of the Council and a deputation was sent to the Governor, asking him to do all in his power to stop a recurrence of the previous night's collision between the police and the masqueraders. Governor Freeling decided to address the people in the Eastern Market and to keep the police out of sight. He explained that he had no desire to stop the people's fun and that the carrying of lighted torches was only forbidden on account of the risk of fire during such a dry season. He told them that if they would undertake to conduct themselves in a proper manner he would withdraw the regular soldiers and police. This was greeted with cries of "We promise" and the Governor ordered the police to be confined to barracks until March 2nd.

On the whole the promise was well kept. Only a few street lamps were broken and private houses stoned, but many people insisted on carrying lighted torches. Just before midnight large numbers paraded with their torches outside the Police Barracks, jeering at the police inside and holding a mock funeral for Captain Baker. The police were unable to take any kind of action and the next morning fifty-eight resigned. Baker was able to persuade them to withdraw their resignations and was authorized by the Governor to publish his great appreciation of their services. When the police returned to duty they were often jeered at and pelted with stones, and for some time had to patrol parts of the town in pairs. By degrees conditions improved but the authority of the police had been undermined and the worse elements of society became very truculent.

As a result of Governor Freeling's report to the Secretary of State, Mr. R. G. C. Hamilton was appointed as a Commissioner to enquire into what had taken place. In his report he stated that the Governor's speech had been received with enthusiasm, but the prohibition against carrying torches was broken with the greatest effrontery. There seemed to be no widespread feeling of dissatisfaction but since Carnival the lower classes were much less tractable than before. Carnival, he considered, should be permitted to continue under strict regulations and to avoid the risk of fire in a wooden town all torchlight parades should be held in such places as the Savannah.

After studying the report, the Colonial Office censured Governor Freeling and commended Captain Baker's action.

In 1884 an Ordinance was passed abolishing Canboulay processions and another in 1891 removed many objectionable features of Carnival itself.

(b) Cricket

Inter-colonial cricket did not start until 1893, following a suggestion that Trinidad might send a team to England. This latter idea was not followed up, but a team from England was invited to visit the West Indies. It arrived in 1895 under the captaincy of Mr. R. Slade and played sixteen matches, winning twelve. In Trinidad they played and beat the Queen's Park Club on the Savannah, but were defeated by an all Trinidad side. In this year the Queen's Park Oval was opened. It was not until 1900 that the first West Indian team went to England with Hon. R. S. Aucher Warner as Captain. It is interesting to note that Lord Harris, son of a former Governor (Lord Harris 1846–54) who was born at Government House, St. Ann's, was the first man born in Trinidad to lead a cricket team representing England. He went as Captain of the side that visited Australia in 1879.

(c) Royal visits

Early in 1883 H.R.H. Prince Henry of Prussia visited the

Island. He was entertained by the members of the Germania Club. In February 1886 their Royal Highnesses Prince and Princess Henri de Bourbon arrived off Trinidad on board the yacht *Aldegonda*. They were entertained by the Governor, and the French population of the colony gave them a very warm reception.

The Prince of Wales (afterwards King George V) visited Trinidad in 1891 when in command of H.M.S. *Canada* on her spring cruise in the West Indies.

(d) *Notes*

In 1886 an exhibition of Trinidad products was held at the Drill Hall, Tragarete Road, Port of Spain as a preliminary to the Colonial and Indian Exhibition held later in London. The following year in San Fernando an Agricultural Exhibition did great credit to the people of Naparima.

Queen Victoria's Golden Jubilee was celebrated in 1887, and special services were held in all churches and chapels. There were dinners for the poor, banquets for the rich, sports and treats for the children. To commemorate the occasion the Victoria Institute was built at the top of Frederick Street. In 1897 when the Queen celebrated her Diamond Jubilee the Institute was enlarged by the addition of a wing to mark the occasion.

(6) *Internal Organization*
  (a) *Fire*

Fire was one of the chief enemies of Port of Spain in spite of regulations passed condemning building in wood. On November 4th, 1881, a fire broke out in the new Police Headquarters in St. Vincent Street. It originated in the lamproom under the wooden staircase where a lighted lamp was overturned and before it could be extinguished had taken such a hold that the building was completely gutted. Two years later the building was restored at great expense, with concrete floors and iron staircase.

On January 27th, 1884, the Union Club caught fire just before midnight. Though the Brigade arrived promptly, it was long before the flames were under control. A young Englishman, who had that morning arrived from Demerara, was burned to death in the club. A jeweller's shop and Crichlow's store underneath the premises were destroyed. Insurance claims amounting to more than £41,000 were settled. The Ice House, Miss Archibald's Hotel, Pineda's Barber shop, Brown's Grocery, and the New Era Printing Office were the principal buildings concerned.

A public enquiry was held early in February by the coroner, but the cause of the fire remained a mystery. The question of arson was raised and though there were suspects none was found to be guilty. The only result was the passing of an Ordinance making arson punishable by life imprisonment.

In January, 1885, Marine Square, Port of Spain, was again the seat of fire, when smoke was seen coming from the roof of a fancy goods store at the corner of Frederick Street. The energy and efficiency of the Fire Brigade confined the fire to one building, which was, however, quickly gutted.

One of the worst fires in Trinidad occurred in Port of Spain on March 4th, 1895. It was believed to have originated in Davidson and Todd's store in Henry Street and swept down Marine Square and into Frederick Street. In all, fifty-four stores were completely destroyed. Had it not been for the presence of British and American naval units in the harbour, the destruction would have been much greater. Parties were put ashore to help with fire fighting and gunpowder was used to blow up buildings in the path of the flames. For four days the fire raged, doing damage estimated at more than two million dollars and causing much unemployment.

(b) *Police*

At the time of the fire at Police Headquarters, Captain Baker, who was head of the force, lost all his furniture and personal belongings. His personal popularity was so great that a public subscription list was opened to make good the loss. The force itself was a very efficient body of about 450 men. Several sergeants were men picked from the Royal Irish Constabulary. The constables were chiefly recruited from Barbados and were not popular with the majority of Trinidadians.

(c) *The Railway*

Once the idea of a railway was accepted in Trinidad, extension followed extension. In 1882, Port of Spain and San Fernando were connected by thirty-five miles of track. A branch was made to Princes Town in 1886, adding another eight miles. Sangre Grande was also connected to Arima during the same year—a further twelve miles. The sixteen-mile section from Tabaquite to Cunupia followed in 1897. It was forecast at the time that the Port of Spain to San Fernando line would lose the colony money, as it would never be able to compete with the parallel sea service.

(d) *Other Transport*

In 1883 the Tramways and Telephone Company was formed, and a system of trams was established in Port of Spain. On La Basse, near the railway station, this company erected large stables to accommodate about eighty mules to draw the trams. This service began in 1884. There were two routes. One was from Queen's Wharf, near the railway station. This was the Red Tram route, running in a north-westerly direction to the top of Tranquillity Street, near the corner of Queen's Park, one and a half miles. The other, the Blue Tram route, ran from Queen's Wharf, up Frederick Street to a terminus near Government House and the Botanic Gardens. The fare was six cents each way or one dozen tickets could be purchased for sixty cents. The trams ran every twenty minutes. This company proved to be a very paying proposition and paid 10% every year. There were no electric trams until some time later, in the 1900's.

(e) *Volunteer Defence Force*

A Royal Commission on Colonial Defence was appointed by the Queen in 1879 to reorganize the system of defence in the scattered colonies. Small isolated detachments existed for the preservation of law and order in the smaller islands and it was felt that in the event of war against an enemy with a large navy these detachments would have to be withdrawn. This sudden withdrawal might cause difficulty and the smaller colonies were advised to form police forces. Some followed this advice. Others revived the old Militia which, through lack of funds and changed circumstances, had been abandoned.

Trinidad already had a Police Force but decided to raise a Volunteer Corps. By an Ordinance of 1879, one Company was raised under Captain Wilson and was permitted to use Police headquarters for parades. In Tragarete Road the Volunteers' own headquarters (the Drill Hall) were built and opened by Governor Havelock in 1885.

A memorandum prepared by Colonel Goodenough was published by the Imperial Government. It pointed out that co-ordinated Imperial defence had never really been contemplated until 1897 and that was based almost entirely on the fortifications and requirements of the past. Conditions in the West Indies had changed during the centuries and no longer were the islands likely to be attacked for their wealth. No European power would wish to add them to its territory, but an enemy might like to capture strategic points which would give advantage in naval warfare.

A Commission suggested that the Imperial Government should decide which such points would be most suitable for the British Navy and that troops should be concentrated there. Men could then be despatched by the Navy all over the British West Indies in case of internal disorders. Shore defences should be built with a view to co-operation with the Navy. A strong naval force in the West Indies would make aggression practically impossible and would reduce the possibility of mounting any formidable attack against the colonies, though it would still leave open the chances of indiscriminate raids from the sea.

The West Indies as a whole did not receive the memorandum with enthusiasm, owing to the likely heavy expenses and the feelings of uncertainty it raised. Modifications were necessary at the turn of the century when the United States Navy was enlarged, and again in 1905, when the Panama Canal was opened.

(7) *Deaths*

In 1887, Charles William Warner died at the age of eighty-one. He was the son of Colonel Warner, owner of the Woodford Dale Estate, and had been born at sea between St. Vincent and Trinidad. After an English education he had started to practise as an advocate in the colony in 1829. He was appointed Attorney-General in 1840. Warner was not universally popular. It was reputed that the riots of 1849 were caused by his mischievous influence. An unrelenting Protestant, he had been most bitterly opposed to Archbishop Spaccapietra and even tried to deprive him of his salary. His Ordinance preventing deathbed marriages had proved unpopular and he had caused general dissatisfaction by his suppression of small distilleries. After his retirement from public service in 1870, though then over sixty, he had continued to practise as a barrister until his death.

The following year saw the death of an eminent Trinidadian, Jean Michel Cazabon, at the age of seventy-five. His parents were both of Negro descent. He was sent to England to school at St. Edmund's, Ware, at the age of nine. On leaving school he moved to Paris to study medicine, but gave this up in favour of art and worked in Paris and in Rome. He won the " Prix de Rome " and was able to live and work for four years in the Villa Medici at the expense of the French Government. In 1850 he returned to Trinidad with his French wife and two daughters and started to paint water colours of his native land.* In 1860

* See plates 1, 3, 4, 5, 6.

he moved to Martinique but after ten years returned to Trinidad, teaching at Queen's Royal College and St. Mary's. Though a good artist he was not a good teacher and had the greatest difficulty in maintaining discipline in the schoolroom. When he died he was actually at work with brush and palette.

On June 30th, 1890, Maxwell Phillip, Solicitor-General, died suddenly at his home, Loyola, in Maraval, at the age of sixty-one. He had been born at Cupar Grande Estate, South Napa-rima, and received his early education in San Fernando. From there he entered St. Mary's Catholic College at Blair in Scotland and later moved to London, where he entered the Middle Temple and was called to the Bar in 1854. On his return to Trinidad he was very successful in his profession, possessing a great knowledge of Spanish and the Spanish Laws. From 1867–69 he was Mayor of Port of Spain and was then appointed an unofficial member of the Legislative Council by Governor Gordon. In 1871 he was made Solicitor-General and under Governor Longden acted as Attorney-General. At his death he was accorded a state funeral attended by the Governor and members of the Council. G. L. Garcia succeeded Phillip as Solicitor-General and was in his turn followed by Eugene Cipriani, a local man with large interests in the colony.

When Sir Sanford Freeling left the colony, he was succeeded as Governor by Sir F. P. Barlee, whose administration was of short duration. He died within two months of his arrival and was buried at St. Ann's on August 8th, 1884.

(8) *Notes*

In November, 1881, the Public Works Department erected a two-storey building in Port of Spain, at the corner of Broadway to house the Commercial News Room and the Harbourmaster's office, with the West Indian and Panama Telegraph Company below. Unfortunately the staircase was omitted from the plans and had to be added as an exterior fitting. The purpose of the News Room was as a meeting place for merchants, shippers and other business men, who could study the latest English and foreign newspapers and periodicals and see telegrams from Europe which were posted on arrival. A membership fee of $12 a year included the introduction of a visitor for his stay in the colony.

Trinity Cathedral installed a private gas lighting plant in 1881, and a new peal of bells, presented by Bishop Rawle, were first rung during this year.

A severe earthquake shook the whole island on January 10th, 1888. Both Cathedrals were damaged and a wall in the Roman Catholic Presbytery collapsed. Much damage was done to houses and in country districts to the chimneys of the sugar factories. Further tremors were reported but no damage was done.

The Queen's Park Savannah, which had been purchased from the Peschier family in 1817* when Woodford was Governor, for " public service " came under review in 1890. A local cricket club (later Queen's Park Club) was given permission by Governor Robertson to enclose an area in the centre for its own exclusive use. A pavilion was also erected. This brought an immediate protest from the general public and the Governor had to withdraw his permission.

Later Governor Broome suggested making the park smaller than its original 232 acres by turning the area to the south of Marli Street and Jerningham Avenue into building lots. Thomas Potter, employed in the Crown Lands Department, persuaded the Sub-Intendent, David Wilson (later Sir David Wilson) to approach the Governor who, as Intendent of Crown Lands, had absolute power, and ask him to reconsider the matter. He pointed out that though the park appeared to be too large for the population of Port of Spain at the time, and not to be very much used, in future it might very well be considered too small as the city grew. Governor Broome reconsidered his proposition in the light of Potter's far-sighted policy and the Queen's Park Savannah was saved for posterity.

* See p. 146.

CHAPTER EIGHTEEN

TOBAGO, 1498–1898

(1) *Early Days*

FOR NEARLY one hundred years after Columbus sighted an island to the north-east as he sailed through the Dragon's Mouth and named it Bellaforma, there is no record of the history of Tobago. Unlike so many other islands of the West Indies, it never became a Spanish possession and in 1580, when first visited by British seamen, it was thought to be uninhabited. This seems hardly likely, as some thirty years later, in 1614, Johannes Roderigo spent some months trying to establish trade between Spain and the island. Roderigo made this effort in spite of the fact that James I had claimed sovereignty of the island in 1608.

In 1628 a grant of the island was made by Charles I to Philip, Earl of Montgomery (later Earl of Pembroke) but the intended colony was never founded.

(a) *The Dutch and English (1627–1660)*

Captain Joachim Gijsz on his way back to Holland from Brazil in 1627 visited Tobago. He found it unoccupied and reported favourably on its suitability for a colony.

In 1628 the Dutch began to take an interest in Tobago when Jan de Moor, Burgomaster of Flushing, sent Jacob Maersz to command his first settlement at New Walcheren, now Plymouth. Though reinforced by fifty-six new colonists, the settlement failed through disease and attacks by the local Indians. In 1632 another abortive effort was made by 200 Dutchmen, under Cornelis de Moor, son of the Burgomaster. In 1636 they were attacked by Diego Lopez de Escobar, Governor of Trinidad. Cornelis with some others were captured and those who escaped returned to Holland.

From 1637, the English made determined efforts to settle Tobago. In this year the Reverend Nicholas Leverton led a party of Puritans from Barbados, but once again disease and the

Indians were stronger than the settlers. The few who remained sailed off to Providence Island. The Earl of Warwick, who had purchased the Pembroke rights in the West Indies, sent out a party of colonists in 1639 under Captain Marsham* but in an attack by Indians in 1640 Marsham was killed and the remainder went to Trinidad. In 1641 James, Duke of Courland, obtained a grant from Charles I of England. He sent an expedition which arrived in Tobago with a number of Courlanders in 1642.

In 1642 the same fate befell another party, led by Captain Marshall of Barbados. The survivors left their tobacco and indigo plantations and withdrew to Surinam. Once again the Duke of Courland sent men to Tobago, this time under Captain Caroon†; a settlement was made at Courland Bay. Once again the Indians proved too strong for their visitors and the few remaining survivors retired to Pomeroon (British Guiana) in 1650.

In 1654 yet another attempt was made by Courland's men. Over 100 families arrived from Courland.‡ Later in the same year Adrien and Cornelis Lampsins§ from Flushing landed with an expedition in another part of the island. The clash of their rights was referred to their respective states, who gave the official patent to hold the island to the Lampsins brothers. Captain Caroon then returned to Tobago, his settlement at Pomeroon having been ruined by the Anglo-Dutch wars. On arrival he requested official recognition of his settlement as distinct from that of the Lampsins, who had received an official patent from the States General. This was rejected but Cromwell supported the claims of the Courlanders against the Dutch, who were exhausted by their recent wars, and Courland remained undisputed master of the island until 1658.

In this year the Duke of Courland was taken prisoner by Charles Gustavus of Sweden and taken to Riga. The Dutch planters at once seized their opportunity, surrounded the Courlanders at Fort James (Plymouth) and forced the Governor, Hubert de Beveren to surrender. Courland was released in 1662, and on November 17th, 1664, Charles II regranted Tobago to him, but he appears to have done little about it.

The Dutch settlers obtained a grant of the island from Louis XIV of France in 1662. The French West India Company surrendered their alleged rights and the King of France created Adrien Lampsins Baron of Tobago.

* Sometimes spelt Massam or Massham.
† Sometimes spelt Coroon. See Appendix XXXIII.
‡ Now Latvia, formerly Kurland.
§ Sometimes spelt Lampsius.

(b) *Holland, England and France (1666–1763)*

The year 1666 was a busy one in Tobago. Four English vessels, under the command of Captain John Poyntz, captured the Dutch settlement. A small garrison was left behind which was forced to surrender to a party of Frenchmen sent by Vincent, the Governor of Grenada, who then abandoned the island.

In the following year Peter Constant was appointed by the Dutch to reform the colony. For five years he was left in peace but in 1672 Colonel Clive Codrington, Governor of Barbados, planned an attack, but, hearing that the Dutch were well defended by a fort and a 30-gun vessel, gave up the idea. However, in December, 1672, a force under Sir Tobias Bridges from Barbados captured Constant and took 400 prisoners and as many Negroes. The settlement was abandoned and the island deserted. After his release Constant again settled in Tobago (1676) with some 600 soldiers and a large number of Negroes captured from the French in Cayenne and Marie Galante.

At the end of the following year the Dutch under Admiral Binkes defeated the French under the Comte d'Estrées in Roodklyp (now Rockley) Bay. The French returned at the end of the year and captured Constant and about 300 prisoners, who were sent to France. The settlement was destroyed and the island abandoned once more. Binkes and many of his officers were killed but the French losses were also high—150 killed, 200 injured, one 70-gun ship blown up and two other vessels stranded.

By the Treaty of Nijmegen (1678) Tobago was once more restored to the Dutch sovereignty. The Duke of Courland tried again to resettle the island but an expedition under Colonel Monck was so badly harassed by local Indians and Frenchmen who had gone native that it was forced to withdraw to Europe. The Duke then granted the title to a company of London merchants headed by Captain John Poyntz. When all was ready to settle the island, an Order of the Privy Council dated December 15th, 1683, held up sailing pending negotiations for the Treaty of Aix-la-Chapelle (1684), making Tobago neutral.

During the next twenty-five years repeated attempts were made to colonize the island by the Duke of Courland, in spite of a Privy Council decision in 1686 that his grant was void. English companies and Frenchmen also made abortive attempts to colonize. Meanwhile the island became a nest of pirates and in 1698 H.M.S. *Speedwell* was sent from Barbados with thirty soldiers on board to suppress those who had established themselves. The Council for Trade and Plantations was opposed to

English settlers leaving for Tobago under the protection of the Duke of Courland and in 1699 the Privy Council again declared his grant to settle in the island null and void and that its settlement was prejudicial to Barbadian enterprise. At the same time the right of the English Crown to both Tobago and St. Lucia was affirmed.

Captain John Poyntz, who claimed to have made eleven voyages to Trinidad and Tobago, was still trying to get permission to settle the colony, but in 1702 his petition signed jointly with Dr. Woodruffe and Professor Stringer was refused.

The island continued to be a no man's land. In 1706 a French squadron was reported to be using it as a base for attacks on the British West Indies. With four ships, each with 300 soldiers on board, they were able to carry out raids all over the southern Caribbean. Meanwhile the paramount Indian chief of Tobago had appealed to the Governor of Barbados for protection against rebellious Negroes. The Governor assured the chief of protection and asserted the British claim to sole sovereignty of the island against the French.

The Privy Council, in 1721, authorized Lord Belhaven, Governor of Barbados, to encourage settlements in Tobago for the cultivation of cacao, indigo and other crops with the exception of sugar, for this would be against the interests of Barbados. When the French withdrew, the pirates once more infested the coast and in 1723 Captain Finn and his men were rounded up by H.M.S. *Winchelsea*.

In 1725 Governor Worsley of Barbados reported to London that the French were persisting in their claim to the island and that until the two countries settled the matter it would be useless to try to persuade Englishmen to settle. In reply he was told that he must maintain the British rights to the colony and at the same time avoid a clash with France.

Matters came to a head in 1748, when the French Governor of Martinique, the Marquis de Caylus, attempted to establish a colony. He landed troops and erected a fort and published an Ordinance authorizing French subjects to settle the island and promising to afford them protection. Governor-General Melville of Grenada, Tobago, St. Vincent and Dominica, at once issued a Proclamation commanding the French to leave and despatched a frigate under Captain Tyrell to remonstrate against the French occupation. The French Government disowned the actions of the Marquis and sent orders for the island to be evacuated. The following year, 1749, both English and French Governments agreed to remove their nationals. The fort was destroyed and the island declared neutral. It was not long, however, before the French had re-established their settlement.

In 1762, Tobago was recaptured by the British and by the Treaty of Paris, 1763, was ceded to Britain.

(2) *A British Colony*
(a) *Colonization*

The British Government had a plan for colonization of the West Indies by which Tobago was included with Grenada, St. Vincent and Dominica under a Governor-in-Chief. By the Royal Proclamation, Governors were appointed with express powers to summon and call general assemblies and with the consent of the Councils and representatives of the people to make laws. The first Governor-in-Chief was General Robert Melville, and the first Lt.-Governor of Tobago, Alexander Brown. The latter arrived in Tobago with his private secretary, Mr. Gibbs, at King's Bay on November 12th, 1764.

An important Proclamation was issued concerning the division of the island into parishes, the setting apart of convenient places for fortifications and other public purposes, the manner in which lots were to be laid out for sale and the obligations of the purchasers. The land sold under this Proclamation amounted to 54,408 acres, which produced £154,050. The first record of land sold by the Crown bears the date March 20th, 1766, made by Governor Melville to James Simpson, 500 acres, Lot 1, at Courland Bay.

Lt.-Governor Brown died in July of this year and was succeeded by Roderick Gwynne, who took office on October 16th, 1767.

According to the original plan of colonization a town was to have been founded in each parish of the island. This was never fully put into effect. Georgetown, Barbados Bay, was the first to be established and there, in April, 1768, the first meeting of the Legislative Council was held. It was decided that Scarborough was a more suitable place for the capital and sittings were transferred there the next year.

Lt.-Governor Gwynne died early in 1769 and during the interregnum Robert (or William) Stewart, President of the Council, acted in his place. During this period there was a six-week insurrection of slaves in the Queen's Bay area. Another feature was the first export of sugar from Tobago from the estate of Mr. Gedney Clarke, Studley Park in St. Mary's parish, in 1770. In 1771 two slave insurrections were put down by the Militia, which was then a well-organized body.

Major William Young arrived to take up duty as Lt.-Governor in 1771 and in the same year General Melville was succeeded by William Leyborne as Governor-General of Grenada, St. Vincent, and Tobago. Dominica was separated from the other islands with an independent government. Another slave insurrection took place in 1774. On the death of Governor Leyborne in 1775, Major Young acted in Grenada and Peter Campbell became Acting Lt.-Governor of the colony. This state of affairs did not last long for Sir George (later Lord) Macartney was appointed as Governor of Grenada and Tobago, St. Vincent having been formed into a separate government. The year of his appointment was disastrous for Tobago, for sugar had to be abandoned for cotton as a staple crop owing to the ravages of ants, which spread across the island from the windward parishes, completely destroying the canes. At this time Tobago was supporting a population of about 2,300 white people, 1,050 free people of colour and 10,800 slaves.

In 1777, Lt.-Governor Young was killed in a duel with P. Franklyn and Peter Campbell once more administered the Government.

(b) *Colony at War*

In the early part of 1778 an American squadron of two ships, three brigs and a schooner determined to capture Tobago. On their way they ran into the British ship *Yarmouth* of sixty guns under the command of Captain Vincent. In the ensuing engagement the American ship *Randolph* of thirty-six guns was blown up with her crew of 315 men and the rest of the squadron withdrew.

Peter Campbell died in 1779 and was succeeded as President of the Council and Acting Lt.-Governor by John Graham. For the first time in the history of the colony, a clergyman, the Reverend Walter Carew, of the established church, began to minister to its people in 1781.

A new Lt.-Governor arrived in the person of George Ferguson in 1781, the Governor-General of the combined colonies having been captured by the French in Grenada two years previously. Ferguson was no more fortunate, for soon after his arrival he had to defend his charge against an attack by a superior French force which took the island and captured the Governor.

Philbert de Blanchelande and René Marie, Vicomte d'Arrot,

were Governors in turn, until by the Treaty of Paris in 1783, the island was ceded to France, and Arthur, Count Dillon (an Irishman) was appointed Governor. The new Government retained the constitution and laws of the colony as laid down by the British and the same form of justice. M. de Jobal became President of the Council, on which Scarborough was for the first time represented. M. de Jobal acted as Governor when Count Dillon went to France as Deputy to the States-General in 1789. His period of office was not a happy one. There was a mutiny amongst the French forces and Scarborough was burned down. Then in 1790 a hurricane swept over the island, causing widespread destruction. Count Dillon returned from France but only stayed two years, leaving to take up military duties in France as a Corps commander. In 1792 he was succeeded by Philipe M. de Maginot, an unpopular choice, as the inhabitants of the island considered that he was antagonistic to the French Republic and started disturbances. To avoid any serious outbreak, both he and M. de Jobal left the colony. Immediately Laroque de Monteil was sent from Martinique to take over the Governorship, but on April 15th, 1793, Admiral Sir John Lefroy and Major-General Cuyler captured the island, taking de Monteil prisoner and appointing William Myers as temporary Governor.

The government of the island now came under a Captain-General and a Governor-in-Chief, with a Legislative Council appointed by the Crown and a representative House termed the General Assembly, and was entirely independent of any other of the West Indian colonies.

Between 1794 and 1800 there were a series of Governors in quick succession. George Poyntz Ricketts was promoted to Barbados in 1795; William Lindsay died in 1796; Stephen de Lancey in 1799. Joseph Robley, President of the Council, then administered the Government, and again on the death of Richard Master in 1800.

In 1801 a threatened insurrection of slaves was averted by the prompt action of Brigadier-General Hugh L. Carmichael who, when he learned of the plot, seized thirty of the ringleaders. One of these he ordered to be hanged on the signal staff and raised and lowered the body twenty-nine times. This sight, witnessed by the insurgents from a distance, decided them to surrender or disperse immediately. Carmichael's prompt action earned him a presentation sword from the Legislature of the island.

Once more Tobago changed hands. By the Treaty of Amiens in 1802, it was surrendered to the French. Brigadier-General

Carmichael, as Acting Governor, handed it over to the new French Governor, General Sabuguet, who took office on November 7th. Again it was decided that there should be no change in the constitution or the law. Sabuguet was a popular Governor and was awarded a gratuity of £4,000 in addition to his salary of £3,300. Though he never lived to enjoy this gift, it was passed on to his widow when he died at the end of the year. During his short spell as Governor he persuaded Tobago to take part in a decision on the question of Bonaparte being elected Consul for life. The Council and the General Assembly voted unanimously in favour of the proposal.

Sabuguet was followed as Governor by General Caesar Berthier. War had already broken out between England and France and a British naval and military force under the command of Commodore Hood and General Grinfield invaded the island on June 30th, 1803, landing at Arnos Vale. There was little opposition. Berthier capitulated on condition that his meagre garrison of about 200 men be allowed to return to France. Brigadier-General Thomas Picton (lately Governor of Trinidad) was appointed Lt.-Governor of the colony. Picton soon had to leave to meet the charges laid against him in England by Colonel Fullarton.*

(c) *Establishment*

From 1803 onwards Tobago was to remain under the British flag, though it was not until 1814 that by the Treaty of Paris it was finally, thanks to the part played by Sir Arthur Piggot (Agent for Tobago), ceded to Great Britain.

After Picton had left the colony there were a series of changes in the administration of the Government, until in 1807 Sir William Young arrived. For eight years he devoted himself to the good of the colony and when he died was buried in the grounds of the new Government House on Mt. William. A tablet was erected in the new Church of St. Andrew, Scarborough, at a later date. The church itself was not completed until 1819. The Society of Wesleyan Methodists had established a mission in the colony the year previously and the Moravians in 1789.

In 1821 a contagious fever spread through the garrison at Fort George, where a large number of officers and men died, and into Scarborough, where many inhabitants suffered a similar fate.

Governor Robinson, who had succeeded Governor Young in 1816, laid the foundation stone of the Court House and public buildings on April 23rd, 1821.

* See p. 59.

Several events in the religious life of the community took place in 1824 and 1826.* In 1824 the Episcopal See was created under the name of the Bishopric of Barbados and the Leeward Islands. It included Barbados, St. Vincent, Dominica, Grenada, Antigua, Montserrat, St. Christopher, Nevis, the Virgin Islands and Trinidad and Tobago. British Guiana was added seven years later. The first Bishop of this West Indian diocese was Dr. Coleridge. In 1826 the new Wesleyan Chapel was completed, built partly by local contributions and partly by the Missionary Society. On May 11th the Reverend John Nelson conducted the first service in the new building.

In 1828 the new Government House at Mt. William was occupied, the previous residence at Orange Hill having been sold on the grounds of its distance from Scarborough.

Major-General Blackwell was appointed Governor in 1828. Exports of the colony in 1830 were 107,946 cwt. of sugar; 400,440 gallons of rum, and 787 cwt. of molasses. When Blackwell left in 1833, Tobago no longer remained a separate government. It was included in the Windward Islands with Barbados, Grenada and St. Vincent. St. Lucia was added in 1838. The islands all came under the general command of Sir Lionel Smith, Governor-in-Chief in Barbados. Major-General H. C. Darling was appointed Lt.-Governor of Tobago.

The colony shared with the whole of the British West Indies in the rejoicing throughout the islands on August 1st, 1834, when all slaves were emancipated and made apprentices to the masters who had previously owned them body and soul. Four years later they were included in the unconditional emancipation of the apprenticed labourers. Education was under consideration and schools were opening.

Trade and commerce in the colony were being encouraged. In 1840, when the West Indian Bank opened a branch in Scarborough (the Colonial Bank had opened three years previously), the exports were 62,208 cwt. of sugar; 174,736 gallons of rum, and 4,735 cwt. of molasses. The Royal Mail Steam Packet Company began operations which included calls at Tobago in 1841.

In 1842 the Diocese of Barbados and the Leeward Islands was divided into three, Tobago being included in the Barbados diocese. In due course three rectories were established in the colony.

In 1843, in an effort to improve the condition of the sugar industry, Mr. Cruickshank of Prospect Estate introduced the

* See Appendix XXXI.

Metayer system of cultivation from St. Lucia. Under this profit-sharing system the labourer was induced to cultivate a definite area under canes, bearing the whole of the cultivation and manufacturing costs. In return he received half of the sugar made and a bottle of rum for every barrel of sugar produced, on condition that all the molasses had been used in the distilling. The system was adopted throughout the whole colony in 1845 and was later modified and extended to cacao.

In February, 1845, Lt-Governor Darling died in office. On October 11th, 1847, a disastrous hurricane, preceded by an earthquake and accompanied by a very severe thunderstorm, struck the colony. This was the first natural disaster since 1790, apart from two minor hurricanes in 1828 and 1831; the inhabitants therefore felt themselves secure and made little or no preparation to face the danger until too late. Property destroyed was valued at £150,000; 26 sugar works were demolished and 33 damaged; 600 dwellings were razed to the ground and 300 damaged. On the night of the 11th, 26 lives were lost and many died later as a result of injuries received. The Home Government granted a loan of £50,000 towards the relief of the victims, but only £20,000 was used.

Lt.-Governor Graeme died after a five year administration and was succeeded in 1851 by David R. Ross. Lt.-Governor Ross was killed when the carriage in which he was returning from a ball to Government House overturned. He was followed by Mr. Dominick Daly, who because of ill-health had to leave the colony after only six months' residence. Henry Yates, President of the Council, administered the Government.

In January, 1854, the garrison troops were withdrawn from Fort George and the colonists were left to make their own arrangements for the defence of the island and the preservation of law and order. However, the Home Government promised to keep a vessel of war constantly within call of Barbados in case its services should be required. At once an Act was passed to strengthen and reorganize the police force, and by another Act the raising of an armed Volunteer Corps was legalized. In February the new Lt.-Governor, Mr. W. J. Shortland, arrived to assume office. Soon after he had come a plot was discovered, the object of which was to burn and pillage the town of Scarborough, murder the inhabitants and violate all females. Thanks to the confession of an accomplice, the plot was discovered. The two ringleaders, immigrant Negroes from Barbados, were tried for conspiracy and sentenced to a fine of £10 each and two

311

years' imprisonment. At the end of their sentences they had to find security for their good behaviour or remain in prison. They were unable to find such security and remained in gaol until released by the exercise of the Royal Prerogative of mercy on the part of the Lt.-Governor.

(3) *Constitutional Changes*
(a) *" The Better Government of the Island "*

In 1855 the constitution of the island was remodelled by an Act of February 9th entitled " An Act for the Better Government of the Island ".

The Act provided for the establishment of a Privy Council and an Executive Committee consisting of one member of the Legislative Council and two members of the General Assembly, appointed by the Lt.-Governor and holding office during his pleasure.* Their duties were to advise and assist the Lt.-Governor in the general administration of the island and to prepare and perfect all estimates of revenue and expenditure. They were the official organs of communication between the Governor and the Legislative Chamber. They formed the Board of Audit and were the Commissioners under the Hurricane Loan Act. The members of the Executive Committee sat as a Privy Council in virtue of their office, but ceased to be members of the Privy Council on retirement from the Executive. For their services they received, along with their secretary, the sum of £100 per annum.

About this time the Comptroller of Customs and other Imperial officers were withdrawn from the North American and West Indian colonies and their duties were transferred to colonial officers. In Tobago the office of Comptroller of Customs was transferred to the Colonial Treasurer, who from then on combined both offices.†

Lt.-Governor Shortland left the colony in 1856 and James Kirk, senior member of the Privy Council, assumed the administration of the Government. Shortly afterwards James Henry Keens received a warrant under the Royal Sign Manual as administrator and assumed office.

In 1857 James Vickery Drysdale became Lt.-Governor.

After the abolition of the apprenticeship system in 1838, some colonies suffered labour difficulties. Some sought remedies whilst others found progress retarded because land went out of cultivation. The lower duties on foreign grown sugar added to the

* See p. 308.
† See p. 255.

difficulties of the time.* Planters were unable to obtain the capital necessary to manage an estate properly and had to find their money by loans or mortgages from capitalists. While the capitalist paid the expenses of the estate, the whole crop was assigned to him. Out of this arose a system of double dealing, for the planter was determined that the estate should not change hands during his lifetime, and further mortgages were entered into. When the limit of advances had been reached from the original source, the planter turned to other sources which were ignorant of the heavy indebtedness of the estate, and raised a second mortgage. A system of "robbing Peter to pay Paul" came about. There was no way in which the planter could be removed from his estate, although he was virtually only the manager. Many estates were badly undercultivated and some abandoned because planters could not keep them in production. Encumbrances were too heavy and uncertain for others to risk buying them and uncertainty of title and heavy legal expenses were against sales. At the same time there was a great need of small plots of land for peasants. The Home Government in 1854 had passed the West Indian Encumbered Estates Act. By this, Commissioners were appointed in London and in any colony which accepted the Act, and to these application for the sale of an encumbered estate could be made either by creditor or owner. When applications had been received, suitable advertisement was made of the intended sale. Expenses were deducted from the proceeds of the sale and an equitable distribution of the surplus was then made to all creditors. When this was completed an entirely new grant, thereafter unassailable, was issued to the property. Legal expenses were obviated and higher prices were offered for estates than would otherwise have been possible. The estates passed into the hands of those who had the capital to exploit them or who were prepared to sell in small lots to the peasants. In January, 1858, Tobago agreed to accept the Act, which was further amended in 1859.

In 1860 the control of the Tobago Post Office was transferred to and invested in the Executive Government of the island.

At this time the population of Tobago was some 15,410 (1861 census) and its exports were 59,052 cwt. sugar, 109,047 gallons of rum, and 1,207 cwt. of molasses.

Lt.-Governor Drysdale had to leave the colony on sick leave in 1860, and Daniel Baynes was appointed from Dominica to administer the Government. Before Drysdale finally left the

* See pp. 234/6 and 258

colony in 1864 he had instituted many important and improving measures. It was during his administration that prisoners were removed from the unhealthy Scarborough gaol to the military buildings at Fort George. He was instrumental in Tobago receiving liberated Africans* to augment the labour force.

Lt.-Governor Kortright followed Drysdale and took office early in 1865. During his administration the franchise was extended to £5 land holders (1871). It was hoped that Tobago might be linked in communication with the rest of the world when in 1872 a subsidy was granted to the West Indian and Panama Telegraph Company for this purpose. Owing to local delays the opportunity was lost and the company took no steps in the matter.

In 1872 Lt.-Governor Ussher succeeded Kortright. The Tobago Concurrent Endowment Act, by which the Church of England ceased to be the established church of the colony was passed in the same year. By the Act the three religious denominations were granted annual aid from the Government; to the Anglican Church, £615; United Brethren (Moravians), £250, and Wesleyan Methodists, £215 per annum. These sums were based on the census returns for 1871, which showed a total population of 18,051. The conditions under which the religious bodies were granted their aid were that they should " maintain in the exercise of their spiritual functions " within the island of Tobago a number of ministers; in the Anglican Church three, Moravian two, and Wesleyan two.

Lt.-Governor Ussher was also responsible for the working of the Single Chamber Act in 1874 by which the cumbersome machinery of Government in the colony was altered. The two Legislative Houses then in existence were done away with and replaced by a single Legislative Assembly. This Chamber consisted of six members nominated by the Lt.-Governor and eight elected members, one from the town of Scarborough and one from each of the seven parishes. Electoral qualification remained as before. The Privy Council was continued but the Executive Committee was reduced to two members, one a nominee of the Assembly, the other an elected member, and their emolument was reduced to £50 per annum.

(b) *Crown Colony*

Colonel R. W. Harley, who on Mr. Ussher's appointment to

---

* These Africans were the slaves taken from foreign vessels by the British Navy in their efforts to curb the slave trade.

314

Labuan took over the task of administering the Government in 1875, was faced with a riot in the Windward district in 1876. The 2nd Company of the West India Regiment was brought in to assist. Though the riot was quickly suppressed, one police officer was killed and others were wounded. Forty persons were indicted for murder, sixteen of whom were sentenced to death. All were eventually reprieved and various terms of penal servitude were provided in place of the death penalty. Shortly all, with the exception of two, were released on "ticket of leave" and none misbehaved himself again. The riot led to the reorganization of the police force, which was increased in number and made a semi-military body. The Volunteer Corps was also organized, consisting of two companies, one in Scarborough and the other in the Windward district.

The most important Act passed during Lt.-Governor Harley's time was the Constitution Act of December 6th, 1876, by which the political constitution of the Government was again changed. The Legislative Assembly was abolished and the Queen in Council left to create and constitute a Legislature in such form and with such power as might seem fitting. This Act was ratified by the Imperial Act 39 and 40, Vict. Cap. 47. Tobago was from then on administered as a Crown Colony and the elective principle abolished. The last meeting of the Privy Council was held on December 5th, 1877.

The Lt.-Governor informed the Privy Council that he had the Royal Instructions on the New Form of Government, dated May 30th, 1877. These instructions stated that the Executive Council was to consist of the officers lawfully discharging the functions of Colonial Secretary, Attorney-General and Treasurer, and such other persons as from time to time might be appointed by Her Majesty, under the Royal Sign Manual and Signet; and further, of such other persons, not being officers, as Her Majesty might appoint. The Colonial Secretary, the Attorney-General and the Treasurer then took the oath.

Until 1880 the Imperial Government paid the salary of the Lt.-Governor but as from March 31st of that year, determined that colonial funds should be responsible for this payment. To minimise expense, an Ordinance was passed by the Legislature combining the posts of Administrator and Colonial Secretary and the officer who had recently held the combined posts of Colonial Secretary and Registrar was retired on pension.

The following year, owing to financial difficulties of the colony no provision was made in the budget for Public Works.

Only the most urgent road repairs were carried out. Difficulties were further increased when the Superintendent of Public Works was transferred to another colony. In answer to an appeal by the Executive, the landowners of the island generously responded and undertook the gratuitous superintendence of the roads. Education at this time only cost the colony £550 a year for thirty-six teachers and 4,767 pupils.

Late in 1882, a Commission was appointed under Royal Sign Manual to enquire into the public debts, revenue, expenditure and liabilities of Jamaica, Grenada, St. Vincent, Tobago, St. Lucia and the Leeward Islands. The Commission, consisting of Colonel William Crossman, Sir George Smyth Baden-Powell and Charles Alexander Harris of the Colonial Office as secretary, arrived in Tobago aboard H.M.S. *Dido* in April, 1883, and spent four days in the island. The time was spent inspecting the public offices, visiting all parts of the island and interviewing people of all classes in the community. They also toured the agricultural districts, in which there were some fifty-six sugar mills, thirty-five worked by steam, six by steam and water, ten by wind and five by cattle.

The report of the Commission supported the recommendation of Sir William Robertson (Governor-in-Chief of the Windward Islands), that Barbados be separated from the Windward group and that Grenada be made the headquarters. The Imperial Government decided to give effect to this recommendation and to unite Grenada, St. Vincent, St. Lucia and Tobago into a single colony, if this were acceptable to the majority of the inhabitants.

Early in 1885, Sir William Robertson visited the islands and laid before the Legislative Councils the Secretary of State's proposals, but met with much opposition from unofficial members, and the matter was allowed to drop. But later in the year, by Letters Patent, Barbados was constituted a separate colony and the other islands became the Windward Islands group under a Governor resident in Grenada. Each island retained its Legislature, presided over by a Resident Administrator.*

The failure of one of the largest sugar estate companies brought about the financial collapse of the island and by an Order in Council of 1888 Tobago became subordinate to Trinidad as from January 1st, 1889. It was to be administered by a Resident Commissioner, who was to be appointed by the Governor of Trinidad and to be an ex-officio member of the

* See Appendix XXXIII.

Trinidad Legislative Council. Sir William Robertson, Governor of Trinidad, appointed Mr. Loraine G. Hay, who was succeeded by Thomas Crossley Rayner (1892) and William Low (1892).

By an Order in Council of October, 1898, Tobago was declared to be a ward of the combined Colony of Trinidad and Tobago as from January, 1899, under the Governorship of Sir Hubert Jerningham.

REFERENCES*

"Select Letters of Christopher Columbus" by H. R. Major
(Hakluyt Society) 1870. T.T.H.S. Pub. [91].
"The History of the Life and Actions of Admiral Christopher
Columbus" and of his discovery of the West Indies called the
New World now in possession of his Catholic Majesty. Written
by his son D. Ferdinand Columbus. Taken from Churchill's
"Collections of Voyages and Travels", Vol. xi. Chap. 68,
1704. T.T.H.S. Pub. [127].
"Admiral of the Ocean Sea—a Life of Christopher Columbus"
by Samuel Morison. Little, Brown & Co., Boston, U.S.A., 1942.
"The Aboriginal Remains of Trinidad and the West Indies"
by J. A. Bulbrook. Pub. by T.T.H.S., 1941.
"The Ierian Race" by J. A. Bulbrook, Lecture delivered to the
Trinidad and Tobago Historical Society, 1939.
"The History of Trinidad" by E. L. Joseph. H. J. Mills, Lon-
don, 1837. Also issued as an appendix to Mills' Trinidad
Almanack, 1840.

* T.T.H.S—Trinidad and Tobago Historical Society.

All references by means of a number in square brackets are references
to the numbers of publications by the Trinidad and Tobago Historical
Society.

CHAPTER TWO

Juan Bono, the slave trader in Trinidad, 1510.
Source : Translated from "Brevísime relación de la destrucción
da las Indias . . ." Part of "Delle costa de las perlas y
d'Paria y la ysla de la Trinidad" British Museum E.
1586. Gift of George III.* T.T.H.S. Pub. [556].
Cedula to the Admiral and Officials of Española ordering them
to cease taking Indians from Trinidad. 15.6.1510.
Source : Colección de Documentos Inéditos. Pacheco y Cardenas
1864.* T.T.H.S. Pub. [73].

Cedula to Admiral Don Diego Colon on taking Indians from Trinidad, 6.6. 1511.

Source : Colección de Documentos Inéditos. Pacheco y Cardenas 1864.* T.T.H.S. Pub. [74].

Cedula to all persons giving permission to wage war upon and enslave the Caribs of Trinidad and other places. 23.12.1511.

Source : Colección de Documentos Inéditos. Pacheco y Cardenas 1864* T.T.H.S. Pub. [75].

Cedula to the Alcaldes of Puerto Rico (on relations with Juan Ponce de Leon). 23.2.1512.

Source : Colección de Documentos Inéditos. Pacheco y Cardenas 1864.* T.T.H.S. Pub. [92].

Appointment of Antonio Sedeno as Governor of Trinidad 12.7.1530.

Source : British Museum, Additional MSS. 36314.* T.T.H.S. Pub. [109].

Instructions from the Queen to Antonio Sedeno, 10.12.1523.

Source : British Museum, Additional MSS. 36314.*
T.T.H.S. Pub. [128].

Report from Juan de la Puente to the King of Spain on the subjugation of Trinidad by Sedeno, 14.7.1534.

Source : Boletín de la Academia Nacional de Historia de Caracas. Vol. 9, No. 23 (1926).* T.T.H.S. Pub. [145].

Summary of report from Antonio Sedeno to the King of Spain, 12.10.1535.

Source : Boletín de la Academia Nacional de Historia de Caracas. Vol. 9, No. 38 (1927).* T.T.H.S. Pub. [166].

Report from Fray Gregorio de Beteta, Bishop elect of Cartagena to the King of Spain, on the pacification of Trinidad, 1540.

Source : Colección de Documentos Inéditos. Pacheco y Cardenas 2nd series, Vol 10.* T.T.H.S. Pub. [185].

Report from Fray Miguel Diosdado to the King of Spain. Account of the settlement of Trinidad. 15.1.1570.

Source : Additional MSS. 36314 British Museum.* T.T.H.S. Pub. [600].

Despatch from Antonio de Berrio to the King of Spain on the settlement of Trinidad, 27.7.1592.

Source : British Museum Additional MSS. 36315 f.251–254.*
T.T.H.S. Pub [14].

Notorial Records of the founding of the Town of San Josephe de Oruña, 3.10.1952.

Source : British Museum Additional MSS. 36316.* T.T.H.S. Pub. [15].

Despatch from Antonio de Berrio to the Council of the Indies on searches for El Dorado and settlement of Trinidad, 1.1.1593.
Source: Arichivo General de Indies. Consejo, Escrivania de Camera Pleiros, 1597–1599.
British Museum Additional MSS. 36315 f.186. et. sq.*
T.T.H.S. Pub. [16].

Despatch from Antonio de Berrio to King of Spain on the settlement of Trinidad, 24.11.1593.
Source: British Museum Additional MSS. 36316, f.230–237.*
T.T.H.S. Pub. [18].

Letter from Licenciado Luxen Asparren to the King of Spain on the administration of de Berrio, 1593.
Source: British Museum Additional MSS. 36315.* T.T.H.S. Pub. [17].

Decree of the Council of the Indies ordering de Berrio to leave Trinidad, 12.1.1594.
Source: British Museum Additional MSS. 36316 f.70–72.*
T.T.H.S. Pub. [19].

Letter from Alvaro Jorge and others to the King of Spain on the Governorship of Trinidad, 12.11.1594.
Source: British Museum Additional MSS. 36316.* T.T.H.S. Pub. [77].

Report of the Discovery of El Dorado by Domingo de Vera, 1595.
Source: Colección de Documentos Inéditos. Pacheco y Cardenas Vol. 6, p. 561.* T.T.H.S. Pub. [94].

Report from the Treasurer of Cumana to the King of Spain, 15.10.1595.
Source: British Museum Additional MSS. 36317.* T.T.H.S. Pub. [95].

Despatch from Simon de Bolivar, Contador of Margarita, to the King of Spain on the capture of de Berrio.
Source: British Museum Additional MSS. 36316 f. 168.*
"The Discoverie of the Large and Beautiful Empire of Guiana" by Sir Walter Raleigh. Edited by Professor Vincent Harlow (Argonaut Press). T.T.H.S. Pub. [20].

Despatch from Pedro de Salazar to the King of Spain on the capture of de Berrio, 10.7.1595.
Source: British Museum Additional MSS. 36316 ff. 151 et. seq.*
"The Discoverie of the Large and Beautiful Empire of Guiana" by Sir Walter Raleigh. Edited by Professor Vincent Harlow (Argonaut Press). T.T.H.S. Pub. [21].

Despatch from Domingo de Vera to the King of Spain on the capture of de Berrio, -.9.1595.
Source : British Museum Additional MSS. 36317 ff. 385 et seq.* T.T.H.S. Pub. [22].
Sir Walter Raleigh's visit to Trinidad, 1595.
Source : "The Discoverie of the Large, Rich and Beautiful Empire of Gviana" by Sir Walter Raleigh Knt.; reprinted from the 1596 edition by the Hakluyt Society in 1848. T.T.H.S. Pub. [24].
Despatch from Licenciade Pedro de Liano to the King of Spain concerning the capture of de Berrio, 15.3.1596.
Source : British Museum Additional MSS. 36317 ff. 61 et seq.* "The Discoverie of the Large and Beautiful Empire of Guiana" by Sir Walter Raleigh. Edited by Professor Vincent Harley (Argonaut Press). T.T.H.S. Pub. [23].
Despatch from the Treasurer of Cumana to the King on the settlement of Trinidad, 18.4.1596.
Source : British Museum Additional MSS. 36317.* T.T.H.S. Pub. [112].
Letter from Domingo de Vera to the King of Spain on the change of Governor, 27.10.1597.
Source : British Museum Additional MSS. 36317.* T.T.H.S. Pub. [131].
Report of the Council of the Indies to the King of Spain on El Dorado, 30.1.1599.
Source : British Museum Additional MSS. 36317.* T.T.H.S. Pub. [132].
"Colonizing expeditions to the West Indies and Guiana, 1623–1627." Edited by V. T. Harlow (Hakluyt Society, Vol 66), 1925.
"Historical Sketches," Vol. 1 by K. S. Wise, 1934. T.T.H.S. Pub.

* Translated from the Spanish.

CHAPTER THREE

"Historical Sketches," Vol. ii, Article 2.
"Tobacco Cultivation in Trinidad, 1600–1614," by K. S. Wise, 1936. T.T.H.S. Pub.
"Historical Sketches," Vol. ii, Article 3.
"Don Fernando de Berrio and the Residencia, 1611–1614," by K. S. Wise, 1936. T.T.H.S. Pub.
"Historical Sketches," Vol. ii, Article 4.

"The final efforts of Don Fernando de Berrio, 1618–1622," by
    K. S. Wise, 1936. T.T.H.S. Pub.

"Historical Sketches," Vol. i, Article 8.

"Sir Henry Colt in Trinidad, 1632," by K. S. Wise, 1934.
    T.T.H.S. Pub.

The Cabildo to Captain Pedro Beltranilla on the treaty against
    the Caribs, 14.1.1603.
Source: British Museum Additional MSS. 36318.*
    T.T.H.S. Pub. [79].

The King of Spain to Fernando de Berrio ordering cessation of
    trade with the enemies, 27.2.1610.
Source: British Museum Additional MSS. 36319.*
    T.T.H.S. Pub. [97].

Report from Sir Thomas Roe to the Earl of Salisbury, Lord
    High Treasurer, on the state of Trinidad, 28.2.1611.
Source: Public Record Office, State Papers Colonial, C.O.25.
    T.T.H.S. Pub. [98].

The King of Spain to Sancho de Alquiza with instructions for
    the Residencia on Fernando de Berrio, 23.3.1611.
Source: British Museum Additional MSS. 36319.*
    T.T.H.S. Pub. [60].

Report from Sancho de Alquiza to the King of Spain concerning
    the Residencia respecting Don Fernando, 11.2.1612.
Source: British Museum Additional MSS. 36320.*
    T.T.H.S. Pub. [57].

Report from Sancho de Alquiza to the King of Spain concerning
    the Residencia respecting Don Fernando, 14.6.1612.
Source: British Museum Additional MSS. 36320.*
    T.T.H.S. Pub. [148].

Report from Pedro de Beltranilla to the President of the Council
    of the Indies on shipping, 8.1.1613.
Source: British Museum Additional MSS. 36320.*
    T.T.H.S. Pub. [150].

Letter from Sancho de Alquiza to the King of Spain on the
    trade of Trinidad, 20.4.1613.
Source: British Museum Additional MSS. 36320.*
    T.T.H.S. Pub. [168].

Report to the Council of the Indies on the Island of Trinidad,
    7.10.1614.
Source: British Museum Additional MSS. 36320.*
    T.T.H.S. Pub. [169].

Report from the Council of the Indies to the King of Spain on
    Don Fernando's deposition, 29.7.1615.
Source: British Museum Additional MSS. 36320.*
    T.T.H.S. Pub. [170].

Letter from the King of Spain to Diego Palameque de Acuña, Governor of Trinidad, on trade with foreigners, 18.11.1615.
Source: British Museum Additional MSS. 36320.*
T.T.H.S. Pub. [189].

The Governor of Cumana to the King of Spain concerning the death of de Acuña, 20.6.1618.
Source: British Museum Additional MSS. 36320.*
T.T.H.S. Pub. [205].

Report by Juan de Viloria y Quinones on the death of Governor de Acuña, 17.3.1619.
Source: British Museum Additional MSS. 36320* 36321*.
T.T.H.S. Pub. [211].

Royal Cedula to Fernando de Berrio on his appointment as Governor, 12.5.1620.
Source: British Museum Additional MSS. 36321.*
T.T.H.S. Pub. [217].

Report from Don Fernando de Berrio to the King of Spain on the Governorship. June, 1619.
Source: British Museum Additional MSS. 36321.*
T.T.H.S. Pub. [214].

Royal Cedula to the Casa de la Contratacion on shipping, 18.2.1620.
Source: British Museum Additional MSS. 36321.*
T.T.H.S. Pub. [216].

Report from the Council of the Indies to the King of Spain on the Governorship of Trinidad, 8.6.1612.
Source: British Museum Additional MSS. 36321.*
T.T.H.S. Pub. [219].

Report from the Council of the Indies to the King of Spain on the death of Fernando de Berrio, 24.5.1625.
Source: British Museum Additional MSS. 36321.*
T.T.H.S. Pub. [222].

Grant to the Earl of Montgomery of Trinidad etc. 20.2.1628.
Source: Record Office, London. Calendar of State Papers Colonial Sign Manual, Cer. 1, Vol. 5, No. 22.
T.T.H.S. Pub. [561].

Letter from Don Juan Eulate, Governor of Margarita, to the King of Spain on the attack against Colt's settlement, 20.7.1633.
Source: British Museum Additional MSS. 36322.*
T.T.H.S. Pub. [61].

Report from Diego Lopez de Escobar, Governor of Trinidad, to the King of Spain on the attack on the Dutch settlement at Toco, -.11.1636.

Source: Relacion de los Particulares Servicion que ha hacho a Vuestra Magestad Don Diego Lopez de Escobar, Gobernador y Capitan General de la Isla de la Trinidad y de les Provincias del Dorado, hijo del Capitan Diego Lopez de la Fuente en el anno de 1636. Published 1637.*
T.T.H.S. Pub. [82].

Report from Diego de Escobar, Governor of Trinidad, to the King of Spain on the attack on Tobago, -.1.1637.

Source: As above.
T.T.H.S. Pub. [84].

Report from the Council of War to the King of Spain on the attack on Tobago, 4.5.1638.

Source: British Museum Additional MSS. 36324.*
T.T.H.S. Pub. [248].

The Cabildo of Trinidad to the Governor of Margarita reporting the sack of San Josef, 17.11.1627.

Source: British Museum Additional MSS. 36324.*
T.T.H.S. Pub. [118].

The Audiencia to the Governor of Margarita concerning the sack of San Josef, 4.12.1632.

Source: British Museum Additional MSS. 36324.*
T.T.H.S. Pub. [120].

The attack on the Island of Trinidad by the Carib Captain Baron, 1640.

Source: "Histoires des Isles Antilles de l'Amérique," Vol. ii, Ch. 3, by M. de Rochefort, 1667.†
T.T.H.S. Pub. [563].

Summary of a report from the Council of War to the King of Spain on the Governorship of Trinidad, 15.6.1640.

Source: British Museum Additional MSS. 36326.*
T.T.H.S. Pub. [269].

Cedula to Martin de Mendoza y Berrio, Governor of Trinidad, on the attack on Tobago, 8.3.1641.

Source: British Museum Additional MSS. 36326.*
T.T.H.S. Pub. [85].

Summary of letter from the Curé of Trinidad to the Bishop of Puerto Rico on the establishment of the Church, 6.1.1645.

Source: British Museum Additional MSS. 36326.*
T.T.H.S. Pub. [86].

Cedula to Nicolas de Velasco on arrest of Escobar, 9.6.1647.

Source: British Museum Additional MSS. 36329.*
T.T.H.S. Pub. [105].

Report from the Council of the Indies on Governorship, 7.2.1657.
Source: British Museum Additional MSS. 36350.*
    T.T.H.S. Pub. [270].
Report of the Comte d'Estrées on what happened in Trinidad in December, 1680, –.12.1680.
Source: Memoirs de Marquies de Villette publié pour la Societe de l'histoire de France par Monmerque, 1844.
    T.T.H.S. Pub. [31].
Report from the Alcaldes of Trinidad to the Governor of Margarita on the capture of Cardenas. 18.6.1684.
Source: British Museum Additional MSS. 36331.*
    T.T.H.S. Pub. [171].
The Alcaldes of Trinidad to the Governor of Margarita on the capture of de Leon, 26.8.1684.
Source: British Museum Additional MSS. 36321.*
    T.T.H.S. Pub. [173].
Diego Suarez Ponce De Leon to the Governor of Margarita on his capture, 4.10.1684.
Source: British Museum Additional MSS. 36321.*
    T.T.H.S. Pub. [174].
Report from Fr. Thomas de Barcelona on Missions in Trinidad, 12.3.1688.
Source: British Museum Additional MSS. 36331.*
    T.T.H.S. Pub. [572].
Sebastian de Roteta to the King of Spain, 4.4.1689.
Source: British Museum Additional MSS. 36331.*
    T.T.H.S. Pub. [575].
The Alcaldes of Trinidad to the King of Spain on the massacre of the Governor, 29.12.1699.
Source: British Museum Additional MSS. 36331.*
    T.T.H.S. Pub. [50].
The Martyrdom of the Fathers and the Lay Brothers at Arena, 1699.
Source: Relaciones de las Misiones de la P. P. Capuchinos en las antiguas provincias espagñoles hoy Republica de Venezuela, 1650–1817.
    Documentos inéditos publicados bajo la dirección y estudio de Fray Froylan de Rionegro, Seville, 1918. Report written by the Official Historian of the Capuchins, Fr. Mateo de Anguiana in 1704.*
    T.T.H.S. Pub. [193].
The Arena Massacre, Trinidad, December 1st, 1699.
Source: Documents relating to the Massacre of the Governor Don José de Leon y Eschales and other officials at San Francisco de la Arena by Indians.
    Collected and translated by Fr. P. J. Buissink, P. P. San Rafael, Trinidad. Published by T. & T. Hist. Soc. 1936.

A guide to Trinidad, 3rd revised edition, by J. H. Collins.
    Elliot & Stock, London, 1888.
The English Puritan Colonies in Trinidad.
    Public Lecture by E. W. Daniel, May 5th, 1939.
    Published by T. & T. Hist Soc. 1940.

* Translated from the Spanish.
† Translated from the French.

CHAPTER FOUR

"History of Trinidad," by E. L. Joseph (H. J. Mills, London),
    1837.
"West Indian Histories," Vol. iii, p. 178 ff. by E. W. Daniel.
"Historical Sketches," Vol. i, Articles 4. 5 and 6, by K. S. Wise
    (Trinidad & Tobago Historical Scy., 1934).
Report from Cristoval de Guzman, Governor of Trinidad, to the
    King of Spain, on his arrival in the colony, 28.9.1714.
Source: British Museum Additional MSS. 36331.*
    T.T.H.S. Pub. [90].
Report from Martin Perez Anda y Salazar, Governor of Trini-
    dad, to the King of Spain, on the Church's difficulties,
    19.3.1722.
Source: British Museum Additional MSS. 36332.*
    T.T.H.S. Pub. [52].
An extract from the Archives of the Cabildo, Trinidad,
    28.4.1757.
Source: "History of Trinidad," Vol. i, pp. 7 and 8, by L. M.
    Frazer.
    T.T.H.S. Pub. [804].
The Governor of Cumana to Josef de la Quintana on the attack
    of the English on Trinidad, 4.1.1741.
Source: British Museum Additional MSS. 36335*.
    T.T.H.S. Pub. [380].
Royal Cedula separating the Province of Venezuela, Cumana,
    Guayana and Maracibo and the adjacent islands of Mar-
    garita and Trinidad from the Vice-Royalty of Santa Fé,
    8.9.1777.
Source: Blanco : Documentos Inéditos, Tomo. 1, p. 129, Docu-
    ment 128.*
    T.T.H.S. Pub. [533].
A report to Lord Macartney, Governor of Grenada, by P. R.
    Roume de St. Laurent, on his visit to Trinidad, –.9.1777.
Source: Public Record Office, State Papers Colonial C.O.
    101–121.†
    T.T.H.S. Pub. [604].

327

Report from the Governor-General of Grenada to the Secretary
of State on St. Laurent's report on Trinidad, 24.10.1777.
Source: Public Record Office, State Papers Colonial C.O.
104–114.
T.T.H.S. Pub. [422].

The Cedula on Colonisation of 1783, 24.11.1783.
Source: "Histoire de la Trinidad," Vol. ii, p. 382,† by P. J. L.
Borde, 1882.
T.T.H.S. Pub. [108].

A Royal Cedula, 1786. Supplementary to that of 1783 making
various minor alterations, 30.1.1786.
Source: Public Record Office, State Papers Colonial C.O. 295/5.*
T.T.H.S. Pub. [704].

A proclamation as to land tenure, by the Governor of Trinidad,
J. M. Chacon, 27.7.1785.
Source: Trinidad Duplicate Despatches, Vol. ii, 1815–16.*
T.T.H.S. Pub. [142].

From the Governor of Barbados to the Secretary of State on
the strengthening of Trinidad, 26.12.1784.
Source: Public Record Office, State Papers Colonial C.O. 28/60.
T.T.H.S. Pub. [427].

A law of Grenada directed at persons from Trinidad who are
suspected of stealing slaves, 7.7.1784.
Source: Laws of Grenada (1763–1805) 1808.
T.T.H.S. Pub. [605].

Instructions given by Don. J. M. Chacon, Governor of Trinidad,
to the Commissaries of Population in the Island, 3.1.1787.
Source: Parliamentary Papers, London. 1826–27, xxxiii.
T.T.H.S. Pub. [470].

Evidence about the Caribs in Trinidad given by Alexander
Campbell before the Committee inquiring into Slave
Trade, 27.5.1788.
Source: Parliamentary Papers, House of Commons, Vol. xxvi.
T.T.H.S. Pub. [628].

The King of Spain to Governor Chacon on the million dollar
loan for development of Trinidad, 20.4.1790.
Source: Parliamentary Papers, 1826–27, xxiii.
T.T.H.S. Pub. [637].

Report by Captain Ricketts of a visit to Trinidad, 20.1.1783.
Source: Public Record Office, State Papers, Admiralty Adm.
1/315.
T.T.H.S. Pub. [175].

The Grant of the Islands of the Bocas to the Illustrious Cabildo,
15.9.1791.
Source: Parliamentary Papers, 1826–27, Vol. xxiii.
T.T.H.S. Pub. [668].
Grant of Patos, Huevos and Monos to the Illustrious Cabildo,
17.9.1791.
Report of the Commission of Enquiry on the subject of Titles,
1827.
Source: House of Commons Papers (Slave Trade) 1826–27, Vol.
xxiii, 883.
Captain Vaughan's Report to Admiral Sir Hugh Cloberry
Christian, H.M.S. *Alarm,* on riots in Trinidad, 9.5.1796.
Source: Public Record Office, State Papers Admiralty 1/318.
T.T.H.S. Pub. [153].
A claim on the Spanish Government by Roume de St. Laurent
for services rendered, 18.1.1796.
Source: Paris, Archives des Affaires Etrangères. Correspondence
Politique Espagne, Vol. dcxxxviii, ff. 403–11.†
T.T.H.S. Pub. [739].
Letter from Don José Maria Chacon y Sanchez, Governor of
Trinidad, to H. E. the Principe de la Paz on disorders in
Trinidad, 16.5.1796.
Source: Galeria Biografia de los Generales de Marina by Fran-
cisco de Paula.
T.T.H.S. Pub. [56].

* Translated from the Spanish.
† Translated from the French.

CHAPTER FIVE

A Report by Dr. A. Williams on the nature and cause of the
fever at Chaguaramas Bay in November, 1796, 20.11.1796.
Source: Public Record Office State Papers Colonial C.O. 205/8.
T.T.H.S. Pub. [501].
A report on the arrival of the Spanish fleet at Trinidad,
13.9.1796.
Source: Public Record Office, State Papers, Admiralty Adm.
1/319.
T.T.H.S. Pub. [178].
Instructions from Secretary of State to Lt.-General Sir Ralph
Abercromby, K.B., 8.10.1796.
Source: Public Record Office, State Papers, Colonial C.O.
153/31.
T.T.H.S. Pub. [200].

List of ships present at the capture of Trinidad, 1797, 17.2.1797.
Source: "Armada Española," Vol. viii, by Fernandez C. Duro
(1895–1903).*
T.T.H.S. Pub. [123].

A return of troops employed in the expedition against the Island
of Trinidad, 20.2.1797.
Source: Public Record Office, State Papers, War Office W.O.
1/186.
T.T.H.S. Pub. [155].

A return of the Spanish garrison to the Island of Trinidad,
20.2.1797.
Source: Public Record Office, State Papers, War Office, W.O.
1/186.
T.T.H.S. Pub. [156].

An extract from the record of Sir James Athol Wood on the
taking of Trinidad, —.—.1797.
Source: The Naval Chronicles for 1810, Vol. xxiv.
T.T.H.S. Pub. [750].

Papers concerning the Council of War held to enquire into the
fall of Trinidad, 1797–1801.
Source: "Armada Española," Vol. viii, Ch. vi, Appendix, by
Fernandez C. Duro (1895–1903).*
T.T.H.S. Pub. [71].

"A Brief History of Trinidad under the Spanish Crown," by Sir
Claud Hollis, G.C.M.G., C.B.E. (late Governor and C.
in C. of Trinidad and Tobago). Trinidad Government
Printer, 1941. Limited Edition.

"History of Trinidad," by Borde, Vol. ii.

Articles of Capitulation for the surrender of the Island of Trinidad, 18.2.1797.
Source: "History of Trinidad," by L. M. Frazer, Vol. i (1781–
1813). Government Printing Office, Trinidad (1891).
T.T.H.S. Pub. [1].

Report from Rear-Admiral Harvey to the Secretary to the
Admiralty on the destruction of the Spanish Fleet,
21.2.1797.
Source: "History of Trinidad," by L. M. Frazer, Vol. i. Govern-
ment Printing Office, Trinidad (1891).
T.T.H.S. Pub. [3].

Instructions issued by Sir Ralph Abercromby to the Commandants of Quarters of Port of Spain, 22.2.1797.
Source: "History of Trinidad," by L. M. Frazer, Vol. i. Government Printing Office, Trinidad (1891).
T.T.H.S. Pub. [4].

Despatch from Sir Ralph Abercromby to the Secretary of State
on the capture of Trinidad, 27.2.1797.
Source: "History of Trinidad," by L. M. Frazer, Vol. i. Government Printing Office, Trinidad (1891).
T.T.H.S. Pub. [5].

Despatch from Governor Chacon to Don Miguel José de Azanca
on the capture of Trinidad, 27.2.1797.
Source: "History of Trinidad," by L. M. Frazer, Vol. i. Government Printing Office, Trinidad (1891).
T.T.H.S. Pub. [6].

* Translated from the Spanish.

CHAPTER SIX

A circular from Sir Ralph Abercromby to the Commandants of
Quarters on the new oath of allegiance, 22.2.1797.
Source: Public Record Office, State Papers, War Office, W.O. 1/86.
T.T.H.S. Pub. [157].

Instructions given by Sir Ralph Abercromby to Lt.- Colonel T.
Picton, 50th Regiment, appointed Commandant of the Island, 1.3.1797.
Source: "State Trials," by J. B. Howell, Vol. xxx.
T.T.H.S. Pub. [341].

◄Commission issued by Sir Ralph Abercromby to John Nihell,
Esq. as Chief Judge, 1.3.1797.
Source: "History of Trinidad," by L. M. Frazer, Vol. i.
T.T.H.S. Pub. [7].

The Commander-in-Chief to John Nihell on his appointment as
Auditor, 1.3.1797.
Source: "State Trials," by J. B. Howell, Vol. xxx.
T.T.H.S. Pub. [844].

Summary of Report on the Island of Trinidad; the dangers that
may result from the permanent occupation by the English; and a scheme for the reconquest of the Island. Circa 1797 in Caracas.*
Source: British Museum Additional MSS. 36350.
T.T.H.S. Pub. [748].

Instructions from Secretary of State to Colonel Picton on trade
with the Main, 8.4.1797.
Source: Public Record Office, Colonial C.O. 153/31.
T.T.H.S. Pub. [505].

The Audiencia of Caracas to the King of Spain in Council, 10.5.1797. (Extract on the proposed reconquest of Trinidad).
Source: Public Record Office, State Papers, War Office, W.O. 1/692.
T.T.H.S. Pub. [506].

An Act making the Port of Trinidad a Free Port, 6.6.1797.
Source: Public Record Office, State Papers, War Office, W.O. 1/93.
T.T.H.S. Pub. [507].

Proclamation by Sir Thomas Picton on trade with the Main. 26.6.1797.
Source: Southey's Chronological History of the West Indies.
T.T.H.S. Pub. [223].

Don J. M. Chacon to the Principe de la Paz, 27.6,1797, concerning the possibility of Picton attacking Spanish possessions, and a proposed remedy.
Source: British Museum Additional MSS. 36351.*
T.T.H.S. Pub. [743].

The Secretary of State to Colonel Picton on Free Trade with the Spanish Main, 5.7.1797.
Source: Public Record Office, State Papers, War Office, W.O. 1/93.
T.T.H.S. Pub. [828].

Summary of a Report from Governor T. Picton to the Secretary of State on relations with the main, 27.8.1797.
Source: Public Record Office, State Papers, Colonial C.O. 298/1.
T.T.H.S. Pub. [509].

Summary of Report from the Governor of Trinidad (Picton) to the Secretary of State on relations with the Main, 11.11.1797.
Source: Public Record Office, State Papers, Colonial C.O. 296/1.
T.T.H.S. Pub. [510].

Summary of Report of Governor of Trinidad to the Secretary of State on threat of attack from the mainland, 17.12.1797.
Source: Public Record Office, State Papers, Colonial C.O. 296/1.
T.T.H.S. Pub. [511]

Despatch from Lt.-General Cuyler to the Secretary of State, on defence of the island, 20.2.1798.
Source: Public Record Office, State Papers, Colonial C.O. 319/16.
T.T.H.S. Pub. [512].

Admiral Harvey to Secretary of State on naval protection, 10.3.1798.
Source: Public Record Office, State Papers, Admiralty Adm. 1/315.
T.T.H.S. Pub. [513].

Summary of Report from Governor of Trinidad to the Secretary of State on death of Captain Souter, 17.3.1798.
Source: Public Record Office, State Papers, Colonial C.O. 296/1.
T.T.H.S. Pub. [514].

Despatch from Colonel Picton to Lt.-General Cuyler on an expedition to the Main, 25.5.1798.
Source: " Memoirs of the Life of Lt.-General Sir T. Picton, G.C.B., etc.," including his correspondence from originals in possession of his family, etc. by H. B. Robinson (2nd edition, Richard Bentley, London), 1836.
T.T.H.S. Pub. [224].

Captain Dickson to Admiral Harvey reporting the loss of the *Regulator*, 3.6.1798.
Source: Public Record Office, State Papers, Admiralty Adm. 1/321.
T.T.H.S. Pub. [515].

Despatch from the Governor of Trinidad to the Secretary of State on defence of the island, 12.11.1798.
Source: Public Record Office, State Papers, Colonial C.O. 296/1.
T.T.H.S. Pub. [516].

Captain Dickson to Admiral Harvey reporting attacks on Corsairs, 6.12.1798.
Source: Public Record Office, State Papers, Admiralty Adm. 1/322.
T.T.H.S. Pub. [517].

Despatch from the Governor of Trinidad to the Secretary of State, on the attack on Campano, 1.1.1799.
Source: Public Record Office, State Papers, Colonial C.O. 296/1.
T.T.H.S. Pub. [519].

Letter from Thomas Picton, Governor of Trinidad, to H. E. General Triggs, on defence of the island, 17.3.1799.
Source: British Museum Additional MSS. 36370.
T.T.H.S. Pub. [62].

Despatch from Secretary of State to the Governor of Trinidad on taxation, 23.2.1799.
Source: Public Record Office, State Papers, Colonial C.O. 296/1.
T.T.H.S. Pub. [521].

333

News of warlike preparations obtained in Trinidad and sent to
Caracas by José Felipe de Inciarte, Commandant of
Guayana, 20.4.1799.
Source: British Museum Additional MSS. 36352.
T.T.H.S. Pub. [752].

Letter from Thomas Picton, Governor of Trinidad, to the Secre-
tary of State on the state of the colony, 21.4.1799.
Source: British Museum Additional MSS. 36870.
T.T.H.S. Pub. [64].

Extracts from the report of a tour of inspection by Lt.-General
Triggs, 4.6.1799.
Source: Public Record Office, State Papers, Colonial C.O.
319/6.
T.T.H.S. Pub. [523].

Letter from Thomas Picton, Governor of Trinidad, to the Secre-
tary of State, on the future of the colony, 30.7.1799.
Source: British Museum Additional MSS. 36870.
T.T.H.S. Pub. [67].

Letter from Thomas Picton, Governor of Trinidad, to H. E.
General Triggs, on defence, 17.8.1799.
Source: British Museum Additional MSS. 36870.
T.T.H.S. Pub. [68].

Letter from Thomas Picton, Governor of Trinidad, to Captain
King of H.M.S. *Gaîté* on defence, 25.8.1799.
Source: British Museum Additional MSS. 36870.
T.T.H.S. Pub. [69].

Letter from T. Picton, Governor of Trinidad, to Judge Bridg-
water of the Admiralty Court in Trinidad on trading
vessels, 14.9.1799.
Source: British Museum Additional MSS. 36870.
T.T.H.S. Pub. [70].

Private letter from Thomas Picton to the Rt. Hon. H. Dundas,
Secretary of State, on the future of the colony, 24.10.1799.
Source: "Memoirs of Lt.-General Sir Thomas Picton, G.C.B.
etc.," by H. B. Robinson (Richard Bentley, London) 1836.
T.T.H.S. Pub. [225].

Letter from Thomas Picton to Sir Ralph Abercromby on the
future of the colony, 30.10.1799.
Source: "Memoirs, etc.," as above.
T.T.H.S. Pub. [226].

Letter from Napoleon Bonaparte, First Consul, to Citizen St.
Cyr, Ambassador at Madrid, 1.12.1801.
Source: "Histoire de Consulate," p. 378, by M. A. Thière,
1865.†
T.T.H.S. Pub. [612].

334

Extract from the King's instructions to Governor Picton, 1.6.1800.
Source: " State Trials," by J. B. Howell, Vol. xxx.
T.T.H.S. Pub. [845].

Report from the Governor of Trinidad to the Secretary of State on appointment of the Council of Advice, 4.11.1800.
Source: Public Record Office, State Papers, War Office, W.O. 1/94.
T.T.H.S. Pub. [528].

A Petition from the Inhabitants of Trinidad to the Secretary of State, asking for Picton to continue as Governor, 15.5.1800.
Source: Public Record Office, State Papers, War Office, W.O. 1/94.
T.T.H.S. Pub. [526].

John Nihell's commission as Judge of the Consulado Court, 18.1.1801.
Source: Public Record Office, State Papers, Colonial C.O. 295.
T.T.H.S. Pub. [833].

The Secretary of State to the Governor of Trinidad on his appointment, 29.6.1801.
Source: Public Record Office, State Papers, Colonial C.O. 296/4.
T.T.H.S. Pub. [179].

A petition from the Illustrious Cabildo of Trinidad to the King of England, 14.12.1801.
Source: Public Record Office, State Papers, Colonial C.O. 295/2.
T.T.H.S. Pub. [158].

Report from the Governor of Trinidad to the Secretary of State on the system of Government, 14.12.1801.
Source: Public Record Office, State Papers, Colonial C.O. 296/1.
T.T.H.S. Pub. [180].

Minutes of the Council on publication of a seditious handbill.
Source: Public Record Office, State Papers, Colonial C.O. 295/2.
T.T.H.S. Pub. [834].

A Proclamation by the Governor, 5.2.1802.
Source: Public Record Office, State Papers, Colonial C.O. 295/2.
T.T.H.S. Pub. [136].

Despatch from the Governor of Trinidad to the Secretary of State on the state of the colony, 18.2.1802.
Source: Public Record Office, State Papers, Colonial C.O. 295/2.
T.T.H.S. Pub. [181].

Despatch from the Secretary of State to the Governor of Trinidad on colonisation, 18.2.1802.
Source: Public Record Office, State Papers, Colonial C.O. 295/2.
T.T.H.S. Pub. [159].

Extract from a Report by the Governor on the administration of the colony, −.2.1802.
Source: Public Record Office, State Papers, Colonial C.O. 295/2.
T.T.H.S. Pub. [201].

The Treaty of Amiens, 1802, 25.3.1802.
Source: The Annual Register, Vol. xliv, p. 608 (1802).
T.T.H.S. Pub. [618].

Despatch from the Governor of Trinidad to the Secretary of State on agriculture, 12.4.1802.
Source: Public Record Office, State Papers, Colonial C.O. 295/2.
T.T.H.S. Pub. [160].

A sworn declaration by William Harrison, Chairman of the seditious meeting at Wharton's Tavern.
Source: Public Record Office, State Papers, Colonial C.O. 295/2.
T.T.H.S. Pub. [839].

Despatch from the Governor of Trinidad to the Secretary of State, with petition, 27.4.1802.
Source: Public Record Office, State Papers, Colonial C.O. 295/2.
T.T.H.S. Pub. [840].

Despatch from the Governor of Trinidad to the Secretary of State, 20.3.1802.
Source: Public Record Office, State Papers, Colonial C.O. 295/2.
T.T.H.S. Pub. [161].

Despatch, with enclosures, from the Governor of Trinidad to the Secretary of State, on the seditious meeting, 21.5.1802.
Source: Public Record Office, State Papers, Colonial C.O. 295/2.
T.T.H.S. Pub. [842].

The House of Commons debate on Mr. Canning's motion concerning Trinidad, 29.5.1802.
Source: Annual Register, Vol. xliv, p. 172.
T.T.H.S. Pub. [753].

A Petition to the King from John Shaw and Thomas Higham, −.3.1802.
Source: Public Record Office, State Papers, Colonial C.O. 295/3.
T.T.H.S. Pub. [843].

Despatch from the Secretary of State to the Governor of Trinidad on the formation of the Commission, 9.7.1802.
Source: Public Record Office, State Papers, Colonial C.O. 295/2.
T.T.H.S. Pub. [162].
" The Life and Administration of Sir Thomas Picton," by E. W. Daniel. Public lecture delivered 27.2.1936.
Published by the T.T.H.S.

* Translated from the Spanish.
† Translated from the French.

CHAPTER SEVEN

Despatch from Secretary of State, instructions to the three Commissioners, 16.10.1802.
Source: Public Record Office, State Papers, Colonial C.O. 295/3.
T.T.H.S. Pub. [163].
Despatch from the Secretary of State to the Commissioners on the use of Chaguaramas, 6.1.1803.
Source: Public Record Office, State Papers, Colonial C.O. 295/4.
T.T.H.S. Pub. [863]
Letter from Colonel Fullarton to John Sullivan on the cost of living, 12.1.1803.
Source: Public Record Office, State Papers, Colonial C.O. 295/4.
T.T.H.S. Pub. [865].
Despatch from the Secretary of State to H.M. Commissioners on collecting taxes, 3.2.1803.
Source: Public Record Office, State Papers, Colonial C.O. 295/4.
T.T.H.S. Pub. [866].
Mr. Woodyear's declaration to Colonel Fullarton on the Duval case, 12.2.1803.
Source: Public Record Office, State Papers, Colonial C.O. 295/4.
T.T.H.S. Pub. [867].
Summary of Motion in the Council by Colonel Fullarton on the Duval case, 19.2.1803.
Source: Public Record Office, State Papers, Colonial C.O. 295/4.
T.T.H.S. Pub. [869].

Despatch from General Picton to the Secretary of State on his resignation, 18.2.1803.
Source: Public Record Office, State Papers, Colonial C.O. 295/4.
T.T.H.S. Pub. [870].

Letter from Colonel Fullarton to John Sullivan, Under-Secretary of State, on his altercation with Picton, 19.2.1803.
Source: Public Record Office, State Papers, Colonial C.O. 295/4.
T.T.H.S. Pub. [871].

Despatch from the three Commissioners to the Secretary of State on colonists and defence, 3.3.1803.
Source: Public Record Office, State Papers, Colonial C.O. 295/4.
T.T.H.S. Pub. [872].

Colonel Fullarton's reply to a letter from General Picton on their disagreements, 19.3.1803.
Source: Public Record Office, State Papers, Colonial C.O. 295/4.
T.T.H.S. Pub. [897].

Letter from the Cabildo to the Commissioners on unrest in the colony, 21.3.1803.
Source: Public Record Office, State Papers, Colonial C.O. 295/4.
T.T.H.S. Pub. [914].

Letter from Archibald Gloster to the Secretary of State on Colonel Fullarton, 26.3.1803.
Source: Public Record Office, State Papers, Colonial C.O. 295/3.
T.T.H.S. Pub. [953].

The suspension of Mr. de Castro, 26.5.1803.
Source: Public Record Office, State Papers, Colonial C.O. 295/4.
T.T.H.S. Pub. [918].

Report from Colonel Fullarton to the Secretary of State on the arrest of de Castro, 29.3.1803.
Source: Public Record Office, State Papers, Colonial C.O. 295/4.
T.T.H.S. Pub. [980].

Report by Mr. Black to the Council on the arrest of Castro, 30.3.1803.
Source: Public Record Office, State Papers, Colonial C.O. 295/4.
T.T.H.S. Pub. [981].

338

An address by General Picton to the Council on his administration of the colony, 14.4.1803.
Source: Public Record Office, State Papers, Colonial C.O. 295/5.
T.T.H.S. Pub. [986].

Petition to the King by W. R. Minchin against his treatment in Trinidad, 22.4.1803.
Source: Public Record Office, State Papers, Colonial C.O. T.T.H.S. Pub. [1019].
295/6.

Despatch from the two Commissioners to the Secretary of State on the confusion caused by Fullarton, 25.4.1803.
Source: Public Record Office, State Papers, Colonial C.O. 295/5.
T.T.H.S. Pub. [164].

Letter from Commodore Hood to General Picton. Notice of rejoining the fleet, 25.4.1803.
Source: Public Record Office, State Papers, Colonial C.O. 295/5.
T.T.H.S. Pub. [1022].

An address to Brigadier-General Picton from the 215 principal residents, 28.5.1803.
Source: Public Record Office, State Papers, Colonial C.O. 295/6.
T.T.H.S. Pub. [1025].

Despatch from the Secretary of State to the two Commissioners on the appointment of Colonel Hislop, 20.5.1803.
Source: Public Record Office, State Papers, Colonial C.O. 296/4.
T.T.H.S. Pub. [228].

A Proclamation by their Excellencies Brigadier-General Picton and Commodore Samuel Hood for the Executing the Office of Governor of Trinidad, etc., 27.4.1803.
Source: "A Refutation of the Pamphlet which Colonel Picton lately addressed to Lord Hobart," by Colonel Fullarton, F.R.S. (John Stockdale, London), 1805.
T.T.H.S. Pub. [227].

Brigadier-General Picton's reply to an address, 4.6.1803.
Source: Public Record Office, State Papers, Colonial C.O. 295/6.
T.T.H.S. Pub. [1026].

General Orders issued from Military Headquarters in Barbados
on the appointment of Brigadier-General Maitland,
11.6.1803.
Source: Memoirs of the late Lt.-General Sir Thomas Picton,
G.C.B. etc., 2nd edition, by H. B. Robinson (Richard
Bentley) 1836.
T.T.H.S. Pub. [229].

A Proclamation by William Fullarton, His Majesty's First Com-
misioner for executing the office of Governor of Trinidad,
16.6.1803.
Source: "A Refutation of the Pamphlet which Colonel Picton
lately addressed to Lord Hobart," by Colonel Fullarton,
F.R.S. (John Stockdale) 1805.
T.T.H.S. Pub. [234].

Notes by an officer of H.M.S. *Ulysses* on a survey of Trinidad,
–.7.1803.
Source: Public Record Office, State Papers, Admiralty Adm.
7/764.

CHAPTER EIGHT

"History of Trinidad," by L. M. Frazer, Vol. i, Ch. 8, p. 264;
Ch. 18, p. 264; Ch. 19, p. 273; Ch. 21, p. 304; Chs. 22,
23, 24.
"History of the West Indies," by E. W. Daniel, Vol. iii, pp.
126–127, p. 131, pp. 217–219.
"Historical Sketches," No. 38.
"The Defence of the Island of Trinidad, 1797–1827," by K. S.
Wise, 1940. Published by the T.T.H.S.

A Proclamation by the Governor on the introducing of improper
persons into the Colony, 14.8.1804.
Source: Public Record Office, State Papers, Colonial C.O.
298/1.
T.T.HS. Pub. [306].

Memorandum by the Colonial Department on Chinese Immigration, 7.4.1803.
Source: Public Record Office, State Papers, Colonial C.O.
295/6.
T.T.H.S. Pub. [1017].

A report on the Cabildo by P. Langton, St. H. de Bégorrat and
John Black, –.8.1804.
Source: Public Record Office, State Papers, Colonial C.O.
295/8.
T.T.H.S. Pub. [278].

A description of the Cabildo, Nihell's Report, –.8.1804.
Source: Public Record Office, State Papers, Colonial C.O.
295/8.
T.T.H.S. Pub. [277].

Sir William Myers, Lt-General, Commander of the Forces to the
Lt.-Governor of Trinidad on defence of the Colony,
12.12.1804.
Source: Public Record Office, State Papers, Colonial C.O.
298/1.
T.T.H.S. Pub. [307].

A Petition from the Council of Government to the Governor of
Trinidad on the expenses of defence, 23.4.1805.
Source: Public Record Office, State Papers, Colonial C.O.
298/2.
T.T.H.S. Pub. [386].

A report on the Pitch Lake etc. in the Island of Trinidad, by
Admiral Alexander Cochrane, 11.10.1805.
Source: Public Record Office, State Papers, Colonial C.O.
295/11.
T.T.H.S. Pub. [301].

General Hislop to the Secretary of State (Summary) on the slave
rising, 17.12.1805.
Source: Public Record Office, State Papers, Colonial C.O.
295/11.
T.T.H.S. Pub. [879]

Summary of despatch from General Hislop to the Secretary of
State on the slave rising, 19.12.1805.
Source: Public Record Office, State Papers, Colonial C.O.
295/11.
T.T.H.S. Pub. [880].

Summary of despatch from Governor Hislop to the Secretary of
State on the slave rising, 8.1.1806.
Source: Public Record Office, State Papers, Colonial C.O.
295/14.
T.T.H.S. Pub. [881].

Summary of report on the health of the Military Posts, by James
Metivier, 8.1.1806.
Source: Public Record Office, State Papers, Colonial C.O.
295/14.
T.T.H.S. Pub. [854].

K. McQueen to the Secretary of State from Calcutta on the
Chinese emigrants, 10.12.1805.
Source: Public Record Office, State Papers, Colonial C.O.
295/15.
T.T.H.S. Pub. [855].

Summary of letter from Archibald Gloster to the Secretary of State on the Picton verdict, 5.3.1805.
Source: Public Record Office, State Papers, Colonial C.O. 295/15.
T.T.H.S. Pub. [858].

Letter from General Hislop to the Secretary of State on the verdict of Picton's trial.
Source: Public Record Office, State Papers, Colonial C.O. 295/14.
T.T.H.S. Pub. [884].

K. McQueen to the Governor in Council on the seizing of the *Fortitude* (Summary), 16.10.1806.
Source: Public Record Office, State Papers, Colonial C.O. 295/14.
T.T.H.S. Pub. [888].

Proclamation by the Governor on the Chinese Immigrants, 18.10.1804.
Source: Public Record Office, State Papers, Colonial C.O. 295/14.
T.T.H.S. Pub. [901].

Summary of despatch from General Hislop to the Secretary of State on the arrival of the Chinese, 26.10.1806.
Source: Public Record Office, State Papers, Colonial C.O. 295/14.
T.T.H.S. Pub. [902].

Summary of despatch from General Hislop to Secretary of State on the administration of justice, 11.11.1806.
Source: Public Record Office, State Papers, Colonial C.O. 295/16.
T.T.H.S. Pub. [904].

General Hislop to the Secretary of State on the Navigation Act, 4.12.1806.
Source: Public Record Office, State Papers, Colonial C.O. 295/15.
T.T.H.S. Pub. [905].

General Hislop to the Secretary of State on the sale of the *Fortitude*, 18.12.1806.
Source: Public Record Office, State Papers, Colonial C.O. 295/15.
T.T.H.S. Pub. [906].

Summary of despatch from Secretary of State to General Hislop, on the settlement of the Chinese, 24.1.1807.
Source: Public Record Office, State Papers, Colonial C.O. 295/15.
T.T.H.S. Pub. [909].

Legal opinion by the Attorney and Solicitor-Generals of England on justice in the colony, 26.1.1807.
Source: Public Record Office, State Papers, Colonial C.O. 295/17.
T.T.H.S. Pub. [910].

Summary of despatch from General Hislop to the Secretary of State on the sale of the *Fortitude*, 8.2.1807.
Source: Public Record Office, State Papers, Colonial C.O. 295/16.
T.T.H.S. Pub. [912].

Summary of despatch from General Hislop to the Secretary of State on the state of the *Fortitude*, 17.2.1807.
Source: Public Record Office, State Papers, Colonial C.O. 295/16.
T.T.H.S. Pub. [913].

Summary of despatch from General Hislop to the Secretary of State on the settlement of the Chinese, 8.5.1807.
Source: Public Record Office, State Papers, Colonial C.O. 295/16.
T.T.H.S. Pub. [958].

Governor Hislop to the Secretary of State on Spanish law, 8.4.1807.
Source: Public Record Office, State Papers, Colonial C.O. 295/16.
T.T.H.S. Pub. [959].

Governor Hislop to the Secretary of State on finance, 25.6.1807.
Source: Public Record Office, State Papers, Colonial C.O. 295/16.
T.T.H.S. Pub. [961]

Representations from the Council to the Governor of Trinidad, 2.7.1807.
Source: Public Record Office, State Papers, Colonial C.O. 295/16.
T.T.H.S. Pub. [962].

Summary of minutes of the Council on Chinese settlers, 20.7.1807.
Source: Public Record Office, State Papers, Colonial C.O. 295/16.
T.T.H.S. Pub. [963].

The Secretary of State to Governor Hislop on the Governor's prerogative, 4.2.1808.
Source: Public Record Office, State Papers, Colonial C.O. 295/19.
T.T.H.S. Pub. [994].

Letter from General Hislop, Governor of Trinidad, to Lord Castlereagh, Secretary of State, reporting the great fire in Port of Spain, 27.3.1808.
Source: Public Record Office, State Papers, Colonial C.O. 295/19.
T.T.H.S. Pub. [72].

An account of the Great Fire at Port of Spain, 3.4.1808.
Source: Annual Register, Vol. l, 1808.
T.T.H.S. Pub. [791].

Losses in the Great Fire, 15.10.1808.
Source: Public Record Office, State Papers, Colonial C.O. 295/20.
T.T.H.S. Pub. [998].

An Order by the Cabildo of Trinidad forbidding the carrying of cudgels by Negroes, 12.9.1810.
Source: An address to the Rt. Hon. Earl Bathurst, by a free mulatto (Dr. Jean Baptiste Philipe), 20.9.1810.*
T.T.H.S. Pub. [653].

Memoires des Ancien Colons a Sa Majesté Britannique on the change from Spanish to English law, 10.8.1810.
Source: Parliamentary Papers, House of Commons, 1831–2, Vol. xxxi.
T.T.H.S. Pub. [792].

The Secretary of State to the Governor of Trinidad on the constitution, 27.10.1807.
Source: Public Record Office, State Papers, Colonial C.O. 298/5.
T.T.H.S. Pub. [184].

The administration of justice in Trinidad in 1811. A debate in the House of Commons, 15.6.1811.
Source: Annual Register, Vol. liii, p. 74.
T.T.H.S. Pub. [793].

" Trinidadiana : being a Chronological Review of events from the Capitulation until 1887," by J. M. Bodu (Blondel, Port of Spain), 1890. Very rare.
A Proclamation concerning currency in Trinidad, 19.6.1811.
Source: Public Record Office, State Papers, Colonial C.O. 298/5.
T.T.H.S. Pub. [308].

An application for a grant of the Pitch Lake at La Brea, 24.6.1811.
Source: Public Record Office, State Papers, Colonial C.O. 295/27.
T.T.H.S. Pub. [302].

*Translated from the Spanish.

344

CHAPTER NINE

The administration of Justice in Trinidad—Debate in the House
of Commons, 13.6.1811.
Source: Annual Register, Vol. liii, p. 74.
T.T.H.S. Pub. [793].
"History of Trinidad," by L. M. Frazer, Vol. i, Ch. 24.
Proclamation of the Patriots at Chacachacare, 11.1.1813.
Source: A traves de la Historia de Venezuela, 1913, by B. Tavere
Acosta.*
T.T.H.S. Pub. [539].
Don Juan Gavazzo, Commandant of Guiria to the Governor
17.1.1813.
Source: Public Record Office, State Papers, Colonial C.O.
298/5.
T.T.H.S. Pub. [303].
Instructions to Lt.-Colonel Lopinot, A.D.C. from the Governor
of Trinidad, 14.1.1813.
Source: Public Record Office, State Papers, Colonial C.O.
298/5.
T.T.H.S. Pub. [387].
"West Indian Histories," by E. W. Daniel, Vol. iii, pp. 217–219.
* Translated from the Spanish.

CHAPTER TEN

"History of Trinidad and Tobago," by L. M. Frazer, Vol. i,
Ch. 24, pp. 357–364.
"West Indian Histories," by E. W. Daniel, Vol. iii, Cha. 13.

CHAPTER ELEVEN

"History of Trinidad," by L. M. Frazer, Vol. ii. Special refer-
ence to Chs. 1, 2, 3, 5, 7, 8, 9, 10, 11, 12, 13, 14, and
pp. 17 ff, 61 ff, 76 ff, 128 ff.
Proclamation on land tenure by the Governor of Trinidad
(Chacon), 27.7.1785.
Source: T.D.D., Vol. ii, 1815–1816.*
T.T.H.S. Pub. [142].

Report on building projects at Pointe Gourde, 8.6.1813.
Source: T.D.D. 41, Vol. i, Red House, Port of Spain.
   T.T.H.S. Pub. [548].

Report on building projects at Pointe Gourde, 10.6.1813.
Source: T.D.D. 41, Vol. i, Red House, Port of Spain.
   T.T.H.S. Pub. [547].

Despatch from the Secretary of State to the Governor of Trinidad, concerning Chief Justice Smith and the new Council, 21.6.1813.
Source: Public Record Office, State Papers, Colonial C.O. 296/5.
   T.T.H.S. Pub. [537].

Report on building projects at Pointe Gourde, 27.6.1813.
Source: T.D.D. 41, Vol. i, Red House, Port of Spain.
   T.T.H.S. Pub. [550].

Report on building projects at Pointe Gourde, 27.6.1813.
Source: T.D.D. 41, Vol. i, Red House, Port of Spain.
   T.T.H.S. Pub. [553].

Report on building projects at Pointe Gourde, 7.7.1813.
Source: T.D.D. 41, Vol. i, Red House, Port of Spain.
   T.T.H.S. Pub. [551].

Report on building projects at Pointe Gourde, 26.7.1813.
Source: T.D.D. 41, Vol. i, Red House, Port of Spain.
   T.T.H.S. Pub. [552].

Memorial from proprietors around Brunswick Square, 6.11.1813.
Source: Public Record Office, State Papers, Colonial C.O. 298/5.
   T.T.H.S. Pub. [535].

Proclamation requiring Judicial Proceedings to be conducted in the English Language, 19.11.1813.
Source: Public Record Office, State Papers, Colonial C.O. 295/31.
   T.T.H.S. Pub. [538].

Proclamation regarding the new Medical Board, 20.12.1814.
Source: T.D.D., Red House, Port of Spain.
   T.T.H.S. Pub. [554].

Secretary of State to the Governor of Trinidad—regulations for making land grants, 5.8.1815.
Source: Public Record Office, State Papers, Colonial C.O. 296/5.
   T.T.H.S. Pub. [389].

Sir Ralph Woodford to the Secretary of State on the death of the Postmaster, 5.8.1815.
Source: T.D.D., Red House, Port of Spain.
   T.T.H.S. Pub. [598].

A Proclamation of neutrality issued by Sir Ralph Woodford, 19.8.1815.
Source: Parliamentary Papers of House of Commons, Vol. xvii.
T.T.H.S. Pub. [655].

Governor Woodford to the Secretary of State on the subject of counterfeit coinage, 21.4.1824.
Source: T.D.D. 541, Vol. iv, Red House, Port of Spain.
T.T.H.S. Pub. [1006].

Report on extension of the eastern settlements, 6.12.1824.
Source: T.D.D., Red House, Port of Spain.
T.T.H.S. Pub. [1008].

Report on provision of clergy for the eastern settlements, 7.5.1825.
Source: T.D.D., Vol. v, Red House, Port of Spain.
T.T.H.S. Pub. [920].

Despatch from Sir Ralph Woodford to the Secretary of State concerning churches and schools in the colony, 17.8.1825.
Source: T.D.D., Vol. v, 1825, Red House, Port of Spain.
T.T.H.S. Pub. [919].

Report on eastern settlements, 10.11.1825.
Source: T.D.D., Red House, Port of Spain.
T.T.H.S. Pub. [921].

Governor Woodford to the Secretary of State on the subject of coinage, 8.11.1825.
Source: T.D.D., Red House, Port of Spain.
T.T.H.S. Pub. [922].

Governor Woodford to the Secretary of State on the subject of grants of land at La Brea—the Pitch Lake, 1.2.1826.
Source: T.D.D., Red House, Port of Spain.
T.T.H.S. Pub. [923].

A Proclamation concerning the Militia, 9.12.1813.
Source: T.D.D., Vol. i, Red House, Port of Spain.
T.T.H.S. Pub. [543].

Governor Woodford to the Secretary of State and a copy of a Proclamation authorizing the Governor to impose certain taxes in the colony, 4.1.1814.
Source: T.D.D., Vol. i, Red House, Port of Spain.
T.T.H.S. Pub. [292].

Reports on settlement and on maintenance costs of American Negroes, 8.11.1815.
Source: T.D.D., Red House, Port of Spain.
T.T.H.S. Pub. [294].

Governor Woodford to the Secretary of State on difficulties of east coast shipping, 9.11.1815.
Source: T.D.D., Red House, Port of Spain.
T.T.H.S. Pub. [599].

Report on settlements of American Negroes at Naparima, 8.11.1815.
Source: T.D.D., Red House, Port of Spain.
T.T.H.S. Pub. [555].

Proclamation constituting new Medical Board, 1.12.1815.
Source: T.D.D., Red House, Port of Spain.
T.T.H.S. Pub. [143].

Proclamation as to security of land tenure, 5.12.1815.
Source: T.D.D., Vol. ii, Red House, Port of Spain.
T.T.H.S. Pub. [144].

Proclamation withdrawing Customs duties on dry goods, 27.1.1816.
Source: T.D.D., 1815–16.
T.T.H.S. Pub. [390].

Governor Woodford to the Secretary of State on the introduction of Venezuelan cattle, 8.2.1816.
Source: T.D.D. 1816, Red House, Port of Spain.
T.T.H.S. Pub. [304].

Proclamation waiving quit rent for certain lands, 7.11.1816.
Source: T.D.D., Vol. ii, Red House, Port of Spain.
T.T.H.S. Pub. [540].

Report on settlement at Naparima and other parts of the island, 31.7.1817.
Source: T.D.D., 1817, Red House, Port of Spain.
T.T.H.S. Pub. [13].

Despatch concerning the great fire at San Fernando de Naparima, 5.5.1818.
Source: T.D.D., Vol. iii, 1818–19, Red House, Port of Spain.
T.T.H.S. Pub. [280].

Governor Woodford to the Secretary of State concerning the building of Trinity Church, 1.6.1818.
Source: T.D.D., Red House, Port of Spain.
T.T.H.S. Pub. [970].

Governor Woodford to the Secretary of State concerning clergy and schools, 26.1.1819.
Source: T.D.D., Vol. iii, No. 316, Red House, Port of Spain.
T.T.H.S. Pub. [1002].

Proclamation concerning smallpox in the island, 26.3.1819.
Source: T.D.D., Red House, Port of Spain.
T.T.H.S. Pub. [300].

Governor Woodford to the Secretary of State concerning con-secration of Trinity Church, 4.6.1823.
Source: T.D.D., Vol. iv, No. 489, Red House, Port of Spain.
T.T.H.S. Pub. [1003].

Governor Woodford to the Secretary of State on the registration
of slaves, 4.1.1814.
Source: T.D.D. 5, Vol. i, Red House, Port of Spain.
T.T.H.S. Pub. [291]

Estimate of value of barracks, hospital, etc., at Peninsula at
Chaguaramas, 2.4.1814.
Source: T.D.D. 41, Vol. i, Red House, Port of Spain.
T.T.H.S. Pub. [546].

Sir Ralph Woodford to the Secretary of State concerning the
financies etc. of the colony, 9.5.1814.
Source: T.D.D. 28, 1814, Red House, Port of Spain.
T.T.H.S. Pub. [295].

Sir Ralph Woodford to the Secretary of State concerning rela-
tions with Venezuela, 25.5.1814.
Source: T.D.D. 25, Vol. i, Red House, Port of Spain.
T.T.H.S. Pub. [250].

Cost of fortifications at Pointe Gourde and Fort George, 1.8.1814.
Source: T.D.D. 41, Vol. i, Red House, Port of Spain.
T.T.H.S. Pub. [297].

Governor Woodford to the Secretary of State on the subject of
immigrants and agriculture, 3.10.1814.
Source: T.D.D. 55, Vol. i, Red House, Port of Spain.
T.T.H.S. Pub. [126].

Despatch from Sir Ralph Woodford to the Secretary of State,
commenting on the military situation in Venezuela and
on emigrants to Trinidad, 23.11.1814.
Source: T.D.D. 64, Vol. i, Red House, Port of Spain.
T.T.H.S. Pub. [298].

The Attorney-General to Sir Ralph Woodford on the subject
of grants of land at the Pitch Lake, 24.1.1826.
Source: T.D.D., Red House, Port of Spain.
T.T.H.S. Pub. [924].

Governor Woodford to the Secretary of State on damage to
Trinity Church, 7.2.1826.
Source: T.D.D., Red House, Port of Spain.
T.T.H.S. Pub. [925].

Code for Slaves. Order in Council, Trinidad, 1823.
Source: "Considerations of Negro Slavery," by Alexander
McDonnell (1825).
T.T.H.S. Pub. [794].

Orders of Government extending time for all petitioners for
confirmation of lands held under Spanish Government,
22.5.1823.
Source: T.D.D. Nos. 3 and 6, Red House, Port of Spain.

Orders in Council for the protection of the slaves, 7.5.1824.
Source: T.D.D. Nos. 545 and 549, Red House, Port of Spain.

Suggestion that complaints of slaves should be published (Burnley), 7.1.1826.
Source: T.D.D. 7, Red House, Port of Spain.

" West Indian Histories," by E. W. Daniel, Vol. iii.
  p. 73, Indian Missions
  p. 163 Negro Settlements
  p. 219 Slavery

Collen's " Guide to Trinidad," Elliot and Stock, London, 1888. Religious Questions and Botanic Gardens.

Catholic Calendar and Directory of the Archdiocese of Port of Spain, 1914.

Trinidad Diocesan Magazine : Bishop Anstey's Silver Jubilee, June, 1942.

Papers relating to the Island of Trinidad. Ordered to be printed by the House of Commons, 1823.

Sunday Duties of slaves, 3.6.1824.
Source: T.D.D. 551, Red House, Port of Spain.

Proclamations and Orders in connection with slavery and the improvement of the conditions of the slaves, 1813–33. Port of Spain Public Library.

Orders and Proclamations, 1813–1833, Port of Spain Public Library.

" History of Trinidad," by E. L. Joseph.

" Historical Sketches of Trinidad and Tobago," by K. S. Wise, Vol. iv, T.T.H.S.

" Trinidad and Other West Indian Islands and Colonies," by D. Hart, 1866.

" The Story of the Queen's Park, Port of Spain," by T. I. Potter. T.T.H.S. Lecture.

Spanish Protocols, 1791–1813, Trinidad Registry of Court.

Governor Woodford to the Secretary of State concerning resignation of Chief Justice, 11.2.1818.
Source: T.D.D. 276, Vol. iii, Red House, Port of Spain. T.T.H.S. Pub. [968].

Trinidad Duplicate Despatches, 1814–1845, indexed and filed in the Red House, Port of Spain. Originals are in the Public Record Office, London.
* Translated from the Spanish.

CHAPTER TWELVE

"History of Trinidad," by L. M. Frazer, Vol. ii.

"West Indian Histories," by E. M. Daniel, Vol. iii.

Reports of the Commission of Legal Enquiry ordered to be printed by the House of Commons, 29.6.1827.

Papers relating to the Island of Trinidad, ordered to be printed by the House of Commons.

Trinidad Duplicate Despatches, 1830, 1831, 1832, 1833.

"Memoirs of the Reverend William Shrewsbury," by Wm. Shrewsbury.

Hansard New Series, Vol. ii, pp. 1273–4.

A Proclamation requiring Judicial Proceedings to be conducted in the English Language, 19.11.1813.

Source: Public Record Office, State Papers, Colonial C.O. 295/31.

T.T.H.S. Pub. [538].

A Proclamation as to the Jurisdiction of the Tribunals of Justice, 19.1.1814.

Source: Trinidad Duplicate Despatches, 1814, Red House.

T.T.H.S. Pub. [124].

Sir Ralph Woodford to the Secretary of State concerning H.M. Commission of Legal Enquiry, 4.8.1824.

Source: Trinidad Duplicate Despatches, Vol. iv, No. 565, Red House.

T.T.H.S. Pub. [1007].

CHAPTER THIRTEEN

"History of Trinidad," by L. M. Frazer, Vol. ii.

"West Indian Histories," by E. M. Daniel, Vol. iii.

"History of the West Indies," by Thomas, as quoted in "At Last," by Charles Kingsley.

"Burnley of Orange Grove, Trinidad," by Sir Norman Lamont, Bt.

Source: Public lecture under the aupices of the Trinidad and Tobago Historical Society.

Extract from the *Port of Spain Gazette* on Emancipation Day, 5.8.1834.

Source: T.D.D. 1834, Red House, Port of Spain, Trinidad.

T.T.H.S. Pub. [256].

Governor Hill to the Secretary of State concerning immigration, 3.11.1834.
Source: T.D.D. No. 29, 1834, Red House, Port of Spain.
T.T.H.S. Pub. [257].

Slavery and Emancipation.
Source: "Truths from the West Indies," by Capt. Studholm (Hodgson, 1838).
T.T.H.S. Pub. [797].

Governor Hill to G. Leferre, Esq., M.P., on the agents to supervise emancipation, 24.7.1834.
Source: T.D.D. 1834, Red House, Port of Spain.
T.T.H.S. Pub. [255].

Governor Hill to the Secretary of State on the abrogation of apprenticeship, 26.7.1838.
Source: Public Record Office, State Papers, Colonial C.O. 295/21.
T.T.H.S. Pub. [813].

Proclamation relating to contracts for agricultural service, 30.7.1838.
Source: Laws of Trinidad, 1831–48. Vol. i.
T.T.H.S. Pub. [8].

Governor Hill to the Secretary of State on labour conditions after apprenticeship, 10.8.1838.
Source: Public Record Office, State Papers, Colonial C.O. 295/121.
T.T.H.S. Pub. [814].

Order in Council regulating rights and duties of masters and servants, 7.9.1838.
Source: Laws of Trinidad, 1831–48. Vol. i.
T.T.H.S. Pub. [9].

Governor Hill to the Secretary of State on labour and immigration, 11.12.1838.
Source: Public Record Office, State Papers, Colonial C.O. 295/122.
T.T.H.S. Pub. [815].

Governor Hill to the Secretary of State on immigration from Fayal, 20.7.1834.
Source: T.D.D. No. 4, 1834, Red House, Port of Spain.
T.T.H.S. Pub. [254].

Governor Hill to the Secretary of State on whaling, 11.2.1834.
Source: T.D.D. No. 19, 1834, Red House, Port of Spain.
T.T.H.S. Pub. [251].

CHAPTER FOURTEEN

" West Indian Histories," by E. M. Daniel, Vol. iii.
Proclamation by His Excellency Colonel John Alexander Mein,
relating to immigration, 24.12.1839.
Source: Laws of Trinidad, 1831–48.
T.T.H.S. Pub. [10].
Colonel Mein to Governor MacGregor of Barbados on the new
Immigration Ordinance, 10.1.1840.
Source: Public Record Office, State Papers, Colonial C.O.
295/129.
T.T.H.S. Pub. [819].
Lt.-Colonel MacLeod to Lord John Russell, Secretary of State,
reporting on the condition of European immigrants,
29.5.1840.
Source: Public Record Office, State Papers, Colonial C.O.
295/130.
T.T.H.S. Pub. [820].
Lt.-Governor MacLeod to the Secretary of State on labour and
immigration, 8.6.1840.
Source: Public Record Office, State Papers, Colonial C.O.
295/130.
T.T.H.S Pub. [823].
Proclamation by the Acting Governor on immigration from
Sierra Leone, 20.1.1841.
Source: Laws of Trinidad, 1831–38, Vol. i.
T.T.H.S. Pub. [11].
Governor of Trinidad to the Secretary of State reporting arrival
of immigrants from Sierra Leone, 20.5.1841.
Source: Public Record Office, State Papers, Colonial C.O.
295/133.
T.T.H.S. Pub. [927].
Governor of Trinidad to Secretary of State reporting progress
of the labouring population, 6.7.1841.
Source: Public Record Office, State Papers, Colonial C.O.
295/133.
T.T.H.S. Pub. [928].
Proclamation by the Governor of Trinidad on the proportion
of males and females among immigrants, 25.11.1841.
Source: Laws of Trinidad, 1831–48. Vol. i.
T.T.H.S. Pub. [12].

Governor of Trinidad to Secretary of State on magistrates' half-yearly returns on agricultural labour, 28.5.1842.
Source: Public Record Office, State Papers, Colonial C.O. 295/136.
Source: Public Record Office, State Papers, Colonial C.O. T.T.H.S. Pub. [938].

Secretary of State to Governor of Trinidad on transport of labourers from West Africa, 15.2.1843.
Source: Public Record Office, State Papers, Colonial C.O. 296/16 and 295/139.
T.T.H.S. Pub. [949].

William Burnley to the Secretary of State suggesting methods of augmenting labour, 13.12.1839.
Source: Public Record Office, State Papers, Colonial C.O. 295/127.
T.T.H.S. Pub. [821].

Summary of letter from William Burnley to the Secretary of State on free labourers from the U.S.A., 19.6.1840.
Source: Public Record Office, State Papers, Colonial C.O. 295/132.
T.T.H.S. Pub. [825].

" Burnley of Orange Grove," by Sir Norman Lamont.
Public lecture delivered under the auspices of the T.T.H.S. 29.11.1946.
" Observations on the present condition of the Island of Trinidad and the actual state of the experiment of Negro emancipation," by William Hardin Burnley (Longman, Brown, Green & Longman), 1842.
Observations made at Whitehall (London) on a report of the Agricultural and Immigration Society (Trinidad), 11.12.1841.
Source: Public Record Office, State Papers, Colonial C.O. 295/135.
T.T.H.S. Pub. [929].

" History of Trinidad," by L. M. Frazer, Vol. ii.
Secretary of State to Governor MacLeod assenting to Indian immigration, 31.7.1844.
Source: Public Record Office, State Papers, Colonial C.O. 296/16.
T.T.H.S. Pub. [951].

Governor MacLeod to Secretary of State enclosing rules for East Indian labourers, 18.10.1844.
Source: Public Record Office, State Papers, Colonial C.O. 294/144.
T.T.H.S. Pub. [952].

354

Correspondence on the Manzanilla settlement of discharged
  soldiers of the 3rd West India Regiment, 14.10.1841.
Source: Public Record Office, State Papers, Colonial C.O.
  295/134 and 296/16.
  T.T.H.S. Pub. [937].

The Acting Governor to the Secretary of State on the problem
  of squatters on Crown lands, 28.9.1842.
Source: Public Record Office, State Papers, Colonial C.O.
  295/137 and 296/16.
  T.T.H.S. Pub. [936].

Governor MacLeod to the Secretary of State enclosing a report
  on a proposed survey of the Colony, 18.8.1841.
Source: Public Record Office, State Papers, Colonial C.O.
  295/134.
  T.T.H.S. Pub. [935].

A protest against immigration from East India and to reduce
  295/144.
Source: Public Record Office, State Papers, Colonial C.O.
  salaries and wages, addressed to the Governor.
  T.T.H.S. Pub. [950].

Observations on the educational needs of the colony by Governor
  MacLeod to the Secretary of State, 1.5.1840.
Source: Public Record Office, State Papers, Colonial C.O.
  295/130.
  T.T.H.S. Pub. [822].

Letter from Governor MacLeod to the Secretary of State on
  education in Trinidad, 8.1.1842.
Source: Public Record Office, State Papers, Colonial C.O.
  295/134.
  T.T.H.S. Pub. [831].

Governor MacLeod to the Secretary of State on increased expenditure of the Roman Catholic Church, 27.11.1841.
Source: Public Record Office, State Papers, Colonial C.O.
  295/134.
  T.T.H.S. Pub. [930].

Governor MacLeod to the Secretary of State on the establishment of the Church of England, 9.6.1842.
Source: Public Record Office, State Papers, Colonial C.O.
  295/136 and 296/16.
  T.T.H.S. Pub. [931].

The Secretary of State to the Governor of Trinidad on the
  Church establishment in the colony, 28.11.1843.
Source: Public Record Office, State Papers, Colonial C.O.
  296/16.
  T.T.H.S. Pub. [932].

Ordinance defining the establishment of the Church of England in the West Indies with particular reference to Trinidad, etc., 17.12.1844.
Source: Public Record Office, State Papers, Colonial C.O. 295/144.
T.T.H.S. Pub. [933].
Governor MacLeod to the Secretary of State concerning the transformation of the Illustrious Cabildo into the Town Council, 5.6.1840.
Source: Public Record Office, State Papers, Colonial C.O. 295/130 and 297/3.
T.T.H.S. Pub. [824].
" Trinidadiana, being a chronological review of events which have occurred in the Island from the Capitulation to the present day," by E. M. Bodu, Blondel, Port of Spain, 1890.
Governor MacLeod to the Secretary of State, enclosing a petition from the cacao growers, 11.7.1840.
Source: Public Record Office, State Papers, Colonial C.O. 295/130.
T.T.H.S. Pub. [926].
" A Guide to Trinidad," by J. H. Collens, 2nd edition, Elliot & Stock, London, 1888.
" The History of Sugar," by Noel Deerr, Vol. ii. Chapman and Hall, Ltd., London, 1950.
St. Ann's Church of Scotland, Port of Spain, Centennial Sketch, 1846–1946.
Ordinance, Trinidad, 1840. Enacted by the Governor of the Island by and with the advice of the Council thereof for regulating the power and constitution, settling mode of election of the members of the Corporate Body called the Illustrious Cabildo of the town of Port of Spain and changing the name thereof to that of Town Council, Port of Spain.
" The History of Sugar," by Noel Deerr, Vol. ii. Chapman and Hall, Ltd., London, 1950.

CHAPTER FIFTEEN

" West Indian Histories," by E. W. Daniel, Vol. iii, Ch. 15.
" Trinidad and other West Indian Islands," by D. Hart.
Immigration.
Source: Parliamentary Papers, Great Britain, Vols. xxvii, xli, xliv, lvi, lxviii. 1846, 1847–48, 1892.
Burnley of Orange Grove, Public lecture, T.T.H.S. by Sir Norman Lamont, 1946.

Notes on the Pitch Lake by Lord Dundonald, 1851.
Source: Notes on the Mineralogy, Government and Condition
of the B.W.I.
T.T.H.S. Pub. [798].
Trinidad Government Ordinance—Education, 1851.
Trinidad Government Ordinance 8, 1849, Division of the Island
into Districts and Wards.
Trinidad Government Ordinance, 14, 1854. Regulations for
appointment of Wardens, defining their duties and
establishing Road Boards.
Trinidad Government Ordinance, 10, 1853. Regulating Munici-
pal Corporations in the Island.
" West Indian Histories," by E. W. Daniel, Customs Depart-
ment, Vol. iii, Cha. 14.
Collin's Guide to Trinidad.
Trinidad Government Ordinance, 1851. Establishing Public
Library in Port of Spain.
" Trinidadiana," by E. M. Bodu.

CHAPTER SIXTEEN

Trinidad's Oil. An illustrated survey of the Oil Industry of
Trinidad. The Petroleum Association of Trinidad, 1952.
Sugar Industry.
Source: " West Indian Histories," by E. W. Daniel, Vol. iii.
" Trinidad and the Other West Indian Islands "—Hart.
Education Commission, 1869. Education in Trinidad.
Keenan Report.
Source: Parliamentary Papers, Great Britain, Vol. L, 1870.
Trinidad Government Ordinance 6, 1870. Education.
Trinidad Government Ordinance 6, 1870. Establishing Queen's
Royal College.
Trinidad Government Ordinance 24, 1875; 14, 1876. Fees to be
charged in all schools.
Trinidad Government Ordinance 13, 1875; 20, 1881. Authorizing
grants in aid to assisted schools.
" Trinidad Reviewer," 1899. Compiled by T. Fitz-Evan Eversley.
Robinson Printing Co., London.
John Morton of Trinidad, Pioneer Missionary of Presbyterian
Church of Canada to East Indians in B.W.I. Journals,
Letters, etc. Edited by Sarah Morton. Illustrations and
maps, Westminster Co., Toronto, Canada, 1916.
Trinidad Historical and Descriptive. A narrative of nine years'
residence in the Islands, with special reference to the
Christian Missions. Yeats & Alexander, London, 1866.

Education.

Source: " West Indian Histories," by E. W. Daniel, Vol. iii. The Legislative Council of Trinidad and Tobago, Hewen Craig, London, Faber and Faber, 1952.

Commission of Legal Enquiry on the Colony of Trinidad, 1827.

Source: House of Commons Papers, Vol. xxiii, No. 53, 1864-65.

Trinidad Government Ordinance of 1849. Restricting Carnival to two days.

Trinidad Government Ordinance of 1868. Permitting masquerading only in conformity with Police Regulations. Torches not to be carried.

CHAPTER SEVENTEEN

" West Indians Histories," by E. W. Daniel, Vol. iii.

Report of the Royal Commission on the Sugar Industry, 1883. London, H.M.S.O.

Report of the Royal Commission on the Sugar Industry, 1896. London, H.M.S.O.

Report on the First Agricultural Conference, Barbados, 1899.

Centenary of the Royal Botanical Gardens, Port of Spain. W. E. Freeman, *Trinidad Guardian,* Christmas Number, 1919.

Trinidad Government Ordinance No. 17 of 1890. Abolishing school fees.

The Churches.

Source: " West Indian Histories," by E. W. Daniel, Vol. iii. " The Church in the West Indies," by A. Caldecott, London. S.P.C.K. 1898.

Report of the Royal Commission on Colonial Defence, 1879. London.

Trinidad Government Ordinance, June 3rd, 1879, Constituting Volunteer Corps.

Proclamation to East Indians forbidding Hosein processions to pass through San Fernando, 1884.

Trinidad Government Ordinance, 1884. Abolishing Canboulay processions.

Trinidad Government Ordinance, 1891. Removing some of the objectionable features of Carnival.

" Trinidadiana," by Bodu.

" Reminiscences of Old Trinidad," by L. D. Inniss. Yuillie's Printerie, 1932.

CHAPTER EIGHTEEN

Duchy of Courland and the Island of Tobago, 1654-1690.
Summary of Events.

Source: Kurland unter den Einflus der Mercantilismus. Walter
Eckart, 1927.
T.T.H.S. Pub. [766].

Cross Road Country, Latvia. "Latvians Abroad," by Edgar
Andersons, pp. 342-347. Kurs (Courlanders) colonizing
enterprises on the Caribbean Island of Tobago, 1654.
Latvju Gramata, Waverley, Iowa, U.S.A., 1953.

Grant of Tobago by the King to the Duke of Courland,
17.11.1664. London.

Source: Public Record Office, State Papers, Colonial C.O. 18,
No. 143.
T.T.H.S. Pub. [87].

Memorial of the Island of Tobago, now called New Walcheren,
how it is situated and of what advantage it may be to the
States of the United Provinces, 1667. No author. No place.

Source: Public Record Office, State Papers, Colonial C.O. 21.
T.T.H.S. Pub. [359].

Pamphlet claiming the unquestionable right of the Duke of
Courland to the Island of Tobago, 1668. Translated from
the French.

Source: Brieve deduction par laquelle il est clairement monstré
que L'Isle de Tobago appartient a Mons. le Duc en
Levine et en Courland, et que la possession que Messrs.
Lampsins prendent sur la dite Isle n'a aucun fondement.
No author. Mittau, 1668.
T.T.H.S. Pub. [731].

Letter from Sir Tobias Bridge, Commander of Expedition to
Tobago, to Governor of Barbados, 22.12.1672.

Source: Public Record Office, State Papers, Colonial C.O. 29.
T.T.H.S. Pub. [39].

John Lucas Lyon, Agent of Duke of Courland to the King,
7.4.1673.

Source: Public Record Office, State Papers, Colonial C.O. 30.
T.T.H.S. Pub. [361].

Account of the attack on Tobago by the French, 1677. Translated from the French.

Source: Dict. historique et Bib. des Généraux Français, Chevalier
de Coucelles, Vol. v., 1822.
T.T.H.S. Pub. [365].

Account of Naval Battle in Rockley Bay, Tobago, 3.3.1677.
Source: Tobago or a geographical description with natural and
civil history. Anon. (1750?).
T.T.H.S. Pub. [364].

Battle of Roodklyp (Rockley) Bay, Tobago, 1677.
Source: "Historical Sketches," by K. S. Wise. No. 40.
T.T.H.S. 1940.

Capture of the island and the forts of Tobago, with the vessels
in the port. December, 1677.
Source: "Histoire Générale des Antilles," by A. Dessalles, Vol. ii,
p. 6, 1847. Translated from the French.
T.T.H.S. Pub. [441].

Governor of Barbados to Lords of Trade and Plantations, Lon-
don, 3.1.1682. Resettlement of Tobago by Duke of
Courland.
Source: Public Record Office, State Papers, Colonial C.O. 48,
49, 29.8.1682, 50, 6.11.1682.
T.T.H.S. Pubs. [367, 368, 369].

" The present prospect of the famous and fertile Island of
Tobago with description of the situation, growth, fertility
and manufacture of the said Island, to which is added
proposals for the encouragement of all those that are
minded to settle there." By Captain John Poyntz, London.
Printed by George Larkin for the Author, and are to be
sold by Thomas Malthus, at the Sun in the Poultry, 1683.
Recently reprinted by Messrs. Yuilles Printerie, Chacon
Street, Port of Spain.

Petition of Captain Poyntz, December, 1683, with reply.
Source: Public Record Office, State Papers, Colonial C.O. 53.
T.T.H.S. Pubs. [371 and 373].

A report on Tobago to the Privy Council, 11.12.1683. Pretensions of the Duke of Courland to Tobago.
Source: Public Record Office, State Papers, Colonial C.O. 53
and 56.
T.T.H.S. Pubs. [376 and 377].

Grant to Duke of Courland void in law. 1.2.1684.
Source: Public Record Office, State Papers, Colonial C.O. 1/66.
T.T.H.S. Pub. [376].

The case of the Island of Tobago by the Envoy from Courland,
13.3.1687.
Source: Public Record Office, State Papers, Colonial C.O. 1/62.
T.T.H.S. Pub. [377].

Petition of Sir Wm. Waller and others to settle Tobago,
21.4.1699.
Source: Public Record Office, State Papers, Colonial C.O. 28/3.
T.T.H.S. Pub. [584].

From the French Ambassador to the Secretary of State, London, 3.11.1699.
Source: Public Record Office, State Papers, Colonial C.O. 28/4 No. 23.
T.T.H.S. Pub. [88].

Claim of English Crown to the Island of Tobago, London, 4.1.1700.
Source: Public Record Office, State Papers, Colonial C.O. 29/7, pp. 15 to 20.
T.T.H.S. Pub. [89].

Title of the Crown of Tobago, 2.6.1709. Council of Trade and Plantations to the Secretary of State.
Source: Public Record Office, State Papers, Colonial C.O. 324/9.
T.T.H.S. Pub. [782].

Secretary of State to the Council of Trade and Plantations, 1731. Summary. Swedish Government would like to settle in Tobago. 11.8.1731.
Source: Public Record Office, State Papers, Colonial C.O. 388/30.
T.T.H.S. Pub. [786].

The Duke of Montague applies for a grant of the Island of Tobago, 5.1.1764.
Source: Calendar of State Papers, Acts of the Privy Council, Vol. vi.
T.T.H.S. Pub. [329].

Recommendations for the settlement of Tobago by the Lords Commissioners of Trade and Plantations, 26.3.1764.
Source: Calendar of State Papers, Colonial Series, Vol. iv.
T.T.H.S. Pub. [330].

Slave insurrections in Tobago, 1770 to 1774.
Source: "Historical Sketches," by K. S. Wise, Vol. iv, Arts. xii to xiv.

G. Franklyn to Secretary of State, Tobago, November, 1781. Capture of Tobago by the French.
Source: Public Record Office, State Papers, Colonial C.O. 101/24.

Capture of Tobago by the French, 1781.
Source: "Historical Sketches," by K. S. Wise, Vol. iv, Arts. i. to iv.
T.T.H.S. 1938.

Major Cuyler to the Secretary of State. Account of attack on capture of Tobago, 18.4.1793.
Source: Public Record Office, State Papers, Colonial C.O. 318/12.
T.T.H.S. Pub. [712].

Minutes of House of Assembly, etc., 1794, et seq.
Source: Tobago Archives, Court House, Tobago.

Slave insurrection in Tobago, 1802.
Source: Annual Register, Vol. xliv, 1802, p. 260.

Despatch from General Grinfield, Commander-in-Chief of H.M.
    Troops in Windward and Leeward Islands announcing
    his capture of Tobago, 1.7.1903.
Source: Annual Register, Vol. xlv, 1803.

Despatch reporting capture of Tobago from Commodore S.
    Hood, R.N., to Sir Evan Nepean, 1.7.1803.
Source: Annual Register, Vol. xlv, 1803.
    T.T.H.S. Pub. [623].

General Caesar Berthier, Governor of Tobago, reports capture of
    the island by the English, 1803.
Source: Paris Archives Nationales, translated from the French.
    Public Record Office, State Papers, Colonial C.10, E.13.
    T.T.H.S. Pub. [620].

" A History of Tobago," by H. I. Woodcock, Chief Justice of
    the Island. Printed for the author by Smith & Grant,
    Ayrshire Express Office, Ayr, Scotland, 1867.

" A Handbook of the Colony of Tobago. Being a brief historical,
    geographical and general account of the island." Com-
    piled by L. G. Hay, Treasurer of the Colony. Printed at
    the Government Printing Office, Scarborough, Tobago,
    1884.

" List of the Governors, Lieutenant-Governors, Administrators
    and Commissioners of Tobago, with contemporary notes."
    Compiled by K. S. Wise. Published by Trinidad and
    Tobago Historical Society, Port of Spain, 1938.

" Archives of Tobago, 1787." Almost all are indexed. Filed in the
    Central Library, Scarborough, Tobago,

APPENDICES

I

The Royal Cedula on Colonization of ~~1873.~~ *1783*

I, THE KING.

Whereas by my instructions of the 3rd September, One Thousand Seven Hundred and Seventy-Six, to Don Manuel Falquaz, Captain of Foot, who was then appointed Governor of my Island of Trinidad to Windward; and by the Commission which I afterward gave Don Joseph de Abalos, appointing him Intendent-General of the Province of Caracas, I thought proper to establish regulations, and to grant various privileges for the population and commerce of the said Island; I have now resolved, on the representation of the said Intendent, and at the instance of certain colonists already established in the said Island, and others who request permission to settle therein, to establish complete instructions in the following articles :

Article 1st. All foreigners, the subjects of powers and nations in alliance with me, who are desirous of establishing themselves, or who are already settled in, the said Island of Trinidad, shall sufficiently prove to the Government thereof, that they are of the Roman Catholic persuasion, without which they shall not be allowed, to settle in the same; but the subjects of these my dominions, or those of the Indies, shall not be obliged to adduce such proof, because no doubt can arise as to their religion.

Article 2nd. All foreigners who shall be admitted, agreeable to the foregoing article, to reside in the said Island, shall take, before the Governor thereof, the oath of fealty and submission; by which they shall promise to obey the laws and general ordinances to which Spaniards are subject; and immediately there shall be granted to them, in my Royal name, gratuitously for ever, the lands proportionally mentioned according to the following rules.

Article 3rd. To each white person, of either sex, four fanegas and two sevenths; and the half of that quantity of land for each Negro or coloured slave, which the settlers shall induce; the lands to be so distributed, that everyone may participate of the good, middling and bad; the assignments of lands to be entered in a book of registry, with insertion of the name of each settler, the day of his or her admittance, the number of individuals composing his or her family, their rank, and from whence they came; and copies of such entries shall be given to them, to serve as titles to their property.

363

Article 4th. Free Negroes and coloured people, who, as planters and heads of families, establish themselves in the said Island, shall have one-half of the quantity of land as is above assigned to the white, and the same portion for each slave they introduce, the proper documents to be given to them, as to the whites.

Article 5th. When the settlers shall have resided five years in the said Island, and bound themselves to an entire residence therein, they shall receive all the rights and privileges of naturalization, as likewise their children, whether brought by them to the Island, or born therein; and consequently shall be admitted to all honourable public employments and to posts in the militia according to their respective capacities and circumstances.

Article 6th. That no capitation money or personal tribute, however small, shall be imposed upon the inhabitants at any time, save and except the annual sum of one dollar for each Negro or coloured slave, to be paid after a ten years' residence in the said Island; and that the said proportional sum shall never be augmented.

Article 7th. During the first five years of residence, the Spanish and foreign settlers shall have liberty to return to their countries or former places of abode; in which case they shall be allowed to take from the said Island, all the goods and property by them introduced into the same, without paying any duties upon exportation; but must pay for all property acquired by them during their residence in the said Island, the sum of 10%. It is to be well understood, however, that the lands which shall have been assigned to such settlers, who afterwards voluntarily quit the Island, shall devolve to my Royal patrimony, to be given to others, or disposed of as shall appear to me most fit.

Article 8th. I grant to the former and recent settlers who, not having necessary heirs, make by last will and testament a disposition of their property, the power of bequeathing their estate to their relations or friends wherever they may be; and if these choose to settle in the said Island, they shall enjoy the privileges granted to the persons whom they succeed; but if they prefer withdrawing the property from the said Island, they may do so, upon paying 15% upon the whole by way of a duty on exportation; that is, if the testator has lived more than five years in the said Island; and if the residence of the testator has been within that period, they shall pay only 10%, as is provided in the last article. And the fathers, brothers and sisters, or relations, of those who die intestate, shall succeed without any diminution to their estate, provided that they are Catholics, and domiciled in the said Island, even should they be settled in foreign countries, and if they should not be able, or do not wish to be enrolled among the inhabitants of the said Island, I do hereby give them permission to dispose of the property of the successions by sale or cession, according to the rules laid down in the foregoing article.

Article 9th. I do also give permission to all settlers, who, according to the Spanish law, have the disposition by testament or otherwise, of their real property, to bequeath the same, if it does not admit of a convenient division, to one or more of their children, provided the legal portions of the others, or that of the widow of the testator, be not injured thereby.

Article 10th. Any settler who, by reason of any lawsuit, or other just and pressing motive, may require to go to Spain, to any other province of my Indies, or to foreign dominions, shall request permission from the Governor, and obtain the same, provided it be not to an enemy's country, or to carry away property.

Article 11th. Spanish and foreign settlers shall be free from payment of tithes, or 10% on the produce of their lands for ten years; and after that period (to be computed from the first day of January, 1785) they shall only pay half tithes, that is 5%.

Article 12th. They shall also be free for the first ten years, from the payment of the Royal duty of alcabala on the sales of their produce and merchantable effects; and shall afterwards only pay an equivalent for the said duty of 5%; but whatever shall be embarked for these Kingdoms in Spanish vessels, shall be forever exempt from any duty on exportation.

Article 13th. As all the inhabitants should be armed even in time of peace, to keep the slaves in subjection, and resist any invasion or the incursion of pirates; I do hereby declare that such obligation is not to render them responsible to the duties of a regular militia, but they are only to present their arms for inspection, in review before the Governor, or some officer appointed by him every two months; but in time of war, or an insurrection of the slaves, they shall assemble together for the defence of the Island, in such way as the Commander-in-Chief hereof may direct.

Article 14th. All vessels belonging to the former or recent settlers, whatever may be their tonnage or make, shall be carried to the said Island and enrolled therein, and the proofs of the property in them enregistered, upon which they shall be accounted Spanish vessels; as also such vessels as may be acquired from foreigners by purchase, or other legal title, until the end of the year One Thousand Seven Hundred and Eighty-six; the said vessels to be free from the duty paid in qualifying foreign vessels for the Spanish Trade. And such as wish to build vessels in the said Island shall have free access to the woods required by Government; save and except those which may be destined for the building of vessels for the Royal Navy.

365

Article 15th. The commerce and introduction of slaves into the said Island shall be totally free of duties for the term of ten years, to be reckoned from the beginning of the year One Thousand Seven Hundred and Eighty-five, after which period the colonists and traders in slaves shall only pay 5% on their current value at the time of their importation; but it shall not be legal to export slaves from the said Island to any other of my Indian dominions, without my Royal permission, and the payment of 6% on their importation into other of my dominions as aforesaid.

Article 16th. The said settlers shall be permitted, having first obtained a licence from the Government, to go to the islands in alliance with me, or the neutral ones to procure slaves, either in vessels belonging to, or freighted by them, being Spanish bottoms; and to export for the payment of the said slaves, the necessary produce, and property, on payment of 5% on exportation; the said duty to be paid by the trader in slaves who, with my permission, imports them to the said Island, besides the duty on their entry; from all which I have freed the settlers, in order to excite agriculture and commerce.

Article 17th. The intercourse of Spain with the inhabitants of Trinidad, and the exportation of licensed produce from the said Island to my American islands and dominions shall be entirely free of all duties for the space of ten years, to be reckoned from the first day of January, One Thousand Seven Hundred and Eighty-five, at the expiration of which time, all the articles which are exempted by the last article of free commerce from payment of duties on entry into these Kingdoms, shall likewise be free, nor shall any more impositions be levied than those which the productions of my other West India Dominions are liable to.

Article 18th. All Spanish and foreign merchandise, and the wine, oil, and spirituous liquors, the produce of these my Kingdoms, which shall be entered and exported to the said Island, shall be free of all duty for the said term of ten years, and shall also be introduced and circulated therein free of duty, but are not to be exported therefrom to any of my other Indian dominions; but if they should be permitted to be exported therefrom, for any urgent or just cause, such permission shall only extend to Spanish goods, and that on payment of the duties fixed by the said article of free commerce.

Article 19th. In order to facilitate every means by which the population and commerce of the said Island can be increased, I do hereby permit, for the said term of ten years (to be computed from the beginning of the year One Thousand Seven Hundred and Eighty-five) all vessels belonging to the same, or to my subjects in Spain, to make voyages to the said Island with their cargoes directly from those ports of France where my Consuls are resident, and to return directly to the said ports with the fruits and produce of the said Island, except money, the exportation whereof by that route I absolutely prohibit; subject however to the following obligation, on the part of the said Consuls, which is not to be dispensed with; that they shall draw up a particular register of everything embarked, and sign, seal, and deliver the same to the care of the captain or master of the vessel, so that he may present the same to the officer charged with the receipt of my Royal Revenues in the said Island of Trinidad; and subject likewise to the payment for the introduction of the goods and merchandise into the said Island, of the sum of 5%, and the same amount on such produce as shall be exported from the same, and carried to France, or to any foreign port, without touching at any one of the Spanish ports which are licensed to trade with the Indies.

Article 20th. In case of urgent necessity (to be attested by the Governor) I do hereby grant to the inhabitants of the said Island, the same permission as is contained in the foregoing article, under the precise condition that the captains or masters of the vessels, do make accurate invoices of their cargoes, and deliver the same to the proper officers in the said Island; so that by comparing the said invoices with the goods imported, the said duty of 5% may be levied on the then current value of the said goods at the said Island of Trinidad.

Article 21st. In order that the former and recent inhabitants may be furnished with the most necessary supplies for their maintenance, their industry and agriculture, I have given the most stringent orders to the Commander-in-Chief of the province of Caracas, to purchase on account of my Royal revenue, and transport to the said Island, horned cattle, mules and horses, to be delivered to the said settlers at first cost, until such time as they have sufficient stock to supply themselves.

Article 22nd. I have likewise given the same order for the supplying the said Island with flour and meal for the term of ten years; and that if, by any accident, a scarcity should take place, the Governor shall permit the inhabitants to go with their own vessels, or those of others my subjects, to the foreign islands to purchase what they stand in need of; and for that purpose to export such produce as may be necessary, paying on exportation, the sum of 5%, and the same proportion on the flour and meal imported into the said Island.

Article 23rd. I have likewise ordered that all matters and things of the manufacture of Biscay and the rest of Spain, which may be required by the settlers for their agricultural pursuits, shall be imported into the said Island, and given to the settlers at prime cost for the said term of ten years; but after that period, each person must provide himself, and if during that period there be an urgent necessity for these matters and things, the settlers

367

shall be allowed to procure them from foreign islands belonging to the Powers in alliance with me, subject to the same duties as the flour and meal.

Article 24th. I have likewise ordered that two secular or regular priests, of known erudition and exemplary virtue, and skilled and versed in foreign languages, shall be appointed to reside in the said Island to serve as new parish priests to the settlers, and I shall assign to them the necessary stipends to enable them to live in the decent manner which their character requires, without being any charge on their parishioners.

Article 25th. I permit former and recent settlers to propose to me, through the medium of the Governor, such ordinances as shall be most proper for the regulating the treatment of their slaves and preventing their flight; and at the same time, to point out such rules as the Governor shall observe relative to this article, and the reciprocal restitution of fugitive slaves from other islands belonging to foreign powers.

Article 26th. I also enjoin the said Governor to take the utmost care to prevent the introduction of ants into the island, which have done so much injury in the Antilles; and for that purpose, to cause the equipage and effects of the settlers arriving at the said Island to be severally examined; and as the inhabitants are the persons most interested in the execution of this order, they shall propose to the Government two of the most active and proper persons to examine the vessels, and zealously watch over the observance of this point.

Article 27th. When the crops of sugar become abundant in the said Island of Trinidad, I shall allow the settlers to establish refineries in Spain, with all the privileges and freedom from duties which I may have granted to any natives or foreigners who shall have established the same; and I will allow in due time the erection of a Consular Tribunal to increase and protect agriculture, navigation and commerce; and I have charged the Governor in his private instructions, and the other judges of the said Island, to take care that all the inhabitants, Spaniards and foreigners, be well and humanely treated, and justice equitably administered to them; so that they may not meet with any molestation or prejudice, which would be greatly to my Royal displeasure.

Article 28th. Lastly I grant to the former and recent settlers the privilege whenever they have questions to ask me worthy of my Royal consideration, of directing their representations to me through the medium of the Governor and the Chief Secretary of States for the Indies; and if the matters are of that nature that require a person to be sent on their account, the inhabitants shall request permission to effect and I will grant the same, if just.

And that the articles contained in this Ordinance be duly carried into effect, I grant a dispensation from all laws and regulations contrary to them, and I command my Council of the Indies, and the chanceries and audiences thereof, Presidents, Captains-General and Commanders-in-Chief, Ordinary Judges in the ports of France, to keep, fulfil and execute, and cause to be kept, fulfilled and executed, all the rules and regulations contained in this my Cedula.

Given at the Royal Palace of San Lorenzo, on the twenty-fourth day of November, One Thousand Seven Hundred and Eighty-three, sealed with my privy seal, and countersigned by my Secretary of State and of the general administration of the Indies, undersigned.

(Signed) I THE KING.
(Countersigned) Joseph de Galvez.

II

Printing in Trinidad

There is no evidence that printing was introduced into the colony until a late stage of the Spanish occupation. It is unlikely that any of the ten skilled tradesmen reported in the island in 1771 were printers. Governor Falquaz (1776–1779) employed a French adventurer, Durand, to write his letters. When St. Laurent visited the island in 1780, he had one copy only of the Royal Cedula, and it seems unlikely that he would have restricted himself to this had there been means of reproducing more.

It would appear that Chacon, who spent some time in Caracas before his arrival in Trinidad, enlisted the services of Juan Cassan as Government Printer. Though Chacon's copy of the Royal Cedula on Colonization was printed in Madrid, it was ordered to be printed locally. The arrival of Cassan would be known officially and this may account for an attempt by the Inquisition to establish itself in Trinidad to carry out its duties of censors of printed documents and books.

It is known that Chacon expelled Jean Villoux (in 1790), editor of a weekly paper, *Gazeta*, from the colony for printing extracts from foreign newspapers without permission. Thomas Gallagher, an Irish immigrant, published the *Trinidad Weekly Courant* in 1796, before leaving for Caracas to establish himself there.

The British Governors or officials exercised a strict control over the Press. Governor Woodford, when annoyed by any articles published, would send a polite note to the editor asking for the loan of the handle of the printing press, thus virtually suspending publication until its return.

Hart, in "Trinidad and Other West Indian Islands and Colonies", lists the following as having been published before 1866:

The Trinidad Weekly Courant
The Trinidad Courant and
    Commercial Gazette
The Trinidad Gazette
Port of Spain Gazette (1825)
The Guardian
The Observer
The Trinidad Standard
The Spectator
The Trinidadian
The Examiner

The Trinidad Reporter
The Herald
The Palladium
The San Fernando Gazette
The San Fernando Reporter
The Sentinel
The Chronicle
The Colonist
The Star of the West
The Trinidad Chronicle
The Free Press

The registration of newspapers commenced in 1834.

III

Return of Troops employed in the expedition against Trinidad.

Headquarters, Port D'Espagne,
20th February, 1797.

Royal Artillery

Officers	12
Staff	3
N.C.O.s	10
Drummers	2
Other Ranks	153

Royal Engineers

Officers	3
N.C.O.s	2
Other ranks	20

2nd Regiment or Queen's—later The Queen's Royal
Regiment, West Surrey, now amalgamated with
the East Surrey Regiment and known as The
Queen's Royal Surrey Regiment

Officers	12
Staff	3
N.C.O.s	28
Drummers	12
Other ranks	551

3rd Flank Company—later The Buffs, East Kent,
England, now amalgamated with the Queen's
Own Royal West Kent Regiment and known as
Queen's Own Buffs

Officers	9
Staff	1
N.C.O.s	9
Drummers	5
Other ranks	150

370

14th Regiment—later The West Yorkshire Regiment
now amalgamated with the East Yorkshire Regiment and known as The Prince of Wales's Own
Regiment of Yorkshire.

Officers	20
Staff	2
N.C.O.s	45
Drummers	20
Other ranks	548

38th Detachment—later The South Staffordshire Regiment, now amalgamated with the North Staffordshire Regiment and known as The Staffordshire
Regiment (The Prince of Wales's).

Officers	11
Staff	2
N.C.O.s	13
Drummers	13
Other ranks	197

53rd Regiment—later The King's Shropshire Light
Infantry, now amalgamated with the King's Own
Yorkshire Light Infantry and the Durham Light
Infantry to form the Light Infantry Brigade.

Officers	22
Staff	5
N.C.O.s	41
Drummers	19
Other ranks	471

60th Detachment—later The King's Royal Rifle Corps,
now the Second Green Jackets, the King's Royal
Rifle Corps.

Officers	10
Staff	1
N.C.O.s	19
Drummers	4
Other ranks	200

Lowenstein's Regiment

Officers	13
Staff	6
N.C.O.s	13
Drummers	6
Other ranks	276

371

Hompsesch's Regiment
Officers	25
Staff	7
N.C.O.s	40
Drummers	16
Other ranks	773

Total Forces
Officers	137
Staff	30
N.C.O.s	220
Drummers	97
Other ranks	3,339

Of the above, 54 were reported as sick.

SPANISH GARRISON
Royal Artillery
Officers	2
Other ranks	43

Engineers
Officers	4

Trinidad Regiment
Officers	24
Other ranks	504
French officers	7

In addition, 50 other ranks sick,
Total	634

IV

List of Ships present at the Capture of Trinidad, 1797.
  Ships under the command of Don Sebastian Ruiz de Apodoca, Jefe of the First Class.

Type of Vessel	Name	Guns	Commander
Ship	*San Vicente*	80	Commandante-Brigadier Don Jeronomio Mendoza
Ship	*Arrogante*	74	Capitan de Navio Don Rafael Bennazar
Ship	*Gallardo*	74	Capitan de Navio Don Gabriel Sorondo
Ship	*San Damasco*	74	Capitan de Navio Don Jose Jordan
Frigate	*Concha*	34	Capitan de Navio Don Manuel Urtizabel

Ships composing the expedition of Rear-Admiral Sir Henry Harvey and Lieutenant-General Sir Ralph Abercromby.

Type of Vessel	Name	Guns	Commander
Ship	Prince of Wales	98	Captain John Harvey
Ship	Bellona	74	Captain George Wilson
Ship	Vengeance	74	Captain Thomas Macnama
Ship	Invincible	74	Captain William Cayley
Ship	Alfred	74	
Ship	Dictator	68	
Ship	Scipio	64	
Ship	Surate	58	
Ship	Ulysses	50	
Frigate	Arethusa	44	
Frigate	Alarm	40	
Frigate	Anna	40	
Corvette	Favourite	20	
Corvette	Zebra	20	
Corvette	Zephyr	20	
Corvette	Thorn	20	
Corvette	Victorious	16	
Bomb Ketch	Terror		

40 transports with 6,750 soldiers.

V

ARTICLES OF CAPITULATION

Articles of Capitulation for the surrender of the Island of Trinidad, between His Excellency Sir Ralph Abercromby, K.B., Commander-in-Chief of His Britannic Majesty's Land Forces, Henry Harvey, Esquire, Rear-Admiral of the Red and Commander-in-Chief of His Britannic Majesty's Ships and Vessels of War, and His Excellency Don José Maria Chacon, Knight of the Order of Calatrava, Brigadier of the Royal Navy, Governor and Commander-in-Chief of the Island of Trinidad and its Dependencies, Inspector-General of the Troops of the Garrison, etc., etc.

Article 1. The Officers and Troops of His Catholic Majesty and his allies in the Island of Trinidad are to surrender themselves prisoners of war, and are to deliver up the territory, forts, buildings, arms, ammunition, money, effects, plans and stores, with exact inventories thereof, belonging to His Catholic Majesty, and they are hereby transferred to His Britannic Majesty in the same manner and possession as has been held heretofore by the said Catholic Majesty.

Article 2. The Troops of His Catholic Majesty are to march out with the honours of war, and to lay down their arms at a distance of three hundred paces from the forts they occupy, at five o'clock this evening, the 18th February.

Article 3. All Officers and Troops aforesaid of His Catholic Majesty are allowed to keep their private effects, and the Officers are allowed to wear their swords.

Article 4. Admiral Don Sebastian Ruiz de Apodoca being on shore in the Island after having burnt and abandoned his ships, he, with the officers and men of the squadron under his command, are included in this capitulation, under the same terms granted to His Catholic Majesty's troops.

Article 5. As soon as ships can be conveniently provided for the purpose, the prisoners are to be conveyed to Old Spain, they remaining prisoners of war, until exchanged by a cartel between the two nations or until peace, it being clearly understood that they shall not serve against Great Britain or her allies until exchanged.

Article 6. There being some officers among His Catholic Majesty's troops whose private affairs require their presence at different places of the continent of America, such officers are permitted to go upon parole to the said places for six months, more or less, after which period they are to return to Europe; but as the number receiving this indulgence must be limited, His Excellency Don Chacon will previously deliver to the British Commanders a list of their names, ranks, and places which they are going to.

Article 7. The officers of the Royal Administration, upon the delivery of the stores with which they are charged to such officers as may be appointed by the British Commanders, will receive receipts, according to the custom in like cases, from the officers appointed to receive the stores.

Article 8. All private property of the inhabitants, as well as Spaniards such as may have been naturalized, is preserved to them.

Article 9. All public records are to be preserved in such courts or offices as they are now in; and all contracts and purchases between individuals which have been done according to the law of Spain are to be held as binding by the British Government.

Article 10. The Spanish Officers of Administration who are possessed of landed property in Trinidad are allowed to remain in the Island, they taking the oath of allegiance to His Britannic Majesty; and they are further allowed, should they please, to sell or dispose of their property and to retire elsewhere.

Article 11. The free exercise of their religion is allowed to the inhabitants.

Article 12. The free coloured people who have been acknowledged as such by the laws of Spain shall be protected in their

374

liberty, person and property, like other inhabitants, they taking the oath of allegiance and demeaning themselves as becomes good and peaceable subjects of His Britannic Majesty.

Article 13. The sailors and soldiers of His Catholic Majesty are, from the time of their laying down their arms, to be fed by the British Government, leaving the expense to be regulated by the cartel between the two nations.

Article 14. The sick of the Spanish troops will be taken care of, but to be attended and to be under the inspection of their own surgeons.

Article 15. All the inhabitants of Trinidad shall, within thirty days of the date hereof, take the oath of allegiance to His Britannic Majesty, to demean themselves quietly and faithfully to his Government, upon pain in case of non-compliance of being sent away from the Island.

Done at Port D'Espangne, in the Island of Trinidad, the 18th day of February, 1797.

> Ralph Abercromby
> Henry Harvey
> José Maria Chacon

VI

375

1688–1690	Sebastian de Roteta
1692–1698	Francisco de Menez
1699	José de Leon Eschales
1701–1705	Francisco Ruiz de Aguirre
1705–1711	Felipe de Alcieda
1711–1716	Cristoval Felix de Guzman
1716–1721	Pedro de Yarza
1721–1726	Martin Perez de Anda y Salazar
1726–1730	Augustin de Arredonda
1730–1735	Bartholomé de Aldunata y Rada
1735–1746	Esteban Simon de Lina y Vera
1746–1752	Juan José Salcedo
1752–1757	Francisco Manclares
1757–1760	Pedro de la Modena
1760–1762	Jacinto San Juan
1762–1766	José Antonio Gil
1766–1773	José de Flores
1773–1776	Juan de Dios Valdez y Varez
1776–1779	(Manuel Falquaz (Military Governor)
	(Martin de Salaverria (Civil Governor)
1779–1784	Martin de Salaverria
1784–1797	José Maria Chacon

IV

The British Governors of Trinidad

1797	Sir Ralph Abercromby
1797	Brigadier-General Thomas Picton
1803	Governed by Commissioners :
	Colonel William Fullarton
	Brigadier-General Thomas Picton
	Commodore Samuel Hood, R.N.
1804	Brigadier-General Sir Thomas Hislop
1811	Major-General W. Munro
1813	Sir Ralph James Woodford, Bart.
1829	Major-General Sir Lewis Grant
1833	Sir George F. Hill, Bart. (Lieutenant-Governor)
1840	Colonel Sir Henry MacLeod
1846	Lord Harris
1854	Sir Charles Elliott, K.C.B.
1857	Robert W. Keate
1864	Hon. J. H. T. Manners-Sutton
1866	Hon. Arthur Hamilton Gordon, C.M.G.
1870	J. R. Longden, C.M.G.
1874	W. W. Cairns, C.M.G.
1874	Sir Henry Turner Irving, K.C.M.G.
1880	Sir Sanford Freeling, K.C.M.G.
1844	Sir F. P. Barlee, K.C.M.G.

1885   Sir A. E. Havelock, K.C.M.G.
1885   Sir William Robertson, K.C.M.G.
1891   Sir F. Napier Broome, K.C.M.G.
1897–1900 Sir H. E. H. Jerningham, K.C.M.G.

VII

*Extracts from a letter of Colonel Picton to Lt.-General Cuyler
dated May 25th, 1798*

" Sir,

Previous to Your Excellency's departure for England, I feel
myself called upon to furnish you with such details and information respecting this island and the neighbouring continent, as
may enable His Majesty's ministers to judge of the means necessary to be employed for the attainment of the objects they may
have in view.

This island, possessing the most extensive, and perhaps one of
the best and finest harbours in all America, wholly free from
hurricanes . . . is so situated as to command the commerce of an
immense continent, extending from the banks of the Rio de los
Amazones to those of La Madaline, including the rich provinces
of Guiana, Barinas, Santa Fé, Venezuela, Caracas and
Cumana . . .

These provinces are inhabited by Spaniards from Europe, who
generally hold all offices and employments under government;
Creoles, or such as are descendants of Spanish settlers; Indians,
who are collected in missions, and kept in the profoundest ignorance by their Capuchin governors; Negroes and a mixed race,
resulting from the communication of all the others; the latter
class and the Indians are by far the most numerous.

Throughout these fine provinces the oppressions and exactions
of these persons entrusted with the government have totally
annihilated all enterprise and industry; and the inhabitants of all
orders are reduced to the most pitiable state of misery. They are
entirely without manufactures of any kind . . . I know a gentleman in the province of Cumana who has 30,000 of horned cattle
and is in absolute want of a coat.

The Government . . . keeps up its authority by arming every
individual against his neighbour . . . so that they appear more as
a set of individuals than as a nation . . . every individual, with
the exception only of those who, placed in the highest offices of
administration, have the means of oppressing and plundering the
inferior ones, looks forward to a deliverance from some foreign
hand with a degree of confident hope. . . .

377

What I have the honour to propose is not in the nature of a conquest, difficult and expensive to be maintained. I have to submit to Your Excellency for the consideration of His Majesty's Ministers, a plan which has for its object the opening of an immense commerce to the industry of His Majesty's subjects, and securing them advantages of an incalculable value, to be obtained by no other means. . . . .

If about three thousand troops could be collected, with a sixty-four gun ship, a frigate, and some forty-four Indian transports to make an appearance or impression—for a squadron would be no otherwise useful—I would propose immediately taking possession of Cumana. The public mind has long been prepared, and the people in general look forward to it as the most favourable event which can befall them. . . . The Governor has no regular force, and the militia have repeatedly signified that they would not expose their families and property to an unavailing resistance . . . A declaration that His Majesty's Government are to give the inhabitants of South America an opportunity of asserting their claim to an independent government and free trade will, I am convinced, decide them at once to forsake a government which has energy only to oppress them . . . The expenses of this expedition I propose would, comparatively, be very inconsiderable. It will not be necessary to employ horses or pioneers, and the ordnance necessary would be a few light field pieces only. The principal objects to be attended to will be arms for infantry and cavalry, for the purpose of arming the inhabitants, and a liberal supply of ammunition. . . .

The beginning of November will be the best time for an expedition to that part of the Main; the dry weather sets in much sooner there than in the islands. The situation is remarkably dry and healthy.

The expedition should go down immediately to its object, without stopping at Trinidad, which would in a certain degree indicate the point menaced; but it will be necessary to apprise me early of the intention, as the success will in great measure depend upon the previous steps I may take to secure it. . . .

A subordinate expedition might be undertaken from Trinidad, with five or six hundred men, up the River Guarapiche, which would essentially contribute to the complete success of the undertaking; and this might be performed without any additional expense, as I should be able to provide the vessels necessary for their transport on the spot.

Having sufficiently enlarged on this subject, and furnished Your Excellency with materials for forming your own opinion from, I shall take my leave, with an assurance that a doubt does not exist in my mind respecting the success of the expedition

378

I have the honour of recommending; and which, if trusted to the command of an officer of prudence and conduct, cannot fail to produce the most extensive and important advantages.

I have the honour to be, etc.,
Thomas Picton."

VIII

Ordinance of the Governor, Lt.-Colonel Thomas Picton, proclaimed June 30th, 1800

"Whereas, in a West Indian Colony settled by different nations, varying in customs and opinions, it is important to incite the inhabitants of every class to mitigate the situation of their slaves, by rendering their servitude as limited and easy as possible and by promoting their natural increase, so as that in course of time the importation of slaves from Africa may be considerably diminished, if not totally dispensed with; and whereas, those desirable ends cannot be more effectually attained, than by compelling owners of slaves to lodge, clothe, and maintain them sufficiently, as well in health, while able to work, as in time of sickness, age and infirmity; by prescribing reasonable grounds to the power of masters and others, having charge of slaves, and by instructing them in the principles of Christianity, to inspire them with some degree of morality.

We have therefore resolved to issue the present Ordinance, by virtue of the authority with which His Majesty has invested us, in order that the regulations it contains may be publicly and generally known, and have their due execution from the date of their publication : charging all persons under our government to pay due obedience thereto, on pain, in cases of negligence or contumacy, of incurring the penalties hereinafter specified.

Article 1. Every proprietor or possessor of a plantation shall provide the slaves attached thereto with good and comfortable houses, well wattled and thatched, so as to be perfectly wind and watertight. The head or chief of every family shall have a house for himself, separated into two or more apartments, according to the number of that family, and there shall be cabanes or bed-places in those apartments, raised at least eighteen inches, to preserve them from the dangerous effects of sleeping on the moist ground. Young Negroes of fourteen and upwards, who have no family, shall be lodged at the rate of three to a house, and they are to have their cabanes raised eighteen inches from the ground as aforesaid. The slaves shall be allowed to enclose their houses with a fence or hedge, to form a little yard for their stock, and defend them from the incursions of the cattle in the pasturage, etc.

379

Article 2. The proprietor or attorney of every plantation shall have one quarree, or three acres, 11/12 of a fanegue of land for every ten working Negroes, planted and cultivated in provisions for the maintenance of his gang, and he shall also, on the Monday or Saturday in every week, distribute to every Negro of fourteen years and upwards under his care, three pounds of salt meat, or four pounds of salt fish (being the weekly allowance), and to all slaves under age, and children, a weekly allowance of salt meat or fish in that proportion.

Exclusive of the allowance of salt meat or fish (in which there can be no exception) every working Negro of fourteen years or upwards, shall have a portion of land allotted to him, adequate to produce, by cultivating it, a sufficiency of ground provisions for himself and his family; and to furnish him more effectively, the means of so doing, he shall be allowed the Saturday from noon, to work his grounds, from the first day of July to the first day of January, if he belongs to a sugar plantation; and from the first day of January to the first day of July, if he belongs to a coffee, cacao or manioc plantation; he will also have his Sundays, and the four great annual holidays of Christmas Day, New Year's Day, Good Friday and Corpus Christi.

The portion of land allotted the slave for his garden cannot be taken from him, or exchanged, without his consent; if the owner or attorney thinks proper to change the situation of the Negro grounds, he must give the slaves a year's warning, unless he prefers obtaining their consent by paying them their improvements and assigning them grounds for gardens, to their satisfaction, elsewhere; And it is a duty most incumbent on managers and overseers, to take care that the Negroes have their grounds in good cultivation, and that they do not lavish or misemploy the surplus time allowed them for that purpose.

Article 3. Owners of plantations whose locality does not admit of allowing Negro grounds, nor having provision grounds, shall furnish weekly to every working Negro under his care, sixty full-grown plantains, or six quarts of manioc, i.e. cassava meal; and in case they cannot procure plantains or cassava meal, it shall be commuted in money, at three bits a week, in lieu of the vegetable allowance, independent of the allowance of salt meat or fish, of which, no pretext, there can be no exemption.

Article 4. To every Negro two shifts of clothing, complete, shall be furnished yearly, one in May, the other in December; and in the case of refusal, there shall be inflicted on the owner a penalty of $12 for every Negro who is not clothed at the time appointed.

Article 5. Owners or attorneys shall not punish slaves by more than thirty-nine lashes;* and managers and overseers shall not

* This by an Order of February 7th, 1815, was commuted to 25 stripes, being the number fixed by the Royal Cedula of May 31st, 1789.

punish by more than twelve lashes for any one offence; the slave who has received thirty-nine lashes shall not be flogged again on the same day, nor until he be recovered from the effects of that punishment; and an infractor of this article will be fined fifty dollars. Should the crime of the slave, however, be of a nature to deserve a severer chastisement, he shall be conducted before the Commandant of the District, who will order such corporal punishment as the case deserves; it being well understood that it cannot extend to death or mutilation, nor shall it be permitted the owner to inflict any further punishment for the same crime, under penalty of fifty dollars.

Article 6. Whoever shall be convicted of having inhumanely struck a slave with an edged weapon, such as a cutlass, axe, sword, or with a bludgeon or loaded beau-stick, will be prosecuted and punished according to law; and if the crime be committed by his master or owner, he (the slave) shall be immediately removed from his (the master's) authority, and deposited with the Commandant of the District, or Alcalde de Barrio, to be sold to some person of known humanity; and the sum arising from the sale shall be applied in whole or in part to the relief of the wounded slave, or in such other charitable purposes as may be deemed proper; and the sale of such slave, it is hereby declared, shall be valid, nor shall the purchaser be disturbed in the possession thereof.

Article 7. The field slave shall have half an hour in the morning for breakfast and two hours at noon for dinner. Nurses having children at the breast shall be permitted to leave the field at noon and night, half an hour before the others, and are exempted of throwing grass. Field slaves are not to go to the field before five o'clock in the morning, nor to work there after six in the evening, except in bringing grass at noon and night for the sick, but it is not meant that this regulation should interfere with the night work on sugar estates in crop time, which cannot possibly be dispensed with.

Article 8. Negroes superannuated, infirm, or invalided by sickness or accident, shall not be abandoned by their owner; on the contrary, he shall lodge, feed and clothe them as usual, and if any person should be so inhuman as to treat them ill, he shall be punished.

Article 9. It has been for many years a custom with some of the inhabitants to give their Negroes Saturday in place of allowance, and with gangs of laborious active Creole slaves, it was found to answer the purpose; but in gangs composed of new Africans, those who adopt it have had reason to repent of the experiment, a new Negro being naturally so lazy and inactive, that he would rather suffer hunger and enjoy his repose than procure himself his subsistence by industry. The increasing opulence of the inhabitants having literally enabled them to augment their force by considerable purchases of this description of Negro, the custom of giving Saturday becomes highly imprudent and would occasion great losses to the Colony: Wherefore it is hereby abolished and prohibited, under penalty of fifty dollars for every delinquent.

Article 10. Owners or managers of plantations shall not oblige their slaves to work on Sundays or holidays hereinbefore specified; but this regulation shall not extend to watchmen or pasture boys (who will continue as heretofore to do that duty in turn), nor to family domestics, the intention being simply to assure the field Negro the free enjoyment of his holiday to work his own grounds.

Article 11. Any Negro who shall assume the reputation of being a spell-doctor or obeah-man, and shall be found with an amulet, a fetiche, or the customary attributes and ingredients of the profession, shall be carried before the Commandant of the District, who will take cognizance of the accusation; and provided the crime be not capital, inflict proper punishment; but should it appear probable that the culprit has been the cause of death of any person by his prescriptions (as very frequently happens), the Commandant will then transmit him to the common gaol, as a criminal, to be prosecuted and dealt with according to law.

Article 12. It is the duty incumbent on Christians, not only to feed and clothe those who are dependent upon them, but also to instruct them in their duty towards their Maker. Planters who have attended this precept have found the benefit of it in the improvement of their slaves' dispositions. It should be therefore the essential duty of the master to teach his slaves the first elements of the Christian religion, to prepare them for Baptism; and we expressly recommend the parish curates the observance of this part of their office, reminding them that it is the principal object of their mission to preach the gospel to the poor.

Article 13. There shall be on every plantation a hospital, proportioned to the number of its slaves, and one or more female attendants attached thereto. The Negro who from sickness is incapable of doing his duty shall there be lodged and attended until he is perfectly recovered; and here it is proper to observe that careful nursing is generally found the most efficacious remedy in Negro disorders. The owner or manager will keep a hospital diary, on which he will note the date of admission and discharge, or decease of the slave; and on giving in the annual enumeration of the estate, he will make also an obituary report.

Article 14. It is a prevalent opinion that owners of plantations, by humane and moderate treatment, might preserve the offspring of their slaves and thereby considerably increase their population. To encourage so beneficial a measure, we have ordained that every mother of a family having more than three children on her master's plantation shall be allowed one day in the week extraordinary, from July 1st to 1st of January, if attached to a sugar or cotton estate, and from 1st January to 1st July, if to a coffee, cacao or manioc estate, and at the end of every year she shall receive from her master a dollar a head, for her future encouragement in the care of her children.

A mother of a family having seven children living on her master's estate shall be exempted from all labour, and she shall be furnished her allowance and maintenance in common with other slaves, and receive the reward, already specified, of one dollar per annum for her children.

The same motive obliges us to prohibit women being put to work before they are perfectly recovered from child-bed, nor shall the infant be carried to the field, but remain under the care of a prudent woman, to be appointed guardian of the children, who will take charge of them in her own house, or a house appropriated to the purpose, until the mothers return from their work, or in their absence.

Article 15. Penalties incurred by infractions of these regulations to be recovered by warrants, signed and sealed by the Commandant of the District in which they have been incurred, which warrants are hereby approved : And all fines recovered in virtue thereof shall be paid into the hands of the Treasurer of the Illustrious Cabildo, to be applied to defray the charges of justice and of public work; for such is our will and pleasure.

Article 16. The present Ordinance shall be printed, and published and proclaimed in all places within our Government; and shall be in full force and execution from the date of publication until further orders.

IX

Extract from a letter from Governor Picton to the Secretary of State, November 4th, 1800

". . . The gentlemen I have selected to form the Council are the most respectable proprietors of the Colony . . .

Don Christoval de Robles is a native of Trinidad, a gentleman to whom I am under great obligation for his advice and assistance on many occasions of difficulty in the administration of justice.

St. Hilaire de Bégorrat, a French gentleman whose zeal and intelligence and indefatigable industry I have successfully employed in terminating an immense mass of intricate litigation which had been unfinished by the Spanish Tribunals.

John Nihell, John Black and John Nugent, Esqs, are of the most respectable and opulent proprietors of the Colony . . ."

X

The Illustrious Cabildo

In the Spanish dominions the Cabildo was made up of persons appointed to conduct the police and government of the chief cities and towns. The Crown had the power to make the laws and appoint the chief Magistrates but at the same time the people had certain rights subordinate to the Crown and its tribunals. The duty of the Cabildo was to support these rights and to represent the people.

Membership of the Cabildo varied according to the size of the city or town in which it belonged. Twelve members were the maximum for the larger towns and six for the smaller communities.

On formation of a Cabildo, two magistrates, the Alcalde of the First Election and the Alcalde of the Second Election were chosen to preside over the courts of justice. To these two Alcaldes the Crown and people entrusted the whole administration of justice for the community, both Civil and Criminal. They were commonly known as the Alcaldes in Ordinary to distinguish them from the other Alcaldes who took their title from their offices.

At the end of each year the Alcalde of the First Election retired from office and was succeeded by the Alcalde of the Second Election and another member of the Cabildo was chosen in his place. This system meant that at all times there was one magistrate who knew the cases pending. After retiring, the Alcalde in Ordinary was not permitted to be re-elected for a period of three years.

All members of the community could take their causes to either of the Alcaldes in Ordinary and their decisions were usually accepted by the Governors of Provinces. If, however, there was a grievance against any judgment of the Alcaldes, an appeal could be made to the Royal Audiencia of the district. Sentences involving corporal or capital punishment, or cases which fixed infamy on the guilty, had to be approved by the Audiencia (In the case of Trinidad, approval had to be sought from the Audiencia in Caracas).

Two Alcaldes del Monte, country members, were also elected to the Cabildo each year and though they had seats on the Board of Cabildo, they had no vote. Other members were the Regidors appointed by the Crown or its representative. They were life members and there was a brisk sale of seats when they became vacant.

By law, all Alcaldes and Regidors were obliged to be of the white race, of good character, upright, honest, and able to read and write. Merchants and craftsmen could be appointed but were unable at the same time to continue with their trade or employment. All persons elected to any office were obliged to carry out their duties unless specially exempted by the Crown.

The Regidors included as officials :

The Alfrez Real, the bearer of the Royal standard on all official occasions.

The Alquazil Mayor, the High Marshal or Chief Constable, whose responsibility it was to see that the decrees of the tribunals were carried out.

The Fiel Executor, who was in charge of the standards of weights and measures, and whose duty it was to see that none imposed upon the public.

The Depositor General, who was responsible for the property of intestate persons, absent persons and for levies made by the Alquazil Mayor.

The Alcalde Provincial or the Alcalde de la Santa Hermandad, who had judicial powers in the country.

These all were called the Regidores Dobles, and had certain privileges by virtue of their offices. They were exempt from serving in the Militia, could not be put in gaol but only confined to the Cabildo building. They could not be cited before a judge but the secretary could take their sworn statement as evidence, and they were in receipt of preference in the choice of purchases in the public markets.

Other members were the Alcaldes de Barrio, appointed to assist in the administration of justice and in the preservation of peace. They were elected by the freeholders of the Barrios into which the town was divided.

Members of the Cabildo elected the Alcaldes in Ordinary, the Alcaldes Provinicial and the Syndic, or Attorney-General, whose duty it was to see that all the proposals of the Cabildo were for the benefit of the public, but who had no vote at the meetings, though he had freedom to speak. Over these elections the Governor had no control but the Crown or the Governor as its representative could sell the other offices.

It was the Governor's right to preside in the Cabildo, though his only vote was a casting one when the voting was equal on any point. If he was absent, his place was taken by his Assessor or Auditor, and in the absence of both, by the Alcaldes in Ordinary or the Regidor Decano, the Dean of the Regidores.

The Cabildo was not a law making body. It could only recommend to the Governor regulations for the police and laws for its own procedure. These had to have Crown approval. Its meetings were secret and great care was taken that only members were admitted. Appeals against the decisions of the Cabildo could be made through the Governor, who could vote any policy or give effect to a minority decision, and through him the Cabildo could address the Crown. They were expected to obey the Governor but had the right to petition for redress.

Their duties included the swearing-in of the Governor, the Lt.-Governor and other high officials. They also inspected and gave approval to qualifications of physicians, surgeons and apothecaries, and to guard against contagious and epidemic diseases. They were responsible for all expenses of the administration of justice, the salaries of its officers, the salary of a physician and surgeon for the poor, and that of a schoolmaster for poor children. In times of public calamities their duty was to assist the distressed from their funds.

In Trinidad as in other colonies, the Governor, as Jeuz Politice, with his Assessor, formed a distinct tribunal trying Civil and Criminal cases brought against planters and others outside the area of San Josef. The Alcaldes dealt only with cases brought by residents of San Josef and Port of Spain against each other.

After the capitulation certain changes were made in the function of the Cabildo and its formation. Appeals in Civil and Criminal cases involving more than £200 came before the Governor. Cases involving more than £500 went to the Privy Council. The British Governors held all the authority which had previously been held by the Audiencia in Caracas. No longer did sentences involving corporal or capital punishment have to be sanctioned outside the colony.

The British Government did not approve of selling the offices of Regidor, and when these became vacant, as the older men who had purchased their office before the capitulation died, the Governor had the right to nominate the new Regidores. An early change had been to increase the number of barrios in Port of Spain from four to eight.

The finances of the Cabildo were left in the hands of a Committee of Public Funds, the Junta Municipal, made up of the Alcalde of the First Election, two Regidores, and the Syndic, who were controlled in their turn by the Junta Superior de Hacienda, until it was superseded by the Governor in Council. There were three keys to the " Public Chest ", one kept by the Alcalde of the First Election, another by the Escribano or Secretary, and the third by the Depositor-General. If there were any funds remaining after expenses had been met, they were spent on public works.

The Assessor or Auditor was the Civil Lt.-Governor who acted for the Governor in civil affairs only. Military affairs were dealt with by the senior officer of the Garrison, who became the

Auditor de Guerro, as all court martial proceedings required his approval.

The income of the Cabildo in 1804 was derived from :

1. Licenses to sell spirituous liquors, @ $10 per month.
2. Licenses for billiard tables @ $12–16 per month.
3. Rents from public flesh and fish markets, about $1,000 per annum.
4. From the Islets of the Bocas, rented to cotton planters at 4–5 reaux a quarree, about $300 per annum. These islands called Monos, Huevos, the Perroquets, Martin Diego and Patos, which were given to the town by the Spanish Government.
5. Rent on lots on Marine Square and the Grass Market, about $1,800–2,000 per annum.
6. Rent of lots at the western extremity of the town called Puerto Cacao and granted to the Cabildo by Governor Picton at $1 per month.
7. Rent of the Coconut Walk granted to the town by His Catholic Majesty. Before the war rented at about $300–500 per annum. Since the war without a tenant.
8. One quarter of 1% obtained from the import and export dues of the wharf, granted by His Catholic Majesty to the town. This amounted to $2,500–3,000 per annum.
9. Rent of new lots east and west of the Mole forming a new part of the town. This was granted by Picton. The streets, 150 feet wide, and the lots, extended the whole extent of the town on the sea side. Several were let at a rent of $50–60 according to the situation.
10. Payments for the use of the public well, pump and aqueduct for the convenience of shipping. This gave about $1,000 per annum.
11. From fines imposed upon delinquents in administration of justice. This amount varied very much.
12. From tax on carts at $2 each month. This farmed out at $1,000 per annum.
13. From duty on foreign liquors, rum, brandy, geneva. A variable amount.

The total revenue of the Cabildo amount to about $14,000 per annum.

The Expenditure of the Cabildo covered :

1. Repairs to public mole and wharf. About $1,600–1,800.
2. Maintenance of slaves employed upon works of public utility.
3. Maintenance of prisoners who had no means of subsistence.
4. Rent and expenses of Town Hall where Courts of Justice and Cabildo met.

5. Repairs to street.
6. The cost of printing.
7. Rent of a public gaol. About $2,000 per annum. The new gaol to cost $20,000.
8. The expenses of the police and the overseers of public works.
9. The expenses of the festival of St. Joseph, the titular saint of the city, and of Corpus Christi, an ancient custom.

Any excess of revenue was required by law to be invested in fixed property to increase the revenue. This was done from 1801–03 by building the flesh and fish markets.

Owners of house property in Port of Spain paid a voluntary tax for the establishment and upkeep of fire engines. This was collected by the Alcaldes de Barrio and paid over to the Director, who in 1804 was Vincent Patrice.

XI

Extract from a letter from the Secretary of State to the Three Commissioners

Downing Street.
16.10.1802.

Gentlemen,

The King having been pleased to appoint you to be His Commissioners for the administration of the Government of the Island of Trinidad, His Majesty's Commission and Instructions are herewith transmitted to you.

The consideration which has principally led to the measure of placing the Government of Trinidad in Commission has arisen from the expediency of preparing for the consideration of His Majesty in Council a system of Government applicable to the peculiar circumstances of this Island where the population though at present limited, is composed of several nations distinct in their languages, customs and prejudices and where a very extensive tract of country remains to be settled under a climate supposed not to be unfavourable to European industry and with the advantages of a soil known to be peculiarly fertile.

It becomes therefore indispensably requisite in the first place to obtain the most accurate information upon the various subjects to which your attention is directed by His Majesty's instructions . . .

In treating of the military situation of the Island you will . . . state your opinion with respect to the force necessary for the internal and external security of the Island in time of war and peace; the proportion of European troops, whether of artillery, cavalry or infantry judged adequate for every service; to what extent the employment of black troops may be advisable; the aid that may be expected from the inhabitants in the form of militia comprising white as well as people of colour; the best mode of providing for the subsistence of all descriptions of force and every other circumstance which may be connected with the defence and safety of the Island.

The naval advantages that may be derived from the possession of Trinidad in a very special manner demand a minute attention and investigation; among other points the following are of material importance; the course of the winds and current at the different seasons of the year; the probably time in which the communication with Jamaica and the different British islands may be effected; the survey of the coasts, harbours and bays; the most eligible place to establish a naval arsenal combining the security of the port in all winds with its fitness for careening or refitting ships of war; the protection it may afford against an enemy, with all other circumstances which may be essentially advantageous to such an establishment; the most secure and convenient place for loading and unloading of ships and the facilitating the commercial intercourse with the Island; how far the rivers may be navigable and to which extent they may be capable of being made so for the purposes of internal communications and commerce; what timber the Island may furnish suitable for naval purposes and the most convenient places for cutting and shipping it; how far the fortifications for the security of the Island can be aided by a naval force in case of its being besieged; the state of and the utility likely to be derived from the bitumen or pitch to be found in the Island and every circumstance relative thereto.

The advantages which might be expected to accrue from the introduction of a European yeomanry at Trinidad are so great that I cannot too strongly recommend that subject to your most serious consideration.

The first object with respect to it will be to ascertain from the information of those who have been longest resident upon the Island the local situations which may be deemed most favourable for European constitution.

It would be proper to consider in what proportion it may be advisable that land should be allotted and what restrictions should be imposed with regard to the future sale or transfer of such land by the proprietors so as on the one hand to check speculation in land and thereby keep the settlers in the class of yeomen, artificers and mechanics, and on the other hand to leave open to them such encouragement as may be requisite for giving a stimulus to their industry.

As this description of persons would for the most part arrive upon the Island without means of providing immediately for their own accommodation and support, you will communicate to me your opinion whether it would be advisable to construct small houses in the situations which may be appropriated for the settlers and also what measures you may judge it necessary to take for their being supplied with a wholesome diet until by their own industry they might be enabled to provide for themselves. You will at the same time transmit to me a list of implements of husbandry which it may be proper to furnish each settler with.

The introduction of any implement that can lighten the field labour or of machinery that may be applied in mills or in the laborious process of any manufacture, would be in the highest degree desirable. In this respect the superior advantages of the steam engine, wherever it can be used, appear only to need a trial to recommend its application ...

In the hope that it may be found practicable to prevail on some of the natives of China to remove their families to Trinidad, it will be proper that tracts of land should be reserved for them in situations most favourable for the plough and calculated for the cultivation of rice as well as the sugar cane.

There is only one subject upon which I have at present anything further to remark, the introduction of British laws into the Colony.

The opinion of Mr. Gloster, who has been appointed Attorney-General in the Island, and the observations which he has had the opportunity of making upon the spot coincide so much with sentiments conveyed in the Memorial of the Inhabitants as to furnish additional argument for the continuing in force of the laws now in existence. In the meantime, Mr. Gloster's suggestion for establishing some temporary tribunal for the more speedy settlement of differences arising in cases of contracts and commercial transactions, merits early and attentive consideration as its adoption might tend to lessen the prejudices which will probably be felt whilst Spanish laws continue to exist.

I am to acquaint you that His Majesty has been pleased to determine that the salary for the First Commissioner should be three thousand pounds per annum, and of the Second and Third Commissioners, two thousand pounds per annum each; which sum you are hereby authorized to appropriate out of the public revenues of the Island ...

I have, etc.,
HOBART,
Secretary of State.

XII

Simon Bolivar, 1783–1830. The Great Liberator. Hero of
South America

Simon Bolivar was born at Caracas in 1783 and descended from
noble Spanish families. He was educated in Madrid and Paris.
He was in Paris during the final stages of the Revolution. On
his return to Spain in 1801 he married a Spanish lady; shortly
after he returned to Venezuela with his bride, and they went to
live on his estates, where his wife died soon after of yellow fever.
Bolivar then returned to Europe, where he travelled extensively.
In 1809, on his way back to Venezuela, he stayed for some time
in the United States of America, where he imbibed revolutionary
ideas, which decided him to devote his life to the cause of independence. After the overthrow of the First Venezuelan Republic, he
offered his services to the revolutionaries of New Grenada, who
in 1813 declared that Vice Royalty to be independent of Spain.
For more than six years he fought against the Royalists. He
experienced many reverses and was obliged to flee no less than
five times. In 1815 he fled to Jamaica, where he was given a
friendly reception by the British Governor. Whilst in Jamaica
he narrowly escaped assassination. Bolivar again returned to
Venezuela. In 1819 his victory over the Spanish Royalists at
Bovaco freed that Province, with the exception of Quito. His
victory at Carabobo in 1821 completed the independence of
Venezuela. When the Provinces of Venezuela and New Grenada
were united, Bolivar was elected President. Besides being a good
soldier, Bolivar was a great statesman. It was due to his efforts
that the Spanish Colonies in South America, the Vice-Royalties
of New Grenada, Peru and La Plata, and the Captaincies-
General of Venezuela and Chile, gained their independence. He
inspired others who followed his example in New Spain and
Guatemala. He died in 1830, having spent most of his life and
his fortune in the service of his country.

XIII

A Proclamation as to the security of land tenure

Port of Spain, Trinidad.
December 5th, 1815.

RALPH JAMES WOODFORD

Whereas it appears that a great proportion of the Titles to
Land in this Colony are defective or absolutely void . . . His
Royal Highness, the Prince Regent, taking these circumstances
into consideration . . . has been pleased to declare as it is hereby
proclaimed and declared.

That in all and every case where, previous to the date of this
Proclamation the lands occupied or granted either under Spanish
or British authority (excepting those hereinafter mentioned) have
been put and are now in a state of cultivation; the Tenures and
Titles of such lands shall be confirmed to the extent of such land
in cultivation together with such a portion as shall be equal to
the quantity in cultivation, provided always that in case the lands
so occupied, granted and cultivated shall be required for the
Public Service the same shall be retained and the Owner or
Occupier thereof shall receive in land, a full equivalent to those
of which he has been deprived : and provided always that from
and after the date of this Proclamation the persons holding or
claiming to hold such lands shall in the month of June in the
ensuing and every succeeding year pay into the Colonial
Treasury for and in consideration of such confirmation, the sum
of Five Shillings Currency for every Quarree of land confirmed
and granted; the said sum to be a perpetual charge and incum-
brance on the lands held and confirmed . . .

And whereas amongst the Grants and Titles herein last recited
there are found to be many, the lands whereof are entirely uncultivated or abandoned contrary to the spirit and letter of the
above mentioned Order and to the present and future disadvantage and inconvenience of the Colony at large; His Royal Highness, the Prince Regent, has been further pleased to declare that
unless the said lands shall within the space of Two Years from
and after the date of this Proclamation be put into a state of
cultivation in a proportion of One-Fourth Part at least to the
whole extent of the land and be so continued; and unless there
shall be placed by the Owner and employed thereon a number
of Negroes or Labourers amounting at least to the proportion of
one Negro or Labourer to every Five Quarrees of land so held,
the Owners thereof shall pay to the Colonial Treasurer in the
month of June next after the determination of the said term

and in the said month of every succeeding year, the sum of Five Shillings Currency per Quarree; And in the case the said Annual Payment shall not be made at the first Annual Period next succeeding the determination of the said term, the said lands shall be taken and considered as abandoned and shall be resumed and seized as forfeited to His Majesty, His Heirs and Successors.

And whereas amongst those persons who from time to time obtain permission from the several British Governors of the Colony to occupy lands under certain conditions and restrictions, there are many who have violated the same, His Royal Highness, the Prince Regent, has been pleased to give a power to His Excellency the Governor to confirm the Grants of such parts of those lands as are cultivated, with the reserve of such portion of them as may be wanted for the Public Service in manner aforesaid, on payment by the Occupiers thereof into the Colonial Treasury of One Hundred Pounds Currency by way of fine and penalty for the violation of the conditions and restrictions of their several permissions of occupancy; the said lands being also held subject to the Annual Quit Rent or charge of Five Shillings per Quarree payable in the same manner and period as are herein more particularly described.

And whereas permissions have also been obtained from the several British Governors to occupy lands in the Colony which said lands have remained and are now uncultivated : His Royal Highness, the Prince Regent, has been pleased to declare that all such grants and permissions shall be considered and taken, as they are hereby declared to be void : with a reservation nevertheless to such nominal occupiers to pray for a grant to the same on such conditions as are hereinafter declared in the case of new settlers.

And His Royal Highness, the Prince Regent, having taken into his gracious consideration the great benefit that might be derived to the inhabitants and others from a cultivation of many parts of the most fertile lands of this Colony, has been further pleased to authorize His Excellency the Governor to confer grants upon the following conditions :

First That it be shown to the satisfaction of the Governor that the persons applying for lands are possessed of the means of cultivating them and rendering them valuable.

Second That no new grant to a resident of the Island shall exceed in the first instance One Hundred Quarrees except in cases where the nature of the intended cultivation shall render a relaxation of this condition indispensable.

Third That if strangers shall be desirous of settling with any great number of slaves from other British Colonies and requiring any greater extent of land than is hereinbefore limited, they will be recommended to His Royal Highness' gracious favour.

Fourth That the said grants of new lands shall in all cases be given upon the condition of cultivating One-Fourth part of the same within the period of five years from the date of the grant; and in failure thereof all title of dominion and of occupancy or otherwise shall revert to the Crown.

Fifth That the right of His Majesty to all minerals as well as quarries, timber, and water when required for the Public Service with free ingress and regress to and from the same, be reserved.

Sixth That the three chains on the Sea Coast (comprehending fifty paces) from the height of the spring tides be held and reserved for the use of His Majesty and the Public Service.

That to avoid all differences or disputes in this respect no building of whatever description shall be erected within the line of this chain without the express permission of the Government first obtained through the Commandant of the Quarter and the Commissary of Population; and in all such permissions the right to demolish and abate at will, shall be reserved.

Seventh That the right of tracing and directing new roads, canals or other means of communications to be opened, shall be preserved to His Majesty.

Eighth That all lands granted to new settlers shall, in like manner, as all other lands, hereafter to be cultivated, be held subject to the payment of the Annual Quit Rent of Five Shillings Currency per Quarree.

Ninth That in case any lands now to be confirmed and granted or hereafter to be granted to new settlers shall cease to be cultivated according to the proportion hereinbefore prescribed for and during the space of Three Years, then and in such case and after notice given by the Attorney-General or Law Officer of the Crown for the time being and the Judgment of Abandonment given in the Court of the Intendent, the said lands shall be resumed by the Crown and become absolutely forfeited to His Majesty, His Heirs and Successors.

And it is hereby further Ordered and Declared that in default of payment of the Quit Rent hereby imposed on all lands granted and confirmed or to be granted into the Treasury of the Island in every month of June, the said Quit Rent shall be sued for, levied and recovered in the same manner as all other debts of His Majesty now are recoverable and under the same privileges, rights and preference which by the laws in force are provided and declared in respect of debts contracted to the Crown; and in default of other property than the lands so granted, the said lands shall revert to the Crown.

By Command of His Excellency,

P. Reinagle,
Secretary.

XIV

A Proclamation waiving the Quit Rent on certain lands

Port of Spain, Trinidad.
November 7th, 1816.

TRINIDAD

Whereas in consequence of a representation made by His Majesty's Council to His Royal Highness, the Prince Regent, through His Majesty's Principal Secretary of State for the Colonial Department, on the expediency of exempting all lands that had been held, granted or occupied previous to the conquest of the Island by his Britannic Majesty's Arms on the 18th of February, 1797, from the payment of the Annual Quit Rent of Five Shillings Currency per Quarree that was imposed by the Proclamation of 5th December, 1815–16 however defective the Grant Tenure or Occupation of the said Lands may have been; His Royal Highness has been leased to signify His gracious Commands that the said Annual Quit Rent on these Lands hereinbefore particularly mentioned should be repealed.

. . . Provided always that the present occupiers of such Lands, shall within the period of Two Months from the date hereof, pay for a confirmation of the same; and provided always that nothing herein contained shall be held to exempt the said occupiers, their heirs or assigns, from the obligation of conforming to the Third Clause of the said Proclamation of 5th December, 1815, and from putting the said Lands into a state of cultivation within a period of two years from the date of the said last Proclamation in a proportion of One-Fourth Part, at least to the whole extent of the Land so held, granted or occupied and from placing and employing thereon a number of Negroes or Labourers to every Five Quarrees so held, granted or occupied; amounting at least, to the proportion of one Negro or Labourer to every Five Quarrees of Land so held, granted or occupied and that in failure thereof, the said Quit Rent of Five Shillings Currency per Quarree* be exacted and the penalty of resumption of the said Land enforced in failure of payment.

By His Excellency's Command,
Geo. Martin,
Acting Secretary.

---

* Five shillings currency was about half its value in sterling.
1 Quarree—3 1/5 acres.
100 Quarrees—320 acres.

XV

Extracts from a Proclamation on land tenure by the Governor of Trinidad (Chacon), July 27th, 1785

First are declared as Crown Lands and belonging to His Majesty all those Lands which have not been alienated by a formal Title of concession, admeasurement and line of boundary in conformity to the Laws of the Indies or Royal Cedulas respecting the colonization and cultivation of the Island.

Second In the decision of the causes or matters now pending with the Fiscal respecting uncultivated Lands, Immemorial Possession will not be admitted as a sufficient Title, it being His Majesty's intentions to possess thereof the property and dominion, against whose interest there is neither occupation nor prescription, as being injurious in this case to the welfare of the State and the common interests of the Nation.

Third That all those inhabitants who hold from a distant period of time, ungranted land whether by inheritance of their ancestors or other relations or because they have taken possession of them by their own will, the same being cultivated and a value thereto given, will be the first entitled to a gratuitous grant thereof of property in preference to other claimants, on condition that in the space of three months they present themselves to this Government in order to obtain their Title of Concession according to the Royal Cedula on Colonization under the penalty to those who shall not so present themselves within the said term, of losing all their right and claim thereto.

Fourth As it happens that many of the inhabitants have inherited of their parents various Lands which although not granted, have been adjudged to them in a certain sum with other co-heirs, it is hereby declared that whenever such Lands by reason of their being uncultivated shall be ceded to some new Colonist, this shall make good the sum in which they shall have been adjudged, the same being proved by proper documents; and the same compensation shall take place under the circumstances of such inhabitants having purchased the Lands of other individuals whose claim is founded on a similar right.

Fifth All the ancient Spanish inhabitants who without Title of Property and Concession, shall claim lands in different parts, covered with wood by their not having the means to clear them, shall within the term of three months make choice of the situation in which they wish to establish themselves and present themselves in order to obtain a grant thereof according to the Cedula on Colonization; the Crown Lands remaining in benefit of His Majesty to bestow them upon others who will clear and cultivate them.

Sixth As the ambition of many Spaniards is carried to such an excess that although they are unable to put a single quarree of land into cultivation, they pretend to be proprietors of considerable portions in different Quarters and quitting these pass over to the Crown Lands and thereon employ the little labour they are capable of, these persons must likewise make election within the said Term of Three Months of the situation most suitable for their establishment whether on their pretended property or on Crown Lands; the surplus land remaining in benefit of His Majesty as provided in the preceding article.

Seventh The spirit of this Proclamation being to remove every impediment whatever in the cultivation of lands, it is declared that should the legitimate possessor not have the means to work them, they shall be granted to others who may demand them, with sufficient strength, these paying to the proprietors the sum or value for which they were obtained, whether in payment of a credit, gift, purchase or other means leaving them such portion of land which they may be capable of cultivating in conformity to the Cedula on Colonization.

Eighth From the preceding article are excepted all those new colonists who possess any land with Title of this Government under conditions conforming to the regulations contained in the said Royal Cedula on Colonization.

Ninth His Excellency not wishing to injure any persons who have bona fide employed their funds by renting lands in the occupancy of Spaniards which have not been granted to them, whenever these shall be granted in consequence of their being abandoned and uncultivated to some other colonists, this shall be bound to secure such rent or tribute on the said Lands so charged or redeem it as may suit his interest.

Tenth Whenever this Government shall grant Crown Lands and any one shall have cultivated a part thereof, he shall be dispossessed of it under condition of his being paid the value of the plantation or provisions that may be found thereon and other expenses he may have incurred on his establishment. And that the above articles might be observed and carried into execution in all their parts, His Excellency ordered them to be published in the usual places of this Port and Copies thereof to be fixed up and others to be sent to the Town of St. Joseph de Oruña, Valley of Tacarigua and to all Commandants of Quarters that they might publish them in their respective districts; and another

397

copy to be transmitted to His Majesty for His Royal Approbation.

And His Excellency decreed, ordered and signed the Act with the advice of his Council in Port of Spain, whereof I certify on oath.

JOSEPH MARIA CHACON.
JOSEPH DAMIEN DE CUENCA.

Before me
LOUIS CENTENO,
Secretary Fiscal.

XVI

Extract of proposals put forward by Sir Ralph Woodford for the amelioration of the condition of slaves, 1823

1. That the condition of the slaves is capable of being ameliorated.

2. That the basis of such amelioration should be religious instruction.

3. That any system of emancipation should be commenced by the manumission of female slaves.

4. That any emancipation of children is not likely to be attended with the advantages that might be supposed to result from such a provision unless preceded by the emancipation of the mothers.

5. That emancipation should be fully indemnified to the owner according to the produce of his estate, allowing for the probable benefit to be expected from any late improvement upon his property.

6. That it be recommended to the proprietors of estates to make the following provisions and concessions :

    1. That religious instruction be afforded and places of worship provided in the several quarters at convenient distances.

    2. That 26 days in the year be granted to the slaves to work their grounds.

    3. That the labour of slaves upon estates be limited to 13 hours out of 24 out of crop time, and 16 hours out of 24 in crop time, such limitation to include the hours appointed for their meals.

    4. That the slaves be permitted and encouraged to deposit their earnings, however small, in Savings Banks to be established in convenient places throughout the island under the care of a Committee, and the receipts to be paid quarterly into the Treasury.

XVII

Summary of the Order in Council of 1825

The first eight clauses of the Order made provision for the appointment of a Protector of Slaves and regulated his duties.

Clause 9. Abolished all Sunday markets.

   „   10. Prohibited the performance of any labour by slaves between sunset on Saturday and sunrise on Monday.

   „   11. Made it illegal to carry any whip, etc., for the purpose of coercing slaves to perform their labours.

   „   12. Prohibited any punishment of a slave until 24 hours after the offence. It required at least one free person to be present in addition to the person who ordered the punishment.

   „   13. Prohibited the use of the whip to any woman for any offence.

   „   14-20. Related to keeping of books of records including one for the recording of punishments.

   „   21. Put the onus on the owner to prove that no punishment had been inflicted, if a slave prosecuted for improper punishment.

   „   22. Related to the encouragement of marriage amongst slaves.

   „   23. Required that no family should be divided upon being sold.

   „   24. Empowered slaves to possess and bequeath property.

   „   25-27. Allowed a slave to manumit himself without his owner's permission.

   „   28. Directed that the fee for manumission should not exceed twenty shillings.

   „   29-33. Regulated appraisement when a slave was affected in a mortgage or law settlement.

   „   34. Required that when a slave under 6 or over 50 years of age was manumitted, the owner should provide gratuitously a bond of £200 to provide sustenance.

   „   35-36. Authorized clergymen to certify that slaves had sufficient religious instruction to understand the nature of an oath, and to be competent court witnesses.

XVIII

My Lord,

In my despatch No. 73, I had the honour to submit for the approbation of His Royal Highness, the Prince Regent, a Proclamation issued by me on 20th December, 1814, constituting a Medical Board in this Island where a number of empyrics and ignorant medical practitioners rendered such a measure extremely advisable.

Such a Board had been constituted by General Picton and renewed by General Hislop but had fallen into disrepute from want of subsequent support on the part of the Government. The Spanish laws which oblige all practitioners of medicine to obtain a licence from the Protomedicate or Medical Tribunal of the great Spanish cities will show to Your Lordship that such a law is fully conformable to the Spanish Code and it had been formerly usual here for all medical persons to enregister their patents with the Cabildo.

Your Lordship not having intimated to me any disapprobation of the measure it has been continued in force and has been universally obeyed except by a Mr. Fitzpatrick Geagan who gives himself out to be a member of the College of Surgeons in London but who refuses to show his Diploma to the Medical Board for registry alleging that he is forbidden to do so by the Act of Parliament incorporating the College of Surgeons and that it is derogatory to him to show the patent which the College has conferred upon him.

. . . .

In consequence of this I am induced to request Your Lordship will be pleased to direct communication to be had with the College of Surgeons that they may perfectly understand that it is only for the purpose of registering genuine Diplomas that gentlemen professing to be Members of their College are obliged to present themselves before the Medical Board of this Colony.

The necessity for such a competent tribunal is, I presume, unquestionable where so many impositions by foreigners are liable to be practised. An American lately produced the certificate of a provincial society in the United States licensing him to practise medicine and surgery in the province and by virtue of which he claimed to be exempt from the examination of the Medical Board here. The Board would not admit the certificate and called upon the American gentleman to submit to examination which he

declined and it is believed from consciousness of his own incapacity to meet it. He has since retired from all practice in this
Colony.

I have the honour to be, My Lord,
Your Lordship's faithful and obedient servant,
RALPH WOODFORD.

XIX

Extracts from a Proclamation forming the Medical Board

Whereas it has become necessary to prevent the indiscriminate
introductions and admission of persons to practise Medicine or
Surgery in the said Island, without due proof of their having
acquired or being possessed of a competent knowledge in such
their profession and practice, and to prohibit in like manner the
Sale of Medicines or Drugs of bad quality, or the Sale of any
sort of Medicine or Drugs therein by persons not duly authorized
or competent in that respect.

And whereas it is expedient for the purpose aforesaid, that a
Medical Board as theretofore existing, should be re-established,
with such powers and authorities as are hereinafter more particularly expressed.

I have thought fit, therefore, to issue this my Proclamation
and to Order, Proclaim, and Declare, as it is hereby ordered,
proclaimed and declared :

First   That the said Medical Board shall consist of Four Members, who shall be from time to time appointed by the Governor,
and Dr. Williams is hereby nominated and appointed to be the
President of the said Medical Board, and that any two Members,
with the President, shall constitute a Board.

Second   That all and every Person or Persons who now practise
Medicine or Surgery, or who act as Apothecaries or sell any
Medicines or Drugs in the said Island shall, within two months
from and after the date hereof, appear before the Medical Board,
at such time and place as the said Board by Notice thereof, to
be inserted in the Island *Gazette,* and signed by the President,
shall appoint, and shall register his and their names, quality,
and profession respectively, in a Book to be kept for that purpose,
and shall at the same time produce any permission, licence or
authority by virtue of which such person or persons now practise
Physic or Surgery or vend any Medicines or Drugs in this Island
under the penalty of FIVE HUNDRED DOLLARS, and being from
thenceforth prohibited from practising Physic or Surgery, or
vending any Medicines or Drugs within the said Island.

Third   That no person who shall not produce and exhibit to
the Medical Board, and by them to be afterwards referred for

approval to the Governor or Lt.-Governor of the said Island, a
Certificate of Medical Degree, duly conferred upon him by some
one or other of the Universities of Europe and America, or some
other Body Corporate, competent and entitled to confer the same,
shall thenceforth be allowed or permitted to practise in this
Island except as is hereafter provided.

Fourth And in case it shall appear that any such person or
persons has or have practised in the Island in the said several
capacities without having any such certificate as is described in
the 3rd Clause of this Proclamation, or any permission, licence, or
authority of any former Governor or Lt.-Governor of the said
Island, and shall be desirous of continuing to practise Medicine
or Surgery, or vend Drugs within the same; such person or persons shall be fully examined by the Medical Board touching their
fitness and ability for the said several Professions and practice,
and if after such examinations it shall appear to the Board that
the said person or persons are in all respects qualified for the
same, they shall, on the Report of the said Medical Board to the
Governor or Lt.-Governor for the time being and an approval
thereof by him, obtain and receive his licence and permission to
practise as aforesaid in the said Island, and such person or persons
as aforesaid who shall be convicted of practising in future, without such licence in writing as aforesaid shall be subject to the
same Fine and Penalty as is provided and ordered in the 2nd
Clause of this my Proclamation.

Fifth That no person shall, from and after the date of this
Proclamation, vend, issue, or otherwise dispose of any Medicines
or Drugs whatsoever, or keep a Shop for the sale thereof, without a licence, in writing from the Medical Board, and the
Report of the fitness of such person or persons in that respect
to be confirmed and approved by the Governor or Lt.-Governor,
under a penalty of FOUR HUNDRED DOLLARS, and total prohibition
to vend such articles in future.

Sixth And it is hereby further ordered, proclaimed, and declared, that the Members of the Medical Board, from time to
time, as to them shall seem expedient accompanied by the Chief
of Police, shall make an inspection of the Shops of all persons
licensed and approved to sell Medicines and Drugs as aforesaid
in the said Island, and shall inspect the quality, state, and condition of such Medicines and Drugs, and if the same appear to
be bad, corrupt, and unfit for sale, they shall forthwith have the
same wholly destroyed, reporting their Proceedings and Remarks,
on every such visit, to the Governor or Lt.-Governor for the time
being take care that such visits shall be made four times at least
during every year.

Seventh That no Medicines or Drugs of what quality and kind
so ever shall be sold, delivered, or issued, by any Apothecary or

Vendor of Drugs, or by his or their Clerk, Shopman, Apprentice, or Servant, to any Slave, without an Order in writing by his Owner, or the Manager, or Conductor of the Estate to which such Slave belongs, or the person who has hired or employed the said Slave, or without the permission in writing of some one or other of the Medical Practitioners authorized and licensed as aforesaid to practise in the said Island, under penalty of TWO HUNDRED DOLLARS for the first Offence, and if convicted of a repetition of the same under that of FOUR HUNDRED DOLLARS, and loss of his or their licence to sell any Medicines or Drugs hereafter in the said Island.

Eighth. That in case any doubt or dispute shall arise at any time hereafter, touching the fairness or justice of any Account or Demand made for Medical attendance or for Drugs and Medicine given and supplied by any person or persons so licensed as aforesaid, either within the Town or Port of Spain or in the said Island, the same shall be referred for decision to the Medical Board, whose determination respecting the same shall be considered final.

Ninth. That no Shops or Laboratory professing to sell Medicine or Drugs shall upon any occasion, in the absence of the Master or Licenciate, be left open for the sale of Medicine or Drugs, without some competent and skilful Person being in attendance therein, who shall be able and fit to supply the Medicine required by the Public, and for whom and whose conduct or ignorance the said Master or Licenciate shall always be responsible.

Tenth. And it is further ordered and declared, that in case of conviction of any person or persons of any of the offences described in the said several Clauses of this my Proclamation, and before any of the Tribunals of Ordinary Jurisdiction of the said Island, the One-Half shall be paid to the person or persons who shall inform and sue the same and the other half shall be paid to the Treasurer of the said Island for the Public uses thereof; and in Default of Payment of any Penalty or Penalties, such person or persons so convicted, shall be imprisoned in the Common Gaol, until the same be paid, at the discretion of the Court or Judge before whom the said conviction or condemnation shall be read.

Eleventh. It is hereby further ordered, proclaimed and declared that the Medical Board shall be authorized to demand and receive the fees that are now established and approved, the Docket of which shall always be produced at any Meeting or Meetings, when any fee or fees shall be charged or taken.

Twelfth. And further, I do hereby will and require, and strictly charge and command the Persons composing the Medical Board, His Majesty's Chief Judge, and the Judges of the Tribunals established in the said Island and all and every Person and Per-

sons practising Physic and Surgery, and vending Medicines
and Drugs therein, to take notice of these Presents, and govern
themselves accordingly.

And last I do hereby order, proclaim and declare, that this My
Proclamation shall, in virtue of the Proclamation of His Royal
Highness, the Prince's Regent, of the 18th of December, 1813, be
registered in the Books of Record thereby directed to be kept
by His Gracious Majesty's Governor and Commander-in-Chief,
and the Judges of the Tribunals established in the said Island.

Given under my hand and seal of Office, at Belmont, in the
said Island, this 20th day of December, 1814, and in the 55th
year of His Majesty's Reign.

By His Excellency's Command,
P. Reinagle, Secretary.

XX

*Extract from a speech by Mr. Brougham in the House of
Commons on the situation in Demerara, 1824*

". . . My opinion ever has been, that it is alike necessary to the
security of our white brethren and just and even merciful to the
Negroes—those victims of a long continued system of cruelty,
impolicy and injustice—to maintain firmly the legal authorities,
and, with that in view to avoid in our relation with the slaves,
a wavering, uncertain policy keeping them in a position of doubt
and solicitude, calculated to work to their own discomfort and
the disquiet of their masters. Justice to the whites, mercy to the
blacks, command us to protect the first from the effect of such
alarms, and the last from the expectation that in the hapless
condition in which they are placed, their emancipation—meaning thereby their sudden unprepared emancipation—or effected
by violent measures or with an unjustifiable haste, and without
previous instruction . . .

It is for the sake of the blacks themselves as subsidiary to their
own improvement that the present state of things must for the
time being be maintained. It is, because to them, the bulk of our
fellow subjects in the Colonies, liberty if suddenly given, and
still more if violently obtained, by men yet unprepared to receive
it, would be a curse and not a blessing, that emancipation must
be the work of time, and above all must not be forcibly wrested
from their masters. . . .

404

Extract from a speech by Wilberforce on the rioting in Barbados, 1823

" . . . At the very time when the prejudices against the Methodists had in some places subsided; when those good men had fairly lived them down by their inoffensive and meritorious conduct; in that very settlement in Barbados, in which the proportion of whites to blacks is largest, and which has been supposed to bear the strongest resemblance to an English community, a chapel lately erected at the expense of several thousand pounds was utterly destroyed, not by a sudden impulse of fury, but after a regular notice, and by a preconcerted collection of people—not by what is commonly termed a mob, the lower orders of the community, but as was boasted, by men of superior rank and property—not at one heat, but after they were wearied by their first day's work, returning again the next day to complete the demolition of the building, of which every trace was swept away, and to drive the Missionary himself out of the Colony. In fact the rage against him was such that had he not been concealed from the fury of his enemies and been able to escape out of the Island, his life could not possibly have been saved. When the Governor of the Island . . . issued a Proclamation offering a reward for the discovery and apprehension of the perpetrators of this outrage . . . it was met by a counter-proclamation posted in all the streets, denouncing the vengeance of the Colony against all who should dare to attempt to bring the destroyers of the chapel to punishment; but reminding the public that they had the cause in their own hands; intimating that they were to be the jury; no one should ever be found guilty on account of so meritorious an action."

XXI

Extract from a letter to the Port of Spain Gazette under the signature "Fore-warned and Fore-armed," March, 1832

" Sir,

The awfully afflicting intelligence which has been received from Jamaica, stating the unprecedented sacrifice which the free inhabitants have been compelled to make of the Negro population, must surely rouse the dormant feelings of the settlers in this Island, as it can be no longer questioned that the dreadful calamity has been the work of the " Saints "* in the hope of effecting the fiend-like object which they have so long had in view, but a merciful Providence has defeated their obvious intentions. Therefore, let us now, under the same Divine Protec-

* The nickname given to the Anti-Slavery Society.

tion, look to ourselves, as surely no further warning can be necessary.

I would therefore suggest that the actions of the emmissaries of the " Saints " who are now in this Colony, should be strictly watched, and on the detection of any well authenticated act which may have a tendency to lead to dangerous results, let the community at once take upon themselves to exercise summary and severe justice; and in such a manner as will strike with terror, the remainder of this infamous gang of vipers whom we are now fostering among us.

We have no time to lose. Let every man be on his guard, and let the moment of detection be the signal for punishment."

XXII

Extract from a letter in the Port of Spain Gazette *from the Secretary of State, August 25th,* 1832

" Sir,

Since the promulgation of the Order in Council of 20th June, 1831, for improving the administration of justice in British Guiana, Trinidad and St. Lucia, I have not ceased to observe with the most watchful attention the progress of that measure . . .

Notwithstanding the opposition with which the Order in Council has had to contend, I am happy in the conviction that in general it promises to advance the great ends with a view to which it was promulgated by His Majesty. Nor is it a just cause of surprise that a system intended, and which, as I believe, will be adapted to diminish the cost and delay of litigation, should, in any part of the world, have had to encounter such hostility; many prejudices which I am bound to respect would, even in absence of less excusable motives, naturally enlist a numerous, active body on the side of abuses sanctioned by long usage, rendered familiar by mere habit. I find, therefore, no cause to regret the course which was pursued on this subject.

I am, however, constrained to admit that the wisdom of so much of the Order in Council as relates to the selection of Assessors in criminal cases has not been justified by the result of the experiments which have hitherto been made. It was supposed, that by drawing those functionaries from a small select body of each Colony, a closer resemblance to former usages might be obtained without any prejudice to the effective admini-tration of the law, and that the best possible security would be taken against a trust so momentous falling into the hands of any improper persons. The high station occupied in the Colonial society by the gentlemen competent to act as Assessors seemed to justify the hope that every influence of party spirit, or of any other improper feelings, would be effectually excluded from the judgment seat, and that in the discharge of their arduous duties the Judges would be assisted by the intelligence and information of those colonists most eminent for their general knowledge, education, and experience. But I am reluctantly compelled to avow my deliberate opinion, that when a disposition to co-operate cordially with His Majesty's Government in improving the administration of the criminal law was attributed to the members of those select bodies, a degree of confidence was placed in them which the result has not justified . . . I cannot on the other hand disclaim too distinctly the intention of imputing to any gentleman who has been called upon to serve as an Assessor a violation or disregard of the sacred obligation which he contracted; yet, on the other hand, the paramount claims of truth, and the duty which I owe to His Majesty and His Majesty's subjects in the Colonies, oblige me to state, without reserve, my convictions that the controversies which unhappily agitate the slave colonies have exercised over the small bodies competent to act as Assessors an influence of which they are probably unconscious, but which has not ceased powerfully to control their conduct, even in the discharge of that high trust. If these feelings had been excited by any slight or transitory cause, I might have permitted myself to hope that they would speedily have subsided, and have given place to more calm and dispassionate sentiments; but when I recollect how deep is their foundation and how strong is the hold which they have taken on the minds of many of the most conspicuous and eminent of the colonists, I cannot avoid the conclusion that they will long continue to render those affected by them unfit for the exclusive enjoyment of a power so momentous . . . In proceeding to the consideration of a remedy fit to be applied to the evil which has been brought to their notice, His Majesty's Government have bestowed their best attention on the various recommendations contained in your despatch, to which I have had occasion to refer. It has been suggested 'that the office and functions of the Assessors might be abolished altogether.' This is a proposal to which nothing but an extreme and paramount necessity could induce His Majesty's Government to accede . . .

The second suggestion is, 'that all trials for capital or transportable offences should be conducted before the judges and Assessors, and all other trials before judges alone.' . . . It presents the further difficulty that it would place the more weighty and important trusts in the hands of those whom it would pronounce incompetent to discharge the lighter and less difficult duty. There might at least be an apparent inconsistency in giving the power of life and death to a Tribunal which had been declared unfit to adjudicate on a question of fine or imprisonment.

' To transfer to the three judges alone the decision of all cases of alleged violation of the Slave Code '—which is the third proposal—would be to attach to the colonists in general a stigma, which would not be unreasonably resisted as an insult and repelled as an immediate injury. The effect would be to aggravate the difficulties with which the administration of the Slave Law is attended, by enhancing its unpopularity. . . .

Having thus adverted to those suggestions which have been deemed expedient, it remains that I should notice more particularly the recommendation to which His Majesty's Government have acceded. It is ' that the selecting of the Assessors, not from any small privileged body, but from the general mass of society.' The plan may be shortly explained by stating that it would render every free inhabitant of the Colonies competent and liable to serve as an Assessor if possessing qualifications corresponding to those of a common Juror in England. This change will leave the judicial system of the three Colonies precisely upon its present footing. . . .

This course of proceedings is powerfully recommended by the circumstances that it negatives, in the most decided manner, the supposition that His Majesty's Government cherish any distrust of the free colonists collectively on the subject of the administration of the Slave Law; on the contrary, by calling on them all to take their share in the discharge of that trust, the highest possible proof is given of confidence in their uprightness and intelligence. I am persuaded that the influence of prejudice and party spirit on this subject, will be found not to have spread through the great mass of society. . . . By calling the entire body of people to act as Assessors in the Supreme Tribunals it may be hoped that a deeper interest in the proceedings of those Courts will be created; that verdicts in which the concurrence of some of their peers is necessary will be received by the public at large with increased deference and respect; and that a preparation will be made for the introduction of Trial by Jury so soon as the distinctions between the different ranks of men shall have disappeared—which for the present would deprive that institution of its essential character and real advantages. This enlargement of the list from which Assessors are to be chosen will I trust be attended with the salutary effect of uniting together in the exercise of one of the most important of all civil rights, the different classes of the free colonists, and thus tend to obliterate the distinctions which the law has now happily abolished. . . .

In determining the qualifications of Assessors, the British Statute, 6 Geo. 4. cap. 50, seems to afford a safe rule of conduct. However different the value of money and of property of every description may be in England and the West Indies, it may without much risk of error be assumed, that the criterion which has been adopted in this country will not be found greatly to fail there. As however, amongst one class of free colonists it is to be feared that the progress of wealth may outrun their advance in knowledge to an extent not usual in Europe, it has appeared not unreasonable to render an inability to read and write a good cause of challenge. . . .

In framing any law in this country on a subject necessarily involving so much minute detail, a difficulty occurs which can only be successfully encountered by delegating to the local authorities the task of completing the general outline of the measure. . . . His Majesty's Council must therefore refer to the Judges of the Supreme Court, and to the Governor, the not less necessary office of prescribing the whole form of proceedings to be observed for compiling accurate lists of persons competent to act as Assessors; the periodical correction of such lists; the citation and empannelling of the Assessors; and the selection from among the persons summoned and attending of a sufficient number to serve on each successive trial. . . .

Before any Rules of Court of this nature are to take effect, your own confirmation of them should be obtained : His Majesty will also reserve to himself the ultimate right of confirming or disallowing them as may be found necessary. Thus it may be expected that the preparation of these important rules of the Court will be effected with all the advantages which the professional knowledge of the Judges and the impartial and deliberate judgment of the Governor, can jointly contribute. . . .

I will not disguise from you the reluctance with which I have advised the introduction of any change in a judicial system adopted so recently, and after so much deliberation. It is a measure to which His Majesty would not have had recourse, except under the pressure of an evident necessity, since there was much obvious advantage in giving the present system in all its parts a full and complete trial; but every other consideration has necessarily given way to the paramount duty of rescuing three Colonies to which the Order extends from the intolerable evils of a denial of justice to the inhabitants or of an administration of justice conducted under undue influence. The change, however, which has been made is the smallest possible innovation which would be attended with any promises of effectual redress of so great an evil. If its tendency will be on the one hand to rescue the law from contempt by securing the infliction of its penalties when justily incurred, it will not on the other hand tend in the slightest degree to abridge any popular franchise; on the contrary, it is to be regarded as an appeal to the great body of society to vindicate the authority of those Tribunals in which the peaceable and well-disposed have their best security. That appeal will, I am happy to believe, be answered in the

same conciliatory spirit with which it is made—an expectation
which His Majesty's Government may justly indulge in on an
occasion when they ask of the people at large nothing more than
to accept and to use aright, the power of defending their own
important social interests.

I have. etc.,

GODERICH."

XXIII

Petition of the Cocoa Planters of May 5th, 1832

" The Petition and Memorial of His Majesty's subjects adopted
and natural born, attached to the cultivation of cacao in the said
Island from time immemorial, respectfully sheweth :

Your Memorialists take leave respectfully to represent that
in order to conciliate and conform to the view of Government
and not to oppose themselves to a powerful party whose ultimate
designs subsequent to the abolition of the slave-trade in 1810
have been too evident to admit of doubt, they adopted that description of cultivation which would least expose them to loss by a
political innovation of the Colonial System established by the
nations and guaranteed to them by the protection of the Laws
which have always considered the property of the subject as
inviolable.

That previous to the year 1827 the crops of cacao gradually
increased in quantity and value, insomuch that a sum in specie
was annually introduced, amounting to from $350 to $400,000
by speculators for the purchase of cocoa, and this prosperous
and lucrative state of the cultivation arose from the industry of
5,720 free subjects and their families and 1,800 slaves, as is by
census established. Yet this once happy and independent population is in the present year 1832, reduced to the greatest poverty
and distress; their properties abandoned, or seized on writs of
execution, or their slaves hired out, the cultivation of cacao not
yielding them bread, and the interest on money being at from
30% to 40%.

In 1828 the state of the cacao cultivation according to Official
Returns was :

	Acres
Land planted in cacao	12,839
Trees on same	5,177,776
Free proprietors	5,720
Slaves	1,816

410

Returns of the cacao crops from 1821 to 1831 were:

lbs.

1821	...	1,214,193
1822	...	1,789,379
1823	...	2,444,703
1824	...	2,661,628
1825	...	2,760,608
1826	...	2,951,179
1827	...	3,695,144
1828	...	2,582,323
1829	...	2,750,603
1830	...	1,300,284
1831	...	1,417,047

By this return it appears that the greatest crop of cocoa since 1821 was that of 33,600 fanegas in 1827, and that the crop of 1830 was only 11,611 fanegas, making a deficit of 21,797 fanegas in the course of only three years, which evinces the deterioration of the culture. In 1830 cocoa was sold as low as 10/- currency ($1) per fanega in the country, and in town at from 15/- to 40/- ($1.50 to $4.00), and the expenses of cartage etc. being deducted, there remained to the planters upon the whole quantity exported of 11,611 fanegas, an average of 34/- ($3.40) per head per annum for their maintenance, whilst the annual expenses of a slave's maintenance is allowed to amount from $50 to $60.

To the free planters and their families who form numerically a fourth part of the free population of the Colony, there remained the resources of hiring out to the proprietors of sugar estates during the period of the sugar crop such slaves as might still chance to belong to them, to assist in taking off the crop; and to the free settlers, not possessing slaves, there in like manner remained the resources of hiring out themselves with the same purpose; from this channel the cocoa planters derived the means of procuring for their families a few of the most pressing necessaries; but these means are now altogether lost to them by the operation of the late Order in Council.

Your Memorialists further beg leave to represent that under those protections of all species of agriculture, the Laws of Spain (and the greater number of Your Memorialists were formerly subjects of His Catholic Majesty), and by their mild and equitable provisions, an individual might under the durable system which protected him in his wants and misfortunes, give himself up in all security during the space of ten years of his life to every species of privation, confident to establish a cultivation which would assure him the means of frugal independence for the rest of his life; and which enabled the cocoa planter to give to an industrious slave his manumission so soon as that slave should, independent of having performed his daily task, have planted one thousand cocoa trees on a spot assigned him for that purpose and delivered them over to his master in a yielding state. These one thousand trees were formerly worth from $400 to $500, the value pretty nearly of the slave himself. There exist few families in the Colony attached to this species of cultivation where instances may not be found of slaves having obtained their emancipation in this manner. These freed men have ever remained attached and grateful to their former masters.

Your Memorialists respectfully submit that the late Order in Council has completely destroyed all sentiment of confidence between master and slave and the respect and obedience that subsisted towards the master.

By the Articles of Capitulation (Clauses 8 and 9) signed on 17th February, 1797, between Governor Chacon and Sir Ralph Abercromby, their properties were guaranteed to capitulants, which was confirmed on the 19th of February of the same year by a joint Proclamation of the General and the Admiral, issued in His Majesty's name.

The 25th Article of the Cedula of His Catholic Majesty, dated 24th November, 1783, grants to the new settlers the faculty of proposing their own regulations for the government of slaves, to prevent marooning,* and prescribes the rules to be observed, which evinces that the capitulants were entitled to be consulted on an event which so nearly affected their security.

Your Memorialists cannot offer Your Excellency or to His Majesty's Ministers a better opinion upon inviolability of their rights as capitulants than that of Lord Mansfield in the case of "Campbell v Hall" pleaded in the Court of King's Bench, on the infraction of the Capitulation of Grenada; it is as follows: The Articles of Capitulation upon which a country is surrendered, and the Treaty of Peace by which it is ceded are sacred and inviolable according to their true intent and meaning. . . ."

XXIV

Currency

Coins of all nations were in constant use in the West Indies, as well as the local currency or " silver Anchor money " and the copper " Leeward Island Dogs " and a few local note issues.

At the time of Governor Hislop the principal current coins in Trinidad were the " douro fuerte ", the quarter dollar, the two bit piece and the " cinq sous clou " or " cinq sous croix ", a small irregular shaped coin impressed with a cross. These coins could be cut into quarters known as " cinq sous coupes " or " moco pa

* Escape of slaves.

Jim ". Halved ten cent coins, " tampes coupes " were also in circulation.

Currency varied in each island of the West Indies. Jamaica had old Spanish doubloons, pistols, gold dollars, Columbian doubloons, sovereigns, joes, macarinis, bits and tenpenny pieces. St. Lucia had sols, deniers, livres Louis d'ors, three man pieces, British pennies and Leeward Island Dogs. British Guiana used predominantly Dutch currency, guilders, stivers and pennings. Grenada had stamped Colonial monetas and moidres. Barbados used chiefly doubloons from the South American countries and British Colonial currency. Trinidad also made use of doubloons, dollars, reals, joes and bits.

During General Munro's Governorship, Trinidad suffered from a shortage of silver and by Proclamation in 1811, $25,000 of cut silver dollars were allowed to circulate. Mr. John O'Brien was appointed to do the cutting. Those buying coin were to receive a piece of silver " escalin clou ", value 1/- and the dollar " gourdes percés " at a value of 9/-.

Woodford found that the currency had become so debased that he was forced to call in all coin and make a fresh issue.

During shortages of small change the shopkeepers issued their own token " marks " to the value of a " demi tempe ". When these private tokens were replaced by coins of the realm, there were so many outstanding and so many forgeries that some merchants were made nearly bankrupt. One Francois Delcos estimated that 500% more " marks " stamped F.D. were returned to him than he had ever issued.

With so much foreign currency in circulation, values were fixed by the Home Government by Proclamation from time to time. The colonists did not agree with this system and fixed their own local rate of exchange at a higher rate than that proclaimed. On the average £100 sterling was the equivalent of £150 Colonial currency.

A great need was felt in the colonies for a banking system similar to that in England, where in country districts advances were made on future crops. In 1824 a petition was presented asking for a bank with a capital of £3,000,000 in £100 shares but no charter was granted until 1836, when the Colonial Bank was set up. Headquarters were in London and branches were opened in Trinidad, Jamaica, British Guiana and Barbados.

XXV

*Petition of Mandingo ex-slaves for return to their own country,
forwarded through Lt.-Governor Hill*

Trinidad No. 4.

12th January, 1838

To the Right Honourable Lord Baron Glenelg,
Her Majesty's Principal Secretary of State for the
Colonial Department, etc., etc.

The Memorial of the undersigned African Subjects of Her
Most Gracious Majesty the Queen of Great Britain and Ireland
humbly sheweth unto Your Lordship :

That Your Memorialists are natives of Africa and of the
Nation or Tribe called Mandingo; that during the existence of
the Slave Trade Your Memorialists were torn from their beloved
Country, their friends and relations, delivered into the hands
of Slave Merchants, who imported Your Memorialists into the
West Indies and sold them as Slaves.

That Your Memorialists, resolving to extricate themselves and
others of their Nation, from the cruel and degraded state to
which they had been reduced, formed themselves into a Society
in this Island; and as the earnings of their honest industry
accumulated, gradually redeemed themselves and their Countrymen from the House of Bondage; hence on the memorable first
day of August one thousand, eight hundred and thirty-four, a
day which will always live in the Annals of Nations, and which
will ever be remembered with feelings of the highest gratitude by
the black man—Your Memorialists can safely, and with truth,
assert, very few, if any of their tribe in the Island of Trinidad
remained in Slavery to partake of the beneficent and humane
achievement of the British Nation.—No!—Your Memorialists
had long before unfettered themselves, their tribe and their
families, by the fruits of their joint and industrious efforts.

That Your Memorialists have always behaved themselves as
quiet and peaceable members of this Community; that they are
proud of the name of British Subjects and feel grateful for the
protection and benevolence which they have experienced from
the Government.

That many generous and praiseworthy attempts have been
made by the enlightened of Europe to introduce and establish
civilization in Africa, but that such attempts have hitherto proved
vain or but very partially successful. That Your Memorialists

414

feel confident that could they but reach the shores of the land that gave them birth, their efforts, as heads of their tribe, would ensure success in progagating Civilization, the benefits of which they so deeply feel themselves, and would give them an opportunity of proclaiming to their Nation the liberality of the British Government.

That there are no means of direct communication between this Island and any of the British Settlements on the Coast of Africa, and if there were, the greater number of Your Memorialists have not the means to defray the necessary expenses attendant upon going there; besides which, Your Memorialists are greatly afraid, that if they were to venture upon the open sea, in any other than a British Armed vessel, they would be exposed to the imminent danger of being captured and again sold into the Iron Hands of bondage by the Nations that still carry on the Slave Trade.

Upon these grounds, and under these fears, and also upon the assurance of their Countryman Mohammed Houssa, otherwise called Philip Filday, who visited England last year and was then introduced into the presence of Her Most Gracious Sovereign the blessing of a long, happy and prosperous reign is and ever will be the prayer of Your Memorialists—

	Signature in Arabic characters
Leonas Bath, for self, wife and children	
Salhin, commonly called *Charles Alexander*	,, ,,
Mahammed Waatra, commonly called *Auguste Bernard* for himself	,, ,,
Mahommed Habin, commonly called *Mahommed Littledale*	,, ,,
Mahommed Sissri, commonly called *Felix Ditt*	,, ,,
Fonta Torre, otherwise called *Sampson Boissiere*	,, ,,
Abouberika Torre, commonly called *Joseph Sampson*	,, ,,
Brahima, commonly called *Adam Balthazar*	,, ,,
Hammadi Torrouke, commonly called *Louis Modeste*	,, ,,
Mahommed Balliah, commonly called *Christopher Picka*	,, ,,
Samba Jaiih, commonly called *Michael Sylvestre*	,, ,,
Malick Job, commonly called *Thomas Jones*	,, ,,

Port of Spain,
11th January, 1838.

Witness : Edward Schack.

Source: Public Record Office, State Papers, Colonial C.O.
295/12.
T.T.H.S. Pub. [811].

This petition was not granted.

XXVI

*Extract from letter from Governor MacLeod to the
Secretary of State, 29th May, 1840*

" My Lord,
It is my duty to request Your Lordship's attention to the
condition of European immigrants who have arrived in this
Island in considerable numbers during the last six months. . . .

I regret extremely to acquaint Your Lordship that nearly the
worst apprehensions that could have been entertained for these
people have been realized.

I have ascertained that in the short space of four months there
has been a mortality of upwards of 10%—very many more cases
have occurred which we have not means at hand of ascertaining.
. . . lead me to fear still greater mortality. But it is not loss of life
alone which has made this immigration peculiarly distressing.

The principal demand for their labour lies in the field. The
employment is new to them, and their constitutions are unsuited
to exposure to a tropical sun—sickness ensues—the estates of this
Island are yet without those conveniences and comforts which a
European looks for when in bad health. . . . many of these people,
the Germans and Prussians, being unable to speak the language
of the country, are, when overtaken with illness, in a very forlorn
and helpless condition.

Instances have occurred, but I am glad to say they have been
rare, in which the master has not only declined to maintain his
servant when overtaken with sickness and unable to work, but
has cast him loose on society in a state of suffering and perfect
helplessness. On the other hand, as would be expected, these
immigrants are not always of good description. . . . This latter
portion of these people has afforded some instances of vagrancy,
and many people have become a serious burden to the community in town, either in the shape of beggars or as suffering
from disease.

. . . Your Lordship may judge how shocked I was by the
arrival here on the 15th inst, of another ship, the *Louise*

from Havre, having on board 190 German and French people . . .

. . . I directed that none of them should be allowed to establish themselves here until they should first find surety, that for twelve months to come, they should not become destitute, or become chargeable to the Public. . . .

Many applications have been addressed to me by individuals desirous of securing their services expressive of their readiness to enter such security and accordingly in every case the parties who have hired them have given the required bond. . . .

But to put a stop to this traffic in human life, I request Your Lordship's assistance. In the case of the *Louise*, I have protested against the exaction of the passage of each immigrant of more than twelve dollars. . . . This may go some way towards checking further speculation of the kind. . . .

. . . I entreat Your Lordship will be good enough to take the necessary measures for calling on the French Government not to permit any vessels to clear from their ports with emigrants to Trinidad at least in ignorance of the disadvantages and other evils with which they will have to contend here. . . .

I would respectfully suggest that a like communication be made to H.M. Minister to the Germanic Confederation. . . ."

XXVII

Summary of Ordinances 18 and 19 of 1844

No. 18

The purpose of the Ordinance was to provide funds to pay the cost of transport of immigrants to Trinidad from India and the repatriation of any who qualified for free return passages, and it further provided :

1. To appoint Agents in London to raise a loan limited to £250,000 by issue not exceeding £50,000 in any one year, of negotiable bonds of at least £200 unit value, bearing interest not in excess of 5%.
2. The Trinidad Government to pay yearly into a Sinking Fund a sum equal to one twentieth of the amount of bonds issued to finance the redemption of the loan.
3. The Agents to attend to the service of the loan; they were also to pay the charges it was primarily designed to meet, as from time to time requested by the Colonial Treasurer, by warrant of the Governor and upon the requisition of the Secretary of State.
4. All the expenses of the loan, whether principal or interest,

to be a charge on the 3½% *ad valorem* export duty of the Colony, which shall not be reduced till the loan has been liquidated.

5. The Agents to invest any balance of the loan not immediately needed, in British Public Stocks or Exchange Bills.

6. Should the guarantee, which Parliament had been asked to provide, be implemented in the form of a supplementary loan or other form of payment to the Colonial Treasury, the same plus 5% interest to be charged to the said export duty or the general revenues of the Colony.

No. 19

The preamble to this Ordinance recites an Ordinance of February, 1843, to raise funds for the cost of bringing immigrants from the coast of Africa. It sets out to make these funds available in regard to " such ports of Asia as may be appointed by Her Majesty."

The Ordinance then specifies more particularly the manner in which the aforesaid funds as well as those raised under Ordinance No. 18 are to be employed.

It defines the conditions under which immigrants who wish to return after residence during five years in the Colony, will be repatriated and the extent to which those who wish to return before that time will be assisted. It is also enacted that every immigrant landing in Trinidad from a vessel hired or licensed by Her Majesty under this Ordinance shall receive from the Agent-General of Immigration a certificate of right to a free passage back to the port of embarkation.

Wages agreed by the Committee of the Immigration and Agricultural Society of Trinidad.

Each				*Per month*
Sirdar	...	...	...	$3.35
Headman	...	...	...	2.90
Male labourer	...	...	...	2.40
Female labourer	...	...	...	1.45
Boy under 12	...	...	...	1.45

Food

Rice	...	...	45 lbs. per month
Peas	...	...	9 lbs. „ „
Ghee or oil	...	...	½ gallon „ „
Salt	...	...	1½ lbs. „ „
Fish	...	...	4½ lbs. „ „
Turmeric or Tamarinds	...	...	4½ lbs. „ „
Onions or chillies	...	...	1½ lbs. „ „

418

Clothing

2	blankets per annum	
2	dhotis	„
1	jacket	„
1	cap	„
1	wooden bowl	„

Medicine and medical attention, house and garden free.

XXVIII

*Extract from a letter from William Burnley, 6 Bryanston Square,
London, to the Secretary of State. 19.6.1840*

In the Ordinance for the encouragement of immigration in
the Colony of Trinidad, approved by Her Majesty in Council on
September 30th, 1839, it is declared that "Whereas it is not
expedient that encouragement be given to any proceedings
whereby the natural proportion between the sexes shall be disturbed in the Colony aforesaid or elsewhere, it is hereby ordered
that the Governor or Lt.-Governor shall not permit the provisions of the above recited Ordinance to be carried into effect
unless it shall ensure an equality in numbers between the male
and female immigrants annually introduced under its provisions.
And with the view of complying with this injunction, the Acting
Governor, Colonel Mein, was pleased to publish a regulation to
the following effect : " That no passage money should be paid for
such male immigrants as might exceed in each vessel the proportion of five males to four females."

As regards immigrants from the U.S., however, the above
regulation is wholly unnecessary and will " throw serious impediments in the way of their emigration." They are shrewd, sensible
people and competent to manage their own affairs, having
already sent delegates to Guiana and Trinidad to report on the
state of the Colonies. Those deciding to emigrate generally embark alone and are prepared to send for their families when
settled. I am so well satisfied with their domestic habits that I
am convinced they will not settle without their families. I do
not think annual emigration from U.S. will exceed 2,000 persons
—which " can never exercise any very mischievous influence
upon our standard population."

The difficulty which the aforesaid regulation creates arises
from its requiring the proportion between the sexes to be observed
in respect of every separate vessel sailing with passengers . . . In
this feeling of hesitation the women naturally participate more
largely than the men, and after every care and precaution, and

419

even extra expense incurred, the attempt to ensure the proportion required between the sexes may ultimately fail, to the entire loss of the whole profits of the voyage. The owners have therefore refused to embark on such a hazardous speculation, without a guarantee for a fixed sum, and a large number of intending emigrants have consequently been prevented from proceeding to the Colony.

I beg therefore to solicit that this regulation as applicable to each separate vessel may be rescinded; and that His Excellency the Lt.-Governor may be simply instructed to watch the general progress of the immigration and to correct by some other process any irregulatities which may threaten to disturb the proper proportion between the sexes; which may probably be more easily adjusted from time to time by raising the passage money paid on account of the females than by the present restrictive clause.

In consequence of the success which has attended the emigration of the first adventurers . . . I have no doubt that a superior class of persons, possessed of education and pecuniary means will now be induced to remove . . . We more especially require in Trinidad this superior class to instruct us in the cultivation of tobacco, which I am now satisfied can with an increased population be most successfully introduced . . .

Men of African descent are not easily to be found amongst us, competent to fill stations to which they now aspire, and their rejection is attributed by themselves to unfair partiality rather than to their own deficiency; whilst their appointment, when not perfectly qualified, creates a feeling of disgust amongst the whites, prejudicial to the success of the object now desired to be accomplished. An immigration of educated Americans would be the means of removing these difficuties, and giving satisfaction to all parties.

I had much communication with men of this description when last in the United States. I assured them that they would be treated and considered in Trinidad as British subjects; that the alien laws were in that colony in abeyance, and that they would be competent equally with naturalized subjects to hold property and fill public situations.

I suggest that the Lt.-Governor be instructed to furnish passports for those of African descent who require them, describing them as residents in the Colony and entitled to British protection, which would meet the requirements necessary for the present population for some time to come. I think it would be advantageous both for the purpose of Government policy of this experiment, if they made the measure general in the Colony, applicable to all leaving the Island and making a passport compulsory.

The principal complaints of the American immigrants arise from the alteration in the nature, and the extreme dearness of their food. At present the duties upon salted provisions from the United States are so high as to operate as a prohibition. It would be very advantageous, and greatly promote the comfort of immigrants in our West Indian Colonies, if these duties were reduced.

At present they serve no purpose as an object of revenue, and no British interest would be injuriously affected by an alteration; whilst the great object of supplying our W.I. Colonies with a sufficient population, and raising tropical produce by free labour would be most materially promoted.

XXIX

Letter from the Reverend J. H. Hamilton, Minister at Tacarigua, to the Governor, describing a tour of the eastern settlements

Tacarigua,
19th March, 1841.
Sir,

I have the honour to inform Your Excellency that I have visited the Settlements of Turure and Manzanilla and beg leave to submit for your information the following report of my visit. I must first direct Your Excellency's attention to the state of the road, which I regret to say is almost impassable; it is overgrown (from Turure to Mt. Calabash) with brushwood, and is literally a continuation of mud thro' which even a powerful horse with difficulty makes his way. From this track (from the extreme depth of the mud), it is frequently requisite to diverge, and to pass for some miles thro' forest; this is a work of difficulty as the trace is scarcely perceptible and is impeded with prostrate trees, of an enormous size. The bridges are in many places equally bad, being constructed of large branches of trees, unwrought and unplaned. The surface is consequently very uneven, and in wet weather slippery and dangerous, especially when unprotected by hand rails.

I was received by the people of the different settlements with evident marks of gratification.

Their religious and social state presents a melancholy picture. From long neglect in so isolated situation, and an entire absence of Clerical instruction, even the outward form of Christianity has almost disappeared among them! Many of them are nominally Mohammedans who are under the influence and guidance of five (so called) Mandingo Priests by whom they are instructed in portions of the Koran; one only of this number can write, to whom they seem to look up to with great reverence. (I enclose a specimen of his writing with the translation, as dictated by him-

421

self for Your Excellency's inspection.) On Sunday, the 14th inst., I had the settlers assemble for Divine Service at the Mico School House (which is a Government building). To the prayers and a plain discourse on their moral and religious duties they paid (including the Priests) the most marked and gratifying attention. I afterwards married 18 couples. There were more applicants for the Sacred Rites, but having exhausted my Licences I was obliged to stop, with a promise of applying to Your Excellency for more and visiting them again. I also baptized 9 children and 3 adults.

I am requested by the settlers to express to Your Excellency their earnest wish to have a clergyman of the Church of England resident amongst them, and I beg to record my opinion that if this desirable measure could be accomplished, they would return to the Christian fold. They also want a regular Physician who (they suggest) might also act as a Superintendent. The repair of the road forms their last demand, so as to enable them to transport their provisions to a market for at present it is almost impossible to traverse it with a heavy burden. Unless these requisitions can be complied with, they have requested me to submit to Your Excellency the expediency of allowing them to remove to Tacarigua and Arouca, stating that they were placed at Manzanilla by the late Sir Ralph Woodford, in order to separate a free black population from Negro Slaves. I am aware that this proposition requires very mature reflection but they certainly are at present exiled in every sense of the word, and are of little use either to themselves or to the state. If such a step should be hereafter taken it would tend greatly to the advancement of the Agricultural prosperity of the Colony, their own temporal welfare and above all to be the means of effecting their moral and religious regeneration. The Mico School at Manzanilla, under the care of Mr. Semper, I lament to say is fast declining. The daily attendance has diminished from 50 children to about 12; a Schism unfortunately existed between the master and some of the most influential people; I addressed on this unhappy difference and left them, I am happy to say, on better terms with Mr. Semper, and many have promised to send back their children to school. The Mico School at Turure, under Mr. Barker's care, is in a satisfactory state. I saw 27 children who are making good progress. I enclose a tabular statement, obtained from the Stipendiary Magistrate of the export of provisions for six months and the mortality among them for nine months. The latter I have reason to think incorrect, as some die, out of the settlements.

In conclusion, I trust my visit to them has been productive of some good, and I only lament that the distance and state of the road preclude my seeing them as often as I could wish.

XXX

" An Ordinance enacted by the Governor of the Island of Trinidad by and with the advice and consent of the Council thereof, for regulating the powers and Constitution and settling the mode of election of the members of the Corporate Body called The Illustrious Cabildo of the town of Port of Spain and changing the name thereof to that of The Town Council of Port of Spain, 1840."

Summary

1. Whereas at the time of the conquest of this Island by British Arms, there was existing, and at the present time still exists, a certain Corporation or Municipal Body known on the Illustrious Cabildo of the Town of Port of Spain, which has from time to time exercised and still exercises certain powers and is possessed of considerable properties, real and personal : And whereas it is expedient that the said Corporation should be continued, but that its name and that of its Officers should be changed, its constitution and electoral methods should be changed, its powers should be ascertained and declared, that after the promulgation of this Ordinance, the said Corporation shall be continued under the title of The Town Council of Port of Spain as a corporate body with perpetual succession, and shall be entitled to use a common seal, and may sue and may be sued, plead and be impleaded under its title aforesaid.

2. The Town Council shall be composed of the Governor, who shall be President thereof and twelve other persons to be styled Town Councillors, of whom four shall retire annually and four others be elected.

3. The twelve existing members of the Cabildo shall assume the title of Town Councillors and continue in office until the 31st December, 1840, after when the names of four who shall retire shall be determined by such means and at such times as the President shall appoint and on the 31st December, 1841, four more Councillors shall so retire and on the 31st December, 1842, the remaining four of the original Councillors shall retire and each of these three groups of four Councillors, when they retire, shall be replaced by a corresponding number of other Councillors, elected by the Burgesses.

4. Every male person over the age of 21 residing within three miles of Port of Spain and having occupied a house therein for the previous twelve months, of a rateable value of two hundred dollars or for which he has paid a rent of two hundred dollars

423

per annum excepting such persons as do not speak and understand the English Language, shall be a Burgess and qualified to vote at the election of Councillors.

5. A list of such Burgesses shall be made before the 1st October, each year.

6. Between the 20th and 30th November each year a Court is to be held by some Barrister of six years' standing in practice in the Colony, to revise the Burgess List and hear applications in relation to it.

7. The aforesaid Court to have authority to examine all persons on oath touching matters on which it deals.

8. The Burgess List shall be signed by the Revising Barrister and deposited with the Town Clerk.

9. Only Burgesses possessed of real or personal property or both to the value of five hundred pounds shall be eligible for election as Town Councillor and no Town Councillor shall be a member of the Council of Government or Officer of Her Majesty's sea or land forces on actual service or shall hold any office of emolument under the Government, or be a Clergyman of the Established Religion, Priest of the Roman Catholic Religion or Teacher of any religious sect, nor shall hold any place of profit under the Council nor have, directly or indirectly, any interest in any contract or employment by or on behalf of the Council under penalty of one hundred pounds and of permanent disqualification for service as Town Councillor.

10. That having once served as a Town Councillor a Burgess shall not be eligible for re-election until at least one year has elapsed since his last terms of service excepting such cases as where temporary vacancies have been filled.

11. On the 20th December, or Monday next following, between the hours of 9 a.m. and 3 p.m. each year, the election by the Burgesses of successors to the four retiring Town Councillors shall be held in the presence of the Chairman of the Town Council, assisted by a practising Advocate, as Assessor. Each Burgess may vote for as many candidates as there are vacancies as well as for two persons to act as Auditors for the ensuing year; then the four candidates who have the greatest number of votes shall replace the four Councillors retiring by vote and, if there are one or more occasional vacancies to be filled, then the candidate having the next greatest number of votes shall fill the vacancy left by him whose unexpired term was the longest and so on till all these occasional vacancies are filled.

12. The Chairman and the Assessor shall at once count the votes and declare the result of the election and the voting papers shall be held by the Town Clerk for inspection of the Burgesses for six months.

13. All Town Councillors shall serve the term for which they

have been elected except they shall cease to comply with the qualifications and in such cases and in the event of death another person shall be appointed ad interim by the President and Town Council until the next election when the person elected to fill the vacancy shall serve the same term as would the Councillor whose place he has taken.

14. All persons elected to the Council shall, within one week, take oath of Allegiance, the penalty for failing to do so without valid reason being four hundred dollars.

15. The Town Council shall, as early as possible each year, elect one of their number to be Chairman of the Council, who shall preside at all meetings of the Council except when the Governor as President is present and shall preside.

16. The Town Council shall have authority to appoint a Town Clerk and Treasurer of the Council at salaries to be fixed by the Council and these officers shall keep all the books and accounts of the Council and shall receive and pay all monies and perform all duties now performed by the Secretary and Treasurer of the Illustrious Cabildo except such duties as are performed by that officer as Registrar of Deeds and the Council shall also have authority to appoint some barrister of six years' standing in the Courts of the Colony to be their standing Counsel. The Town Clerk and Treasurer shall be bound to give security to the satisfaction of the Governor. Nothing shall prevent the same person being appointed Town Clerk and Treasurer and also standing Counsel.

17. The Town Council shall establish Rules for the regulation of its proceedings which shall be valid if approved by the Governor : Provided that in all such Rules it is provided that all questions shall be decided by a majority of votes of members present, not being less than six and that no acts of Council shall come into force until approved by the Governor as President.

18. The Town Council shall have authority to make Bye-laws for the Government of the Town of Port of Spain.

(Here follows a lengthy list of what these Bye-laws are intended to regulate, e.g. streets, transport, markets, etc.)

19. All real and personal property, profits and advantages of every description formerly belonging to the Cabildo shall be transferred and vested in the Town Council, and shall likewise assume all debts and liabilities of the Cabildo, and shall become responsible for the maintenance of schools, markets and all other institutions and services formerly maintained by the Cabildo.

20. This clause enumerates in detail the financial and executive responsibilities of the Town Clerk and Treasurer.

21. The Town Council shall not have the power to sell or otherwise alienate any property or emoluments belonging to it,

or lease or demise the same for any longer period than five years without the consent of the Governor and the Council of the Government.

22. After the Promulgation of this Ordinance the titles and Offices of Corregidor, Alcaldes in Ordinary, Alcaldes de Barrios, Alcaldes de Marina, Perpetual Regidors, Regidors and Syndic Procurador of the Illustrious Board of Cabildo shall cease and determine.

23. Nothing in this Ordinance shall abolish or in any way change the duties of the Secretary and Registrar of the Board of Cabildo under order of the Prince Regent in Council dated the 6th day of April, 1818, or in the taking of acknowledgements of deeds or in registration and care and custody of debts, mortgages, wills, manuscripts public and private or other duties relating thereto but that all such duties shall continue to be performed by the Registrar of Deeds who, for the purpose of such duties shall retain the title of Secretary and Registrar of the Cabildo but for other purposes the said office and title of Secretary of the Board of Cabildo shall cease.

24. The limits of the Town of Port of Spain shall be as follows :

North: The line of the north side of Barrack Street.

South: The sea.

East: The Dry River.

West: The west side of Richmond Street extended to the eastern boundary of the Tranquillity Estate and the Tragarete Road and including Corbeau Town.

25. The limits of the " Town of Port of Spain and Suburbs " shall be as follows : On the north—a line drawn from east to west from the bed of the St. Ann's River on the north side of the Circular Road until it meets the turn to Maraval : On the south —the sea; On the east—a straight line drawn from the spring at Madame Monerau's to the end of the Causeway over the River St. Ann's near Orange Grove Barracks and from thence over the bed of the River St. Ann's northwards until it meets the eastern point of the northern boundary above described; and on the west—a line drawn from the turn to Maraval and running south upon the west side of the Tragarete cross road and thence over the land of Woodbrook Estate to the sea.

26. This Ordinance shall have effect from the date of Promulgation.

Passed in Council this first day of June in the year of Our Lord one thousand eight hundred and forty.

Thomas F. Johnston,
Clerk of Council.

XXXI

Trinidad (89)
17th December, 1844.

AN ORDINANCE

No. 16, 1844.

For the better regulation of the duties of the Clergy of the United Church of England and Ireland in this Colony and for ensuring the more effectual performance of the same.

WHEREAS Her Most Gracious Majesty Queen Victoria was pleased to grant Letters Patent under the Great Seal bearing date at Westminster the twenty-first day of August in the sixth year of Her Majesty's Reign, which Letters are to the tenor and effect following, that is to say :

Victoria by the grace of God of the United Kingdom of Great Britain and Ireland, Queen Defender of the Faith to all whom these presents shall come greeting.

Summary

The preamble comprises references to the following Acts, which are herinafter revoked with the exception of those of William IV, 4th March, 1831, and Victoria, 1841 :

George IV, 24th July, 1824.   Constituting Barbados, Grenada, St. Vincent, Dominica, Antigua, Montserrat, St. Christopher, Nevis, the Virgin Islands, Trinidad, Tobago and St. Lucia a Bishop's See entitled " The Bishopric of Barbados and the Leeward Islands " and appointing William Hart Coleridge Bishop for life.

George IV, 2nd April, 1825.   Creating two Archdeaconries, respectively of Barbados and Antigua, the former to embrace Barbados, Grenada, St. Vincent, Trinidad, Tobago and St. Lucia, and the latter to embrace Antigua, Montserrat, Dominica, St. Christopher, Nevis and the Virgin Islands.

George IV, 11th May, 1826.	Proclaiming Demerara, Essequibo and Berbice to be parts of the See of Barbados and the Leeward Islands.
William IV, 4th March, 1831.	Constituting the above mentioned settlements on the Coast of S. America one Colony to be known as British Guiana.
1831.	Creating an Archdeaconry of British Guiana subordinate to the See of Barbados and the Leeward Islands.
Victoria, 24th September, Victoria, 1841.	Legalizing an increase of the number of Bishoprics and Archdeaconries within the territorial limits of the existing Sees of Jamaica and Barbados and the Leeward Islands.

In the preamble, reference is next made to the resignation of Bishop Coleridge on 6th April, 1842, leaving the See of Barbados and the Leeward Islands vacant.

The purpose of the Ordinance is then declared to be to create a new See to be known as the Bishopric of Barbados, with two subordinate Archdeaconries, namely of Barbados and of Trinidad. The new See shall include the City of Bridgetown and the Island of Barbados and the Islands of Trinidad, Grenada, St. Vincent, Tobago and St. Lucia. The Archdeaconries shall include respectively, Barbados, St. Vincent, St. Lucia and Trinidad, Grenada and Tobago.

The parochial church of St. Michael in Bridgetown, Barbados, is ordained a Cathedral Church and Bishop's See and the Town of Bridgetown is proclaimed a City.

The Hon. Thomas Parry, D.D., formerly Archdeacon of Barbados, is nominated Bishop of Barbados for life, subject and subordinate to the Archepiscopal See of Canterbury and " the most Reverend Father in God William by Divine Providence Archbishop ", an oath of due obedience to whom he and his successors shall, at their consecration, take.

The Bishop and his successors shall perform the functions peculiar to their office, within their Diocese, according to the Ecclesiastical Laws in force in England.

The " Bishop of Barbados " shall be a body corporate and may own property, may use a corporate seal, may plead and be impleaded in all manner of Courts and shall have perpetual succession. The Bishop and his successors shall for ever hereafter be called and known by the title of " Lord Bishop of Barbados ".

Of the sum of money payable out of the Consolidated Fund as the salaries of Bishops and Archdeacons, the sum of £2,500 per annum is assigned for the maintenance of Thomas Parry and his successors and the sum of £500 per annum for the Archdeacon of Barbados and the sum of £250 per annum for the Archdeacon of Trinidad. The sum of £2,000 per annum is assigned to the Bishop to apportion among the Ministers, Catechists and School Masters of his Diocese, subject to the approval of the Commissioners of the Treasury or the Principal Secretary of State.

Witness Ourself at Westminster the twenty-first day of August in the sixth year of Our Reign.

By the Queen Herself.

. . . .

The sense of 39 amplifying clauses enacted by Lt. Governor in Council follows :

Summary

1. The Ecclesiastical Laws of England to be in force in the Colony and the Judges of the Supreme Courts to assist in carrying processes into execution.
2. As regards the Established Church of England, the Colony shall be divided into the following Sixteen Parishes, namely :

Holy Trinity, town of Port of Spain, and Suburbs, with the Quarters of La Ventille, Tragarete, St. Ann's and Maraval.

St. Paul, town of San Fernando and the Quarter of North Naparima.

St. Michael, the Quarter of Chaguaramas, Carenage, Diego Martin, and Mucurapo, with the Islands of the Bocas.

St. Mary, the Quarters of Tacarigua and Arouca.

St. Jude, the Quarters of Arima and Guanapo, with the settlements of Cuare, Touroura and La Seiva; and such parts of the Quarter of Caroni as lie to the eastward of the junction of the Caroni and Tacarigua Rivers.

St. John, the Quarters of Cimaronero, Acarigua, Santa Cruz and St. Joseph and such parts of the Quarter of Caroni as lie westward of the junction of the Caroni and Tacarigua Rivers.

St. Thomas, the Quarter of Chaguanas.

St. Andrew, the Quarters of Carapichaima, Barancon, Cascajal and Couva.

St. Philip, the Quarter of Savonetta.

St. Peter, the Quarter of Pointe-a-Pièrre.

St. Luke, the Quarter of South Naparima.

St. Stephen, the Quarter of Savanna Grande.

St. Matthew, the Quarters of Oropouche, Le Brea and Guapo.

Christ Church, the Quarters of Cedros, Icacos, Erin and Irois.

St. Mark, the Quarters of Moruga and Guayaguayare.

St. Batholomew, the Quarters of Mayaro, Nariva, Toco and the settlement of Manzanilla.

3. The five several Parishes of the Holy Trinity, St. Paul, St. Mary, St. Stephen and St. Luke shall be constituted into five several Rectories, and the Parishes of St. Andrew and St. Philip shall be constituted into one Rectory, to be called the Rectory of the United Parishes of St. Andrew and St. Philip.

4. If the need arise, in a Parish which is not attached to a Rectory, the Government may allow an Island Curate, who shall be licensed to officiate there under the direction of a neighbouring Rector.

5. The patronage of every Rectory and Island Curacy shall be vested in Her Majesty.

6. For each Rectory, it shall be lawful for the Governor in Council to allow a Curate as Assistant to the Rector; such Curate to be licensed by the Bishop of the Diocese on the nomination of the Rector and approved by the Governor.

7. There shall be allowed to the Archdeacon and the Rectors, Island Curates and Assistant Curates appointed under this Ordinance, from the Colonial Treasury, the following stipends payable quarterly :

To the Archdeacon, £500 per annum.
To the Rector of the Parish of Holy Trinity, £600 per annum. And to every other Rector, £350 per annum.
To the Island Curate, who shall be appointed to act for the Parish of St. Michael, £300 per annum.
To every other Island Curate, £150 per annum.
To every Assistant Curate, £100 per annum.

8. The Governor in Council may, on the decease of any Archdeacon, Rector, or Island Curate, alter the annual stipend attached to any such Archdeaconry, Rectory or Island Curate.

9. For each Church or Chapel, duly consecrated or licensed, there shall be allowed a Clerk and Sexton who shall be paid from the Colonial Treasury, an annual salary of £20 16s. 8d. payable quarterly.

10. Where Churches shall be built, a convenient house shall be built at the common charge; and the Rector, except the Rector of the Parish of the Holy Trinity, shall keep the Rectory house in good repair, for which purpose an annual sum of £20 shall be allowed him; and the Archdeacon shall once in each year inspect each Rectory house in the Island, and shall certify to the Government the state of repair of the same.

11. To each Rectory house, except that of the Parish of Holy Trinity, shall be given 3 acres of land.

12. The present Rectory house of the Parish of Holy Trinity shall be kept in repair at the expense of the Colonial Government.

13. Every Rector and Island Curate shall reside in his parish, unless otherwise permitted by the Bishop.

14. It shall not be lawful for any Rector or Curate to act as attorney in the management of any estate or plantation, or as receiver of any Court in this Island or any Estate on any pretence whatever.

15. It shall not be lawful for the Bishop to permit any Incumbent to absent himself from his duties without an approved Locum Tenens; and the Bishop shall not permit any Incumbent to absent himself for more than one year together; or the Governor may declare the Rectory or Curacy to be vacant.

16. Any Incumbent irregularly absent from his Parish for more than three months in any year may forfeit a proportionate amount of his salary.

17. Empowers the Bishop to replace an Incumbent incapable of officiating and defines procedure.

18. Empowers the Governor to suspend salary or proceed to deprivation of an Incumbent whose competence or conduct may be proved unsatisfactory to his Vestry.

19. Registers of baptisms, marriages and burials shall be made and kept by the Rector or officiating Minister of every Parish, in well bound books, to be provided at the expense of the vestries of the respective Churches and Chapels, in which every officiating Minister shall record in a legible hand the several particulars and sign the same; and in no case, unless prevented by unavoidable impediment later than within three days after any such ceremony shall have taken place.

20. The Registry Books in the several Parishes shall belong to every such Parish and shall remain in the custody of the Incumbent of such Parish, and the said books shall not be removed from his custody.

21. A certified copy from the Registry Books shall be admitted in all Courts as legal evidence.

22 to 31. Deal with the election, duties and proceedings of the Vestry to be established in every Church and Chapel.

32. The two wardens, appointed respectively by the Incumbent and the Vestry, shall be treasurers and receive the pew rents for which they shall account to the Vestry, and shall have the same power as any church warden has by the Law of England.

33. The Church Wardens shall be allowed to retain to their own use a commission, at the rate of six per cent, on the amount of monies actually received by such Church Wardens respectively.

34. Of every church in any Parish under this Ordinance, one-fifth part of the seats or sittings shall be free seats for the use of the poor; and the remaining seats may be let out. Provided always that seats free of rent be set apart in the Church of the

Holy Trinity, for the Governor and his family, and the Archdeacon and his family, and in each Church or Chapel for the Incumbent and his family and for strangers.

35. The Vestry shall have authority to settle and alter the rates at which the rented seats shall be let.

36. The amount of rents received in respect of the sittings shall be divided into two equal portions, one portion to be applied to defray church expenses, and the other portion shall form a building fund, to be applied to the keeping the body of the Church in repair.

37. All sums due for pew rent may be recovered before any competent Court, by an action in the name of the Church Wardens.

38. The several fees mentioned in the schedule to this Ordinance shall be paid to the Rector, Curate or officiating Minister and Clerk, for the several services performed in the Church or Chapel; and none others shall be demandable by them.

39. Authorizes the Incumbent to appoint clerks and sextons.

Passed in Council this second day of December in the year of Our Lord, 1844.

JAMES PORTER,
Acting Clerk of Council.

Bishops of Barbados and the Leeward Islands

William Hart *Coleridge*	1824	to 1842
Parry	1842	to 1872

Bishops of Trinidad

Richard *Rawle*	1872	to 1888
James Thomas *Hayes*	1889	to 1904

XXXII

The Roman Catholic Church, Trinidad

In the early days the whole of the West Indies had been included in the Roman Catholic See of Santo Domingo, but later when some of the islands became British Possessions, so far as the Roman Catholic Church was concerned they came under the spiritual jurisdiction of the Roman Catholic Bishop of London, whose Vicar-General up to 1815 was the Abbé Planquais. Trinidad, however, was still regarded as being under the jurisdiction of the Bishop of Guiana. In 1820 the Rt. Rev. James Buckley was created Bishop of Olympus and 1st Vicar Apostolic with jurisdiction over Trinidad and the Lesser Antilles. On his death he was succeeded as follows :

1828   Daniel MacDonnell, 2nd Vicar Apostolic. Assumed duty June 21st, 1829.

1844	R. Patrick Smith, 3rd Vicar Apostolic.
1850	R. Patrick Smith, 1st Archbishop of Port of Spain.
1855	Vincent Spaccapietra, 2nd Archbishop of Port of
1860	Ferdinand English, 3rd Archbishop of Port of Spain.
1863	Louis Joachim Gonin, 4th Archbishop of Port of
1887	Patrick V. Flood, 5th Archbishop of Port of Spain.

Note : During the period 1828 to 1887 three Apostolic Administrators held temporary office at Port of Spain, viz. from 1852 to 1855 Michael Monaghan, Bishop of Roseau, Dominica; 1859–1860 James Etheridge and 1862–1863 François Cuenat.

Roman Catholic Establishment, Trinidad, 1899

Archbishop.
Vicar-General.
Parish Priests 42. Assistant Curates 5.
Jurisdiction of the Archbishop extended over St. Lucia, St. Vincent, Grenada, Trinidad and Tobago.
1 Cathedral.
67 Churches.
Archbishop's Residence.
Cathedral Presbytery, also one attached to each church.
Schools 59, with 7,686 children enrolled.
Formerly the Roman Catholic Clergy were paid salaries directly from the Treasury and were entitled to pension. This was changed and a grant made from the Treasury to the Archbishop in aid of the Roman Catholic Church.

XXXIII

Commanders in and Governors of Tobago

1627		Captain Joachim Gijsz visited the island
1628–29		Captain Jacob Maersz (or Maertz)
1632–34		Cornelis de Moor
1639–40		Robert Marsham (Massham or Massam)
1642–43		Captain Edward Marshall
1643–50		Captain Cornelius Caroon (or Coroon)
1654		Adrien Lampsins (or Lampsius)
1655–58	Governor	Hubert de Beveren

1667–72		Peter Constant appointed Governor by the Dutch.
1676–77	Governor	Peter Constant
1681	”	Colonel Monck
1684	*Tobago declared neutral by Treaty of Aix-le-Chapelle*	

English Governors and Lt.-Governors

1764–66	Lt.-Governor	Alexander Brown (or Browne)
1767–69	”	Roderick Gwynne
1771–77	”	Major William Young
1781	”	George Ferguson

French Governors

1781		Philbert de Blanchelande
1782		René Marie, Vicomte d'Arrot
1784–92		Arthur Count Dillon
1792		Philipe M. de Maginot
1793		Laroque de Monteil

English Governors

1794–95	Governor	George Poyntz Ricketts (Tobago formed a separate Government).
1795–96	”	William Lindsay
1797–99	”	Stephen de Lancey
1800	”	Richard Master
1802	Lt.-Governor	Brig.-General Hugh Lyle Carmichael

French Governors

| 1802 | Governor | F. Sabuguet |
| 1803 | ” | General Caesar Berthier |

English Lt.-Governors and Governors

1803 June	Lt.-Governor	Brig.-General Thomas Picton
1803 July	”	William Johnson
1803 Aug.	”	Donald MacDonald
1804 June	”	James Montgomerie
1804 July	Governor	J. Halkett
1807–15	”	Sir William Young, Bart.

| 1816–27 | Governor | Sir Frederick P. Robinson, K.C.B. |
| 1828–33 | „ | Major-General Nathaniel Blackwell |

Ceased to be separate Government in 1833

1833–45	Lt.-Governor	Major-General Henry C. Darling
1845–50	„	Major Laurence Graeme
1851	„	David R. Ross
1852	„	Dominick Daly
1854–56	„	W. J. Shortland
1857–64	„	James Vickery Drysdale
1865–72	„	Cornelius Kortright
1872–75	„	H. T. Ussher, C.M.G.
1875–77	„	Col. R. W. Harley, C.B., C.M.G.
1877–80	„	Lt.-Col. Augustus Frederick Gore

Administrators

1880–82	Administrator	Edward Laborde*
1883–84	„	John W. Carrington, D.C.I.*
1885	„	Loraine G. Hay*
1885–87	„	Robert B. Llewelyn*
1888	„	Loraine G. Hay*
1889–92	Commissioner	Loraine G. Hay
1892	„	Thomas Crossley Rayner
1892	„	William Low

* Also Colonial Secretary

XXXIV

The Islands of the Bocas

In 1791, Don Gaspar Antonio de la Guardia, Procurator Syndic of Port of Spain, presented a petition to Governor Chacon praying that the Islands of Patos, Huevos, Monos and Chacachacare be granted in order to increase the revenue of the town. This petition, dated June 27th, 1791, and signed by Guardia, Chacon passed to the First Commissary of Population, Don Pedro Ybarrate, requesting him to submit a report on the Islands.

Ybarrate reported that as the King of Spain had " no occasion for the Islands Monos, Huevos and Patos, Your Excellency may be pleased to concede them to the Illustrious Cabildo of this Island (Trinidad), that the produce they yield may serve as funds to the Board wherewith to defray the expenses; but it is the opinion of the Commissary that His Excellency should reserve the proprietorship in case the same should in future be wanted for some Royal Service; in which case he will take possession, without being obliged to pay for any labour expended thereon, whenever it may happen."

Chacachacare, which was prayed for in the petition, had already been granted to Sir Gerald Fitz-Patrick Carry by the King of Spain for services rendered to the Spanish Crown on the mainland. He had been presented with a proper title deed, with a proviso that whenever His Majesty required the island, it should be returned to him. Ybarrate went on to say that the island was too large for one man to cultivate, and that Carry rented part of it to others. He considered that in future these annual rents should be paid to the Cabildo and that the Cabildo should pay expense of clearing or other works which had to be done. "Whenever the same shall be wanted for the King's use, always exempting Don Geraldo Carry from such contribution, in consideration of the document of proprietorship given to him by the King, from this results that the King is released from his obligation given in the title of Geraldo Carry, that the Cabildo is served and this inhabitant enjoys his property without prejudice to his interests. Should Your Excellency approve of my report, it will be proper for Your Excellency to send back this report to this office, in order that the necessary entries may be made in the books of this office."

This report was dated July 9th, 1791. Chacon then decreed "that in virtue of the authority vested in him by the Real Cedula de Poblacion of 1783, and that provided and ordered by the Laws respecting the funds of towns and cities, and those respecting pastures for cattle belonging to the said town and villages, he was pleased to grant and he hereby does grant in proprietorship of this town, by way of funds (propios) the Islands of Patos, Huevos and Monos in perpetuity that the same may be administered, their rents and produce applied to the public wants of the said city, conformably to the order of the aforecited laws and succeeding Royal Ordinances; for which purpose regular titles are to be granted, taking faithful copies of these proceedings for the information of His Majesty and to obtain His Majesty's sovereign confirmation thereof, the same being likewise passed in duplicate to the office of the Commissary, and by which His Excellency, Don Josef Maria Chacon, Colonel of the Royal Army, Governor, Commander-in-Chief and Intendant of the Island of Trinidad, resolved, be ordered and signed with the advice of Don Josef D. de Cuena, Honorary Oyder, Lt.-Governor and Auditor of War in Port of Spain, the 15th day of September, 1791."

436

This was signed by Chacon, sealed with his arms, counter-signed by the under written Secretary of the Cabildo, Josef Ant. Perez, Essio. Ryl. y de Cabildo.

Chacachacare, at the west of the first Boca, is horseshoe shaped and very hilly. The hills slope towards the inside of the horse-shoe. On the west side the hills are precipitous, descending abruptly to the Caribbean Sea. At the junction of the arms of the horseshoe, the land is flat and marshy. At times of spring tides or in rough weather the sea often passes over the isthmus. Boats can be hauled from calm water on the east to La Tinta Bay in the west. La Tinta, so called on account of the colour of the sand, which is black, the water being clear, but the sand beneath makes it look like ink.

In 1791, there were many people living on this island, culti-vating ground provisions and sugar apples (Annona squamosa). During the time of slavery large quantities of cotton were grown, which after emancipation was abandoned. Later, when the price of cotton was very high, the industry was re-established by Messrs. Gerold and Urich. There were also three or four whaling stations carried on by Messrs. Gerold and Urich, Tardieu and F. Urich and Partners.

Looking across the Boca Grande there is a view of the Vene-zuelan mountains eight miles away. On a clear day they appear to be much closer. On the land side of the bay there is a fringe of deadly manchineal trees (Hippomana Mancinella). Tall cacti and aloes grow on the cliffs on the southern shore. There is a pebbly beach—Bande de Sud—inside which there is a lagoon of salt water from what in the early days the islanders attempted to extract salt.

About 1887 a stone pier and a large house for the use of a sanatorium was erected in the island by S. Chittenden. At present there is only a lighthouse on the west and the Leper Asylum on the island.

Patos (Goose Island), south west of Chacachacare, is the first island to be sighted on entering the Boca Grande. It is about one mile long and about three-quarters of a mile wide. In 1822 Joseph Felix petitioned the Acting-Governor, A. Young, to be allowed to settle on Patos to raise cattle and to fish in the sur-rounding sea. A Commissary enquiry was set up and it was reported that there were sheep on the island, but probably they were goats; also that there was no water. As the island belonged to the Cabildo, the petition was turned down.

In 1876 a deed, No. 262, was made out by the Port of Spain Borough Council, granting the island to L. Dennis O'Connor for thirty years at a rental of $12,000 per annum. O'Connor and his brother started to raise stock and to catch fish, which they salted. They found the life not to their liking, being too isolated. In

1890 it reverted to the Crown, because the ward rates, amounting to £11. 10. 0d. had not been paid.

At the north-west of Patos there is a cylindrical crater about eighty feet deep and fifty feet in diameter, accessible from a small cove near the edge of a cliff reaching almost to sea level. Here some old guns were found. The only vegetation on the island is a few small trees and a great many cacti. There are also some birds.

Monos (Apes' Island) lies west of Trinidad between it and Huevos. The soil is poor and there are many parasol ants.

Huevos (eggs) lies west of Monos. On this island there is an interesting cave. It is not easy of access, the entrance being narrow, rocky and steep. Hundreds of night birds called Guacharo, or Diablotin, live in the cave, which is always dark. There is no fresh water on either of these islands.

The Guacharo (steatoinis caripensis), a species of goat sucker, is considered by Trinidadians to be a very great delicacy. There are also a few smaller caves inhabited by a species of fishing bats, which emerge at dusk to catch small fish.

The Five Islands, originally called Perroquets, are about five miles west of Port of Spain and two miles from the village of Carenage. They originally belonged to the Crown but some grants have been made to various people from time to time.

The first island, Caledonia, was granted to Lt. Herbert Mackworth, R.N., who was Marshal of Trinidad. This island was then known as Marlin Spike Hall. The Craig, a rock at the west end of Caledonia, was joined to it, but the sea has washed out a narrow passage between them. A Mr. Caldwell built a house on Craig and purchased Caledonia and Craig from Mackworth when he left Trinidad. Caldwell also built a house for his own use on the island, which he renamed Caledonia. The original house was where Lord and Lady Harris spent their honeymoon.

The second of the Five Islands is Lenegan's Island. The third is Stephenson's, better known as Neilson's, was granted to Dr. Thomas Neilson, who called it Bel Air. It is the largest of the Five Islands and later was used as a place where Indian immigrants on their arrival in the colony were looked after until allotted to estates.

The fourth is Pelican, which was first granted to C. Hobson. Later it was the property of G. Revell, to whom it belonged in 1866.

The fifth is Rock Island, granted to T. F. Johnston, who sold it to Dr. Mercer, who gave it to Thomas Laughlin. This island was later used as a Quarantine Station.

The two islands west of the Five Islands are about a mile from them. They are Carrera and Creteau, originally Diego

Martin Islands. Carrera was at one time called Long Island. It is near the entrance to Chaguaramas Bay. Creteau was sometimes called Bégorrat's Island. In the early days these islands were used as holiday resorts. A convict prison was built on Carrera in 1877 and on Creteau there are stone quarries. Gaspar Grande, Gasparillo or Gasparee, lies a few hundred yards north of Creteau. It is one mile and a half long and half a mile wide. It was off the east end of this island that the Spanish Admiral Apodoca scuttled his ships in 1791. There was a small fort at Bomb Shell Hill, where British troops were garrisoned after the capitulation. The bay at the foot of the hill is still known as Bomb Shell Bay.

In 1856 a party of Americans with diving apparatus arrived on board the *Silver Arrow*. They anchored off Chaguaramas and made attempts to recover the Spanish ships that had sunk there. They did not find much of value. Amongst the articles salvaged were two guns.

Many years ago cotton was grown on Gasparee and there were two whaling stations—a large one at Pointe Baleine, managed by a sea captain from Bermuda, and the other by Mr. Tardieu. The earliest residences were two villas, one of which was the property of J. P. Tuttleby, and the other known as *Silver Bay* belonged to Mr. Liddle. The west point of this island is made on entering the Boca. On this island there is an interesting limestone cave, which is light on account of a hole in the roof. Long stalactites hang from the roof and there is water at the bottom of the cave which comes in from the sea, the depth of which depends on the tide. Colonies of bats live in this cave.

INDEX

Compiled by G. Norman Knight, M.A., M.S.Ind., Barrister-at-Law

Page numbers in italic type indicate main references. Places in Tobago are distinguished by having the name of the island in brackets.

441

Ballena, Gulf de la (= Gulf of Paria), 13
Band d'Este plantation, 71
Baptists, the, *230, 252*
Barataria Estate, 247
Barbados, 284, 285, 316
—hurricane, 1831 . . . 179; immigrants from, 188; Lady Harris's death in, 1853 . . . 246; Tobago and, *305*
Barbados, Bishopric of, 222, 228, 293, 310, *427-9, 432*
Barbados Bay (Tobago), 306
Barlee, Sir F. P. (*Governor,* 1884), 300, 376
Barrios (*town divisions*), 50
Barry, Edward (*litigant*), 143, 144-5
Barry & Dawson (*estate owners*), 143
Barton, A. E. V. (*Secretary, W.I.C.*), 10
Basanta, Dr., 256
Basanta, Joseph (*civil servant*), 176
Bastidas, Captain Roderigo de, 17
Bathurst, Henry, 3rd Earl (*Secretary of State*), 121, 124, 126, 154
Baynes, Daniel (*A./Lt.-Govr. of Tobago*), 313
Bear, The (privateer), 24
Beckwith, Sir George (*C.-in-C.*), 140
Bee (H.M. sloop), 47
Beet sugar, competition from, *258-9, 282*
Bégorrat, St. Hilaire de (*First Alcade*), 50, 51, 58, 87, 383
—cocoa petition presented by, *176*; on constitutional question, 154
Bégorrat's Island (= Creteau), 439
Behrens (*sculptor*), 257
Bel Air (= Neilson's Island), 438
Bellaforma (*first name for Tobago*), 14, 302
Belmont, Government pasture at, 259
Belmont Hill, Governor's house on, *143-5,* 147, 277
Benson, D. V., 287
Berlin Decree, 1806 . . . 234
Bermuda:
Apprenticeship scheme rejected by, 196; settlers from, 29
Berrio, Antonio de (*Governor*), 22-5, 29, 375
Berrio, Fernando de (*Governor*), 25, 26-7, 28, 29, 375

Berrio, Mendoza de la Hoz y (*Governor*), 29-30, 375
Berthier, Gen. Caesar (*Governor of Tobago,* 1803), 309, 434
Betata, Fray Gregorio de (*Bishop*), 21
Beveren, Hubert de (*Governor of Tobago,* 1654), 303, 433
Bideau, Jean Baptist ("*Patriot* "), 108, 109
Biggs, John (*Chief Justice*), 135, 144
Binkes, Admiral, 304
Birch, Mariana, picture by, 133
Bishop (*Commissary-General*), 217
Bitumen from Pitch Lake, 248-50
Black, John (*Councillor*), 50, 68, 87, 93, 383
—Chairman of Building Committee, 114; death of, *203*
"Black Corps of Dragoons," the, 198
Blackwell, Major-Gen. Nathaniel (*Govr., Tobago,* 1828-33), 310, 435
Blanchelande, Philbert de (*Governor of Tobago,* 1781), 307-8, 434
Board of Trade, U.K., 282
Boca del Dragon, 14, 302
Boca Grande, 14, 47, 437
Boca de la Sierpe, 13, 14
Bocas, Islands of the, 429, 435-9
Bodu, E. M.: *Trinidadiana, 251,* 357
Bohitos (*Arawak priests*), 16
Boissiére, Jean (*estate owner*), 141, 145
Boissière Village, 73
Bolivar, Simon ("*the Liberator* "), 102, *391*
Bomb Shell Bay, Gasparee, 439
Bonaparte, *see* Napoleon I
Bonaventure Estate, 247
Boneta, H.M. Sloop, 38
Borde, Hypolite, 275
Botanic Garden and Government Farm, Tobago, 289
Botanic Gardens, Trinidad, 146, *147,* 259
Bounties for B.W.I. sugar in U.K., 80
Bounty system, Continental beet, *258-9, 282*
—countervailing duties, 282, 284; Select Committee on, 1880 . . . 282
Bridgens, Robert (*Dir. of Public Works*), 178, 230

442

443

444

447

450

457

459